Consuming Audiences?
Production and Reception in Media Research

INTERNATIONAL ASSOCIATION FOR MEDIA AND COMMUNICATION RESEARCH

This series consists of books arising from the intellectual work of IAMCR sections, working groups, and committees. Books address themes relevant to IAMCR interests; make a major contribution to the theory, research, practice and/or policy literature; are international in scope; and represent a diversity of perspectives. Book proposals are submitted through formally constituted IAMCR sections, working groups, and committees.

Series Editors
IAMCR Publication Committee

Coordinator: Annabelle Sreberny

Members:
Naren Chitty
John Downing
Elizabeth Fox
Virginia Nightingale

Consuming Audiences?
Production and Reception in Media Research

edited by

Ingunn Hagen
University of Trondheim, NVST

Janet Wasko
University of Oregon

 HAMPTON PRESS, INC.
CRESSKILL, NEW JERSEY

Printed in the United States of America

Library of Congress Cataloging-in-Publication Data

Consuming audiences? : production and reception in media research / edited by Ingunn Hagen, Janet Wasko.
    p. cm. -- (International Association for Mass Communication Research)
  Includes papers presented at a round table held Sydney, Australia, 1996, during a meeting of the International Association for Mass Communication Research.
  Includes bibliographical references and index.
  ISBN 1-572-73175-3 -- ISBN 1-572-73176-1 (pbk.)
  1. Mass media--Audiences--Congresses. 2. Mass media--Research--Congresses. I. Hagen, Ingunn, 1959- II. Wasko, Janet.

P96.A83 C65 1999
302.23 21--dc21

                                99-043816

Hampton Press, Inc.
23 Broadway
Cresskill, NJ 07626

Contents

1

INTRODUCTION

1

Introduction: Consuming Audiences? Production and Reception in Media Research

Ingunn Hagen
Janet Wasko

For individual media researchers as well as for specific research projects, there are often limited resources; time, money, and capacity. Naturally, this limits the empirical focus of research and also the field of study or tradition to which researchers attach their academic identity. Still, most researchers agree in principle that it is useful and necessary to pay attention, at least theoretically, to the entire communication process. A more holistic understanding requires that the interrelationship between factors or moments in the communication process—however defined—is taken into consideration.

In this book we aim to explore the intersection between two such areas of research—political economy and reception analysis; in other words, the interaction between media production and audience reception/consumption. Although these research traditions have included serious critiques of each other in the past, there is also an argument to be

3

made that they should be complimentary, corespective and even symbiotic. As Graham Murdock points out in this volume: "Since modern communication is self evidently both a symbolic and economic system, its analysis has to be a matter of both/and rather than either/or."

Our efforts to initiate this book were inspired by ongoing debates at the International Association for Mass Communication Research (IAMCR), especially the panel entitled "Cultural Imperialism or the Active Audience? A Debate about Power in Global Communication," at the conference in Seoul, Korea, in 1994.[1] The panel was sponsored by the Political Economy section and the Network for Qualitative Audience Research (NEQTAR) and produced a provocative and lively debate at the time. The general interest in the topic, as well as our own concerns, suggested that this was a theme worth further attention.

In order to pursue such a goal, we envisioned a collection of articles focusing on aspects of media production and consumption.[2] We also invited potential contributors to participate in a panel/round table at the IAMCR, Sydney, 1996. Again, the event was sponsored by the Political Economy Section and NEQTAR. And again, the discussion was lively and provocative. However, not all the book contributors were able to participate at the panel in Sydney. The contributors have been chosen because we thought they were doing very interesting work—from a political economy perspective or related to audience reception or ethnography.

We have defined the following themes or questions that we feel are particularly important in the current and ongoing discussion related to the interrelationship between media production and consumption:

- How much freedom does the audience have to interpret messages produced by media institutions?
- What role does textual analysis play in the study of production contexts and audiences' reception?

---

[1]The panel was initiated by James Lull and was to include participants representing the two perspectives—political economy and reception analysis. Herbert Schiller and Vincent Mosco, and James Lull and Ingunn Hagen were scheduled to participate. However, the political economy scholars were unable to make it to the conference, so Eileen Mahoney and Gerry Sussman replaced Schiller and Mosco.

[2]This work took place when Janet spent a semester in Copenhagen as a Fulbright scholar. Thus, we were able to have working meetings in Norway and Denmark. "Distance makes the heart grow fonder" is a common expression, but "Closeness makes cooperation easier" is more appropriate here. When developing ideas, it is very valuable to meet personally, even in the age of Internet. We would like to thank Dan Y. Jacobsen for contributing the idea for the book's main title.

- Are there similar theoretical assumptions and political alliances that can and should be developed between reception analysis and political economy? Or are there still irreconcilable differences, due to academic backgrounds and traditions, between these two areas of research? Is it possible that some conflict might even be necessary and even productive?

These rather broadly defined questions are both overarching and controversial in communication studies. Although each of the contributors to this volume deal with aspects of them, either explicitly or implicitly, these questions need to be addressed more specifically. We do so in this introduction, based on our different backgrounds; Janet has done work from a political economy perspective and Ingunn has concentrated on reception studies in later years.

But before we discuss these overarching questions, we will provide brief sketches of reception research and political economy. Our aim is not to achieve conclusive answers—an introduction and even a book can hardly achieve that. However, we do hope to inspire further debate and work related to the intersection of production and reception among researchers and students.

RECEPTION ANALYSIS OVERVIEW

Recent Audience Research

In the last 10 to 15 years, great changes have taken place in the field of audience research. Qualitative research has become more legitimate, much due to the acceptance of reception analysis. Cultural studies has been a major source of inspiration towards this development. The most recent tendency in audience research is the so-called "ethnographic turn." In the following, we discuss some of these changes.

To many, cultural studies and reception analysis are more or less the same. We see cultural studies and reception analysis rather as overlapping categories. However, some distinctions can (and should) be made.

Cultural Studies' Audience Research

Cultural studies has a much broader concern than reception analysis—especially as this "school of thought" was developed at the Centre for Contemporary Cultural Studies in Birmingham (CCCS, often referred to as the Birmingham Centre). Stuart Hall, the most vocal spokesperson and theoretician at the Centre during the 1970s and 80s, however, emphasizes that the Centre was not a "school" in the scientific meaning of the term.

Cultural studies at the Centre can be characterized as certain common themes and focus points related to the study of contemporary cultural practices. For many of the early studies, like the ones of Richard Hoggart and Raymond Williams in the 1950s and 60s, working class culture was a major concern.[3] In the 1970s, an interest in the (sub)culture of minorities and women was central.[4]

Cultural studies' most important contribution to audience research is the so-called encoding/decoding model developed by Hall, based on the political meaning systems of Parkin.[5] This model was proposed as a semiotic alternative to the more linear communication model (sender-message-receiver) underlying the dominant traditions of audience research (see, Hall 1980a, 1980b).

Hall emphasizes the paradigmatic break with earlier traditions; the encoding/decoding model is supposed to open up "a new and exciting phase in so-called audience research, of a quite new kind" (1980a: 131). The model is an attempt to theorize the role of ideology in textual production under certain social, economic and historical conditions. According to this encoding/decoding model, TV programs are constructed as "meaningful" discourses or texts, structured in dominance.

The audience, on the other hand, in their decoding can accept this preferred meaning. Or they can resist the program's dominant meaning structure by producing negotiated or oppositional readings. The audiences' various modes of interpretation obviously relate to the polysemic nature of the TV program/text. However, Hall warns against confusing this with pluralism, as the producing institutions still lay the premises for reception.[6]

Hall's encoding-decoding model has been very influential and the article in which it is described is regarded as almost a "classic." This model has been the point of departure for numerous studies. One of the

---

[3]See, for example, Hoggart (1957) and Williams (1958). Another example is Thompson (1968).

[4]Hebdige (1979) is often mentioned as an example. The same is the case with the Hall and Jefferson (1976) anthology.

[5]Hall outlined this model in 1973, in one of the CCCS Stencilled Papers. A abbreviated version was printed in 1980, in *Culture, Media, Language*, a collection of cultural studies working papers from the 1970s. The same article was also reprinted in 1993, in *The Cultural Studies Reader* (During, 1993).

[6]Pluralism is defined here as different producing institutions constructing texts or messages representing distinctly different values.

first and probably most quoted applications of the encoding/decoding ✓ model is David Morley's study of *The "Nationwide" Audience*. Morley's study, published in 1980, is regarded as a pioneer work in this kind of audience research. The "Nationwide" study has been interpreted as critical studies' "rediscovery" of the empirical audience. Morley himself presents this work as an alternative to the "screen tradition"—dominant in English film and TV research in the 1970s—where the focus is on "implied readers" in the text; how the text positions audiences.

Morley's "Nationwide" study is often mentioned as the starting point of reception analysis. However, Morley himself seems more concerned to stress his cultural studies affiliation.[7] With regard to audience research, a cultural studies approach continues its focus on culture, defined as meaning production (*cf*. Fiske, 1982; 1987), where the interest is in the signification process related to mass mediated texts.[8]

Reception Theory: Posing a Challenge?

Reception analysis has become established as a field of research during the last 10-15 years. Although the tradition had to fight for legitimacy in the early 1980s, it has since the mid-1980s demonstrated a number of interesting results. In the 1990s, there is a tendency to do meta-analysis of the field. That means to examine what the theoretical claims of reception theory and its supportive evidence really mean (*cf*. Condit, 1989; Livingstone, 1993; Morley, 1992).

In their article "In Search of the Audience," Jensen and Rosengren (1990) distinguish between cultural studies and reception analysis. However, these authors acknowledge that cultural studies and reception analysis often blend. Several researchers, like Ang (1985), Jensen (1986), and Morley (1980; 1986) give credit to cultural studies and especially to Hall's encoding-decoding model as influential for their work.

The label "reception analysis" is taken from reception theory or reception aesthetics, the German branch of literary theory that focuses ✓ on the role of the reader in reading process.[9] Several attempts have been made to define reception analysis as a field of research in mass communication.

---

[7]This affiliation is clear in Morley 1980 and 1986. But the cultural studies perspective is especially emphasized in his 1992 publication.

[8]McQuail (1994) in the last revision of his much used *Mass Communication Theory: An Introduction* labels this "a culturalist approach."

[9]This tradition, *Rezeptionsesthetik*, was developed at the University of Constanze in Germany. Two of the best known representatives are Wolfgang Iser and Hans Robert Jauss (for an overview, see Holub, 1984).

Reception analysis in our view should refer to studies that focus on the meaning, production, and experiences of audiences in their inter-action with media texts (see Hagen, 1992). This focus on the process of decoding, interpretation, and "reading" is the core of several conceptual-izations of reception analysis (e.g., Höijer, 1990; Höijer, Nowak and Ross, 1992). Other definitions are broader, like the one proposed by Jensen and Rosengren, where reception analysis refers to "various forms of qualitative empirical audience research which, to different degrees, seek to integrate social-scientific and humanistic perspectives on reception" (1990: 213, see also Jensen, 1986).

Reception analysis has mainly been performed on TV viewers, although the perspective is well suited for studying other kinds of audi-ences as well. As in mass communication generally, researchers have backgrounds from different academic disciplines. Obviously, it is possi-ble to study the TV viewers' interpretation without paying tribute to Hall's encoding/decoding model. However, with the semiotic presuppositions of the model, and also with the interdisciplinary nature of cultural studies and its openness to qualitative research, many find the encoding-decod-ing model enlightening.

Moreover, the academic reception of Morley's book *The "Nationwide" Audience* has made the encoding/decoding model unavoid-able for reception researchers. The fact that Morley's book is attributed such a pioneering role "forces" researchers to discuss its influence as part of the expected academic discourse. The "smart move" of Morley (1992) to summarize his "Nationwide" findings, as well as the discussion that followed, together with extracts of his later work, have even strengthened this position.

Ethnographic Audience Research

Ethnography has become the "new fashion" in audience research during the latter part of the 1980s and the 1990s. James Lull—often considered a pioneer within ethnographic media research with his early article, "The Social Uses of Television" (1980)—ironically described media ethnogra-phy as "an abused buzzword in our field" (1988: 242). Ethnographic media research can be defined as "an interpretive enterprise whereby the investigator uses observation and in-depth interviewing to grasp the meaning of communication by analyzing the perceptions, shared assumptions, and activities of the social actors under scrutiny" (Lull, 1990). This definition indicates that ethnographic audience research might have much in common with reception analysis; the significance of the communication process is still in focus.

The central distinction is that whereas reception research's emphasis is on the process of interpretation, ethnographic audience research is more focused on media use as practice. Thus, the recent ethnographic turn in qualitative audience research has been characterized as a change in focus from decoding to context (Morley's book *Television, Audiences & Cultural Studies* from 1992 illustrates this well).[10] Methodically, ethnographic work often also incorporates observation, in addition to interviewing.

Still, different researchers disagree about what ethnographic audience research is and should be. Many view ethnographic audience research as a special branch of reception analysis.[11] Drotner (1993) labels this a broad definition of ethnography. Personally, she prefers a narrower conceptualization, reserving the word ethnography for research that is more truthful to the ideals of ethnography developed in social anthropology. She argues that media ethnography is most usefully seen as an epistemological alternative to reception analysis, rather than as a broadening or variation of the latter. What is disagreed upon is the depth and time period required to get inside the culture of the audience ("the other"). Geertz's notion of "thick description" has inspired many researchers. But the question remains how this is possible to achieve by a few visits in people's homes doing interviews.

Generally, ethnographic audience research means that audiences are being interviewed and observed in their "natural environment" or context. Although we find a narrow definition of ethnography theoretically interesting, we think it is most relevant for studies of, for example, youth groups or other subcultures. With regard to studying normal family or household viewing, for example, the ideals of classical anthropology might function as a "tight-rope."

The notion of decoding also is central in ethnographic research. But in this latter tradition the social situatedness of meaning production is more acknowledged. Thus, ethnographic research also overlaps with cultural studies. At the same time, ethnographic audience research continues cultural studies' interest in cultural practices. As indicated earlier, ethnographic audience and reception analysis also blend, with the degree of overlap dependent upon a narrow or broad conceptualization of ethnography.

---

[10]This ethnographic turn is not just a tendency in mass communication and audience research. Rather, similar trends can be seen in several social science disciplines.

[11]Such thinking is exemplified by the Nordic research course, "Mass Media and the Ethnography of Everyday Life—New Departures in Reception Research," held in Denmark during the fall of 1992.

POLITICAL ECONOMY OVERVIEW

The study of the political economy of communication has a long and varied history that would be difficult, if not impossible, to present in this brief introduction. Only a short description of the tradition and some recent developments will be offered before we contrast political economy and reception analysis and the positions these approaches take on the previously mentioned themes of this volume.

"We Told You So"

The study of communications as an economic process has not always been a respectable endeavor, even in mainstream circles. However, the role communication plays in an economic system is no longer considered as radical as it may have been in the 1950s and 1960s. Although there should be no smugness or delight, there may be some satisfaction among political economists in finding that their analysis of communication's role as a vital economic force in society has been on target and is now receiving public recognition, as well as scholarly acknowledgment. The recent intensification of media concentration and globalization has drawn much more serious attention to the economic characteristics of the communication process. Indeed, the understanding of the development of communication and media as industries—as capitalist industries, that is—and the implications of this development for democratic and human values, has finally gone beyond a small circle of friends who call themselves radical or critical political economists.

Defining the Tradition

In his recent book, *The Political Economy of Communication* (1996), Vincent Mosco begins with a discussion of the general field of political economy, which he defines as "the study of the social relations, particularly power relations, that mutually constitute the production, distribution and consumption of resources" (p. 25). Mosco draws on the foundations of political economy in 18th-century Scottish enlightenment thinking, as well as current theorists, to delineate four central characteristics of political economy: (1) an interest in social change and history; (2) an emphasis on the social totality; (3) a grounding in moral philosophy; and (4) an orientation towards praxis. Although there have been other classic discussions of the approach, Mosco's definition—informed by those discussions—would probably be acceptable to most critical political economists. Indeed, Graham Murdock and Peter Golding (1996) suggest quite similar characteristics in defining a critical political economy as distinguished from mainstream economics: (1) holistic; (2) historical; (3) centrally concerned with the balance between capitalist enterprise and public intervention; and, (4) goes beyond technical issues of efficiency to engage with basic moral questions of justice, equity, and the public good.

In the broadest sense, the political economy of communication is interested in analyzing the allocation of communication resources in society and the implications of that process, or what Nicholas Garnham (1979) has called "the modes of cultural production and consumption developed within capitalist societies"—in other words, the entire communication or cultural process.

Despite these broad definitions, the study of political economy of communications is still often considered narrow and deterministic, focusing primarily on the economic or the production side of the communication process. However, the tradition is actually much more complex. For instance, a common misconception is that the approach is concerned primarily with ownership and control questions. Though studies of ownership patterns and the dynamics of control are essential, political economic analysis is much more extensive than merely identifying and then condemning those who control media/communication resources.

It is important to remember that the study of political economy encompasses political as well as economic analysis. Understanding interrelationships between communications industries, the State, other economic sectors, and key power bases is crucial for a complete analysis of the communication process, and thus involves research issues that are not always related directly to audiences or consumption.

Rethinking Political Economy

As noted previously, ongoing critiques of political economy continue to point to a narrow and deterministic focus and the lack of attention to audiences and the consumption process in general. Over the years, political economists have defended their research and theories from extreme and inaccurate accusations, but also have attempted to respond to reasonable criticism of the approach (cf. Murdock and Golding, 1974; 1996). Some of this discussion has taken place in the flurries of theoretical debates between political economy and cultural studies (e.g., Garnham, 1995; Grossberg, 1995).

In addition, a few political economists specifically have directed attention to the process of "rethinking" political economy (Meehan, Mosco and Wasko, 1994). Mosco's volume (1996) is subtitled "Rethinking and Renewal," with an attempt to redefine political economy in the broad terms of commodification, spatialization, and structuration, as well as examining political economy's relation to cultural studies and policy studies.

Others have combined political economy with other approaches, such as textual and audience studies or ethnographies. It is obvious, then, that current thinking by political economists includes those issues that also concern reception analysts.

Although it may be a challenge to trace the evolution of reception analysis and compare it to other approaches, such as cultural studies (as presented in the first section of this introduction), it is nearly impossible to briefly trace the rich history and wide range of communication theory and scholarship that draws on a political economic tradition, much less contrast it with other approaches.[12] One might argue that political economy is much more broadly conceived than reception analysis, thus more difficult to summarize. Political economists have examined a wider range of communication and media practices than reception analysts, including a wider range of the traditional mass media to (more recently) computers, information technologies, and users.

Therefore, as the aim of this volume is to look at issues relating to the intersection of reception analysis and political economy, we will limit more detailed discussion of political economic theory and research to specific issues relating to media audiences, audiences' relations to texts, and so forth, which will be addressed in the following sections.

RECEPTION ANALYSTS MEET POLITICAL ECONOMISTS

Most of the authors in this volume probably identify with one of these research traditions more than with the other. In other words, they are either primarily political economists or primarily reception analysts. Obviously, their discussions of the themes we have delineated are flavored by their own positions and perspectives. We might suppose that all would agree on the need to analyze the communication process in its entirety, understanding both production and consumption. Yet, there may still be important differences in where one begins that analysis and, to some extent, what conclusions are drawn.

---

[12]Mosco (1996) presents an overview of political economic approaches to communication research in different regions, including North America, Great Britain and Europe, and the Third World. Mosco also observes (pp. 72-3) that there are four generations of communication scholars who call themselves political economists. This may need to be revised soon, as a fourth generation of scholars is introducing their students to the political economy tradition.

Audience Freedom or Deconstructing the Notion of the Active Audience

Audiences As Viewed by Political Economists

The most confounding and controversial issues that confront these traditions revolve around the nature of the audience, and especially the question of "active" or "passive" audiences.

In the 1980s, it may have been a fair critique to point to the disappearing audience in much political economic research (see Fejes, 1984). On the other hand, one might argue that the audience has never been totally absent from the political economy of the media, at least at a theoretical level. Although specific attention to studying audiences—especially in terms of amassing audience numbers or in the analysis of individual audience members' responses to messages—has been noticeably missing, the audience has been conceptualized as a key component of the media commodification and consumption process.

Nevertheless, for some political economists, even the notion of an audience—much less an active audience—may be seen as problematic, needing much more careful attention, as indicated in Mosco and Kaye's article in this volume. In their genealogy of the word, they point out that the term audience was created by the media industry itself, yet has become a central concept for communication research.

Indeed, their argument is reminiscent of an important debate within political economy. In 1977, Smythe argued that the most important commodity produced by the media industry is the audience, which is constructed and sold to advertisers. Programming is only important in that it constructs audiences, which contribute their labor as the primary product of the media process.

Certainly, Smythe's formulation fueled further criticism of the political economic approach as (again) reductionist and economically determined, or vulgar. Yet Smythe's argument started a lively debate among political economists in communication, importantly, drawing attention to the role of the audiences in political economic theory and research. (Jhally, 1990; Livant, 1979; Meehan, 1984; Murdock, 1978) As Mosco (1996) points out, "Neglected in the debate about whether the audience labors, or whether it is the sole media commodity, is arguably the central contribution that Smythe made to our understanding of the media commodification process. For him, the process brought together a triad that linked media, audiences, and advertisers in a set of binding reciprocal relationships." And it is this relationship that political economists cannot ignore when they consider media audiences.

Although the labor metaphor may not be totally appropriate, Smythe's notion of audience labor also draws attention to the question of audience activity or power. Although not wholly analogous to labor in a literal sense, audience activity still can be contrasted in some ways to labor power. Again, as Mosco (1996) observes, "As with labor, which the literature on work demonstrates brings a wide range of responses to the point of production, from full compliance to withholding labor power, the audience exercises power, but also, like labor, it is power circumscribed within terms largely, though not entirely, set by capital." Thus, political economic analysis allows for the notion of audience power. But, again, just as political economists cannot separate capital from labor, they have difficulty separating audiences from capital.

This point is well-represented in this volume in the articles by Murdock, Meehan, and Maxwell.

Murdock reminds us that audience members are not only responding to individual media programs, but are part of "a dense network of consumption relations." He points to marketing strategies that "interlaced promotion and spectacle," acknowledging the "thicket of signs accreting around commodities." Murdock briefly revisits the "audience commodity" debate and calls for more attention to the history of commodity culture and shifts in everyday life, as well as an approach that acknowledges "the interlacing of culture, economy and identity and the interplay between local, national and transnational dynamics."

In her discussion of fan ethnography, Meehan echoes Smythe in tracing the transformation of leisure time to work time and the industrial strategies that have promoted "cultural consumption as a name brand, ritualized activity." Meehan focuses on examples of audience members who demonstrate the most overt or obvious responses to this process, or the fans who move beyond the typical consumer to participate in a wide range of activities relating to media products. Although fans have been studied by ethnographers, typically there is little or no analysis of the important industrial context in which fandom operates, thus providing an example of the need to integrate political economy and audience studies.

Richard Maxwell links political economy and audiences through his work on marketing research, and in his essay in this volume, identifies consumer surveillance as an empirical problem that deserves the attention of political economic and cultural analysis. In his discussion, Maxwell confronts some of the "sins of political economists"—reductionism, instrumentalism, functionalism, and pessimism—and argues that "to focus on how assessments of media audiences range dumbly between pessimism and optimism only serves to divert the discussion of audiences away from politics—away from the conflict between corporations' and people's sense of life's meaning and value."

Although the audience may not be explicitly discussed in some political economic studies, to conclude that political economists consider audience members "dopes" or "passive victims" ties the tradition too closely with mass society theorists and may not even be a fair assessment. The work that probably receives the most attention from those making these claims revolves around the notion of cultural imperialism, which, as Schiller notes in his article, has been harshly critiqued or virtually absent in recent audience research. It might be recalled that many accounts in the 1970s and 1980s describing the dominant role of Western communications in Third World countries came from the Third World itself, thus representing a kind of resistance in itself. There are also examples of studies grounded in political economy that examined audience resistance (see Mattelart and Siegelaub, 1983).

And, more recently, much more attention has been paid by some political economists to audience studies and ethnographies, although this analysis is carefully situated within a strong political economic context (e.g., Pendakur 1993; Wasko, 1996). But even though some political economists are more deliberately studying audiences and the consumption process, the notion of a sovereign or active audience is still a troubling notion, as discussed in several of the chapters in this volume.

Reception Analysis and Audiences

For reception analysts, not only is the study of audiences the fundamental focus of research, but the notion of sovereign or active audiences is an often unquestioned assumption in much of recent reception research (*cf.* Evans, 1990; Hagen, 1992; Morley, 1993). But it is necessary to examine what the notion of active audience means for audience theory and research. With regard to reception analysis, "active" characterizes the role of the audience in the process of meaning construction.

Much reception research presupposes a semiotic understanding of communication. Thus, "active" refers to the role of audiences or viewers in meaning construction. Rather than the common meaning of the term active (as opposed to passive), viewers are seen as actively participating in the process of signification. Such emphasis on audience activity also counters ideas of direct influence and of audiences as passive victims. Thus, the notion of audiences as active agents of meaning production serves rhetorical purposes; it is proposed as a reconceptualization of the concept of audience, often used to differentiate reception analysis from the effect research tradition.

One model in particular can be seen as a milestone for this conceptualization of the audience as active producers of meaning. Stuart Hall's earlier mentioned encoding/decoding model (1980) has provided the point of departure for both empirical studies and much theorizing of audiences' reception. As already discussed, the model was proposed as a reaction to the linearity of the traditional mass communication research's conceptualization of communication, that was seen to underlie the existing perspectives in audience research. Hall's political concern was the hegemonic influence exercised by the media's ideological content, and the fact that their texts provide the audience with preferred meanings. But the model also accounts for the audiences' abilities to resist this ideological structuration and to produce negotiated or even oppositional readings.

The active role of audiences in decoding messages and constructing meaning has become a trademark for reception studies. In commenting on this, it has been pointed out that the notion of an active audience is nothing new in mass communication research. In a critique of what he labels the "new revisionism" in audience research, Curran (1990) tries to demonstrate that the notion of the audience as active and creative also formed the basis for studies done in the 1940s and 50s. However, many of the early studies seem to define active audiences in term of selective use, rather than as meaning constructing. Still, it is probably correct to recognize that the notion of an active audience has been swinging like a pendulum (*cf.* Morley, 1993). We find it important to ask about the implications and limitations of conceptualizing the audiences as active.

One issue in particular should be further reflected upon, namely the potential danger in emphasizing the active role of audiences in making meaning from texts. Much recent work on audiences' reception celebrate the interpretative resistance of audience groups, which are as often presumed as demonstrated. Such studies often take as their point of departure an overemphasis on the polysemic qualities of the text. This might result in a conception of exaggerated audience autonomy.

By focusing on audiences' active role in decoding polysemic texts, one runs the risk of overlooking the fact that media texts are not produced according to the choice of audiences. Thus, an overemphasis on the polysemic quality of texts risks the apologetics that uses and gratifications research was often accused of: "It does not matter what is broadcast, because audiences interpret it in multiple ways, anyway!" Excitement over the "creativity" of empirical audiences at times easily results in exclusion of other aspects, such as the power of producer institutions to provide the premises for consumption. Of course, political economists would agree that there is also little attention paid to historical, social, and cultural power relations (*cf.* Gripsrud, 1988; 1990; von Feilitzen, 1988).

There are further problems related to characterizing the audience as active. When pursuing the notion of the active audience too far, one risks the romanticism that Fiske (1987) is often accused of (e.g. Murdock, 1991; Silverstone, 1990). There is also the danger of "senti-

mentalizing audiences as they exist in certain inhumane social conditions" (Schudson, 1987: 64). The problem is that the emphasis on the
ability of audiences to create meaning and experience pleasure ultimately results in confusing audiences activity with power.

Several of the articles in this volume address this issue. For
instance, Svein Østerud asks "how can audience research overcome the
divide between macro- and microanalysis, between social structure and
action?" He describes how ethnography represents a change from
decoding and textual ideologies to viewing practices. In his article,
Østerud pays attention to the double function of television, as a technology and as a provider of program content. He calls for a combination of
an emic and etic perspective in media reception studies. In his study of
Norwegian television audiences, the author uses the Janus metaphor—
the two-faced Roman god guarding the entrance to the house—as a
sensitizing concept. Østerud claims that this location of television
between the interior and the exterior, between the private and the public
sphere leads to ambiguity in the way it functions for viewers. For some
viewers, television is used "to shut themselves in," engaging in a face-to-
face communication with the talking heads on the screen. Others, at the
opposite side of the scale, use television to undertake imaginary long-
distance "travels," thus using the medium to extend their horizon.
Østerud also draws on Schutz and Luckmann's lifeworld phenomenology
and Gidden's structuration theory to make sense of his data.

Meanwhile, Monteiro and Jayasankar discuss how global satellite television is received by the urban middle class in Mumbai (Bombay),
in what they characterize as "the post-liberalization period" in India. That
means a period of less state control, also over television. The interviewed families draw upon content from cable channels to construct their
identities. This active process of constituting the spectator-self, as these
authors call it (drawing on Foucault), is effected by constructing "others,"
above and below the spectator-self, and in relation to the "imaginary"
and the "normal." Whereas Doordarshan (Indian television) often is perceived to represent the normal, cable and satellite television are seen to
be beyond the normal. Monteiro and Jayasankar's study shows how
satellite television, both through the programming and through its entry
into the domestic sphere, results in renegotiation of family relations and
also in moral panic among parents. In the interview accounts these
authors identify a sense of agency on the part of the viewer. This means
that the effects of television on the spectator-self are seen to be under
their conscious control. Monteiro and Jayasankar feel that the contrary is
the case; precisely this sense of "agency" makes the viewers vulnerable
and facilitates the incorporation of the spectator-self into the consumer
culture. Television commercials even play on this theme of the "active
discerning consumer" to promote further consumption.

John Sinclair, Kee Pookong, Josephine Fox, and Audrey Yue report on a project aimed to find out how audiovisual media—especially television and video—are used in diasporic communities such as the Chinese in Australia. The research group is interested in how these communities maintain their cultural connections with the Chinese world while they negotiate a space for themselves in their host culture, Australia. The point is how these immigrant communities will try to maintain their cultural identity while simultaneously adapting to a new environment. The notion of "hybridization" is introduced to capture this transcultural process, whereby a new form of culture evolves, related to but different from both the home and the host cultures. The preliminary results indicate that knowledge of English is an important determining factor for their choice of mainly English or mainly Chinese media. But the respondents' preference for nonfiction television and for serious film suggest that people use audiovisual media deliberately, both to improve their English, and to gain factual information and cultural insight about their new home society.

Ingunn Hagen explores how people present themselves as television viewers and what discourses are drawn upon to create such identities. Hagen uses interview accounts in Norway that reveal a moral tone related to everyday television viewing. The article provides an attempt to locate the significance a person attributes to his or her television viewing in the intersection between the individual and the cultural. The meaning of watching television was negative for several of the interviewees, even though many of them also enjoyed it. Television viewing was regarded as something passive, a waste of time—the opposite of life quality. It was especially the role of television as a "time stealer" that created dilemmas in people's daily lives, something that relates to the expectation of productive use of time (the Protestant work ethic). Viewing television was also a direct source of conflict in some families. Such conflicts also related to the value hierarchy that respondents had with regard to television, and also the hierarchy of genres with which they were operating. Interviewees were often eager to disclaim their dependency relationship to television. The similarity in interviewees' accounts regarding television use suggested that they were drawing upon some common discourses or cultural scripts. Some of these discourses related to television are: television is a time waster; it is a cultural invader; television is a source of taste debasement; it is an extremely influential medium; it may cause cognitive impairment; and it could result in antiliteracy. Such discourses related to television may also be familiar in other countries as well.

The Role of Textual Analysis in Studying Media Production and Reception

The media texts are obviously a meeting point in order to understand the intersection between media production and consumption. Let us first address the concern with texts in reception analysis. Two basic assumptions of reception analysis relate to the status of texts. The focus in reception analysis on the text-reader relationship lead to a concern with the meaning potential of texts. Texts are assumed to be polysemic, to have many possible meanings. The medium studied in reception studies is often television.

A central assumption in reception analysis is that the meanings programs have for viewers arise in the program/audience interaction (*cf.* Dahlgren, 1988). This implies that reception analysis often combines empirical interest in the audience as meaning producers with analysis of media content. Thus, reception analysis can be referred to as audience-cum-content analysis (Jensen and Rosengren, 1990). Both the audience data and the content are normally analyzed through qualitative means and then compared. In other words, "reception analysis can be said to perform a comparative reading of media discourses and audience discourses in order to understand the processes of reception" (*op. cit.*, p. 222). This research tradition focuses on the processes where audiences are involved with texts, rather than on the results, which had been the focus of earlier audience research.

Several researchers, such as Morley (1980), argue that one should give due weight to both the text and the audience. The point is that a text, such as a TV program, provides both potential and limitations for the audiences decoding it. Hall attributes these limitations to the production of the text: "encoding will have the effect of constructing some of the limits within which decodings will operate" (1980: 135). But still, several possible meanings can be generated through the reading process. Thus, the ideal is the assessment of "the relative influence on meaning production exerted by the text and the receiver, respectively. (Höijer, Nowak and Ross, 1992). Or as Corner argues: "the researching together of interpretive action and textual signification is still the most important thing for audience research to focus upon" (1991: 14).

The aim of this book is the analysis and researching together the conditions for encoding and for decoding media texts. Thus, we will take another look at Hall's influential encoding/decoding essay. According to this model, the television discourse will be structured to provide a dominant or "preferred meaning"—a so-called "structured polysemy" (see also Morley, 1980). Audiences can negotiate or oppose this meaning in their decoding, but only within the limits of the text. But Hall warns against confusing this polysemy with pluralism. Pluralism requires that the viewpoints of all important groups and subcultures are represented. This is hardly the case in many countries.

It is the polysemic nature of the television text that enables the audiences to go beyond the "preferred reading." However, this is not an indication of audience power. In his discussion of Hall's position on polysemy, Jensen argues that "the polysemy of media texts is only a political potential, and the oppositional decoding of media is not yet a manifestation of political power" (1990: 74).

There is, however, a certain theoretical inconsistency when linking the ideas of the resisting viewer to the notion of polysemic text. The logic in this is indeed contradictory as Corner (1991) points out; a viewer actively resisting the meanings and values of a program—presumably intended by the program makers—seems to presuppose the determinateness of a text rather than its polysemic character.

In this volume, Kirsten Drotner argues that media ethnography is most fruitfully defined as an epistemological alternative to reception studies rather than as a continuation or supplement, as it is often regarded. She uses her own ethnographic fieldwork among teenagers who produced video in their leisure time to demonstrate the difference between talk and action; if there is a discrepancy between what informants say and what they do, this is significant in itself. Drotner discusses different traditions of media ethnography and how they deal with key problems like the contribution of text and context to meaning. She advocates, as indicated, a more narrow or restricted definition of media ethnography. In such a conception, the analytical point of departure is a particular group of people, not a particular medium. In this way one may follow how "different types of media constitute intertextual registers of meaning." The author sees methodological processuality as a major strength in media ethnography. A main difference between media ethnography and reception analysis is the time spent with informants. Drotner finds it difficult to specify how long it takes to do media ethnography. However, the researcher needs to stay long enough with the group of informants that her or his own preconceptions are being questioned. But she feels that processes of signification still should be the core of the investigation.

Thomas Tufte's article is based on his fieldwork in Brazil and is based on Martin-Barbero's theory of social-cultural mediation. Tufte attempts to go beyond the classical dualism of active/passive audiences that has been haunting reception research as well as other approaches to media audiences. The author presents two examples where audiences' consumption of TV fiction sparked spectacular events of mass social movement. First, the mini-series *Rebellious Years*—about the Brazilian student movement's political resistance against the military dictatorship in the late 1960s and early 1970s—was broadcast a few weeks after President Collor had been accused of corruption (by his own brother, on the newscast of the same Rede Globo television that broadcast the miniseries). The TV series sparked a massive mobilization against President Collor—demonstrations that eventually led to his removal. The second event, the real death of the popular telenovela actress Daniela Perez, led to a social movement to revise the Penal Code to arrest the suspected murdered more quickly and efficiently. Tufte concludes that rather than focusing on the narrow relationship between the media text and the audience, the aim should be a mediation ethnography, offering a broader analysis of cultural practices and everyday life.

Meanwhile, Birgitta Höijer reports from several studies of audiences' consumption of three popular genres in television: news, social-realistic fiction, and prime-time soap opera. Höijer describes—building on Bruner—how narratives are not only to be found in texts, but are a general form of organizing experiences in the mind. She describes how the audiences' expectations of fiction differ quite a bit from the expectations they have towards news. Thus, different frames of reference are used as interpreting schemas. In the reception of the social-realist genre, processes of recognition and identification lead to a process this author calls creative illusion—an imaginative impression of reality. In reception of more glamorous popular fiction, less of the viewers' own social reality is brought into the interpretation. Since intertextuality dominates in meaning making of such narratives, Höijer calls this process pleasurable forgetfulness. The news genre is seldom seen to mediate personal identity building. Reception of news is directed towards reality testing in the public sphere. This author emphasizes that whereas a text constrains what meanings viewers make from it, it also invites viewers to make different individual and cultural readings.

How audiences create alternative cultures and texts is the concern of Robert A. White. He proposes a more comprehensive framework of audience interpretations to avoid the dichotomy of either textual determinacy or audience freedom. He focuses on current research dealing with interactive networks around particular genres, and how such networks organize their cultural practice around the media text. White is concerned with some of the central questions of the critical studies tradition: how can mass media contribute to human liberation and to democratization of the social structures? He sees mass media as contributing to the continual creation and maintenance of the mythos that connects and unites a certain society. The constituting factors of mass media and audiences' practices are seen to be: political-economic factors; strategies of attracting audiences; the textual discourse; the audience subjectivities; the social mediations; the deconstruction of the text; and the reconstruction of the text in terms of identities. White also draws a distinction between the notion of "active audience" and a "political active audience."

White's approach echoes the attitudes of some political economists towards textual analysis. In other words, it is mandatory that media
texts are analyzed within the context of production and consumption.
Although none of the representatives of a political economic approach in
this volume specifically present textual analysis in their contributions,
there are numerous examples of such studies (e.g., Dorfman and
Mattelart, 1975; Schlesinger, Murdock and Elliott, 1983). More recently,
some political economists also are working with cultural analysts to produce more comprehensive analyses of media products (e.g., Byars and
Meehan, 1995; Jhally and Lewis, 1992).

INTEGRATING PERSPECTIVES: COOPERATION, CONTROVERSY OR COOPTATION?

In political economy, the primary focus is most often on macro structures, whereas the audience has been assumed as part of the consumption process. Although political economists would want to make the
argument that there are implications for consumption that they have at
least understood and pointed to theoretically, too often these points have
not been explored empirically. They would further argue that the economic context sets the limits and boundaries for reception/consumption
and it is important to begin analysis with a solid understanding of this
context. Yet, it may be true that those adapting a political economic
approach have spent less time studying what happens within those
boundaries, that is, looking at the specific texts that are produced and
audiences' responses to them.
On the other hand, most reception studies have focused on the
micro levels on the consumption side, without always relating them to
larger cultural and political frameworks that set the premises for both
media institutions and for consuming audiences.
In much recent writings on reception theory, there is enthusiasm
regarding the interpretive abilities of the audience or viewers and in
empirical reception work from different countries, the creative abilities of
viewers are often demonstrated (see Katz and Liebes, 1987).
Reception analysis has a different point of departure than political economy. Its sources of inspiration are literary reception theory and
cultural studies, and to some extent uses and gratifications research
(see Hagen, 1992). Thus, its focus of analysis tends to be the text/read-
er interaction and to various extent, in a broader cultural framework.
Theoretical insights are often drawn from phenomenology, hermeneutics, and semiotics. The new ethnographic turn has resulted in a concern
with the "politics of the living room."

Political economy has developed from a social scientific background, drawing on economics, political science, and sociology, most often from Marxist or Marxian perspectives. Thus, its project is often more critical and more macropolitical in nature than reception studies. In order to analyze the mechanisms of capitalism, researchers have aimed to understand power structures relating to communication, both at a global and national level. Not surprisingly, such analysis leads to more pessimistic conclusions than those in the field of reception analysis.[13]

What political economists and reception analysts may have in common is an interest to understand where power is located. For political economists, it is often assumed that power is related to ownership structures, hierarchies and political alliances of media corporations. One of the most populist and controversial notions related in reception research, Fiske's term "semiotic democracy" implies that there is also power (to interpret) on the side of audiences. However, in his celebration of semiotic democracy, Fiske ". . . enthusiastically embraces the central themes of sovereign consumer pluralism" (Curran, 1990: 140). The acknowledgment of audiences' ability to create a variety of meanings and pleasures from media texts tends to confuse audience activity with power. But as Morley (1992; 1993) claims, it would be foolish to compare the power of viewers to reinterpret meaning with the power of media institutions to create the text.

Not everyone applauds the boom of reception studies since the 1980s, as some regard these empirical studies to be too obsessed with the micro level. In this volume, Schiller joins the previous critiques, arguing that inequality and class have disappeared from active audience research, which "weakens, actually undermines, any effort to tangibly resist corporate cultural domination." We understand this skepticism, as studies of micro processes need to be situated within a broader framework. But the macro level should not be understood as static structures; macro structures as Giddens (1991) formulates in his theory of "structuration," both reflect and transform micro processes. Thus, one needs to examine how the micro processes are integrated into the macro structures.

We think research that offers only an understanding of the micro process of consumption without referring to broader cultural, social, and political patterns will have limited value. Researchers need to maintain a critical awareness of the kind that Seiter et al. demonstrate in their study of television audiences: "In our concern for audiences pleasures in such programs we run the risk of continually validating Hollywood's domina-

---

[13]For example, the often quoted study by Liebes and Katz (1990) is taken to support the notion of audiences' sovereignty towards the text. Consequently, the study is interpreted as a refutation of the cultural imperialism thesis, even though it could be argued that a demonstration of variety in audience readings does not necessarily contradict claims of cultural dominance through media.

tion of the worldwide television market" (1989: 5). Instead, the relationship between pleasure and politics should be specified in terms of history and context. In order to understand this relationship, one has to analyze the structural inequalities of media ownership and control, and the consequences for what is available for consumption.

At the same time, analysis of macro processes easily becomes oversimplified if the complexities of consumption in various cultures and subcultures are overlooked. For example, the working class in several European countries have found great pleasure in consuming American popular culture products because these products offered alternatives to their own, elite-dominated culture provided by often paternalistic media institutions (*cf.* Morley, 1989). Or an Indian young woman might enjoy programs that do not portray (and promote) the caste and gender roles of her own society. Through examining the specificities of local consumption processes one can better understand the implications of global communication structures.

The conditions of consumption is a part of the story that should be included, as structures are reproduced in everyday consumption habits. Thus, how audiences interpret and use what they have access to is important to understand. But whether there is any progressive potential in their "resistance" is another part of the story. As Schiller (1989) eloquently demonstrates, a massive, ideologically unanimous and repeated message can be hard for audiences to resist. One of the central questions remains, then, to what extent audiences' decodings constitute any liberating pleasure or social empowerment? For answers, we need the insights offered by political economic and reception analysis to help us understand media, as Meehan has noted in her chapter, as "both manufacture and expression, as consumption and interpretation, as cultural constriction and cultural springboard." We hope that this volume helps further such understanding.

REFERENCES

Ang, I. (1985) *Watching Dallas. Soap Opera and the Melodramatic Imagination.* London: Methuen.

Byars, J. and E. R. Meehan (1995) "Once in a Lifetime: Cable Narrowcasting for Women," *Camera Obscura,* Fall, 13-41.

Condit, C. M. (1989) "The Rhetorical Limits of Polysemy," *Critical Studies in Mass Communication, 6*(2).

Corner, J. (1991) "Meaning, Genre and Context: The Problematics of 'Public Knowledge' in the New Media Studies." In James Curran and Michael Gurevitch, eds. *Mass Media and Society.* London: Edward Arnold.

Curran, J. (1990) "The New Revisionism in Mass Communication Research," *European Journal of Communication, 5*(2-3), June, 135-65.

Dahlgren, P. (1988) "What is the Meaning of This? Viewers' Plural Sense-Making of TV News," *Media, Culture and Society, 10,* 285-301.

Dorfman, A. and A. Mattelart (1975) *How to Read Donald Duck.* London: International General.

Drotner, K. (1993) "Medieetnografiske problemstillinger—en oversikt" [Media Ethnographic Problematics—An Overview], *Mediekultur, 21,* Dec. 5-23.

During, S., ed. (1993) *The Cultural Studies Reader.* New York: Routledge.

Evans, W. A. (1990) "The Interpretive Turn in Media Research: Innovation, Iteration, or Illusion?" *Critical Studies in Mass Communication, 7*(2), 147-68.

Fejes, F. (1984) "Critical Mass Communication Research and Media Effects: The Problem of the Disappearing Audience," *Media, Culture & Society, 6,* 219-32.

Fiske, J. (1987) *Television Culture: Popular Pleasure and Politics.* London and New York: Methuen.

——— (1982) *Introduction to Communication Studies.* London and New York: Methuen.

Garnham, N. (1979) "Contribution to a Political Economy of Mass Communication," *Media, Culture and Society, 1,* 123-46.

——— (1995) "Political Economy and Cultural Studies: Reconciliation or Divorce?" *Critical Studies in Mass Communication, 12*(1), 62-71.

Giddens, A. (1991/84) *The Constitution of Society. Outline of the Theory of Structuration.* Cambridge: Polity Press.

Gripsrud, J. (1988) "Hvorfor skal man kommentere dansk resepsjons-forskning?" [Why comment on Danish reception research?]. *NordicomInformation, 4,* 15-18.

——— (1990): "Toward a Flexible Methodology in Studying Media Meaning: Dynasty in Norway," *Critical Studies in Mass Communication, 7*(2), 1-15.

Grossberg, L. (1995) "Cultural Studies vs. Political Economy: Is Anybody Else Bored with This Debate?" *Critical Studies in Mass Communication, 12*(1), 72-81.

Hagen, I. (1992) *News Viewing Ideals and Everyday Practices: The Ambivalences of Watching Dagsrevyen.* Ph.D. Dissertation, Department of Mass Communication, University of Bergen.

Hall, S. (1980a) "Encoding/Decoding." In Stuart Hall, Dorothy Hobson, Andre Lowe and Paul Willis, eds. *Culture, Media, Language.* London: Hutchinson.

———— (1980b) "Introduction to Media Studies at the Centre." In Stuart Hall, Dorothy Hobson, Andre Lowe and Paul Willis, eds. *Culture, Media, Language*. London: Hutchinson.

Hall, S. and T. Jefferson, eds. (1976) *Resistance Through Rituals: Youth Subcultures in Post-War Britain*. London: Hutchinson.

Hebdige, D. (1979) *Subculture: The Meaning of Style*. London: Methuen.

Hoggart, R. (1957) *The Uses of Literacy*. Fair Lawn, NJ: Essential Books.

Höijer, B. (1990) "Studying Viewers' Reception of Television Programmes: Theoretical and Methodological Considerations," *European Journal of Communication, 5*(1), March, 29-57.

Höijer, B., K. Nowak and S. Ross (1992) "Reception of Television as a Cognitive and Cultural Process (REKK)," *Nordicom Review, 1*, 1-15.

Holub, R. C. (1984) *Reception Theory—A Critical Introduction*. London: Methuen.

Jensen, K. B. (1986) *Making Sense of the News. Towards a Theory and an Empirical Model of Reception for the Study of Mass Communication*. Aarhus: Aarhus University Press.

———— (1990) "The Politics of Polysemy: Television News, Everyday Consciousness and Political Action," *Media, Culture & Society, 12*(1), January, 57-77.

Jensen, K. B. and K. E. Rosengren (1990) "Five Traditions in Search of the Audience," *European Journal of Communication, 5*(2-3), June, 207-39.

Jhally, S. (1990) *The Codes of Advertising: Fetishism and the Political Economy of Meaning in the Consumer Society*. New York: Routledge.

Jhally, S. and J. Lewis (1992) *Enlightened Racism: The Cosby Show, Audiences, and the Myth of the American Dream*. Boulder, CO: Westview Press.

Katz, E. and T. Liebes (1987) "Decoding Dallas: Notes from a Cross-Cultural Study." In Horace Newcomb, ed. *Television: The Critical View*, 4th ed. New York and Oxford: Oxford University Press.

Liebes, T. (1984): "Ethnocriticism: Israelis of Moroccan Ethnicity Negotiate the Meaning of 'Dallas,'" *Visual Communication, 10*(3), 46-73.

Liebes, T. and E. Katz (1990) *The Export of Meaning. Cross-Cultural Readings of Dallas*. New York and Oxford: Oxford University Press.

Livant, W. (1979) "The Audience Commodity: On the 'Blindspot' Debate," *Canadian Journal of Political and Social Theory, 3*(1), 91-106.

Livingstone, S. M. (1993) "The Rise and Fall of Audience Research: An Old Story With a New Ending," *Journal of Communication, 43*(4), 5-13.

Lull, J. (1980) "The Social Uses of Television," *Human Communication Research, 6,* 197-209.

—— (1988) "Critical Response: The Audience as Nuisance," *Critical Studies in Mass Communication, 5,* 239-43.

——— (1990) *Inside Family Viewing: Ethnographic Research on Television's Audiences.* London and New York: Comedia.

Mattelart, A. and S. Siegelaub, eds. (1983) *Communication and Class Struggle, Vol. 2: Liberation, Socialism.* New York: International General.

McQuail, D. (1994) *Mass Communication Theory: An Introduction,* 3rd ed. London: Sage.

Meehan, E. (1984) "Ratings and the Institutional Approach: A Third Answer to the Commodity Question," *Critical Studies in Mass Communication, 1*(2), 216-25.

—— (1986) "Conceptualizing Culture as Commodity: The Problem of Television," *Critical Studies in Mass Communication,* December.

Meehan, E., V. Mosco and J. Wasko (1994) "Rethinking Political Economy: Change and Continuity." In Mark R. Levy and Michael Gurevitch, eds. *Defining Media Studies: Reflections on the Future of the Field.* New York: Oxford University Press.

Morley, D. (1980) *The Nationwide Audience: Structure and Decoding.* London: British Film Institute.

—— (1986) *Family Television: Cultural Power and Domestic Leisure.* London: Comedia.

—— (1989) "Changing Paradigms in Audience Studies." In Ellen Seiter, Hans Borchers, Gabriele Kreutzner and Eva-Maria Warth, eds. *Remote Control. Television, Audiences, & Cultural Power.* London: Routledge: 16-44.

——— (1992) *Television Audiences & Cultural Studies.* London and New York: Routledge.

——— (1993) "Active Audience Theory: Pendulums and Pitfalls," *Journal of Communication, 43*(4), 13-20.

Mosco, V. (1996) *The Political Economy of Communications.* London: Sage.

Murdock, G. (1978) "Blindspots About Western Marxism: A Reply to Dallas Smythe," *Canadian Journal of Political and Social Theory. 2*(2), 109-119.

—— (1989) "Critical Inquiry and Audience Activity." In Brenda Dervin, Lawrence Grossberg, Barbara O'Keefe and Ellen Wartella, eds. *Rethinking Communication. Volume 2: Paradigm Exemplars.* Beverly Hills, CA: Sage.

—— (1991) "Communications, Modernity and the Human Sciences." In Helge Rønning and Knut Lundby, eds. *Media and Communication. Readings in Methodology, History and Culture.* Oslo: Norwegian University Press.

Murdock, G. and P. Golding (1974) "For a Political Economy of Mass Communication." In Ralph Miliband and John Saville, eds. *Socialist Register*. London: Merlin Press: 205-34.

—— (1996) "Culture, Communications, and Political Economy." In James Curran and Michael Gurevitch, eds. *Mass Media and Society*, 2nd ed. London: Arnold.

Parkin, F. (1973) *Class, Inequality and Political Order*. London: Paladin.

Pendakur, M. (1993) "Political Economy and Ethnography: Transformations in an Indian Village." In Janet Wasko, Vincent Mosco and Manjunath Pendakur, eds. *Illuminating the Blindspots: Essays Honoring Dallas W. Smythe*. Norwood, NJ: Ablex.

Schiller, H. I. (1989) *Culture, Inc. The Corporate Takeover of Public Expression*. New York and Oxford: Oxford University Press.

Schlesinger, P., G. Murdock and P. Elliott (1983) *Televising Terrorism: Political Violence in Popular Culture*. London: Comedia.

Schudson, M. (1987) "The New Validation of Popular Culture: Sense and Sentimentality in Academia," *Critical Studies in Mass Communication, 4*, 51-68.

Seiter, E., H. Borchers, G. Kreutzner and E. M. Warth (1989) "Introduction." In Ellen Seiter et al., eds. *Remote Control. Television, Audiences and Cultural Power*. London: Routledge.

Silverstone, R. (1990) "Television and Everyday Life: Towards an Anthropology of the Television Audience." In Marjorie Ferguson, ed. *Public Communication: The New Imperatives*. London: Sage.

Smythe, D. W. (1977) "Communications: Blindspot of Western Marxism," *Canadian Journal of Political and Social Theory, 1*(3), 1-27.

—— (1981) *Dependency Road: Communication, Capitalism, Consciousness and Canada*. Norwood, NJ: Ablex.

Thompson, E. B. (1968) *The Making of the English Working Class*. New York: Vintage Books.

von Feilitzen, C. (1988) "Den fula ankungen. Om dansk resepsjonsforskning" [The Ugly Duckling. About Danish Reception Research]. *NordicomInformation, 4*, 9-15.

Wasko, J. (1996) "Understanding the Disney Universe." In James Curran and Michael Gurevitch, eds. *Mass Media and Society*, 2nd ed. London: Arnold.

Williams, R. (1958) *Culture and Society, 1780-1950*. New York: Columbia University Press.

II

DEFINING THE AUDIENCE

2

Questioning the Concept of the Audience

Vincent Mosco
Lewis Kaye

WHERE'S THE BEEF? *How disgusting! CALM DOWN*

The concept of the audience is one of the governing ideas in mass communications research. It is also one of the most hotly contested. Even
scholars offering a critical view of the notion acknowledge its significance. In a widely cited assessment of the term, Allor (1988: 217) concluded that "the concept of the audience . . . is the underpinning prop for
the analysis of the social impact of mass communication in general."
Moores starts his assessment of the term by seriously questioning its
value. In answer to the question, "What is an audience anyway?" he
concludes (1993: 1-2):

> There is no stable entity, which we can isolate and identify as the
> media audience, no single object that is unproblematically "there" for
> us to observe and analyze.

31

The plural "audiences" is preferable, he maintains, but recognizes that it, too, is lacking. He poses the question more starkly: "So given the lack of an easily identifiable thing to be researched, how is it that we have come to accept the category of 'the audience' as a self-evident fact?" His answer (1993: 2) is equally stark (and refreshing):

> An important reason for the word's naturalization has undoubtedly been the vested interests of media institutions (as well as many academic researchers) in imagining such a fixed entity to measure and monitor.

Nevertheless, after even more refreshing candor ("there are careers to be made and books to be written about 'the audience'!"), he proceeds to write a book about *Interpreting Audiences.*

To Moores' credit, one can safely conclude that his explicit questioning of why the term is used and his reference, however brief, to the institutional reasons for its perpetuation, are long overdue. Admittedly the concept has been far from uncontested. There is no shortage of debate about whether the audience is best viewed as active or passive (and if so, how active or passive), as singular or plural, as a commodity, a form of labor, or as an ensemble of social practices. Similarly, we find no lack of argument about whether the audience is best viewed through the lens of the postmodernist, the political economist, the ethnographer, or some combination of these and other perspectives. There is no denying the value of these debates because they have expanded the scope of media studies. Nevertheless, they all miss a fundamental point because none will address the question of why we continue to use the term. This is especially significant for the audience concept because it has no particular warrant in intellectual or disciplinary history. This is unlike concepts such as race, gender, social class, culture, or the state, whose histories are complex but traceable to extensive debate across a range of disciplines. The concept of the audience was hatched largely out of the marketing departments of companies with a stake in selling products through the media. This is not news to media scholars. What is puzzling, however, is why the term continues to be used. Why does scholarship claiming a disciplinary warrant for communication studies continue to more or less rely on a marketing term as a central conceptual linchpin?

Admittedly, one of the most frequently used names of the discipline, *mass communication,* implies large groups of people exposed to common media texts. In other words, we see an inherent concern with what is commonly known as the audience. Yet the *concept* of the audience is something that has taken on a specialized life of its own within this field of study. From a primarily quantitative concern of broadcasters—that is, the need for commercial broadcasters to determine as accurately as possible just how many people are "tuned in" to their broadcasts—the term *audience* has over time become embedded within the literature of mass communications studies. How has this ostensibly industrial term come to its central position as a key analytical category within the academic lexicon of mass communications?

This chapter is a brief and modest effort to trace the usage of the term *audience* within the field of mass communications. It is an attempt to clear some ground by exploring the roots of the word itself, how it entered the English language, and how it has been used. By doing this, we can provide a foundation from which to investigate how *audience* entered into the specialized lexicon of mass communications studies. Its adoption as a social research category by commercial broadcasters has effectively set an agenda for determining the meaning of the social relations of mass media.

AUDIENCE: GENEALOGY OF A TERM

The English word *audience* can be traced to the Latin root *audire,* meaning to hear. According to *The Oxford English Dictionary* (Simpson and Weiner, 1989: 779), the earliest uses of the word are found in the 14th century. At this point, there was no conception of the audience as a group to which a communication is directed; that is, our common understanding had not yet made an appearance. Rather, audience referred primarily to formal hearings in front of a magistrate, court official, or sovereign. It is interesting to note the power dynamics implicit in this usage of the term. Individuals are *granted* audience, with such a meeting implying a favor or privilege bestowed by a superior. It is also useful to note that technically this represents a reversal of the activity of hearing specified by the Latin root. Although a commoner may be granted audience, it is actually the official who is listening. This reversal may well refer to the grantee's right to hear the official response. Thus we see the emergence of a passive, and in a sense subservient, role attributed to those given audience, a role consistent with the power dynamic inherent in the magistrate/commoner relationship.

This definition of audience is tied quite closely to other early uses that appear directly linked to the Latin root. *The Oxford English Dictionary* (Simpson and Weiner, 1989: 779) lists a 14th-century use, specifically in Chaucer, referring to the act or condition of hearing. This has singular and general dimensions, referring to both an individual's actions or ability to hear or be heard, and to the ability of a specific public, such as a church congregation, to hear a common speech. It is this latter, more general sense of audience that likely gives rise to the considerations of audience as object: in other words, considerations of an audience. Indeed, by 1708 John Kersey (1969 [1708]), in his *Dictionarium Anglo-Britannicum* defined audience as "the hearing of one that speaks, or the Assembly of Hearers." This notion of audience as object is to a degree faithful to earlier definitions. Those who are granted audience can refer to themselves as having had an audience, and might well be able to call themselves the audience, albeit an audience of one.

It is in this latter definition that uses of *audience* within the study of mass communications find their lineage. It is quite apparent that references to television, radio, and print audiences can be usefully compared to notions of an "Assembly of Hearers." Indeed, its usage in this sense may well be an extension of considerations of theater audiences. The earliest reference in *The Oxford English Dictionary* (Simpson and Weiner, 1989: 779), specifically with respect to an audience for cultural activities, in fact refers to the readers of a book, a reference from 1855. The book noted was one with a religious theme, and we may speculate that it draws the term audience from its application to a congregation, or those witness to a sermon. However, with the emergence of these and certain other media of communications throughout the 19th and 20th centuries, the term audience was to find successive applications.

The fundamental experience constituting the audience is the exposure of a group of people to a common message. The key distinction between this notion of audience and earlier ones is in fact based on the form of communication: no longer does an audience have to be a physical assembly of people. New media technologies allow for physically separated groups of people to be exposed to identical texts. With the advance of industrial, mass society in the West, and the concurrent diffusion of literacy and media technologies of communication, we can see the emergence of a very distinct notion of audience. At this point we need to distinguish between common, everyday usage of the word and more specialized and specific meanings employed by researchers. With the rise of commercial radio broadcasting came the first attempts to systematically investigate the dimensions of a hitherto unknown and amorphous entity referred to as the audience. This research essentially transformed a common word into a statistical, and fundamentally institutional category, a transformation carrying significant social, political, and economic ramifications.

MASS MEDIA AND THE CONSTITUTION OF THE AUDIENCE

From the beginning, commercial broadcasters referred to their listeners as an audience. Indeed, H.P. Davis, a Vice President of Westinghouse Electric and Manufacturing Company and the man responsible for establishing Pittsburgh's KDKA, one of America's first commercial radio stations, spoke of the station's first broadcast and of the need to "draft" an audience:

> A broadcasting station is a rather useless enterprise unless there is someone to listen to it. Here was an innovation, and even though advertised, few then, other than possibly some of the amateurs who had receiving sets, could listen to us. To meet this situation we had a number of simple receiving outfits manufactured. These were distributed among friends and to several of the officers of the company. Thus was the first audience drafted. (cf. Stamps, 1979: 22-3)

One can easily infer an objectified audience from the passive role assigned to it by Davis. The audience is here contrasted with "amateurs," or those who often took a technical interest in radio for its own sake, individuals not necessarily content with passively consuming broadcast material. Yet an implicit assumption in Davis' statement is that people who have a radio must be listening: audience members are not constituted simply out of the fact they *possess* a radio. The audience is an assumed entity, unknown and certainly unquantified which, while objectified in word, remains amorphous, still defined as the Assembly of Hearers, albeit an anonymous assemblage.

It was not until broadcasters needed to determine the actual size of the unknown audience that the analytical objectification of the audience began. Critics of this institutional need of broadcasters to "know" their audience (Ang, 1991; Gandy, 1990) point to the desire of broadcasters for some degree of control over the audience, whether out of the economic incentive of attracting advertisers or the cultural incentive of legitimizing their activities. If broadcasters could have knowledge of how many people are listening (or viewing), programming success could be determined by comparing the audience sizes of different shows. This was to have important consequences, fundamentally transforming a common word into an institutional term, and eventually bequeathing to the field of mass communications an analytical category loaded with meaning.

The roots of systematic audience research can be traced to the early activities of radio broadcasters in attempting to count listeners. Other mass media such as print and film could rely on circulation numbers or box-office receipts respectively to tell them how large their audience was. But the anonymity of radio broadcasting necessitated a different approach, one that would call for systematic research techniques. This need to determine how many people were listening was one shared by commercial (primarily American) and public service broadcasters (notably British and Canadian). Although the underlying rationales between public service and commercial broadcasting may differ, the impetus behind audience research remained the same: broadcasters needed to know that their programming was reaching people. These concerns are summed up well in a statement made by Val Gielgud, the British Broadcasting Corporation's Director of Drama in 1930, ". . . it must be of considerable disquiet to many people beside myself to think that a very great deal of our money and time and effort may be expended on broadcasting into a void" (cf. Silvey, 1974: 14).

AUDIENCE AS PASSIVE MASS

The first part of this chapter examined how the word audience entered into common usage in the English language, and how this word itself became an institutional term. We now turn to how the audience became a specialized academic signifier. One way of answering the central question posed by this paper—how did an ostensibly industrial term become central to the academic study of mass communications?—is to briefly examine the origins of the "field" of mass communications itself.

The rise of media studies in the early 20th century came about because of worries over the proliferation of new forms of mass communications. Newspapers, films, radio, and even comic books became objects of popular worry and scholarly study. The reach of the mass media, and the anonymity of the consumers of media content were unprecedented features of social life, and gave many cause for grave concern. Sexual promiscuity, violence, and juvenile delinquency were seen as social ills fueled by exposure to media content. Regardless, some conception of an audience, whether explicitly stated or implicitly assumed, underpinned much of this early concern over the effects of the mass media. Stamps (1979 [1956]), in his historical-descriptive study of the concept of the mass audience in American broadcasting notes this feature as well, and cites it as a difficulty in locating the earliest use of the term in reference to broadcasting. Indeed, any concern with media effects necessarily presumes the existence of an audience being affected.

Early worries over the influences of media content can be roughly paralleled with concerns over the effects of propaganda. Thus the earliest uses of the term *audience* in academic discourse generally share the belief in the audience as a passive mass easily swayed by powerful media messages. In itself this is not totally surprising, considering the common definition of audience as an Assembly of Hearers; this objectified Assembly lent itself well to considerations of the audience as a mass, with no relations other than common exposure to a text. At this time, much play can be also seen between the notions of public, listeners, readers, and audience. These terms were often used interchangeably, and as such no specifically academic use of audience was present. The audience, as a social category on a par with class, race, gender, or even mass, can not really be said to exist, but the perception that it is an analytical entity grew with the legitimacy of sustained academic analyses of the mass media.

An early and important attempt to document the effects of media content upon viewers was conducted between 1929 and 1932 through the philanthropy of the Payne Foundation. Known as the Payne Fund studies, these investigations were in response to the popularly held belief that risqué movie content contributed to juvenile delinquency and other social ills. According to Lowery and DeFleur (1995: 24), these studies had two main objectives: "In one category, the goals are to assess the content of the films and to determine the size and content of their audiences. The second category attempts to assess the effects on those audiences of their exposures to the themes and messages of motion pictures." These studies concluded that media content did indeed have an effect on audiences, a conclusion that served to reinforce public perceptions of the dangers of uncontrolled media content.

The importance of this study to the field of mass communications cannot be underestimated. Lowery and DeFleur (1995: 24) go so far as to say the Payne Fund studies, by combining the popular concern over media content with quantitative social science techniques, effectively "gave birth to the scientific study of mass communication." Although this should not be confused with the disciplinization and institutionalization of mass communication, the conceptions of the audience employed by Payne Fund researchers and by self-conscious communications scholars such as Lazarsfeld are quite similar. What we find is a direct consideration of the audience as an important and legitimate object of social research. Although their raison d'être differed, both the Payne Fund studies and Lazarsfeld's Princeton Radio Research Project agreed upon an audience that is knowable; this assumption would help to legitimate the study of audiences.

Utilizing the audience as a primary unit of analysis results in an implicit privileging of this one social relationship over others, such as class, race, and gender. Giving the audience priority within the discourse of scientific communications research served to help legitimate the sender, commercial broadcasters, and the power relations inherent in the broadcaster-audience relationship. Ruggles (1994: 146) reminds us of the social and political consequences of such an assumption, and its corresponding sense of audience:

> The mature development of commercial mass communications institutions has occasioned large-scale change in the structure of public discourse. . . . [T]he organization of mass audiences as a tool for reducing the unit cost of message distribution and the high degree of control of message context which commercial firms were able to offer preferred clients radically changed the relative communicative power of competing interests.

Ruggles is arguing that the communicative power of commercial broadcasters and their "preferred clients" was enhanced by the organization of the mass audience, an organization conducted through the use of systematic audience research and academically legitimated through analyses focusing on the effects of media on such audiences.

The notion of the audience as a passive mass is one that recurs throughout the history of mass communications studies. The propaganda function of the commercial mass media posited by Marxist cultural theorists, such as those of the Frankfurt School, often assumes a passive, consuming role for the audience by emphasizing the relative power of ideologically loaded media content. Mass society theorists make similar assumptions, arguing that media content reinforces the existing social order and that people are generally resigned to this fate (McQuail, 1983).

The passive role ascribed to audiences is often needed to justify a particular political worldview. Yet if this is true here, then is not interpretation of the audience, in terms of a statistical, institutional or demographic category, itself a political act, suggesting the legitimation of the broadcaster-audience power relation? This legitimation is achieved partly by the academic acceptance of such a relationship, through its consequent use as a basis for investigation and interpretation. However, the passive view of the audience has been challenged over time by communication scholars arguing for a more active sense of audience. Although perhaps worthy in intent, debate such as this further legitimates a term by entrenching its use within the discourse of mass communications.

THE ACADEMY AND COMMERCIAL AUDIENCE RESEARCH

The earliest self-conscious and systematic academic studies of mass communications were conducted by researchers such as Paul

Lazarsfeld, Wilbur Schramm and others affiliated with commercial research initiatives, such as those supported by the Princeton Radio Research Project. A number of academic studies conducted throughout the late 1930s and early 1940s frequently engaged in analyses of radio audiences, simultaneously, as Buxton (1994: 148) notes, "accepting the framework of commercial broadcasting as a given . . ." Gitlin (1978), in his critique of early mass communications research, argues that an "administrative" agenda derived from the needs of commercial broadcasters drove much of this research, and thus these needs in a sense are responsible for determining much of the so-called "dominant paradigm" of mass communications studies.

Quantitative and qualitative knowledge of the radio audience became a central concern to both broadcasters and academics during the 1940s. It is here, in this historically important period, that the commercial orientation of much early mass communications research is readily apparent. Indeed, Lazarsfeld and Kendall (1948: 82) explicitly call for a connection between the research activities of commercial media and academic researchers:

> We can hope that as time goes on it will increasingly become clear that continuing social research is one of the responsibilities incumbent upon the large communications media. As a matter of fact, it is to the credit of the radio industry that it has led the other media of mass communication in showing what can be done. . . . The research student, on his part, has the responsibility of showing the implications of his data, however fragmentary they may be at any given moment.

This suggests a direct relationship between the goals of commercial broadcasters and the research activities of academics. A concrete example of this is given by Eaman (1994), who cites the participation in 1935 of Lazarsfeld, then professor at Columbia University and director of the Bureau of Applied Social Research, along with Frank Stanton, the first head of CBS' research department, in the development of the CBS Program Analyzer, a device designed to gauge audience reactions to specific CBS programs.

Early academic studies of the audience often focused on questions of audience composition, a subject of obvious appeal to commercial broadcasters. One such study, *Social Stratification of the Radio Audience* (Beville, 1939), provides an excellent illustration. The title of this study suggests an analysis focused on investigating audience members based on social class affiliations. In actuality, Beville's work reads more like a demographic analysis, subdividing program audiences by income group and attempting to determine which programs appeal to whom. Indeed, Beville's study explicitly uses commercial audience data and research techniques in an attempt to draw scholarly conclusions. The directors of the Princeton Radio Research Project wrote in the foreword of the study's twofold purpose:

> The first was to acquaint a larger public, presumably one interested in educational broadcasting, with the vast fund of material which commercial agencies have been collecting for years and which is quite astounding as to the amount and regularity of canvass. There are few areas of social research which could boast such a large collection of data. But because they are collected for commercial purposes, they have never received attention from educators. The second purpose behind this report was to show the useful sort of information which can be gained from it. The ratings are used by sponsors and producers to test whether their programs are successful at the time of the canvass, and are then usually filed away. The student would like to see them further used as indices of human behavior in the important field of communication research. (Beville, 1939: i)

This quotation highlights the overt commercial underpinnings of early communications research. The "social research" noted deals primarily with the determination of program popularity, and "human behavior" is here crudely defined as little more than the selection of programs.

The convenience of using pre-existing commercial data for academic research should not be underestimated when considering how a commercially defined term such as the audience entered into wide academic usage. Indeed, if commercial data were to play a large role in academic research, so too would commercial determination, whether implicit or explicit, of legitimate analytical categories.

We must also here consider how in the 1920s and 1930s private funding helped to shape social research in general, as well as specific initiatives such as the Princeton Radio Research Project. Gitlin (1978: 226) argues that research agendas at this time were substantially influenced by the "mutually indispensable partnerships" between universities, corporations, and private trusts such as the Rockefeller Foundation. These relationships served to secure funding for universities partly by putting "sociological methods at the service of a brash, expanding consumer capitalism . . ." (Gitlin, 1978: 228). The "audience," as defined by broadcasters, would thus seem to naturally become an object of scholarly investigation.

AN ACTIVE AUDIENCE IS STILL AN AUDIENCE

Notions of audience activity came quickly after the academicization of mass communications studies. The early focus on ratings research was not sufficient to sustain prolonged academic investigation. Likewise, the deepening sophistication over the approach to questions of media effects required theories that would have to go beyond simple quantitative and passive models of the audience. Yet the focus on audiences remained. As such, we see a rise in theoretical perspectives stressing the active nature of audiences and the relative lack of power of media texts, and hence broadcasters.

One of the earliest of this type of theoretical perspective was the "two-step flow" model of communication offered by Lazarsfeld and Katz in 1948. This model introduced the intervening variable of the "opinion leader" to help explain why media texts do not necessarily have the desired, direct effect. Although the merits of this approach have been widely debated and critiqued, the important feature is that for the first time people were seen as playing an active, albeit institutionally circumscribed, role in the consumption of media texts. This broke somewhat with the history of "audience" as a numerically defined entity, transforming what was essentially a statistical entity into an organic and reflexive social grouping. The political significance of this was not only to theoretically diminish the power of the mass media, but to further elevate the audience to the status of a legitimate feature of social life.

Just as the consideration of the audience as a passive mass is a fundamentally political decision, so too is investing the audience with all manner of discriminating and active qualities. For Ang (1991), it represents a reclamation of the audience from the ratings charts of institutional audience researchers. Cantor and Cantor (1986: 223) reinterpret the audience as "aggregates or clusters of taste segments," envisioning them as being selective about their media intake. Uses and gratification theory in general attempts to downplay the power of media texts, preferring to concentrate on the question of how audiences make use of the media. Ethnographic research observes audiences in a natural setting to determine how they constitute their relationship to media. What all of these approaches share is the desire to reformulate a pre-existing theoretical construct, albeit according to different political and scholarly motivations. But again, by doing so they serve to reinforce the concept's status, further entrenching what was originally a statistical marketing device as a legitimate object of analysis.

The concern here is not to confront each of these positions, but to ask why the audience is still the focal point for analysis. All of these approaches start with a central consideration of the audience, and proceed to draw their conclusions based upon this feature. The attempt at the theoretical reclamation of the audience simply serves to further legitimate it as an important and central concept, despite its origins as a marketing term. Angus (1994: 234) rues the fact that much contemporary cultural studies emphasizing audience activity offers little more than earlier pluralist approaches that stress "the ingenuity of people to use the products of mass culture." This may well be due to the theoretical weakness of focusing on the audience, a focus that leaves little room for any activity other than the consumption of media texts.

This is is particularly unfortunate because the very term *audience* is not an analytic category, like class, gender, or race, but a product of the media industry itself, which uses the term to identify markets and to define a commodity. References to audience activity have given the term an analytical and experiential reality that has not been documented and which should therefore warrant greater care in use. At the very least, it is premature to assert that the demographic category "audiences" *act* when we have not established the conceptual value of the term, particularly its relationship to social class, race, ethnicity, and gender, which are more than demographic groupings—*they are lived experiences.* People, organized as social actors in various class, gender, race, and other social dimensions, carry out activities, including resistance to media presentations, the significance of which is an empirical question testable through a range of procedures.

BEYOND THE AUDIENCE

Following from this position, one way out of the audience morass is to consider alternative approaches to the interpretation of media consumption, approaches that decline to accept audience status as a fundamentally determinant social relation. One such example is provided by Press (1991; see also Tichi, 1991), who situates the experience of television viewing within the wider social relations of gender, class, and age. The analysis of media effects remains the focus here, but it does not treat women as a specific audience, constituted in their relationship to television. Rather, what is important is the lived experiences women bring to television viewing, and how these experiences help one to interpret the social relations of media activity.

Press acknowledges that the process of media reception is complicated and her approach allows her to avoid the extreme conclusions that viewers are passive in the face of dominant media ideology and that viewer interpretation is automatically valorized. Using ethnographic research on women's television use, she argues that not only does gender influence media consumption and interpretation, but class and generational affiliations further shape such media habits. When approached along these lines, the fact that different groups of viewers interpret media content differently is not altogether surprising. In a sense she could be said to be documenting an "active audience." However, Press' approach has the conceptual strength to sidestep this intellectual dead-end and ask the questions that deal with why such differences emerge. Lived experiences such as gender, class, and age are what constitute us as human beings, and it is this identity that is brought to the viewing experience.

Long (1994) provides another useful example in her project that confronts the image of the solitary reader, reconceptualizing this cultural act as a fundamentally social one. Her research entails an examination of women's reading groups, analyzing how these groups have allowed women to come together to determine meaning from media texts and how this social activity has served to transform their own image of women's role in society. As with Press (1991), Long's approach allows her to move beyond a simplistic conception of women as audiences for reading materials instead seeing how they actively constitute themselves in relation to the media. By focusing on the reading groups themselves, Long provides us with a deeper understanding of how particular groups of people organize themselves into specific audiences. This approach also leaves room for class and race considerations, and how these identities play a part in the choice of texts to be read, how interpretation is achieved collectively and what, if any, political and social agenda is behind such activities.

Long also exhorts us to pay attention to what she terms the "social infrastructure of reading." This consideration has two basic dimensions. First, we need to remember "that reading must be taught, and that the socialization into reading always takes place within specific social relationships" (Long, 1994: 192-3). This is an important reminder for those who study the mass media. Applying this observation we can say that one's socialization into viewing also takes place within specific social relationships, be they familial, gendered, racial, generational, or otherwise. This leads us, as Press does, to consideration of the social relations that constitute us as social human beings prior to our membership in any particular audience. The second dimension of this social infrastructure Long refers to as the "social base" (1994: 193), comparing this to the physical infrastructure required for transportation systems. This consideration is vitally important, for it directs us to the spheres of production and distribution. This reminds us that what is available for consumption is often institutionally circumscribed, something that political economists, among others, have long argued. Audience "activity," however conceptualized, is constrained by both factors of socialization and what fundamentally amounts to the social distribution of power.

A final example of an intellectual approach that transcends the traditional treatment of the audience is offered by Davis (1986), who provides us with an analysis of the uses of parades and street theater in antebellum Philadelphia. Spectacles such as these can be considered as precursors of 20th-century media texts. Parades provided an essential form of public communication. Their organization also reflected social status and power relations. For instance, parades such as those celebrating civic occasions were often organized by those in the upper classes, such as budding industrialists, wealthy merchants, and skilled artisans. The excessive pageantry of these parades was meant not only as a celebration but as a display of social power and an attempt to legitimize the existing social order. Parades from those of the lower classes, such as the Mummers or striking workers, often lacked such excessive displays of wealth and formal organization and were meant as a challenge to the existing social order.

This observation reminds us that the processes of production involve an attempt, whether implicit or explicit, to construct meaning. Audience members' relations to such spectacles often depended on the meanings implicit in each particular parade, and their responses often depended on their position in the social hierarchy. One of the most interesting responses noted by Davis was the ability of parade watchers to actually participate in the parade itself. Excessive pageantry, garish displays of wealth, and quasi-militaristic order worked to prevent audience members from participating, instead relegating them to the sidelines as the dominant classes' vision of the legitimate social order flowed past. Working class parades, on the other hand, tended to have far less formal organization and at times actively encouraged parade watchers to march and otherwise participate in the event. This observation forces us again to consider the institutional limitations of the production process itself. Audience members, we must constantly remember, exist not only in relation to the media text itself but are constituted out of the entire set of social production relations.

CONCLUSION

There is no denying the value of the manifold debates about the audience, because they have expanded the scope of media studies. Nevertheless, they all miss a fundamental point, because none will address the question of why we continue to use the term. This is especially significant for the audience concept, because it has no particular warrant in intellectual history. This is unlike concepts such as race, gender, social class, culture, or the state, whose histories are complex but traceable to extensive debate across a range of disciplines. The concept of the audience was created largely out of the marketing departments of companies with a stake in selling products through the media. What continues to be puzzling is why the term continues to be used. Why does scholarship claiming a disciplinary warrant for communication studies continue to more or less rely on a marketing term as a central conceptual tool?

This chapter provided a modest effort to trace the usage of the term audience within the field of mass communications. It cleared some ground by exploring the roots of the word itself, how it entered the English language, and how it has been used. By doing this, it offered a base from which to investigate how *audience* entered into the specialized usage of mass communications studies. Its adoption as a social research category by commercial broadcasters has effectively set an agenda for determining the meaning of the social relations of mass media. This is unfortunate, because the central concern with audiences from researchers involved with the Princeton Radio Research Project and other business-sponsored programs has bequeathed to the field a concept ill-equipped for the critical analysis of media consumption and interpretation.

The chapter concluded by providing a few exemplars of attempts to move beyond the audience. These join a growing group of scholars who aim to recover the lived experience of people's use of the media and demonstrate how this is constituted in the social relations of class, gender, and race.

REFERENCES

Allor, M. (1988) "Relocating the Site of the Audience." *Critical Studies in Mass Communication, 5,* September, 217-33.

Ang, I. (1991) *Desperately Seeking the Audience.* London: Routledge.

Angus, I. (1994) "Democracy and the Constitution of Audiences: A Comparative Media Theory Perspective." In J. Cruz and J. Lewis, eds. *Viewing, Reading, Listening: Audiences and Cultural Reception.* Boulder, CO: Westview Press: 233-52.

Beville, H. M. Jr. (1939) *Social Stratification of the Radio Audience.* Princeton, NJ: Princeton University, Office of Radio Research.

Buxton, W. J. (1994) "The Political Economy of Communications Research." In Robert Babe, ed. *Information and Communication in Economics.* Boston: Kluwer Academic Publishers: 147-75.

Cantor, M. G. and J. M. Cantor (1986) "Audience Composition and Television Content: The Mass Audience Revisited." In S. J. Ball-

Rokeach and M.G. Cantor, eds. *Media, Audience and Social Structure* . Newbury Park, CA: Sage: 214-25.

Davis, S. (1986) *Parades and Power: Street Theatre in Nineteenth-Century Philadelphia.* Philadelphia: Temple University Press.

Eaman, R. A. (1994) *Channels of Influence: CBC Audience Research and the Canadian Public.* Toronto: University of Toronto Press.

Gandy, O. H. Jr. (1990) "Tracking the Audience." In J. Downing et al., eds. *Questioning the Media.* Newbury Park, CA: Sage: 166-79.

Gitlin, T. (1978) "Media Sociology: The Dominant Paradigm," *Theory and Society, 6*(2), 205-53.

Kersey, J. (1969[1708]) *Dictionarium Anglo-Britannicum.* Menston, England: The Scolar Press.

Lazarsfeld, P. F. and P. L. Kendall (1948) *Radio Listening in America.* New York: Prentice-Hall.

Long, E. (1994) "Textual Interpretation as Collective Action." In J. Cruz and J. Lewis, eds. *Viewing, Reading, Listening: Audiences and Cultural Reception.* Boulder, CO: Westview Press: 181-211.

Lowery, S. A. and M. L. DeFleur (1995) *Milestones in Mass Communication Research,* 3rd ed. White Plains, NY: Longman.

McQuail, D. (1983) *Mass Communication Theory: An Introduction.* London: Sage.

Moores, S. (1993) *Interpreting Audiences: The Ethnography of Media Consumption.* London: Sage.

Press, A. L. (1991) *Women Watching Television: Gender, Class, and Generation in the American Television Experience.* Philadelphia: University of Pennsylvania Press.

Ruggles, M. A. (1994) *The Audience Reflected in the Medium of Law: A Critique of the Political Economy of Speech Rights in the United States.* Norwood, NJ: Ablex.

Silvey, R. (1974) *Who's Listening?: The Story of BBC Audience Research.* London: George Allen & Unwin.

Simpson, J. A. and E. S. C. Weiner, eds. (1989) *The Oxford English Dictionary.* Oxford, UK: Clarendon Press.

Stamps, C. H. (1979[1956]) *The Concept of the Mass Audience in American Broadcasting: An Historical-Descriptive Study.* New York: Arno Press (reprint of the author's doctoral thesis, Northwestern University, 1956).

Tichi, C. (1991) *Electronic Hearth: Creating an American Television Culture.* New York: Oxford University Press.

3

Peculiar Commodities: Audiences at Large in the World of Goods

Graham Murdock

THE DEATH OF THE READER

In 1968, a year of ruptures, Roland Barthes declared the "death of the author." Texts, he argued, should no longer be seen as messages dispatched by their inventors, but as sites of "multiple writings . . . entering into mutual relations of dialogue, parody, contestation." And since their socially active meanings were constructed "not in [their] origin but in [their] destination," it was time to announce the demise of the producer and "the birth of the reader" (Barthes, 1977: 148). Reception was no longer a simple act of tearing open the packaging to get to the present inside. There was no gift. There were only layers of wrapping that could be cut up and made into collages.

This view resonated strongly with the growing anthropological interest in goods as means of expression (e.g., Douglas and Isherwood, 1979) and with work in the newly emerging field of contemporary cultural studies. This refused any suggestion that popular media had simple, direct, "effects," and continually emphasized the creativity of everyday consumption. In one of the first ethnographies of this "new wave," Paul Willis explored how a group of motor bike boys assembled clothing, music, and machines into a distinctive expressive style (Willis, 1978). This idea of consumption as bricolage was also central to Dick Hebdige's general account of subcultures, published the following year. His argument that popular culture offered "a set of symbols, objects, and artefacts, which can be assembled and reassembled by different groups in a literally limitless number of combinations," proved immediately attractive and the book's success gave it wide currency (Hebdige, 1979: 104).

It did not seem to work so well for television viewing, however. Yet it was television that many researchers in cultural studies were most interested in as by the late 1960s in Britain, the box in the corner had established itself as the undisputed center of contemporary cultural life. The problem was that television's texts were public goods not commodities. Before the arrival of the video recorder they could be consumed but not owned, altered imaginatively but not "customized" or reassembled. Because viewers appeared to be at one remove from the world of goods, the notion that they were "reading" a text seemed entirely appropriate. Through letters, depth interviews, and group discussions, people were asked to talk at length about their involvement with particular programs and the sense they made of them, but not about their relations to the products they featured, the merchandise that clustered around them, or the advertisements that might frame them. In Britain and Europe, this narrowing of focus reproduced the strong separation between programming and advertising within the broadcasting system itself.

National advertising-supported channels arrived relatively late in a number of European countries, and even in Britain, where terrestrial commercial television had been launched in the mid 1950s, product placement was banned, sponsorship was tightly controlled, and spot advertising was confined to clearly demarcated "natural" breaks within and between programs. Although advertisers made repeated attempts to evade or bend these rules (see Murdock, 1992), commercial promotion remained far less extensive that in the United States, and the two BBC channels carried no spot advertising at all. Even so, British television, including public broadcasting, was thoroughly enmeshed in the world of goods. In the interests of "realism" contemporary dramas—from single plays to situation comedies and soap operas—continually demonstrated what goods could say about their owners. They celebrated consumption in the cars characters drove, the clothes they wore, the drinks and food they enjoyed, and the objects that furnished the kitchens, bathrooms, and living rooms they moved through. From the outset, the pleasures of viewing were inextricably bound up with the pleasures of looking at other people's chattels and the styles of life they supported. It was the medi-um's hidden curriculum.

Television was also locked into the world of goods through the "box" itself. Sets were major consumer items that carried powerful mes-sages about economic arrival, being "in touch," and looking to the future. As ownership climbed towards saturation point however, and viewing became routine, these connotations slipped from view. They have been recovered only recently, through historical work on the arrival of television in the home (Tichi, 1991) and anthropological studies in "transitional" societies where the simple possession of a television set carries potent meanings even when the lack of an electricity supply keeps the screen permanently blank (Gell, 1986). The continuing importance of screens and boxes as sites of struggle over meanings and uses has also been confirmed by recent research on the domestic careers of video recorders (Gray, 1992) and home computers (Murdock, Hartmann and Gray, 1992).

This work reminds us of something that much interpretive com-mentary on television audiences has forgotten or pushed to one side. When people watch television they are not only trying to formulate their response to particular programs, they are also entering a dense network of consumption relations. To unpick this web and its links to interpretive practices we need to think of audiences as actors at large in the world of goods and to announce the death of the "reader" as the lone heroine of audience activity.

Because we are focusing here on late capitalist societies, the obvious place to begin is with Marx's celebrated analysis of commodities in the first chapter of Volume One of *Capital*. However, the more we examine his formulation, and its best-known applications in communica-tion studies, the more problematic it becomes as a guide to contempo-rary research. In a famous sentence, Marx argued that though "a com-modity appears, at first sight, a very trivial thing, and easily understood" its analysis shows that it "is in reality, a very queer thing" (Marx, 1946: 41). With the benefit of hindsight, we can now see that it was even more peculiar than he imagined.

CURIOUSER AND CURIOUSER

Marx followed Locke in arguing that all goods that "supply the necessi-ties, or serve the conveniences of human life" have a use value (Marx, 1946: 2). They could be a product of self sufficiency, like a piece of furni-ture someone has made himself; a gift, like a pair of woolen gloves a mother has knitted for her daughter; or a public good, like a park, that everyone can use. Commodities, on the other hand, are goods designed to be sold in the marketplace. Consequently, they have exchange values as well as use values. Capital's central impetus is to commodify more and more areas of everyday life, relentlessly transforming use values into exchange values (Mosco, 1996: 141). Public goods are sold to private developers, gifts are easier to buy than to make, and domestic craftsmanship is annexed by the do-it-yourself industries. However, Marx insisted, prices should not be taken at face value, as simple counters of exchange, as they actively conceal "instead of disclosing, the social character of [the] labour" that has produced the objects offered for sale (Marx 1946: 47).

In a capitalist economy, he argued, the principal source of value is the labor that goes into transforming raw materials into saleable goods and services. Like other commodities, the capacity to work (labor power) is traded in the market and purchased by employers with wages and salaries. By enabling workers to enjoy a standard of living above the bare minimum (as defined by prevailing social standards), these payments ensure that they are able to continue working. But, Marx argues, it is in capital's interest to keep these "socially necessary" labor costs as low as possible. In his analysis, they are met by the value produced in only part of the working day. The rest of the time is additional and produces "surplus value" that can be appropriated as profit. There are constant struggles over the distribution of this added value. Employers seek to restrict wage rises and to get workers to produce more in the same time. Workers press for guaranteed minimum wages, reductions in working hours, and productivity bonuses. And political parties argue over what constitutes a "decent" standard of living.

From this perspective, the structures of inequality and exploitation that give the lie to capitalism's promise of fair dealing, are buried, or in Marx's phrase, "congealed," inside commodities. Underneath the marketplace is the production line, the sweatshop, and the regimented office. As consumers we are encouraged to look at a commodity and ask, "Is it worth the money?" (exchange-value) and "What will it do for me?" (use-value). As workers and citizens, however, we might also ask "Who made it?" "Under what conditions?" and "At what social cost?" These uncomfortable questions crowded in on the French journalist, Maurice Tameyr, as he walked around the Indian pavilion at the great Paris exposition of 1900. Despite the lavish display, the piles of carpets, plates, fabrics, and sacks of rice spoke to him "only of an incomplete and truncated India, that of the cashiers. . . . For this land of enormous and sumptuous trade is equally that of horrifying indigenous misery. . . . India is not only a warehouse, it is a cemetery" (quoted in Williams, 1982: 62-3). Successive campaigns for human, environmental, and animal rights have battled to keep these questions on the public agenda. But, Marx argued, because we mostly encounter commodities only as finished products for sale, we are tempted to "put out of sight . . . the . . . character of the various kinds of labour embodied in them" (Marx, 1946: 5). This amnesia is actively encouraged by a commodity culture that fixes firmly on the convenience, opportunity, and pleasure of consumption, projecting attention forwards to the moment of purchase and possession rather than backwards to the organization of production. This "incomplete and truncated" meaning system is central to the way capital "covers its own tracks" (Burke, 1996: 9). At its heart is what Marx called "commodity fetishism."

A fetish is an object believed to have magical powers. As a confirmed atheist Marx had no difficulty in arguing that gods and spirits were entirely imaginary, and that religious believers were mistaken in seeing them as "independent beings endowed with life, and entering into relation both with one another and the human race" (Marx, 1946: 43). Having grown up as a Jew in a Christian culture, he was also well aware of the powers often attributed to religious relics, statues, and images. Commodities he argued, worked in the same way. Once made and put on display, they assumed a life of their own and were invested with the power to change people's lives. They were a modern form of religious fetish. Victorian advertisers, who were developing their strategies as Marx wrote, grasped this immediately. Taking their cue from the Christian evangelical movements they promised that "life could be perfected. . . . The consumer could keep the wolf from the door. Assurance could be hers. All that was required was one single choice" (Loeb, 1994: 184).

Commodity fetishism, then, worked to conceal the origins of commodities. Consequently, as Marx put it in a striking metaphor, "value does not stalk about with a label describing what it is," but appears as a "social hieroglyphic" written in a forgotten language, inscribed very faintly across the surface of goods offered for sale. The task of critical analysis is to "try to decipher the hieroglyphic, to get behind the secret of our own social products" (Marx, 1946: 45). By 1867, however, (when Marx completed the first volume of *Capital*) this act of recovery and decoding was becoming steadily more difficult, as the continuing reorganization of production and consumption removed goods from their local sites of production and inserted them into a rapidly expanding system of generalized promotion and display.

EMPORIUMS OF THE SIGN

As people moved into waged work they increasingly purchased the things they used to make themselves. At one level, their entry into the world of commodities was a liberating experience, a release from the personal obligations that enveloped barter and gift relations. As Lewis Hyde has noted, "the excitement of commodities is the excitement of possibility, of floating away from the particular to taste the range of available life" (Hyde 1983: 67-8). This recognition strikes Mrs. Crowell, a character in Inez Irwin's 1917 novel *The Lady of the Kingdoms*, with the force of a revelation, as she walks past the glittering department stores of San Francisco at night. It was, Irwin writes, as though this dowdy woman from "a little dead country village" was "trying to fill out the shape of her soul with a new cargo, a cargo which should make up in degree of its colour and strangeness for all the lost greyness and familiarities" (quoted in Leach 1984: 341-2). Irwin could not have known how apposite her idea of "cargo" was. The new commodity culture was very similar to the cargo cults that anthropologists would later discover in the Pacific during World War II. Like the goods that islanders saw stacked in the holds of American transport planes, the commodities in the new stores seemed to have arrived from nowhere. This impression was carefully constructed.

In 1898, for example, the recently formed National Biscuit Company was searching for a brand name for their new octagonally shaped crackers (Ohmann, 1996: 100). After considering a range of possibilities they finally settled on "Uneeda." From a marketing point of view it was an inspired choice. By evoking an entirely "natural" product meeting basic biological needs, it cleverly directed attention away from the product's manufactured origins while avoiding the suggestions of hucksterism and greed implied by contending suggestions, such as "Hava Cracker" and "Wanta Cracker." Employing an advertising agency to organize every aspect of the new product's launch, from the name to the promotional campaign, was relatively novel, but the wider shift of which it was part had been gathering momentum for some time.

The movement from craft production to mechanized mass production removed all marks of human labor. It promised "manufacturing without tears" (Gilloch, 1996: 119). Its products were standardized, not singular, made anonymously and usually somewhere else, rather than by someone local, whom you knew and whose skills you understood and respected. This process of disembedding was accelerated by the completion of the great railway networks and the arrival of national markets. The greater the distance commodities travelled from the point of production to the point of sale, the more difficult it became to recall how and where they were made. This impersonality was further reinforced by the introduction of price tags. In traditional retail stores "the price of goods was determined by their visible and tangible qualities, as evaluated by the customer and the shopkeeper in the sales conversation" (Schivelbusch, 1980: 184). Both use-values and exchange-values were negotiable, but once haggling had begun, the customer was expected to make a purchase. The new department stores cancelled this social contract by imposing fixed prices with no obligation to buy. Customers arrived at values not by bargaining but by looking. They were no longer coproducers but audiences, beckoned to become shoppers by increasingly spectacular displays. The pleasures offered by these new sights were progressively uncoupled from the satisfactions of possession. It was possible to browse, window shop, or just to look, without buying.

The formative moment in this transition came with the Great Exhibition of 1851, at the Crystal Palace in London. The architects used the new technologies of steel and glass to build the first wholly modern cathedral of capitalism and to flood it with light. Although the exhibits did not carry price tags and were not offered for sale, the scale and lavishness of the event "synthesized a new spectacular mode for the representation of commodities, thereby opening a new public arena for them" (Richards, 1991: 60). This mode was taken up and refined in the selling techniques of the new department stores that "emerged slowly and unevenly in the retailing world between 1850 and 1890" (Benson, 1986: 13). The stores displaced the local relations that had previously surrounded goods and drew new maps of the connections binding everyday life to the world of goods. The social tableaux carefully staged in shop windows and floor displays dramatized novel links between styles and looks, objects and identities, that were later elaborated on by the advertising industry (see Marchand, 1985: Chapter 6). They were freeze frames in an unfolding film of modern life. Stores had become emporiums of the sign.

Settings that made the mundane appear exotic were particularly popular. "Stores were decorated to look like . . . Egyptian temples, semitropical refuges in the middle of winter, Japanese gardens" (Leach, 1984: 322) and often "used images of the Orient to give clothes, chinaware, furniture . . . a distinctive 'look'" (Laermans, 1993: 91). In 1903, the Siegel-Cooper store rounded off its Oriental Week with a series of tableaux that included a Turkish harem. This iconography, with its deep roots in Orientalism (Said, 1991), has proved remarkably resilient. Margaret Crawford found it recycled in a contemporary shopping mall, in a display that placed an ordinary pot in another harem, this time Moroccan. These representations allowed "noncommodified values to enhance commodities," but they also reversed the process so that "previously noncommodified entities become part of the marketplace" (Crawford, 1992: 15). This second movement was fed by modern tourism, which expanded alongside the department stores. It packaged adventure and made it available to all, with the added guarantee that the product would be entirely reliable. Travel had been about relating to other cultures. Tourism was about looking at them. The stores offered the spectacles of tourism without the inconvenience of leaving town. They were day-trips to the exotic.

They were also part of a thickening web of connections between marketing and new forms of visual display. Instances appeared everywhere. In 1895, Australian officials in the state of Victoria provoked an outcry when they allowed advertisements for Havelock Tobacco and Foster's Lager-Beer, to be printed on the postcards they had issued to raise revenue (Holt and Holt, 1971: 120). The following year, one of the first productions made by the pioneering German film-maker, Max Skladanowasky, showed his daughter advertising "Liebigs Fleischextract" (Hansen, 1983: 176). Four years later, Talmeyr was shocked to find a brand name inscribed on the lovingly reconstructed ruins in the Spanish pavilion at the 1900 Paris exposition. Having enjoyed the sense of "five centuries of mystery and sunshine" evoked by old walls, crumbling columns, and an almost obliterated coat of arms, he noticed, "above the door, in the patina of the stone, the tracing of Gothic letters. . . . I approach, and what is it I make out? Simply: *Menier Chocolate*" (quoted in Williams, 1982: 63). It was one of many company brand names that proliferated in the last two decades of the century (see Tedlow, 1996). They reinvested goods with personalities, but carried the names of capital not labor. Commodities appeared as gifts from on high. As Lord Randolf Churchill remarked at the time, "We live in . . . the age of Holloway's Pills, of Colman's Mustard, and of Horniman's pure tea" (quoted in Richards, 1991: 249).

THE NEW LOOK

By interlacing promotion and spectacle, the pleasures of the new consumer system became as much about looking as about possession. Commodity culture stood at the center of late capitalism's general emphasis on show. Department store showrooms jostled for attention with show places, fashion shows, beauty shows, and show girls (Leach, 1984: 325), and drew on a uniquely powerful cluster of new technologies of vision to enhance their impact. The introduction of chromolithography and new chemical dyes crowded the streets with vivid posters in colors never seen before. The spread of electricity filled shops with heat and illumination and lit up the night with glowing window displays and shining billboards. The rise of moving pictures and their stars offered powerful new images of fashion, comfort, and luxury. The cinema screen became a universal "display window . . . occupied by marvellous mannequins" (Eckert, 1978: 4). As Will Hays noted in 1920, it carried "to every American at home, and to millions of potential purchasers abroad, the visual, vivid perception of American manufactured products" (Eckert, 1978: 5). In a short story, published seven years earlier, Scott Fitzgerald had pictured his young heroine, Yanci, in a picture palace, fascinated by this new theater of styles, watching "Mae Murray swirl through splendidly imagined vistas . . . she calculated the cost of the apartment. . . . She rejoiced in the beauty of Mae Murray's clothes and furs, her gorgeous hats, her short-seeming French shoes" (quoted in Fuller, 1996: 162).

The connections between wishing and having were anchored by carefully orchestrated promotional ploys. Manufacturers paid to have their products featured in films, and tie-ins transferred their aura to the shops that surrounded movie theaters in town centers. The publicity pack that accompanied the release of *Now Voyager* (1942), a film that celebrated a dull spinster's transformation into a woman of elegance and sophistication, for example, urged local clothing stores to devise "special windows showing travelling ensembles and accessories" under the slogan, "Now Voyager, Buy Wisely . . . Now!" (quoted in La Place, 1987: 142). In fact, all the central milieux of high modernity—department stores, cinemas, railway stations, the city streets themselves—were not only sites of consumption but *sights* of consumption (see Ewen and Ewen, 1982: 68). They furnished a new way of looking at goods, at other people, and at oneself. By the century's turn "the experience of consumption had become all-encompassing [and] inseparable from knowledge of the self" (Richards, 1991: 7).

This emerging identity was anchored in popular consciousness by another new technology of vision—vernacular photography. George Eastman's easy-to-use Kodak cameras, first launched in 1888, enabled people to put themselves in the big picture and record their roles as actors in the world of goods. By showing them out and about against a backdrop of commodities and promotions, or at home or on holiday surrounded by appliances and branded goods, snapshots provided potent visual markers of changing relations between domestic life and material "progress," intimacy, and appearance.

Despite the clarion calls of socialism, the communalities of consumption seemed more seductive to many than the solidarities of labor, and the equality of the mass marketplace more easily attainable than the full entitlements of mass democracy. By celebrating "a community redefined by the shared experience of being consumers" (Loeb, 1994: 142) so comprehensively, commodity culture increasingly pushed the identities of worker and citizen to the margins of popular representation.

Marx hints at the essential visuality of commodity culture in his metaphor of the hieroglyphic (a picture language), but he never develops the point. This is not particularly surprising, as he died in 1883 at precisely the moment when the new technologies of promotion and display were beginning to emerge in their fully modern form. The 17 years to the century's end saw the spread of the department store and the illustrated mail order catalogue, the rapid diffusion of electric light, the development of chromolithography, and the beginnings of cinema. They also saw modern advertising agencies take control of promotion and move "to privilege visual impressions and play down discursive appeals" (Ohmann, 1996: 180).

Marx's lack of interest in the thicket of signs accreting around commodities is clear from his thoroughly utilitarian discussion of consumption. He concedes that human wants may "spring . . . from fancy" (Marx, 1946: 1) but he never explores the cultural construction of demand and desire. His near contemporary, Emile Zola, had broached the erotics of commodity culture in his novel, *Au Bonheur des Dames*, set in a fictional Parisian department store whose "marketing principle is the arousal of feminine desire" and whose logo shows two laughing, bare-breasted, confident women, "unrolling the name of the house that promises an erotic paradise on earth" (Vinken, 1995: 247-8). But it was left to later European Marxists, strongly influenced by Freud, to explore these connections in detail, through explorations of male desire. In his essay of 1910 on Leonardo da Vinci, Freud confessed that he experienced his own "intensive desire to look" as "an erotic activity." The implications of this admission were pursued with vigor by his nephew, Edward Bernays in his path-breaking handbook of 1928, *Propaganda*, which urged advertisers to tap the powerful "motives which [men and women] conceal from themselves" (quoted in Douglas, 1996: 47). His advice fell on ground already well prepared. Combining the erotics of looking and anticipation with the sexual connotations of possession became a stock-in-trade of promotional campaigns, particularly for items that worked on or through the body. An ad for Camel cigarettes showing a young man lighting a woman's cigarette, captioned "Pleasure Ahead," was typical. Marx had regarded the fetishism of commodities as a form of metaphysics. Later observers saw that it was also thoroughly carnal. For writers like Walter Benjamin, it was a process of redirecting "desire and passion towards lifeless manufactured products . . . [in which] the commodity is transformed into an object of sexual desire, and to consume is to consummate this desire" (Gilloch, 1996: 120). Moving through the world of commodities was no longer simply a secular form of religious worship, it was a series of intimate encounters with objects charged with some of the same erotic intensity that devotees of sexual fetishes might derive from high-heeled shoes or rubber clothing.

This idea that fetishism "is more than the meanings invested in goods" and includes "the accumulated power of commodities . . . to contain within themselves [all] the forms of consciousness through which capitalism manufactures its subjects" (Burke, 1996: 5) has been most fully elaborated in Jean Braudrillard's notion of "sign values." As with many of his arguments, he chews rather more than he bites off. In his enthusiasm for provocation he pushes a good idea some way beyond its useful limits, arguing in his key revision of Marx, *The Mirror of Production,* that nowadays "the super ideology of the sign . . . has *replaced* political economy as the theoretical basis of the system" (Baudrillard, 1975: 122) [emphasis added]. This notion has been welcomed by some scholars in cultural studies because it confirms their view that the circulation of texts and meanings is the defining feature of the world of goods. But it has attracted strong criticisms from political economists who claim that by consigning struggles over the production of value to the dustbin of history, it offers at best, only a very partial reading of contemporary capitalism (Mosco, 1996: 156).

Baudrillard may be largely wrong, but he is also partly right. We can no longer analyze the process of commodification without paying careful attention to the multiple meanings that gather around goods as they move through time. Contemporary commodities are caught up in a triangular field of forces that generates increasingly complex relations between exchange-value (profits), use-values (everyday acts of consumption), and sign-values (meanings and identities). Interpretive studies are strong on the relations between meanings and consumer activity but weak on the third term. Political economy is strong on the tensions between use- and exchange-values but relatively uninterested in sign-values and their relations to identity. Combining these perspectives would offer us a much richer account of the life of goods in contemporary capitalism, but the prospects are not encouraging. Many scholars in cultural studies refuse to consider any move that defines texts as also cultural commodities, seeing this as one of the fundamental breaks between their interests and those of political economy (see Fiske, 1994: 197). For their part, political economists tend to resist any dilution of their central focus on the progressive annexation of use values by exchange values. However, if we look carefully at the strongest expression of this position within communication studies, the idea of the audience itself as a commodity, we find rather more points of contact with interpretive research than its advocates have been prepared to recognize.

ASSEMBLY ROOMS

Contemporary observers quickly understood that the core business of commercial newspapers was assembling audiences for sale to advertisers. As the English commentator Thomas Bowles noted in 1884: "Newspapers are in reality in a false position. They profess to sell news and give advertisements to boot. What they really do is sell publicity for advertisements and . . . give news to boot" (quoted in Jones, 1996: 136). The popular press' dependence on advertising increased sharply over time. In the United States in 1880, newspapers in major cities gained 35% of their revenues from ads. By 1900 this figure had climbed to 55%, and by 1920 it stood at over 70% (Weaver, 1994: 45). Advertising was even more central to the economics of commercial broadcasting. Unlike a newspaper (or a cinema seat or gramophone record) an evening's programming could not be bought directly. It was available to anyone with the right receiving equipment. Hence, apart from earnings from associated merchandise (such as program guides) and selling programs to other stations, broadcast revenues depended entirely on marketing audiences to advertisers. Suitably packaged into ratings points, listeners and viewers were the principle commodity traded.

In his seminal analysis of the "audience commodity," published in the late 1970s, Dallas Smythe pursues this point, arguing that what television advertisers are buying is viewers' ability to understand the ads and their willingness to act on them. Like the "potato chips and peanuts given to customers of the pub bar, or cocktail lounge," the programs sandwiched between the advertising breaks offer a "free lunch" designed to keep people relaxed, receptive and in their seats (Smythe, 1981: 37-8). For Smythe, the pleasures of looking and the exercise of "audience power" (Smythe, 1981: 26) were an integral part of people's never-ending labor of "marketing consumer goods and services to themselves" (Smythe, 1981: 34). Audiences might be active, but their activities reproduced the consumer system. In this bleak vision, the basic "material reality under monopoly capitalism is that all non-sleeping time of most of the population is work time" and that of this "off the job work time, the largest single block is the time of the audiences which is sold to advertisers" (Smythe, 1977: 3). Living rooms had become extensions of the factory assembly line, subject to industrialized regimes of time and motion.

This novel application of Marx's analysis of labor was taken a step further by Sut Jhally and Bill Livant, who argued that in the same way that profits in production come from "surplus labour," so profits in the commercial broadcasting system come from the "surplus watching time" undertaken after the viewing needed to cover costs has been completed (Jhally and Livant, 1986: 127). In their hypothetical example, audiences only have to watch four of the 12 ads in a half-hour show to meet its costs. Their attention to the remaining eight is pure profit.

These explorations of the audience commodity were written very much against the prevailing grain of critical analysis, which had largely followed earlier Western Marxists in focusing on the cultural meanings carried by communications and their role in reproducing existing relations of power. Smythe and his supporters pressed for a decisive change of direction, arguing that "mass media are not characterised primarily by what they put into audiences (messages) but by what they take out (value) " (Jhally and Livant, 1986: 143). By posing the issue in this way, they reinforced the formidable perimeter fence that had already been built between critical political economy and cultural studies. I did not, and do not, accept this separation (see Murdock, 1978). Because modern communications is self-evidently both a symbolic and an economic system, its analysis has to be a matter of both/and rather than either/or. Despite their truculent stance, however, a careful rereading of the key contributions to the audience commodity debate, reveals loopholes through which questions of meaning and audience action continually reappear only to disappear.

Jhally and Livant offer an immediate concession when they argue that it is only during "commercial time" that "audiences create meaning for capital" and that during "programming time they create meaning for themselves" (Jhally and Livant, 1986: 142). They then dismantle this neat division by highlighting the ways that product placement, long-form advertising, and other techniques of "embedded persuasion" are eroding the line separating advertising from programming. This suggests that the battle between commercial speech and public discourse is waged across the whole of the schedule and that viewers may move between domains of meaning and reference when watching any "text" (Allor, 1988: 221). The increasingly fluid traffic in images, styles, and personalities between ads and programs, which is part of television's increasing penchant for self-referral, actively encourages this. Also, when we compare viewing to labor it is important to remember that life on the factory floor is more complex than it first appears. Ethnographic research shows that workers bring "a wide range of responses to the point of production, from full compliance to witholding labour power," engaging in small acts of sabotage, or "borrowing" materials to make something of their own (Mosco, 1996: 149). So do audiences.

Dallas Smythe acknowledged this, arguing that "most people embody a dialectical tension: they feel it necessary to cooperate with the monopoly-capitalist system in a variety of ways and for a variety of reasons; yet at the same time . . . they resist such cooperation in a variety of ways, for a variety of reasons" (Smythe, 1981: 43). This concession moves him within hailing distance of the research on audience activity being developed within cultural studies at the same time and announced in Stuart Hall's seminal paper on encoding and decoding (Hall, 1981) and David Morley's study of differential interpretations of the current affairs program, *Nationwide* (Morley, 1980). As Morley has recently pointed out, the aim of this work was not to celebrate the "polysemy of media products" or to argue that "forms of interpretive resistance are more widespread than subordination," but to explore the interlacing of opposition and complicity (Morley, 1993: 14).

Television is a notoriously hungry and parasitic medium. It continually trades on materials it does not originate. It recycles, reorganizes and recombines, calling on interpretive skills it does not provide. So where do the capacities and meanings that audiences bring to viewing come from? Smythe followed socialization theory in nominating the family as one of the "powerful institutions" that "feed the audience production process" (Smythe, 1981: 29). Through their everyday life, inside and outside the home, he argued, children learn how to talk about commodities, how to look at and relate to them, and how to use them as extensions of self. By presenting the family as a simple conduit, however, he misses the complexity of the relations between television and domestic life. Living rooms are not simply assembly sites for completing the circuit of production, they are "an industrial technology" for producing meanings "that in deeply contradictory ways" serve "experientially and ideologically not as the marketplace, but as its counterpoint" (Streeter and Wahl, 1994/95: 252-53). The meals prepared for friends, the commodities given as presents, the favors done for neighbors, reintroduce gift and barter relations alongside the daily forays into the commodity system. All three are rooted in a complex network of ties "between the history of production and that of consumption, between the history of wage work and that of domestic labour, and between the development of national industry and the changing structure of the family economy" (Coffin, 1996: 113). As a consequence, "the uses and understandings inherent within any commodity 'in any given time and place' are likely to be the result of the intersections of macropowers and micropowers, the partial and challenged hegemony of rulers and the episodic creativity of the ruled, the logics and disjunctures of everyday life" (Burke, 1996: 7) .

In asserting that the labor of viewing extends the relations underpinning waged work in the factory, writers on the audience commodity forget the strongly gendered nature of the connections between these domains. While the business of mass production was unequally centered around men, the system of mass consumption turned from the outset on the work of women. Henry Foster Adams spoke for the emerging advertising consensus when he noted in 1916 that "Many commodities are strictly women's propositions, and the advertiser, to secure the largest returns, should . . . base his campaign upon that knowledge" (quoted in Bowlby, 1996: 381). The principal target of this promotional offensive was the "housewife," married to the task of turning a dwelling into a home. As a French marketing magazine proclaimed in 1908, the "home" was the "umbilical cord" of the new "economic and social world," the suspension bridge slung between the promotion of branded commodities and the reorganization of intimate life (Coffin, 1996: 129). The American-born entrepreneur Gordon Selfridge understood this perfectly. When he opened his London department store in 1909, his publicity brochure was headed "Selfridge's 'at home'" and promised that the rest rooms, writing rooms, and dining rooms had been expressly designed to "create and cherish that comfortable sentiment " of being entirely "at home" in "the hundred or more departments" with their "displays of Manifold Merchandise" (quoted in Nava, 1996: 72-3). Though a number of the great department stores have gone now, their carefully orchestrated combination of comfort and spectacle left an enduring legacy. It cemented a way of looking, at things and at people, and a set of relations between domestic space and public display that broadcasting took up and embellished. By the time that regular commercial radio services arrived in the mid and late 1920s, women were already full citizens of the republic of goods. The modern housewife celebrated in interwar advertising "is not bound to the past or tradition: she is neither fussy nor old-fashioned. She is efficient, up to date, knowledgeable about domestic technology and an expert consumer" (Pumphrey, 1987: 191).

The department stores enticed prospective shoppers to venture into town by promising a "home away from home." Early advocates of commercial broadcasting reveled in their ability to overcome respectable fears about moving through the city streets, and reach into the innermost recesses of domestic life. As Frank Arnold, a particularly vocal enthusiast of radio advertising put it in 1931, "for the first time in the history of mankind" it is possible to enter "the homes of the nation through doors and windows, no matter how tightly barred," and to deliver "the message of advertising [into] the midst of the family circle, in moments of relaxation" when people are likely to be at their most receptive (quoted in Smulyan, 1994: 87). Radio advertising was careful to conceal the aggression expressed in the central image of audiences as "targets," however. It presented itself as an imaginary friend and advisor and learned from corner stores and travelling salesmen to wrap its appeals in easy banter and common sense sayings.

Television combined this new intimacy with the attractions of "just looking" that the big stores had pioneered (See Bowlby, 1985). As an environment of mass consumption commercial television, like the store, was a place "where consumers are an audience to be entertained by commodities, where selling is mingled with amusement, where arousal of free-floating desire is as important as immediate purchase of particular items" (Williams, 1982: 67). Despite the regulators' best intentions, television's promotional impetus could not be confined to the "natural" breaks in programming. "The desirousness constructed by advertising" was never "finally or completely linked to any one object." It was mobile, transferable, "designed to last in perpetuity" (Nightingale, 1997: 141). Moving with the flow of the evening's schedule of viewing (whether on one channel or several) was like walking through the various departments in a large store. The objects and tableaux on display ranged from the mundane to the exotic, from staples to luxuries, but they all held out the promise that commodities could remake the self. In this system of secular transubstantiation, "material spoils become spiritual benefits" (Conrad, 1982: 105) and use and exchange-values become inextricably bound up with sign-values. Questions of utility and value for money could no longer be uncoupled from lifestyles and social identities. As consumers, viewers shifted continually between the pleasures of looking and the pleasures of being looked at.

This movement was most obviously cemented in the game shows in which contestants vied for prizes. *The Price is Right*, which was launched in the United States in 1956 and went on to enjoy one of the most successful and well-travelled careers of any television program, celebrated the postwar world of merchandise with particular vigor. In a virtuous circle of consumption, contestants who most accurately guessed the retail prices of the commodities paraded in the studio, were allowed to take them home. Their evident joy in possession whispered in the audience's ear, "As you slog and slouch your way through your daily circuit of consumption chores, the logica runs, how can you possibly resist a programme that is so obviously about you" (Holbrook, 1993: 55).

Like the stores, television massively expanded the range of goods and people on open view. It was domestic panopticon, a massive machine for seeing more and further from the concealment and comfort of home. Whatever the genre, " the effect was a visual, visceral dazzle, an absorbing sense of pleasure in the act of perusal. Costumes. Things. Things to look at. New things. The latest things . . . the only thing wrong with movies was that they weren't TV, offering a free look at the contents of other people's lives, and houses, on demand" (Marling, 1994: 5). Commercial television constructed viewers as consumers twice over, as browsers and as buyers, as audiences for the medium's endless parade of commodities and as potential customers for the goods on display. The screen was "a shop window, the box a warehouse" and "every prop" was "purchasable" (Conrad, 1982: 122). Television reinforced the fetishism of commodities in both its main senses. It presented goods as independent actors in a theater of styles and it invested the pleasures of possession and looking with a strongly erotic charge. As the English critic, Peter Conrad noted, with studied distaste, "People on television ads have carnal congress with their appliances. The man who announces in satiated tones 'Boy, did I get stroked this morning' is complimenting his razor. The woman who confesses 'I like to start my day with a couple of swift strokes' is referring to her roll-on deodorant" (Conrad, 1982: 107).

In postwar Britain, this unabashed celebration of the intimate pleasures of possession had contradictory impacts. In a landscape still marked by austerity, the promise that anyone could remake themselves through mundane acts of purchase was deeply seductive. It offered release from British norms of self denial and asexuality, a chance to look and to feel different, to embrace a more glamorous, self-confident world (see Stacey, 1994: 238). At the same time, its increasingly powerful gravitational field pulled people even more securely into orbit around commodities.

HAUNTINGS AT THE FEAST

Commodification has accelerated markedly over the past 15 years of so. Successive moves towards privatization have transferred huge volumes of assets from the public sector to the corporate domain. A new enclosure movement has progressively fenced in the cultural commons. Shared resources have become private properties. At the same time, brand names, corporate logos, and company slogans have permeated more and more areas of public space, appearing on the doors of police cars and the roofs of schools and hospitals. Political economists have devoted a considerable amount of time to tracing the first process, and a number of textual analysts have welcomed the second as part of postmodernism's creative destruction of cultural boundaries. Commentators in both areas, however, have preferred to focus on ruptures and breaks rather than continuity. But, as I have argued here, to properly understand these processes we need to retrieve their concrete histories. The narrative of commodification is relatively easy to write, as we are on familiar institutional terrain. Successive movements to turn use-values into exchange-values have left thick trails of documentation. The history of commodity culture's relations to shifts in everyday life and ways of looking is much more difficult to compile. The evidence is scattered, fragmented, and often elusive. Yet, if we are to properly understand contemporary interpretive activity we must recover it. As Timothy Burke has argued, the "forms of knowledge, subjectivity, identity and consciousness produced by or through the process of commodification . . . cannot be understood without a detailed map of . . . the cultural and social raw material from which the 'social life of things' was shaped" (Burke, 1996: 3). He is talking particularly about the recent history of consumption in Zimbabwe, and it is certainly easier to trace these connections in societies that have only recently been exposed to the full force of commodity culture. They are nearer the surface. It is impossible to make sense of consumption in contemporary China, for example, without exploring the ways that commodity culture collides and colludes with legacies of Confucianism and memories of Maoism (see Zhao and Murdock, 1996). In our own societies, because commodity culture has accumulated over a century and half, links have become obscured. I have suggested that thinking of television audiences as actors at large a world of contemporary goods whose visual field has been shaped by a range of prior institutions, raises important questions for analysis. I have paid particular attention here to department stores. That is one thread worth following, but there are many more. The ways that new modes of popular transportation, particularly railway travel, reconstructed ways of looking and helped prepare the ground for the visual experience of cinema, and later television, is an obvious case in point (see Schivelbusch, 1980: Kirby, 1997).

The fact that commodification has successfully annexed the high ground of contemporary culture, however, does not mean that its colonization of everyday life is complete. "A world dominated by the spectacle of commodity culture is a world awash in representations of commodities, but it is not a world that has ceased to exist" (Richards, 1991: 15). "Saying that commodity relations are important or even primary" does not mean that "we can ignore the existence of other sorts of relations" (Carrier, 1992: 203). "Haunting the commodity and the market are noncommodity production and non market exchange" (Gibson-Graham, 1996: 244). The constitution of friendship and solidarity in the private sphere and the continuing struggles to extend citizenship rights in the public sphere, offer other ways of looking and other relations to the world of goods (Mosco, 1996: 163).

Citizens' rights and responsibilities and the resources needed to underwrite them have been a major theme in recent critical work on communications, and for good reasons. Not only are the disputes highly visible, with strong roots in a vision of democracy that has continually pitched the claims of citizenship against the promises of consumerism. They have also been central to the defense of public broadcasting as an essential counter to the increasing commodification of public culture (Murdock, 1996). As the dramatist Dennis Potter insisted, not long before his death, in an impassioned speech to professional broadcasters, television "is not a business trying to distribute dosh to its shareholders . . . but something held in trust and in law for every citizen" (Potter, 1993: 3). For all its failings, public broadcasting is important precisely because it struggles to keep commercial speech at arm's length and to provide a public space that is available to all and hospitable to diverse ways of talking and looking. When people offer help and comfort to strangers, or campaign for a safe children's play area in the local park, they are absent without leave from commodity culture. At its best, public broadcasting provides symbolic resources that help sustain these other ways of acting in the world of goods. It helps revivify habits of the heart that nurture other values and other identities. But in a commodity culture these alternatives are never secure.

Interpretive studies are right to argue that "in action, meanings are always at risk" (Shalins, 1985: ix) but wrong to assert, often on the basis of very selective evidence, that audience activity almost always affirms alternative or oppositional meanings (see Evans, 1990). They have written a declaration of the rights of difference and refusal without stopping to ask where these "other" meaning systems come from or how access to them may be changing as a result of shifts in the underlying organization of capitalism. Many researchers have been carried along by an evangelical belief that "the sins of the industry (or the message) are somehow [always] . . . redeemed in the after life of reception" (Morley, 1993: 16). But "after a decade of research documenting the relative autonomy of audiences" an increasing number of researchers are now acknowledging the "need to explore the structural limits of autonomy" (Jensen, 1994: 293, 303). A critical political economy that examines how shifts in capitalism impact on the meanings carried by local traditions and by national and transnational media is indispensable to this enterprise.

Early work in cultural studies, such as Phil Cohen's (1972) analysis of subcultures in London's East End, combined ethnography with elements of political economy to launch speculations about the possible connections between street style, shifts in local working class culture, and the wholesale restructuring of neighborhoods and occupational communities. It was an eminently practical response to C. Wright Mills' call for work that ranged "from the most impersonal and remote transformations to the most intimate features of the human self" and struggled "to see the relations between the two" (Mills, 1970: 14). Unfortunately, very few later writers in communications or cultural studies have taken up this challenge. Critical political economists have tended to work at a high level of generality, charting the structural transition from Fordism to Post-Fordism, the shifting relations between state and capital, and movements in the world system. In contrast, interpretive studies have focused down on the micropolitics of everyday life. They might relate television viewing to the material and moral economies of the household, but have shown little interest in exploring how patterns of domestic life are being reshaped by the restructuring of labor markets and urban space.

A political economy that helps to explain how the material, social, and symbolic resources for everyday action are assembled and allocated and how patterns of access are shifting as a result of the recomposition of contemporary capitalism and commodity culture, is essential to any attempt to explain patterns of creative consumption. By the same token, ethnographies that detail how these altering conditions are encountered, worked through, and challenged "on the ground" are indispensable to any account of change and inertia. Combining these modes of inquiry will not be easy. In the era of global capitalism the interlacing of culture, economy, and identity and the interplay between local, national, and transnational dynamics are becoming more and more difficult to see clearly. Which is all the more reason to take up Mills' call for a perspective that disregards disciplinary borders and moves freely between analytical levels "from examination of a single family to comparative assessment of the national budgets of the world" (Mills, 1970: 14). Since intimate life and capitalist economics intersect with particular force in the world of goods, it offers a particularly good place to start .

REFERENCES

Allor, M. (1988) "Relocating the Site of the Audience," *Critical Studies in Mass Communication, 5*, September, 217-33.

Barthes, R. (1977) "The Death of the Author." In Roland Barthes. *Image/Music/Text*. London: Fontana Press.

Baudrillard, J. (1975) *The Mirror of Production*. St. Louis: Telos.

Benson, S. P. (1986) *Counter Cultures: Saleswomen, Managers, and Customers in American Department Stores, 1890-1940*. Urbana: University of Illinois Press.

Bowlby, R. (1985) *Just Looking: Consumer Culture in Dreiser, Gissing, and Zola*. London: Methuen.

———— (1996) "Soft Sell: Marketing Rhetoric in Feminist Criticism." In Victoria de Grazia and Ellen Furlough, eds. *The Sex of Things: Gender and Consumption in Historical Perspective*. Berkeley: University of California Press: 381-87.

Burke, T. (1996) *Lifebuoy Men, Lux Women: Commodification, Consumption and Cleanliness in Modern Zimbabwe*. Durham: Duke University Press.

Carrier, J. G. (1992) "Occidentalism: The World Turned Upside Down," *American Ethnologist, 19*(2), May, 195-212.

Coffin, J. G. (1996) "Consumption, Production and Gender: The Sewing Machine in Nineteenth-Century France." In Laura L. Frader and Sonya O. Rose, eds. *Gender and Class in Modern Europe*. Ithaca: Cornell University Press: 111-141.

Cohen P. (1972). "Subcultural Conflict and Working Class Community." *Working Papers in Cultural Studies, 2*, Spring, 5-52.

Conrad, P. (1982) *Television: The Medium and its Manners*. London: Routledge and Kegan Paul.

Crawford, M. (1992) "The World in a Shopping Mall." In Michael Sorkin, ed. *Variations on a Theme Park: The New American City and the End of Public Space*. New York: Hill and Wang: 3-30.

Douglas, A. (1996) *Terrible Honesty: Mongrel Manhattan in the 1920s*. London: Picador.

Douglas, M. and B. Isherwood (1979) *The World of Goods.* New York: Basic Books.

Eckert, C. (1978) "The Carole Lombard in Macy's Window," *Quarterly Review of Film Studies, 3*(1), 1-21.

Evans, W. A. (1990) "The Interpretive Turn in Media Research: Innovation, Iteration, or Illusion?" *Critical Studies in Mass Communication, 7*, June, 147-68.

Ewen, S. and E. Ewen (1982) *Channels of Desire.* New York: McGraw-Hill.

Fiske, J. (1994) "Audiencing: Cultural Practice and Cultural Studies." In Norman K. Denzin and Yvonna S. Lincoln, eds. *Handbook of Qualitative Research.* London: Sage.

Fuller, K. H. (1996) *At the Picture Show: Small-Town Audiences and the Creation of Movie Fan Culture.* Washington, DC: Smithsonian Institution Press.

Gell, A. (1986) "Newcomers to the World of Goods: Consumption Among the Muria Gonds." In A. Appadurai, ed. *The Social Life of Things.* Cambridge: Cambridge University Press.

Gibson-Graham, J. K. (1996) *The End of Capitalism (As We Knew It): A Feminist Critique of Political Economy.* Oxford: Blackwell.

Gilloch, G. (1996) *Myth and Metropolis: Walter Benjamin and the City.* Oxford: Polity Press.

Gray, A. (1992) *Video Playtime: The Gendering of a Leisure Technology.* London: Routledge.

Hall, S. (1981) "Encoding and Decoding in Television Discourse." In Stuart Hall et al., eds. *Culture, Media, Language.* London: Hutchinson: 128-38.

Hansen, M. (1983) "Early Silent Cinema: Whose Public Sphere?" *New German Critique, 29,* Spring/Summer, 147-84.

Hebdige, D. (1979) *Subculture: The Meaning of Style.* London: Methuen.

Holbrook, M. B. (1993) *Daytime Television Game Shows and the Celebration of Merchandise: The Price is Right.* Bowling Green, OH: Bowling Green State University Popular Press.

Holt, T. and V. Holt (1971) *Picture Postcards of the Golden Age: A Collector's Guide.* London: MacGibbon and Kee.

Hyde, L. (1983) *The Gift: Imagination and the Erotic Life of Property.* New York: Vintage Books.

Jhally, S. and B. Livant (1986) "Watching as Working: The Valorization of Audience Consciousness," *Journal of Communication, 36*(3), Summer, 124-43.

Jensen, K. B. (1994) "Reception as Flow: The 'New Television Viewer' Revisited," *Cultural Studies, 8*(2), May, 293-305.

Jones, A. (1996) *Powers of the Press: Newspapers, Power and the Public in Nineteenth-Century England.* Aldershot: Scolar Press.

Kirby, L. (1997) *Parallel Tracks: The Railroad and the Silent Cinema.* Durham, NC: Duke University Press.

Laermans, R. (1993) "Learning to Consume: Early Department Stores and the Shaping of the Modern Consumer Culture (1860-1914)," *Theory, Culture and Society, 10*(4), November, 79-102.

La Place, M. (1987) "Producing and Consuming the Woman's Film: Discursive Struggle in Now Voyager." In Christine Gledhill, ed. *Home is Where the Heart Is: Studies in Melodrama and the Woman's Film.* London: British Film Institute.

Leach, W. R. (1984) "Transformations in a Culture of Consumption: Women and Department Stores, 1890-1925," *The Journal of American History, 71*(2), September, 319-42.

Loeb, L. A. (1994) *Consuming Angles: Advertising and Victorian Women.* Oxford: Oxford University Press.

Marchand, R. (1985) *Advertising the American Dream: Making Way for Modernity, 1920-1940.* Berkeley: University of California Press.

Marling, K. A. (1994) *As Seen on TV: The Visual Culture of Everyday Life in the 1950s.* Cambridge, MA: Harvard University Press.

Marx, K. (1946) *Capital: A Critical Analysis of Capitalist Production-Volume One.* London: George Allen and Unwin.

Mills, C. W. (1970) *The Sociological Imagination.* Harmondsworth: Penguin Books.

Morley, D. (1980) *The "Nationwide" Audience.* London: British Film Institute.

—— (1993) "Active Audience Theory: Pendulums and Pitfalls," *Journal of Communication, 43*(4), Autumn, 13-19.

Mosco, V. (1996) *The Political Economy of Communication.* London: Sage.

Murdock, G. (1978) "Blindspots about Western Marxism: A Reply to Dallas Smythe," *Canadian Journal of Political and Social Theory, 2*(2), 109-19.

—— (1992) "Embedded Persuasions: The Fall and Rise of Integrated Advertising." In Dominic Strinati and Steven Wagg, eds. *Come on Down? Popular Media Culture in Post War Britain.* London: Routledge.

—— (1996) "Rights and Representations: Public Discourse and Cultural Citizenship." In Jostein Gripsrud, ed. *Media and Knowledge: The Role of Television.* Bergen: University of Bergen, Department of Media Studies: 9-26.

Murdock, G., P. Hartmann and P. Gray (1992) "Contextualising Home Computing: Resources and Practices." In Roger Silverstone and Eric Hirsch, eds. *Consuming Technologies: Media and Information in Domestic Spaces.* London: Routledge.

Nava, M. (1996) "Modernity's Disavowal: Women, the City and the Department Store." In Mica Nava and Alan O'Shea, eds. *Modern Times: Reflections on a Century of English Modernity.* London: Routledge: 38-76.

Nightingale, V. (1997) "Ad-Sick, Love-Sick, Home-Sick." In Maryanne Dever, ed. *Australia and Asia: Cultural Transactions.* Richmond Surrey: Curzon Press: 122-42.

Ohmann, R. (1996) *Selling Culture: Magazines, Markets and Class at the Turn of the Century.* London: Verso.

Potter, D. (1993) "Occupying Powers," *The Guardian,* 28 August, 3.

Pumphrey, M. (1987) "The Flapper, the Housewife and the Making of Modernity," *Cultural Studies, 1*(2), May, 179-94.

Richards, T. (1991) *The Commodity Culture of Victorian England: Advertising and Spectacle, 1851-1914.* London: Verso.

Said, E. (1991) *Orientalism.* London: Penguin.

Schivelbusch, W. (1980) *The Railway Journey: Trains and Travel in the 19th Century.* Oxford. Basil Blackwell.

Shalins, M. (1985) *Islands in History.* Chicago: The University of Chicago Press.

Smulyan, S. (1994) *Selling Radio: The Commercialization of American Broadcasting 1920-1934.* Washington, DC: Smithsonian Institution Press.

Smythe, D. W. (1977) "Communications: Blindspot of Western Marxism," *Canadian Journal of Political and Social Theory, 1*(3), 1-27.

—— (1981) *Dependency Road: Communications, Capitalism, Consciousness and Canada.* Norwood, NJ: Ablex.

Stacey, J. (1994) *Star Gazing: Hollywood Cinema and Female Spectatorship.* London: Routledge.

Streeter, T. and W. Wahl (1994/95) "Audience Theory and Feminism: Property, Gender and the Television Audience," *Camera Obscura, 33-34,* May/September/January, 243-61.

Tedlow, R. S. (1996) *New and Improved: The Story of Mass Marketing in America.* Boston, MA: Harvard Business School Press.

Tichi, C. (1991) *Electronic Hearth: Creating an American Television Culture.* New York: Oxford University Press.

Vinken, B. (1995) "Temples of Delight: Consuming Consumption in Emile Zola's Au Bonheur des Dames." In Margaret Cohen and Christopher Prendergast, eds. *Spectacles of Realism: Body, Gender, Genre.* Minneapolis: University of Minnesota Press: 247-67.

Weaver, P. H. (1994) *News and the Culture of Lying.* New York: The Free Press.

Williams, R. H. (1982) *Dream Worlds: Mass Consumption in Late Nineteenth-Century France.* Berkeley: University of California Press.

Willis, P. (1978) *Profane Culture.* London: Routledge.

Zhao, B. and G. Murdock (1996) "Young Pioneers: Children and the Making of Chinese Consumerism," *Cultural Studies, 10*(2), 201-17.

4

Leisure or Labor?: Fan Ethnography and Political Economy

Eileen R. Meehan

In the United States, media scholars rarely use the terms "ethnography" and "political economy" in the same sentence. This has been particularly true for that branch of media ethnography focusing on fans. The term refers to individuals (fans) who utilize a particular media artifact (novel, comic book, film or television series) as the basis for organizing affinity groups (fandoms), conventions, social hierarchies, personal interactions, and amateur productions (artwork, criticism, videos, newsletters, novels, etc.). Ethnographers of fans explicate these activities largely in terms of viewer autonomy, pleasure, and creativity (Amesley, 1989; Jenkins, 1992; Penley, 1991; Tulloch and Alvarado, 1983). These accounts are generally optimistic and often identify the ethnographer as an active member of the community under study, thus classifying such ethnographies as "within the group" or "emic" in focus. These fan ethnographers question both administrative and critical theories of enculturation, arguing that viewers exercise considerable power over messages delivered by commercial media. Among viewers, fans exemplify this autonomy in its purest form: not only do Trekkers read against the grain but they appropriate and rework *Star Trek* to suit themselves through their own, noncommercial media and social activities. Fans, then, are the most active of active audiences, bearing no resemblance to the stereotypes of "couch potatoes" or "hopeless nerds" that are circulated in American media.

In contrast, political economists analyze media in terms of ownership, relations of production, and institutional structures. They trace processes by which corporations routinize, commercialize, and commoditize both cultural expression and cultural consumption (Anderson, 1995; McAllister, 1996; Schiller, 1989; Wasko, 1994). Their accounts examine not only how the process of industrialization effects cultural expression, but also how advertising interests define the pool of acceptable messages that are drawn from the larger cultural fund. Both style and content are at issue here. Innovation in either follows standard patterns that maintain proconsumerist, procapitalist ideologies (Budd, Entman and Steinman, 1990; Gitlin 1983; Meehan, 1986). Political economists assume that enculturation occurs: people are most influenced by messages naturalized through constant repetition (Curran, Gurevitch and Woollacott, 1982). As conglomerates increasingly integrate operations in publishing, film, broadcast television, cable channels, pay channels, and new media, they create internal markets that foster recycling and repackaging artifacts for distribution in each of the conglomerates' operations. For successful product lines like Paramount's *Star Trek,* the result can mean decades of profits mined from the elaboration of a single television series. These structural patterns in the media sector militate against cultural diversity—a tendency that is reinforced by the intrusion of advertising into films, books, and most media previously supported by audiences alone. From this point of view, little in the media justifies optimism.

From this contrast, fan ethnographers and political economists seem to have little cause to communicate with each other. Clearly, I do not believe this to be the case. Rather, I suggest that each approach has a significant contribution to offer the other. On the one hand, fan ethnographers document the activities and handicrafts of a self-aware subculture that appropriates and reworks mediated ideology. On the other, political economists document the activities and structures that generate this ideology. Put in these terms, the connection between fan ethnographers and political economists seems obvious: whereas ethnographers explain how fans deal with media, political economists provide a larger context for understanding fandom as a social and economic phenomenon. Understanding both subcultural practices and industrial contexts serves to balance optimism and pessimism by identifying sites where people exercise their agency in the cultural sphere as well as identifying the economic structures that limit such exercises.

In this essay, I use the notion of leisure time to bridge the two positions. I begin with a discussion of fan ethnographers' implicit notion of leisure time, connecting it to dominant ideology. I next sketch the logics behind this notion and behind the provision of leisure time to workers. The transformation of leisure time to work time, as noted by Smythe (1975), leads to a discussion of industries organized to profit from leisure time. Here I focus on the impact of changes in corporate structure on marketing strategies, particularly on the promotion of cultural consumption as a name brand, ritualized activity. I note that these changes have increased fans' economic importance, though not their social stature. Finally, I reflect on the power of political economic analyses to contextualize ethnographic observations and the need for "etic" (outside the group) ethnographies to bridge the analytic gap between "emic" ethnography and political economy. By integrating these approaches, we can better understand media as both manufacture and expression, as consumption and interpretation, as cultural constriction and cultural springboard.

ETHNOGRAPHY: EMIC OR ETIC?

Fan ethnographers work with complex theories of reception, pleasure, and viewer autonomy as their frequent citations of De Certeau and Bourdieu attest. Most rely on a mixture of textual analysis, informant interviews, personal experience, and participant observation (Fiske, 1990; Jenkins, 1992). Basic to their ethnographies is their own identification with, or membership in, the fandom under study. As one of the group, the ethnographer already knows the group's core beliefs and values, its sacred practices and rituals; further, the emic ethnographer is impervious to both derogatory stereotypes of fans, often circulated through the media, and elitist attitudes towards mass culture. Thus fan ethnographers articulate fans' shared understandings in the fans' own terms. While constructing such ethnographies, researchers present the ongoing account to the group in order to ensure that they have gotten it right.

This notion of insider privilege, and the emic ethnographies associated with it, has long been debated in U.S. cultural anthropology (Pike, 1966). Much of that debate centers on issues of power and otherness, particularly in relations between European-descent anthropologists and Native Americans (Harris, 1968; Rosaldo, 1989). For U.S. anthropologists, the academic debate is rooted in the research paradigm that dominated cultural anthropology. Founded by Franz Boas, this paradigm theorized culture as an expressive totality in which core values formed the basis of a unique way of life. Central to Boasian ethnography is the premise that ethnographers can discern underlying structures within a culture—structures hidden from most participants—and thereby determine the core values driving that culture (Benedict, 1934; Mead, 1928). Boasians describe cultures using analytic categories that might be foreign to any particular culture but were capable of describing all cultures.

The resulting accounts rarely connected to the lived experience of the people being observed. This fact is the basis for several parodies written by Boasians in which the odd customs of the few "Nacirema" were described. Thus Miner (1967) describes the American bathroom as an isolation chamber in which natives enact rituals using magical liquids, pastes, and wands to defeat the demons of bad breath, tooth decay, and germs. Such parodies demonstrated how etic ethnography could make anything exotic. In the mid-1960s, paradigmatic struggles in anthropology, which questioned Boasianism, coincided with activist movements in the academy and among Native Americans. The critique argued that etic ethnographies were colonialist because they decontextualized native cultures, transformed subjects into exotic others, and implied that native peoples were cultural dupes who needed white experts to explain native cultures.

As the critique spread across the social sciences, researchers began theorizing emic positions designed to reproduce the understandings of the culture member, not of the outsider (Berger and Luckmann, 1966; Glaser and Strauss, 1967; Mehan and Wood, 1975; Schutz, 1967, etc.). In the U.S. academy, emic approaches became axiomatic in programs where the "object of study" had been "othered" due to gender, race, ethnicity, religion, or sexual orientation. The belief that people who had been silenced should speak for themselves had considerable appeal to progressives both inside and outside the academy.

Fan ethnographers locate themselves within this emic tradition, although they deal mainly with fans who are middle class, white, heterosexual, and college educated. Emic ethnographers report that fans fear censure from nonfans ("mundanes") and discrimination by mainstream institutions. Jenkins (1992) claims that fans suffer from the same low social status as homosexuals prior to the emergence of the Gay Liberation Movement. Presumably, fans would view etic researchers with suspicion; etic researchers would construe fandom in alienating or prejudicial categories; the resulting accounts would be skewed, inaccurate, and biased. In contrast, emic researchers could be trusted to tell their shared story in a full and acceptable manner. Ultimately, the fan ethnographers' defense of emic ethnography turns on the claim that insider status guarantees accuracy and objectivity.

That claim, however, is not easily validated. Reporting on one's own community poses difficulties, especially when the community perceives itself as targeted for censure. Such perceptions encourage a positive portrayal of one's community and discourage portrayals that are unflattering or critical. To the degree that fan ethnographers share concerns regarding censure and define authenticity as acceptability, they are limited by their insider status. This may explain the optimism typical of emic ethnographies. Being an insider may also render some topics outside the group's consciousness or taboo. For example, a community may not recognize or may not wish to discuss economic barriers that systematically exclude some types of people. Emic ethnographers share the taboos of the group under study. This may prevent them from placing U.S. fandoms in the context of U.S. culture and from exploring the degree to which fandom's values and fan's experiences are shaped by dominant ideology.

In the U.S., this is crucial: dominant ideology celebrates notions of individuality, freedom, and self-determination. These values are connected to the consumption of goods and services, and to the media as the mainstays of leisure. "Common sense" tells us that the best society is a consumer society, that freedom is a choice between brand name products, and that democracy is a function of the marketplace. Freedom, individuality, and consumption all happen in leisure time; work time is constrained, corporate, and limiting. For fans, leisure time is spent in fandom, work time in the "mundane world" of nonfans. An emic approach accepts this division as authentic, lived experience and thereby as a unique feature of fandom. Thus, emic ethnographers overlook the constructedness of "leisure time" and the role that dominant ideology plays in that construction. The implications of that oversight are explored in the following discussion of leisure time as a cultural and economic category developed in the context of American capitalism.

LEISURE TIME: WORK OR PLAY?

In American culture, leisure time has strong, positive connotations: freedom *from* work; freedom *to be* one's self; freedom *to do* as one pleases. This sense of leisure infuses the work of fan ethnographers who pursue the same pleasures as the subjects of their research. These ethnographers attend conventions, talk with other fans, read amateur publications, participate in Internet chat groups, watch television shows, acquire relevant artifacts, and so forth. For fan ethnographers, work and play meld together. Unsurprisingly, fan ethnographers and fans share a positive valuation of fan activities.

Fans consistently report to their ethnographers that fandom is more fulfilling than the mundane world. In fandom, they are free to be and do as they please with like-minded people away from the drudgery of the workplace. This sense of leisure as freedom seems integral to fans and fandom. It is reflected in their use of "mundane" to describe life outside of fandom: mundane world, mundane job, mundanes (non-fans). By contextualizing fan culture in terms of the larger American culture, however, this identification of leisure with life, and work with drudgery, puts fandom in the ideological mainstream. Similarly, the belief that one's preferred leisure is superior to that of others replicates the hegemonic practices that so effectively reinforce hostility among affinity groups in the interests of capitalism.

None of this is visible from the perspective of emic ethnography, specifically because the approach has forsworn abstractions and analytic categories that do not appear in the community under study. In capitalism, a great deal of hegemonic machinery is in place specifically to discourage abstract thinking about, or systematic analysis of, one's immediate experience. Yet, researchers should be able to integrate their experience of leisure with an abstract analysis of leisure. To this end, I will sketch an analysis of leisure from a political-economic perspective and then discuss connections between analytic and lived notions of leisure.

Following Marx (1984), political economists have conceptualized leisure time as rooted in the capitalist regimen of work and in the human need to recover from that intensive regimen. In Fordist industrialism, capitalists utilize multiple shifts of laborers to keep factories running around the clock and organize each shift to extract the maximum output of labor over the greatest number of productive hours for a minimum payment. But workers who toil too long make mistakes, thereby becoming inefficient and expensive even at rock-bottom wages. Tired workers endanger the individual machines that they tend and may disrupt the interplay of machines within the factory. Capitalists recognize the material need for rest and attack this inefficiency first through automation (Braverman, 1974; Kraft, 1996) and second by granting leisure time. The former process generates various "revolutions" in capitalist economies (steam and electrical; industrial and postindustrial; Fordist and post-Fordist) with varying effects on leisure time and unemployment. For example, post-Fordism expands the deskilling regime to managers and professionals (Clement, 1988; Harvey, 1990; Mosco, 1989).

In the human need to recover from work may lay one key to the development of commercial media, advertising, and consumerism. Time spent in recovery is not necessarily insulated from capitalism. Food, sleep, sexual intercourse, social activities, household chores, intellectual work, cultural performances, and so forth, may involve objects and interactions that can be commoditized into goods and services. By transforming recovery time into consumption time, capitalism reforms the worker into consumer and recovery into leisure.

In the United States, this transformation was facilitated in the 1800s by governmental and corporate campaigns seeking to "Americanize" the working class (Gutman, 1977). Using zoning laws, urban architecture, educational institutions, and religionist organizations, Americanization movements attacked the ability of working class households to raise and process their own food, sew their own clothing, and so forth (Braverman, 1974). Americanization campaigns promoted the purchase of decorative plants, processed foods, household appliances, and single-family houses. Real Americans, it seemed, bought their soup in cans and their crackers in boxes. Modern packaging ensured that the contents had been scientifically processed according to strict rules regarding sanitation and nutrition—or so the promotional campaigns alleged. Such claims were reiterated by the Advertising Council in campaigns connecting patriotism (and anti-Bolshevism) with the purchase of nationally advertised, name-brand products. These messages saturated public schools, private factories, social welfare offices, and public exhibitions: to be American was to be a consumer.

Thus, leisure time was transformed into work time. Time away from one's workplace was spent increasingly in the workplace of others: music halls, department stores, movie theaters, and fairs in the 19th century—joined by supermarkets, theme parks, sports arenas, shopping malls, and cybercafes in the 20th century. To attract spenders and differentiate often identical goods and services, companies hired advertising agencies and launched media campaigns. Leisure time spent at home increasingly depended on mass-produced media: first, sheet music, trading cards, newspapers, magazines, books; then, recorded music, radio, comic books, television, and video cassettes. Corporate media cultivated the association of consumption with modernity, desirability, and individuality. Such corporate media enculturate: they teach us what we ought to need. When advertising is added, these media also teach us which brands will satisfy those needs.

Thus Smythe argues that all time is work time in capitalism (1975, 1978). He demonstrated that people's labor with media generates a product for which there was significant demand: the audience commodity. All advertiser-supported media manufacture audiences, which are sold to advertisers. Here Smythe links people's leisurely uses of media and their production of surplus value. Even as we pay for access to media and learn what to need and buy, advertisers pay media corporations for access to us. Thus media corporations set out the cheapest cultural bait available to attract us. Because advertisers are willing to pay high prices for dedicated consumers, media corporations try to attract audiences comprised of people who augment their regular purchases of brand names with impulsive purchases of brand names (Meehan, 1990). In this way, the superstructural role of media is subsumed to their economic role. As media corporations increasingly integrate advertising into films, novels, songs, and other "audience-supported" media, artifacts take on a more uniformly commercial purpose in which the significance of artistic or cultural expression diminishes (Murdock, 1978; Wasko, Phillips and Purdie, 1993). Leisure time spent working with media, then, becomes a necessary element of contemporary capitalism.

WORK EXPERIENCED AS FUN

Smythe's analysis, however, does not invalidate our experience of leisure as different from work. In a secular capitalist society like the United States the unpaid nature of leisure ensures that it has no official regimen. Because of this, media corporations and retailers flood the media system with advertising. The lack of a work regimen for leisure also motivates campaigns by governmental entities, religionist institutions, social welfare groups, and manufacturers associations trying to limit our choice of leisure activities. Despite the efforts of such organizations, underground markets persist, providing goods, services, and media artifacts that are marginally or entirely illegal.

Further, even in the United States, people can avoid commercialized leisure. Various movements (ecological, progressive, and religious) have organized specifically to combat the commercialization of leisure by providing cultural opportunities and activities that are noncommercial. This provides competition for commercial media. No single entity can commandeer our leisure in the same way that an employer commandeers our labor. We must be persuaded—or enculturated—to prefer one activity over others. For media corporations, enculturation is the key to lessening competition. By gaining direct access to the household via the newspaper, radio, television, computer, and so forth, media corporations weave images and advertisements into the household's daily life.

From infancy, most Americans live in a highly mediated, highly commercialized domestic sphere. This entails fairly constant contact with media products. Because domestic chores fill much leisure time, the presence of media technologies in the home takes on a special significance. Media products become the background for doing laundry, cleaning house, cooking, talking with family members, and so forth. Media products may also function in the foreground: radios, recorded music, television, or video recorders play as newspapers, magazines, books, or web sites are read. Throughout those commercial songs, shows, films, papers, magazines, and books runs the assumption that consumerism is good, that consumption is leisure.

The resulting hegemonic effect requires no conspiracy. Simple self-interest leads media corporations and their advertisers to portray "the good, the true, and the beautiful" as consumption. Spending time with media or spending time shopping become the most obvious ways to spend leisure time. The seeming naturalness of this—at the level of lived experience—cannot be overstressed. Within lived experience, leisure is obviously connected to consuming entertainment. Going to the movies or watching television or renting a video or going on-line are constructed as leisure—as fun, not work. Thus, we pay for access, enduring direct advertisements and product placements in order to be entertained. In that process, advertisers pay media corporations to constantly repeat the pantheon of brand names within the "cheap bait" of programming. Our enculturation, then, generates direct and indirect revenues for media corporations. This duality is strongly masked; media corporations have little interest in explaining how the commodity audience generates surplus value while paying for "mere entertainment."

The strength of that masking fosters a belief that entertainment has no significance beyond the moment of amusement. This belief is not without competition, however. Some social, religious, and professional organizations argue that the media have serious effects, ranging from the cultivation of violence to the erosion of morality. When covered by commercial news sources, such groups are treated as special interests, opposed to free speech or out of step with public taste. Research supporting claims of strong effects is always counterbalanced by research showing highly diffused effects. Public discourse, then, remains muddled and the commercial media distributing some of that discourse have little impetus to clarify the issues.

When audience members organize themselves and treat media products as culture—as expressions to be appropriated, reinterpreted, and reexpressed—the commercial media's response is particularly intriguing. Such avid fans are represented as fools in news coverage and as sexually unattractive fools in entertainment programming. Yet media corporations have long cultivated fans in order to organize audiences and routinize consumption. With intensive conglomeration, these firms now have a compelling, structural reason to target fans as reliable and undiscriminating consumers for specific product lines associated with particular titles (*Star Trek*, *Star Wars*, *The Simpsons*, etc.). Indeed, corporate cultivation of fans as reliable consumers predates the current emphasis on product lines and corporate synergy. In the next section, I will briefly sketch the economic logic undergirding this interest in fans.

SHAPING CONSUMPTION:
VERTICALLY INTEGRATED FIRMS AND FANS

Long before the invention of film, the star system (with its legions of fans) was well established in vaudeville, musical theater, opera, and legitimate theater. The names of entrepreneurial impresarios and their favored employees (performers, authors, composers) operated as brand names promising a certain kind of experience to ticket buyers. Even outside the cities and away from the theater circuits, a recognizable "name" was a significant advantage in terms of drawing people to performances (Kraft, 1996). Given the uncertainties of performance, where each rendition necessarily differed from any other, brand names promised an acceptable experience to ticket buyers.

This simplified advertising: ads need only to invoke the names of those involved. The names themselves promise certain production values, standards of performance, styles of representation, and generic forms. Such invocations organize ticket buyers into taste publics and rationalize purchases. This decreases competition by generating niches. Whereas all possible ticket buyers are a large, disorganized, and unreliable target requiring extensive advertising, fans of light musical revues with plenty of patter comprise a smaller, more organized, and more reliable audience that advertising can target directly. By invoking the relevant names, ads could motivate fans—ticket buyers who attend anything that features particular names—and provide comparative information for more discriminating ticket buyers selecting from the few items offered within a particular performance niche. Different combinations of names signified different degrees of novelty or experimentation. Although companies paid higher salaries to stars, firms traded that inefficiency for guaranteed revenues from fans and comparative advantages gained with more discriminating buyers.

During the film industry's first decade in the United States, studios largely avoided the costs and complications attached to actors (and to their off-screen lives) by refusing to name them in the credits. By 1909, some actors appeared with sufficient frequency that moviegoers nicknamed them (e.g., "the Biograph Girl" for Florence Lawrence, "Dimples" for Maurice Costello). The press also used those nicknames to identify players. Whereas anonymous players had little bargaining power, nicknamed players closely identified with a studio became de facto stars. By 1910, many studios promoted their recurring actors by name. Before long, studios were designing genres of stars, assembling stables of actors, and promoting some for stardom through fan clubs and publicity campaigns.

The studios' short-lived resistance to naming performers was briefly replicated by radio stations and networks with news reporters and announcers. That quickly changed: an identifiable voice on radio assumed the same economic significance as an identifiable profile in silent movies (Barnouw, 1966). Replacing silent movies with talkies, studios integrated network radio into their promotional strategies. Networks developed their own stars, some of whom developed secondary careers in the talkies. Similarly, recording companies moved their stars onto radio and into movies.

Because all three media could be deployed to promote purchases and to assemble the commodity audience, major corporations moved swiftly to integrate recording, radio, and film in their operations. This process intensified with the introduction of television by CBS and RCA's NBC in the 1950s. By the 1960s, the economic connection between studios, networks, and record labels was mirrored by an iconographic integration of stars from film, television, radio, and recording.

The circulation of stars across media served three main goals. First, it cultivated fans for individual stars and types of stars across integrated industries. Second, it allowed companies to promote the immediate consumption of particular records, films, and broadcast programs. Third, it guaranteed that most individual stars and particular titles would quickly fade due to oversaturation. Novelty, fads, and fashions (Hirsch, 1972) were key elements of corporate strategies attempting to control demand and guarantee steady revenues in broadcasting, film, and recorded music. Although stars, styles, and titles constantly changed, the corporate firmament remained stable.

These corporate policies were supported by extent technologies, which were oriented around immediate, time-based, and limited consumption of media artifacts. Broadcasting required audiences to attend in "real time"; programs could not be recorded and collected for subsequent reviewing. Film distribution was limited to theatrical performance and television reruns; personal collections of films were not technologically or economically feasible. Technologies and substances used to record and replay music were unstable and short-lived. In brief, media artifacts were ephemeral and markets for subsequent embodiments of old movies, old television programs, and old songs were limited to specialized collectors. Media corporations had little incentive to preserve old product and little expectation that a market for recycled product would develop. Lacking the replay technologies that would make multiple moments of consumption and reconsumption of media artifacts possible, media firms emphasized "the latest thing" —stars with new titles and newer stars with newer titles.

All this changed with corporate decisions about, and scientific advances in, media technologies. From the 1970s to the 1990s, electronics manufacturers—many like Philips or RCA involved in media production—have developed multiple technologies designed to allow households to collect once "ephemeral" television shows and movies. This created a new market in which old movies and old television programs are recycled as "new" titles for household video, laser disc, and DVD collections. For recorded music, the development of laser technologies and CDs made vinyl records obsolete, generating a similar opportunity to reissue old music in new formats. However, electronics manufacturers were not the only force behind media corporations' new interest in fostering consumption of "old stuff" along with "the latest thing."

SHAPING CONSUMPTION: MEDIA CONGLOMERATES AND FANS

Another force behind the recycling of obsolescent materials into new markets was conglomeration. In the 1960s, U.S. companies experimented with conglomeration by absorbing firms in other industries to protect overall revenues from the business cycle: an expanding market in one industry would offset a contracting market in another. Some companies targeted firms in widely disparate sectors; others targeted firms in related but separate industries to ensure that the parent firm had the necessary expertise. Our interest here is in a strategy of conglomeration across related industries and its effect on the economic standing of fans.

When a media company becomes a media conglomerate, it creates internal markets that encourage the recycling and repackaging of product from one operation to another and thereby from one medium to another (Meehan, 1991). Further, once a company commits to transindustrial conglomeration, it acquires companies whose operations supplement and extend these internal markets. Such conglomeration, then, encourages a film studio to buy a book publisher in order to recycle the publisher's list into screenplays and to publish novelizations of the studio's films. This is the logic of conglomeration across industries that comprise a single sector of the economy. Such transindustrial conglomerates can invest considerable sums in a blockbuster title, knowing that the title will feed most of its media operations.

Consider the blockbuster film. A conglomerate with subsidiaries in the music industry can generate the soundtrack by assigning talent to write and perform new music, or by rerecording old songs, or by reusing old recordings. The conglomerate's music operations repackage the sound track as a CD. Sales of the CD mean that the film earns indirect revenues prior to its release. Radio airplay promotes the CD, its singer, and the film. Adding to the promotional effort is the music video, often comprised of scenes cut from the film and mixed with footage of the singer. That video advertises the film, the CD, and the singer's other CDs. Further, decisions to take these steps can be announced as "news," which will be covered by magazines like Time Warner's *Entertainment Weekly,* television shows like Paramount's *Entertainment Tonight,* and so forth—all of which earn revenues from advertisers. As a conglomerate expands its media holdings, it adds ways to further recycle and promote a blockbuster title across other media, into other external markets, and through other retail outlets.

Licensing is crucial to earning indirect revenues. By selling the right to use images from a film, the conglomerate earns revenues from other companies while saturating retail markets with objects that advertise the film. For most blockbuster films, these objects include tee shirts, dresses, underwear, sweat shirts, sleep wear, sheets, comforters, pillow cases, posters, jewelry, cups, glasses, plates, utensils, dolls, stuffed animals, toys, board games, computer games, statues, trading cards, clocks, watches, hats, pin ball machines, paper goods, and so forth. Deals with fast food chains guarantee advertising on site and on television for souvenirs and special meals bearing logos from the film. Such deals increasingly mean that the fast food restaurants and all ordinary paper goods (mats, napkins, cups, wrappers, take-out bags, etc.) are decorated with images from the film.

Media conglomerates increasingly rely on secondary markets and on product lines tied to a master title. Whereas the latter encourages the generation of film sequels and television spin offs, the former encourages the cultivation of fans who will purchase any item connected to the title that is sold across the secondary markets. As collectors, fans can be counted on to purchase objects connected to the product line's title regardless of the quality of any individual product. The emergence of a collectors' ethos fosters the emergence of resale markets in which collectors and dealers trade old comic books, dolls, trading cards, and so forth. In the United States, speculation in these items has become a major hobby. The media promote this with tales of Ovaltine decoder rings and similar trivia that have sold for thousands of dollars. The age and rarity of these items has made them valuable, especially if kept in pristine condition.

Such tales also foster secondary markets for dolls ("action figures") and other items connected with titles like Paramount's *Star Trek,* Lucasfilm's *Star Wars,* and Time Warner's *Batman.* From the collector's perspective, buying Captain Picard dolls and storing them in the original packages for resale in 2050 constitutes a sensible investment. This fuels purchases by dealers and fans, often multiple purchases of a single item. Dealers may purchase a certain doll en masse in order to corner the supply. This pushes up the price that some fans will pay for the doll, thus allowing dealers to reap immediate profits. Recognizing this dynamic, some manufacturers now specify how many copies of a doll can be bought at one time. This sends two messages: first, the company is "pro-fan" and "anti-dealer"; second, the doll is a sound investment. Of course, if most dolls survive in pristine condition, they will be worthless. This analysis falls outside the discourse of speculation found in magazines for collectors.

Here, then, emerges the economic logic for a conglomerate's cultivation of fans. Transindustrial conglomeration, recycling of content across internal markets, and licensing only works if each recycled artifact has some hope of being purchased. The traditional marketing of media artifacts as novelties suggests that recycling the screenplay from film to novel to comic book to cassette is irrational. However, recycling the title can make sense for a media conglomerate if the cost of recycling is less than the cost of new product, if each recycled product earns revenues from buyers untapped in other venues, and if fans routinely purchase recycled products associated with a title. Fans, then, guarantee revenues across all recycling operations if the conglomerate can cultivate them as reliable and undiscriminating purchasers of a product line.

STAR TREK, FANS, PARAMOUNT

An undiscriminating and reliable fandom has been the basis of Paramount's *Star Trek* product line, which is now over 30 years old. The line is rooted in the original television series *Star Trek* (1966-69), which was recycled as a cartoon on television and then as a film with multiple sequels. Paramount subsequently launched three related television series (*Star Trek: The Next Generation, Star Trek: Deep Space Nine,* and *Star Trek: Voyager*), and a second film series based on *The Next Generation.* Paramount syndicates *Deep Space Nine* and airs *Voyager* on the United Paramount Television Network.[1] All of these materials are recycled as video cassettes for rent or purchase. As technologies shift, Paramount reissues the films in new playback formats (video cassette, letter box, DVD, etc.). Periodically, it also reissues recordings of old shows with new introductory material to celebrate *Star Trek* anniversaries. Besides owning Paramount and UPN, Viacom also owns the nation's largest video retailer, Blockbuster Video. Given this relationship, Blockbuster has no difficulty in getting *Star Trek* product. Because *Star Trek* fans are repeat consumers and ardent collectors—in cultural terms, these Trekkers are close viewers who ritually reimmerse themselves in the *Star Trek* canon—they provide a steady stream of revenues for reformatted and reissued copies of films and shows that they already own. This is a crucial element shaping Paramount's recycling of *Star Trek* film and video.

---

[1]Paramount itself is owned by National Amusements Inc., which is privately held.

In print, *Star Trek* feeds five different book series for adult readers, one per television series and one that has originated its characters and placed them within the *Star Trek* universe. Although some "favorite episodes" are recycled as novels, most of the books in each series is an original, paperback novel published by Pocket Books. A separate series of hardbound books is published by Simon & Schuster, which includes novelizations of the more recent films, the last episode of *The Next Generation,* and some "extended length" original novels. Both publishers were acquired by Paramount in 1975 and the *Star Trek* books were launched in 1979 with Pocket Book's publication of the first film novelization. By moving *Star Trek* into print, Paramount ensured that a steady supply of cost-efficient product would be routinely available for Trekkers to purchase. To recruit young readers, Paramount maintains a separate line of *Star Trek* books.

Paramount's use of *Star Trek* characters in these books is limited neither by the aging nor the cost of the principle actors—whose identification with their characters allow them to monopolize those roles. In the first *Star Trek* films, Paramount paid hefty salaries and granted perquisites to William Shatner (Captain Kirk) and Leonard Nimoy (Mr. Spock) that have not always been balanced by box office revenues. With the novels, Paramount generates revenues from Kirk and Spock regardless of Shatner and Nimoy. Giving each *Star Trek* television series its own line of books allows Paramount to feed its publishing operations by recycling characters whose very presence in a book will guarantee some sales. And those sales require no advertising.

The degree to which Trekkers are reliable consumers should not be underestimated. Paramount is so sure of these fans that it released the hardbound novelization of *The Next Generation*'s last episode prior to its broadcast. Trekkers could be trusted to snap up the book *and* watch the episode. Such ardent fans could also be relied upon to purchase the "official" video for its cover art and additional, unbroadcast material. Besides books and videos, Trekkers have been offered a wide variety of licensed *Star Trek* merchandise including toys of all types, commemorative plates, medallions, clothes, albums, comic books, bed linens, mugs, CD-ROMs, figurines, trading cards, jewelry, fine china, posters, screen savers, costumes, "official" "signed" plaques, and "official" Federation regalia. This suggests only the most rudimentary notion of the official *Star Trek*'s product line. Given repeated iterations of each type of product over a 30-year period, the traditional admonition to "collect them all!" takes on a somewhat sinister quality.

This only scratches the surface of Viacom's ability to exploit the *Star Trek* product line to feed its transindustrial operations. Among Viacom's holdings in cable television is the SciFi Channel (50%), which specializes in science fiction, fantasy, and horror programming. The

SciFi Channel has celebrated *Star Trek* anniversaries, airing various *Star Trek* films with Leonard Nimoy as host and running specials comprised mainly by *Star Trek* clips and host segments. Ads for SciFi have featured Majel Barrett, the widow of *Star Trek*'s creator Gene Roddenberry, who herself portrayed Nurse Chapel in *Star Trek*, Ambassador Troi in *The Next Generation,* and the voices of several *Star Trek* computers. Barrett has also appeared on SciFi's talk shows. This synergy recruits *Star Trek* fans for the SciFi audience, promotes the *Star Trek* product line to mundanes, and provides the channel with inexpensive product to fill its schedule.

Paramount's *Star Trek* line earns millions of dollars and, when other Paramount ventures fail, the *Star Trek* line subsidizes those losses. This depends on Trekkers' willingness to buy anything marked *Star Trek* and that willingness has been remarkable indeed. Ironically, that both contributes to and limits Trekkers' economic significance for Paramount.

THE (UN)IMPORTANCE OF BEING EARNEST

As a media conglomerate, Paramount cultivates its *Star Trek* fandom to ensure a reliable base of consumers. Paramount arranges the appearances of its *Trek* stars at fan conventions, operates the official *Star Trek* fan club, and generally tolerates minor infractions of its copyright as long as fan-creators make no profits. In return, Paramount receives a considerable flow of income—as well as commentary—from Trekkers. To the degree that fans buy *Trek* products indiscriminately, Trekkers provide little incentive for Paramount to either produce items that respond to fans' comments or exert greater quality control over items in the product line. As long as Paramount can assume its revenues from fans, Trekkers can be safely ignored. The very significance of *Star Trek* to its fans encourages Paramount to target the population from which revenues are not guaranteed—the dreaded mundanes.

Outside fandom, the *Star Trek* title functions like any other brand name. In those two words lie the promise of space opera with a humanist twist, of a vision blending militarism and egalitarianism on a galactic scale. Within the brand name, individual characters nuance that promise: more sex with Captain Kirk, more literary references with Captain Picard. Such promises may influence purchases when costs are comparable, commitment is minimal, and buyers are unwilling to take risks—as when one rents a video, buys a book at an airport, or channel surfs on cable. In such circumstances, mundane buyers may opt for the reliable promise of *Star Trek* over similar products whose promises are less certain. The unreliable buyer, then, is the source of revenue growth.

As long as unreliable mundanes must be wooed and fans can be ignored, Trekkers will not be the primary market for *Star Trek*. To guarantee fan revenues, Paramount attends conventions, engages in dialogues, and offers sops to Trekkers—even as it targets materials for nonfans. This attend-and-ignore policy often frustrates fans. But as long as Trekkers routinely buy the product line, they can be taken for granted.

This violates "common sense" about how capitalist markets work in general and how U.S. media work in particular. Markets are supposed to be demand driven and thereby to give people what they want. In media markets, the audiences' demand guarantees that what we see is what we want. In the United States, media corporations argue that they are not responsible for the content of their films, television shows, and so forth, because they must give us what we want in order to stay in business. This argument is circular but simple. If people didn't want *Star Trek* products, Paramount wouldn't produce them. But Paramount does produce them so *Star Trek* products must respond to our demand for them. By the logic of a demand-driven marketplace, fans should have the most influence over *Star Trek*.

Common sense, however, fails to recognize that U.S. media markets have long been oligopolized and integrated (vertically, horizontally, and now transindustrially). The logics of the demand-driven market simply do not apply. Instead, for a transindustrial conglomerate like Paramount, synergy and brand name consumption allow supply to subordinate demand as long as Trekkers buy indiscriminately. Given *Star Trek*'s reliability as a revenue generator, Paramount's problem becomes revenue growth, which comes from impulse buyers purchasing a particular *Star Trek* product. In television, the situation is complicated by the A.C. Nielsen sample, which gathers data on demographics but not subcultural affiliations. This means that Trekkers are not identifiable within the sample. As long as advertisers of cars, tampons, or athletic shoes have no reason to target Trekkers, Nielsen need not identify any who crop up in the sample. Trekkers are too few in number—and too disorganized in their non-*Trek* buying—to be targeted by advertisers. This further complicates Trekkers' economic status. Their devotion to *Star Trek* translates into revenues from the product line for Paramount, but not necessarily into ratings for either *Star Trek: Deep Space Nine* or *Star Trek: Voyager*. For these series to become ratings hits, they must target the dreaded mundanes.

These conundrums leave Trekkers' economic status unsettled, which opens Trekkers to ridicule. Interestingly, Trekkers are not criticized for being name-brand consumers; such criticism remains a taboo in U.S. commercial media. Instead, Trekkers are scorned for the very activities that fan ethnographers celebrate. Trekkers are ridiculed for taking *Star Trek* too seriously. They are portrayed as fools for immersing themselves in *Star Trek*'s fictional universe, for treating *Star Trek* as a symbolic system worthy of interpretation, and for utilizing the elements of that system to generate new artifacts. Such activities violate the dominant ideology's precept that media are mere entertainment. The fans' earnestness about *Star Trek* as culture makes them fools to the corporations that profit from them and to the mundanes who surround them. Without this economic and ideological context, emic ethnographers can only report that Trekkers and other fans feel scorned. Emic research does not illuminate the larger context that fosters such scorn; to do so, requires abstract analysis. Let us turn, finally, to a consideration of this challenge to integrate emic and analytic research.

LEISURE AND LABOR: TOWARD AN INTEGRATION

To paraphrase Marx (1972), human beings make culture but not in the circumstances of our choosing. In the U.S., the industrialization of cultural production and consumption must be factored into any account of what people do with media. Subcultural groups, like fandoms, are situated within a radically commercialized media system that naturalizes and privileges the interests of advertisers and transindustrial conglomerates. Thus subcultural practices, unsanctioned by corporate interests, are portrayed as foolish, bizarre, and peculiar. But alternative practices persist, given their linkage to the root dynamics of culture: people collectively play with given symbols, recombining and reinterpreting the given, as part of the process of maintaining and making culture. These abilities remain despite the industrialization and privatization of culture.

However, the transformation of culture into big business changes the circumstances in which we make culture. Playing with corporate property is not the same as playing with a given cultural heritage. For commercial media, the enculturation process is limited to teaching people what they ought to need and what they ought to buy. Beyond that, any learning is incidental. Limiting cultural play to corporate property means restricting the cultural fund to those representations believed to sell name brands, maintain routine consumption, and trigger impulse buying. This corporate enculturation costs us time, money, and labor. The surplus value that we create as the unpaid audience commodity earns revenues for media conglomerates from advertisers. Further, if we buy name-brand items from product lines or pay access/ticket fees, we again generate revenues for these media conglomerates. With transindustrial structure, corporate synergy guarantees that the content of a limited, commercialized cultural fund will be recycled across multiple outlets so that commercial enculturation is reinforced by our personal adornment, decor, and so forth. At the same time, however, people may interject cultural play into the work of commercial enculturation, thus generating noncommercial meanings from commercial messages or creating entirely new expressions using commercial characters. Similarly, we may reject consumerist isolation by building subcultures—as the fans and fandoms demonstrate.

Given this analysis, the linkage between the experiential category of leisure and the analytic category of leisure-as-labor should be clear. However, it should also be clear that a methodology adequate to enact that linkage is yet to come. I have indicated some directions for such an integration and will briefly discuss them.

As emic ethnographies of fandom show, the most active audiences are deeply immersed in the duality of culture and commodity that constitutes the media product. Their lived experience of this duality is central to their subcultural identity as well as to their participation in the mainstream of American life. Yet that mainstream discourages the development of analytic skills that would foster a reasoned critique of consumerism, never mind capitalism. With emic scholars committed to articulating the vision of subcultures rooted in media products and with the hegemonic system (including the media) operating to circulate dominant ideology, emic ethnography is effectively blocked from creating an analytic, contextualized account of fandom. Although emic accounts are enriched by their intimacy with and respect for the fandom under study, they are limited to descriptions that are predisposed to celebrate fandom.

That predisposition may be useful to a subcultural community's self-esteem, but not to the creation of knowledge. Some analytic distance is required if we are to see how fandoms work as subcultures, how subcultures relate to dominant ideology, and how subcultures operate in terms of the entertainment/information sector of a capitalist economy. However, too much analytic distance can be as debilitating as too much intimacy. A balance must be struck between emic and etic ethnographies so that we can both understand the vision of the subculture and see how the subculture fits within capitalism.

That brings me to my final point: our accounts must recognize the larger circumstance that serves as the context of subcultures, media, and commercial culture: capitalism. By using political economy, we can discern the economic relationships that govern how corporations are structured, what cultural elements they select, what audiences are targeted, what behaviors are expected, and what meanings are privileged. By integrating emic ethnography, etic ethnography, and political economy, we will better address the actual phenomenon that we experience daily: cultural expressions packaged as media products designed to earn profits— yet capable of exciting the imagination and of motivating individual "consumers" to create subcultural communities. In studying subcultures, we must be very cognizant of the "raw" materials provided by media corporations and of the economic system that constitutes the circumstances in which we act. As human beings living in social collectivities, we do make culture—but in the context and within the limitations of capitalism.

REFERENCES

Amesley, C. (1989) "How to Watch Star Trek," *Cultural Studies, 3*, 323-39.

Anderson, R. (1995) *Consumer Culture and TV Programming.* Boulder, CO: Westview Press.

Barnouw, E. (1966) *A Tower of Babel: A History of Broadcasting in the United States, 1933-1953.* Oxford: Oxford University Press.

Benedict, R. (1934) *Patterns of Culture.* New York: Houghton Mifflin.

Braverman, H. (1974) *Labor and Monopoly Capital: The Degradation of Work in the Twentieth Century.* New York: Monthly Review Press.

Budd, M., R. M. Entman and C. Steinman (1990) "The Affirmative Character of U.S. Cultural Studies," *Critical Studies in Mass Communication, 7*(2), 169-84.

Berger, P. and T. Luckmann (1966) *The Social Construction of Reality.* New York: Doubleday.

Clement, A. (1988) "Office Automation and the Technical Control of Information Workers." In V. Mosco and J. Wasko, eds. *The Political Economy of Information.* Madison: University of Wisconsin Press: 217-46.

Curran, J., M. Gurevitch and J. Woollacott (1982) "The Study of Media: Theoretical Approaches." In M. Gurevitch et al., eds. *Culture, Society, and the Media.* London: Methuen: 11-29.

Fiske, J. (1990) "Ethnosemiotics: Some Personal and Theoretical Reflections," *Cultural Studies, 4*(1), 85-99.

Gitlin, T. (1983) *Inside Prime Time.* New York: Pantheon.

Glaser, B. and A. Strauss (1967). *The Discovery of Grounded Theory.* Chicago: Aldine.

Gutman, H. G. (1977) *Work, Culture, and Society.* New York: Vintage Books.

Harris, M. (1968) *The Rise of Anthropological Theory.* New York: Thomas Y. Crowell.

Harvey, D. (1990) *The Condition of Postmodernity.* Oxford and Cambridge, MA: Blackwell.

Hirsch, P. (1972) "Processing Fads and Fashions: An Organization-Set Analysis of Cultural Industry Systems," *American Journal of Sociology, 77*(4), 639-58.

Jenkins, H. (1992) *Textual Poachers: Television Fans and Participatory Culture.* New York: Routledge, Chapman, and Hall.

Jhally, S. (1982) "Probing the Blindspot: The Audience Commodity," *Canadian Journal of Political and Social Theory, 6*(1-2), 204-10.

Kraft, J. P. (1996) *Stage to Studio: Musicians and the Sound Revolution, 1890-1950.* Baltimore: Johns Hopkins University Press.

Livant, B. (1979) "The Audience Commodity," *Canadian Journal of Political and Social Theory, 3*(1), 91-106.

—— (1982) "Working at Watching: A Reply to Sut Jhally," *Canadian Journal of Political and Social Theory, 6*(1-2), 211-15.

Marx, K. (1984) *Capital: A Critique of Political Economy, Volume I.* New York: New World Paperbacks.

—— (1972) *The German Ideology.* New York: International Publishers.

McAllister, M. P. (1996) *The Commercialization of American Culture: New Advertising, Control and Democracy.* Thousand Oaks, CA: Sage.

Mead, M. (1928) *Coming of Age in Samoa.* Morrow: New York.

Meehan, E. R. (1986) "Conceptualizing Culture as Commodity: The Problem of Television," *Critical Studies in Mass Communication*, 448-57.

—— (1990) "Why We Don't Count: The Commodity Audience." In P. Mellencamp, ed. *Logics of Television.* Bloomington: Indiana University Press: 117-37.

—— (1991) "'Holy Commodity Fetish, Batman!': The Economics of a Commercial Intertext." In W. Uricchio and R. E. Pearson, eds. *The Many Lives of Batman: Critical Approaches to a Superhero and His Media.* New York: Routledge, Chapman, and Hall: 47-65.

Mehan, H. and H. Wood (1975) *The Reality of Ethnomethodology.* New York: Wiley.

Miner, H. (1967). "Body Ritual among the Nacirema." In F. J. Zulke, ed. *Perspectives of Social Science.* Berkeley: McCutchan

Mosco, V. (1989) *The Pay-Per Society: Computers and Communication in the Information Age.* Toronto: Garamond.

Murdock, G. (1978) "Blindspots about Western Marxism: A Reply to Dallas Smythe," *Canadian Journal of Political and Social Theory, 2*(2), 109-19.

Penley, C. (1991) "Brownian Motion: Women, Tactics, and Technology." In C. Penley and A. Ross, eds. *Technoculture.* Minneapolis: University of Minnesota Press.

Pike, K. L. (1966) "Etic and Emic Standpoints for the Description of Behavior." In A. G. Smith, ed. *Communication and Culture.* New York: Holt, Rinehart and Winston: 152-163.

Rosaldo, R. (1989) *Culture and Truth: The Remaking of Social Analysis.* Boston: Beacon Press.

Schiller, H. I. (1989) *Culture, Inc.: The Corporate Takeover of Public*

Expression. New York: Oxford University Press.

Schutz, A. (1967) *The Phenomenology of the Social World.* Evanston, IL: Northwestern University Press.

Smythe, D. (1975) "Communications: Blindspot of Western Marxism," *Canadian Journal of Political and Social Theory, 1*(3), 1-27.

Smythe, D. (1978) "Rejoinder to Graham Murdock," *Canadian Journal of Political and Social Theory, 2*(2), 120-29.

Tulloch, J. and M. Alvarado (1983) *Dr. Who: The Unfolding Text.* St. New York: Martin's Press.

Wasko, J. (1994) *Hollywood in the Information Age: Beyond the Silver Screen.* Austin: University of Texas Press.

Wasko, J., M. Phillips and C. Purdie (1993) "Hollywood Meets Madison Avenue: The Commercialization of U.S. Films," *Media, Culture, and Society, 15,* 271-93.

III

STUDYING THE AUDIENCE

5

Surveillance and Other Consuming Encounters in the Informational Marketplace

Richard Maxwell

One cannot resist on behalf of someone else. The very idea of resistance implies an aggression felt in the very heart. . . . But to challenge the choice of battlefield and the use of words, without relating them to the conditions of their selection, is surely to prevent oneself from identifying the historical origin of resistance, to understand the language it speaks and therefore to communicate.

Each form of resistance has its own language.
—Mattelart, Delcourt and Mattelart (1984: 13)

Times are bad for all but the rich, and yet leftist communication scholars find it more interesting to fight among themselves. At some point during the last 10 years, many of us who study communication and culture from the critical left perspective were invited to take part in a debate that hinged on a dispute over how two "camps" of critical communications research, defined for convenience rather than conceptual accuracy as cultural studies and critical political economy, identify and analyze media audiences. In my view, those of us who immersed ourselves in this debate have so far produced only one outcome: we've forgotten who our common enemy is. This is not to say that the tension between political economists and cultural studies professors hasn't led to some interesting thinking, which the authors in this book discuss as well as represent. But surprisingly few writers on either side have used this productive tension to modify the theory and practice of struggle against antidemocratic and exploitative transnational corporate media. Instead, the debate has more often sparked the desire to fundamentalize the tenets of each approach (Garnham, 1995; Grossberg, 1995). This inward gaze might be good for stabilizing the boundaries around beleaguered disciplinary identities, but it can also lead to a kind of narcissism that sees one's own advances as the other's failings. Hence, political economists lack cultural sensitivity, and cultural studies professors suffer from false consciousness that mistakes popular coping strategies for systemic resistance to capitalism.

This opposition has always been nonsense, of course, but such nonsense has nevertheless run deep in the vocabularies and selected genealogies that each "camp" used for self/other descriptions throughout the debate. This has contributed to forgetfulness about the issues and theoretical puzzles that set the heading for leftist communication research almost a decade before the debate heated up. For some of us, that common heading can be traced to the practical and theoretical limits reached by critical international communication research sometime in the 1970s. If studies on cultural imperialism gave rise to new questions about reception and resistance, they also provided the clearest examples of where critical international research models and theories were in need of modification, particularly in analyses of global media audiences and cultural consumption (Roach, 1997). This point was not lost on political economists of international media like me who were committed to sustaining the radical critique of the cultural imperialism thesis while taking into account advances made by (primarily British) cultural studies. In my case, this meant combining an internationalized approach to cultural studies with a localized understanding of cultural imperialism. This boiled down to conducting research at the point of contact between transnational cultural industries and popular cultures (at national, regional, and local scales of cultural practices).

This chapter indicates how theory, field work, and analysis can rely on questions and analytics drawn from both political economy and cultural studies. By focusing on encounters in the informational and cultural marketplace I hope to show where a space of theoretical and methodological alliance can be produced for leftist political economy and cultural studies (and consequently, where political solidarity enables better research). In order to get to that point, however, it's important to explain why the drive to purify the critical study of audiences is counter-productive for a leftist critique of audiences and audience analysis. The focus will then widen to take stock of the larger problem of consumer surveillance, but the links to narrower issues of audience analysis will be evident.

THE SINS OF POLITICAL ECONOMISTS

This essay will no doubt be considered an abomination by some post-marxists and liberal cultural studies professors, for my aim is to unfasten the stigma they've attached to some of the contested moves that are basic to writing a political economy of media audiences. The list of political economy's wrongs includes reductionism, instrumentalism, functionalism, and pessimism. Unfortunately for serious students of media audiences, moral arguments overshadow substantive theoretical debate over what these terms mean and why or when they're bad/good for analysis of media audiences. We can all use healthy criticism that exercises our brains, shakes the foundations of our thinking, and keeps our imaginations fresh. But moral injunctions are rarely salutary; they usually end up chucking bathwater and baby together. In this essay, I want to argue that the absolutist drive to purify political economy of its supposed sins depoliticizes thinking about media audiences and the contexts of audience research.

Let me first say that I'm agnostic when it comes to media audiences and consumers generally. I don't believe we can know as much about the thing called audiences as we can about the purposes of "expert" thinking that has given audiences an enduring presence within media institutions. Fortunately, for this writer at least, our venerable concepts cannot contain the variety, unruliness, and surprises erupting from groups of people who get together to enjoy or "dish" the sights and sounds of electronic media. In addition, there's the ethical predicament faced by most researchers of media audiences: seeing people as audiences, masses, or consumers, is already downright disrespectful. However, another problem with such research is that it also requires knowing more about people's tastes, tendencies, desires, and so on—that is, it calls for surveillance.

Media researchers are an imperious lot. As experts on media, we persist in finding ways to describe people as audiences, using a bountiful supply of both common sense and esoteric models. We can report, for example, on aggregate numbers of individuals watching a particular TV program or consuming a specific brand of mineral water. We can break those numbers down further and detail demographic differences, geographical concentrations, and obvious correlations between these descriptions. We can also sit down with groups of teenagers or families, chatting in an open interview format until our tape recorders and notepads are full. Inferences can be made from all of these reports and, depending on the analytics we use to explain things, we might draw a picture of an unyielding structure of an audience or decide that audiences are thoroughly contingent, unstructured. Using such knowledge, we can make up rules about media influence and even persuade politicians to write these rules into law. We can picture audiences as a mathematical equation and show their probability of being lodged within industrial time and cadastral space (obviously, marketers and their academic counterparts will care more about these dimensions of modern life). Whatever we do, we are conducting surveillance for the purpose of classifying people into audiences.

All inferences about audiences will begin with an assumption that individuals possess essential characteristics that make them into audiences as opposed to something else. Suppose we're talking about questionnaires designed to correlate media usage with a person's life. Despite the dynamics of most lives, forced-choice questions have to render personal information into reputed essences like age and sex; and such properties as education and income are likewise essentialized as aspects of personhood. The institutional identity, the media audience, forms by recombination of these component categories. A composite creature comes into being, with features that often mirror our own so well that our self-definition gets tied up with the way a media audience is said to behave.

Despite all this, the audience remains merely an institutional identity, an impossibly restrictive notion of collective belonging. Nobody goes around in the form of an audience as such, singing their way to audience-work like the seven dwarves. We are only audiences in the eyes of experts like those Western media critics who, since Hegel, have compared daily communion to reading the morning newspaper. We are only audiences when someone other than ourselves associates us with a publicized measure of attention given to some medium of expression like a TV, book, play, movie, painting, and so on.

Within this agnostic approach, the question for a political economy of audiences is simplified: What is the purpose of allying us, or other people, with any medium? As Dallas Smythe taught us, there is always more than just an electronic gadget or performance determining the conditions for inclusion and exclusion in audiences. This means, at a minimum, that audience analysis must account for the context that sustains both its own enterprise and a social presence for the institutional identity it has invented. With this departure from a mediacentric worldview, the contested moves of political economy can begin to make more sense.

TO MUDDY IS TO COME CLEAN

I'm a class reductionist because I begin from a perception that people's material living conditions determine basic things like time for media use and availability of media hardware. Such a move ascertains a significant part of the "causal nexus" (McLennan, 1996: 59) that delimits the fund of expressive and informational resources people draw from to cultivate their values and the meanings they ascribe to life. Writing about lives structured by economic pressures like the unequal distribution of the media consumption fund competes with two fatalistic determinisms that have erased class from mainstream media analysis: technological determinism and methodological individualism. Compared to these, class analysis of media audiences is a form of "weak reductionism" (McLennan, 1996: 59-61).

In this attenuated sense, the analysis of ordinary experiences of class does not reduce personal and collective identity to ideologies anchored to an internal and unchanging class nature. Instead, it confronts the hard edges in the political economy that cut the world into haves and have-nots and—far from fundamentalizing an identity essence in class—delights in the variety of ways people find to elaborate personal and collective identities within and across the boundary narratives provoked by class and social stratification. There is no single genre nor pure story line; the incitement to tell a life marked by class leads to many semiotic possibilities and intersects with other grand narratives of collective identity. This opposes mainstream, authoritative representations of audiences that take for granted that tastes and values can be judged and interpreted according to their fixed location in vertically ordered space—where, for example, cultural superiority and political authority are affixed to the first of paired terms like high/low, stage/street, North/South, modern/primitive, and center/margin.

By comparison, post-marxist and liberal cultural studies writers who intone against class reductionism appear theoretically misguided; or worse, they propagate a faith in capitalist social relations by ex-nominating the political economy. In practice, if such prejudgment against class reductionism silences analysis of the cultural sensibilities that class divisions engender it also ignores an important interpretive struggle that issues from a decisive conflict between capital and labor, one that pits corporate against popular interpretations of life's value.

Take a look at the accompanying chart. Table 5.1 illustrates the magnitude of strategic surveillance over tastes and values which U.S. market research firms carry out for commercial enterprises worldwide. It lists the top 50 U.S. companies engaged in consumer surveillance in 1995, stating each firm's take of the estimated $4.6 billion in revenues

Table 5.1. Top 50 U.S. Marketing, Advertising, Opinion Research Firms.

Company	1995 Revenues (millions $)	Yr. Change (percent)	Non-U.S. Revenues (percent)	Countries
1. Dun & Bradstreet MIS	$2388.1	9.0	63.9	90
A.C. Nielsen	1286.0	6.0	76.0	87
Nielsen Media Res.	283.0	13.5	—	—
IMS Int'l Inc.	819.0	11.0	67.0	—
2. Information Resources	399.9	11.0	11.0	—
3. The Arbitron Co.	137.2	11.5	—	—
4. Westat Inc.	124.0	4.2	—	—
5. Maritz Marketing Research Inc.	122.4	12.0	21.4	U.K./U.S./Can.
6. Walsh Int'l, PMSI	(228.9)	—	—	—
Research-only	111.6	6.5	25.1	5
7. The Kantar Group USA	91.9	6.5	6.5	—
Research Int'l USA	20.6	-12.0	29.3	—
Millward Brown Inc, USA	42.9	34.1	—	—
(The Kantar Group Ltd.)	(432.9)	19.2	79.0	—
(WPP Group, Plc.)	—	—	—	—
Millward Brown Int'l UK	(137.4)	—	—	—
Research Int'l Group	(233.3)	—	—	—
MRB Group Ltd., London	(28.4)	-8.7	—	—
8. The NPD Group Inc.	85.8	24.6	15.0	—
(foreign research)	(99.8)	—	—	—
9. NFO Research Inc.	73.1	17.4	2.7	17
10. Market Facts Inc.	64.6	13.0	9.9	U.S./Can.
11. Audits & Surveys Worldwide Inc.	54.6	24.4	24.0	—
12. The M/A/R/C Group	(74.4)	—	—	—
Research-only	52.1	3.2	—	U.S./Can.

Table 5.1. Top 50 U.S. Marketing, Advertising, Opinion Research Firms (con't.).

Company	1995 Revenues (millions $)	Yr. Change (percent)	Non-U.S. Revenues (percent)	Countries
13. Opinion Research Corp.	44.1	0.9	23.1	23
14. Abt Associates Inc.	42.9	-8.1	2.3	5
15. The BASES Group	41.6	11.0	20.0	47
16. Intersearch Corp.	41.1	12.3	—	—
17. MAI Information Group	38.0	12.0	—	—
(MAI, Plc.)	(125.0)	13.0	—	—
18. Macro Int'l Inc.	(45.0)	—	—	
Research-only	37.8	7.1	40.7	7
19. Walker Information	(42.0)	-11.2	—	—
Research-only	37.7	-10.9	15.3	—
20. Elrick & Lavidege	34.6	21.7	1.5	—
21. Burke Inc.	32.0	10.3	5.0	—
22. Roper Starch Worldwide Inc.	31.5	18.0	5.7	—
23. J.D. Power & Associates	30.3	6.3	—	—
24. Creative & Response Research	27.1	8.0	—	3
25. Lieberman Research Worldwide	23.4	20.0	11.9	68
26. Chilton Research Services (Disney)	23.3	5.7	—	—
27. Yankelovich Partners Inc.	23.2	12.6	6.0	—
28. M.O.R.-PACE Inc.	22.5	22.2	13.1	—
29. Wirthlin Worldwide	22.3	21.2	3.8	U.S./U.K./HK
30. ASI Market Research Inc.	21.1	14.4	—	—
31. Total Research Corp.	20.9	16.4	26.3	U.S./U.K./Arg.
32. Market Strategies, Inc.	19.3	6.6	—	—
33. Data Development Corp.	18.6	11.1	—	—
34. Custom Research Inc.	18.5	9.5	—	—

Table 5.1. Top 50 U.S. Marketing, Advertising, Opinion Research Firms (con't.).

Company	1995 Revenues (millions $)	Yr. Change (percent)	Non-U.S. Revenues (percent)	Countries
35. ICR Survey Research Group	17.9	7.1	—	—
36. Response Analysis Corp.	17.2	11.3	—	—
37. IntelliQuest Inc.	17.0	30.7	29.2	—
38. Market Decisions	15.1	8.0	—	—
39. Research Data Analysis	14.4	10.9	20.0	—
40. Matrixx Marketing Research	14.1	28.7	52.9	U.S./U.K./Fr.
(Matrixx Marketing Inc)	(271.1)	—	—	
41. Conway/Milliken & Assoc.	12.4	6.9	—	—
42. National Analysts Inc.	12.0	-6.8	—	—
43. Guideline Research Corp.	11.7	20.1	—	—
44. Gordon S. Black Corp. Louis Harris & Asc.	11.5	13.5	—	—
45. Ross-Cooper-Lund Inc.	10.3	35.7	1.0	—
46. Behavioral Analysis Inc.	10.0	2.9	10.8	—
47. Newman-Stein Inc.	8.6	-3.3	5.0	—
48. TVG Inc.	8.6	4.9	—	—
49. Marketing Research Services Inc.	8.5	23.8	—	—
50. FRC Research Corp.	8.4	3.8	3.0	—

(Honomichl and American Marketing Association, 1996: H2)

they collectively controlled that year. Out of this conservative estimate, which excluded revenues from public relations and advertising agencies, about $1.8 billion, or 39%, were revenues that came from research done outside the United States. Many on the list interlock with public relations, advertising, and communications corporations that form part of one global conglomerate. Between 1990 and 1995, the number of U.S. firms studying consumers outside the United States increased from 12 to 29, and the number of employees grew to roughly 40,500 full-timers and about 11,500 part-timers worldwide. With most smaller U.S. marketing firms added to the list, the combined revenues for 1995 were around $5 billion (Honomichl and American Marketing Association, 1996: H2).

These 50 firms routinely engage in a variety of ad hoc and continuous consumer studies, many of which involve contact with people through random telephone interviews, mixed focus groups, and fixed demographic panels. Such interviews and encounters can take place over very long distances. For example, Lieberman Research has a network of interviewing stations covering 68 countries in Europe, Asia, Mexico, and North and South America; interviews are conducted in 60 different languages. Many of these firms boast of high-tech telecommunications centers using computer-aided telephone interviewing systems. Others use, sell, and license for use a variety of proprietary software that is supposed to predict, model, or otherwise track people's tastes and shopping habits. They track banking and credit card use. They conduct litigation research, setting up mock juries to pretest people's attitudes in order to help corporations prepare court cases. They watch people buying cars, computers, telephones, drugs, health care, financial services, insurance, and packaged goods. Some companies focus less on products and services and more on corporate reputation and image in order to manage the public perception of big business. Others work for the U.S. government, such as Macro International, which did a demographic and health survey of more than 60 countries for the U.S. Agency for International Development. Roper operates the RISC (Research Institute on Social Change) system in the United States for a Paris-based consultancy group that measures and monitors social change. In addition, many new services have started to monitor the Internet, where they're observing purchasing patterns and, I suspect, compiling lists of World Wide Websters.

In saying all of this, I'm pointing out how much capital and labor it currently takes to make expert knowledge about consumers or audiences work to the corporate advantage. When I write about how the cultural industries use the figure of consumers or audiences as an instrument to extend a capitalist interpretation of the value of people and things, I'm making an instrumentalist move. Were I to suppress this instrumentalism, I might find it harder to notice how audiences get used.

This is because audience instrumentation is buried deep in the foundation of mainstream media audience analysis—that is, under the paradigm of consumer sovereignty.

Consumer sovereignty makes sense of the world like this: people are competent and free to reflect upon the kinds of media or commodities best for them; as such, they're empowered as sovereign consumers. It follows that what is brought into public culture through print, television, film, and so on results from autonomous consumer demand. From this perspective, people cannot be instruments of corporate design. By extension, the market is anthropomorphized: it has freedom and it makes demands on corporations that in turn supply it with meaningful and valuable goods and services.

Consider the ideology of consumer sovereignty in the context of the interpretive conflict from which it arises. Despite the rhetoric of empowerment, consumer sovereignty in effect disavows the aggressive corporate defense against divergent, popular assessments of value and meaning. By far, market research's most widespread purpose for consumer surveillance is the protection of symbolic assets that give money value to a commodity's brand name—this is called brand equity. Marketers want to know all about the fluctuations in product purchases and therefore monitor the attention that people pay to a particular brand. The information doesn't describe people's demand for a product; it tells market researchers if advertising, public relations, and promotions have built up the money-value of the product's image. That's what drives the billion-dollar A.C. Nielsen company to hire people to scan barcodes of their daily purchases. That's why IMS International, another Dun and Bradstreet property, tracks physicians' prescription patterns and pharmacy sales of over-the-counter drugs, monitoring OTC brand switching in more than 60 countries. Walsh and many others do the same. None of this is meant to give people what they want, but to generate a data image that defines people in terms of what is wanted from them. In that sense, the representational authority of consumer sovereignty renders people into identity categories that give corporations and their publicists an advantage in the interpretative conflict over the value and meaning of the things they sell.

They need the advantage, too, because the corporate assessment of value is not robust enough to survive by itself. What is fragile about the corporate design for life is that it's based on routine preferences organized around exchange value. According to this business orthodoxy, life should be compatible with commerce, human relationships should be judged on a cost-benefit model, and, moreover, life only gains social value when it is lived in a commodity form—as something that can legitimately be bought and sold, as are television viewers when they are rendered into ratings, or market-interview subjects when their life stories are sold as indices of consumption trends. Such reflex commoditization can never fully contain all competing valorizations, no matter how hard it hammers life into its pea-sized framework. Enter market research: because corporations can't get a firm grip on everybody's hearts, minds, and pocketbooks, billions of dollars go into the continuous surveillance of people's values and desires. Adjustments are made, merchandising ensues, people lose interest, "brand equity" deflates, and the research cycle begins again. In short, people's mercurial tastes in things are the driving force behind market research. Market research keeps a highly paid, watchful eye on people through surveillance networks that stretch around the globe with the singular purpose of arraying unwieldy personal tastes and desires to suit the corporate fondness for treating people and the things people value as marketable goods and services.

Now I've become a functionalist, for I've treated the instrumentation of audiences as a function of the corporate drive to make the corporate view of the meaning and value of things the social norm. Note, however, that I'm not professing the sort of functionalism that assumes that audience behaviors support a self-generating, homeostatic social structure. It is extremely important to remind political economists and cultural studies professors alike that it was that kind of functionalism, structural-functionalism, which both camps of critical communication scholars once sought together to jettison from theory and from the academy. The point I want to underscore here is that the structure that privileges capital is not self-sustaining. This is precisely why businesses are forced to surveil competing value assessments of life while propagating their own value system by, among other strategies, defending the commodity form.

I've made a functionalist move, then, on an as-needed basis in order to posit a preliminary question about the manner in which audiences achieve and sustain a social presence. What happens in a society in which marketers measure "audiences," not against the contradictory and complex lives of ordinary people, but rather as functions of their corporate client's purpose, which is to preserve a society that is congenial with capitalist relations of production and exchange?

To begin to answer this, you can study the ways market research links notions of nationality, or family, or race to shopping patterns in order to make identity functional for the corporate definition of collective life. Quite a few firms listed in Table 5.1 keep specialized panels that represent this view in terms of "lifestyles" or the component elements of a lifestyle. NFO maintains groups it calls "The Hispanic Panel," "The Baby Panel," and "The Mover Panel"; it also has a beverage consumption panel it calls "SIP." Yankelovich's "Monitor" identifies and predicts consumer behavior by tracking so-called "consumer values and motivations," and includes such samples as the "African American Monitor," "Asian American Monitor," "Hispanic Monitor," "the Nickelodeon Youth Monitor," and "MTV Young Adult World Monitor."

Despite the tropes of everyday life that might register calamitously from such panels and "monitors," people's values and tastes are instead assigned categorical definition as the lifestyles of predetermined market segments. Notions of identity and difference shrink to bits of data about shopping pattern diversity. In a way perhaps peculiar to them, marketers bend social and cultural differences into the commodity form's shape, pulling on collective loyalties from the side of a corporate valorization of things. They brand, package, and advertise goods and services to look familiar, until those strange things resemble something or someone already known. Corporations favor people who see themselves as the consumer type that marketers have allied with the commodity form.

We may or may not incorporate this institutional identity into our sense of common cause; but if we did, the functionalist move I've made could not say what action or event would happen next. As McLennan argues, a "functionalist explanation is not a failed request for causal information; it is rather a different way of 'making sense' of a phenomenon's coming-to-be" (1996: 65). The injunction against functionalism should therefore be taken with a grain of salt.

Finally, I'm a pessimist—sort of. I would rather argue that pessimism-optimism is a false and diversionary dichotomy. Surely, the analytical moves I've been making have led to some disturbing claims, yet the words break off where reductionism, instrumentalism, and functionalism reach the question: What next? But, then, I cannot see how neoliberal economics, for example, along with its media and telecommunication policy regime have reduced the agonies of the world's population; on this score, I'm deeply pessimistic. Yet I recognize early stages of political reversal, where bottom-up and progressive uses of media technologies multiply in the Third World and within the poor and oppressed zones of the First World. Does that make me an optimist or just better informed? I also think it's unwise to dismiss thrills and good feelings offhand, even those associated by many post-marxists and liberal cultural studies professors with shopping and commercial entertainments. However, I cannot think of such joys separately from the way, in my experience at least, that class, race, gender, and nationality weave together pleasure, agony, hope, anxiety, arousal, security, fear, melancholy, hatred, and a myriad of other complex sentiments. If structures of feeling cannot be essentialized down to a single sensation or desire, then why insist on pleasure as a defining property of any experience, let alone the experience of consuming or TV viewing?

To focus on how assessments of media audiences range dumbly between pessimism and optimism only serves to divert the discussion of audiences away from politics—away from the interpretive conflict between corporations' and people's sense of life's meaning and value.

As Herbert I. Schiller has long demonstrated by his work, the question is not whether we're pessimists or optimists about media audiences, but rather what kind of society we want to live in.

In short, if there are problems with political-economic approaches to media audiences, I don't think they necessarily flow from the contested moves of reductionism, instrumentalism, and functionalism. They come, I think, from the drive to install these or any analytical moves within a fundamentalist moral vision of the political economy of media audiences. For me, it doesn't matter whether this fundamentalizing drive comes from within or from outside the discourse of political economic analysis. I believe that any moral injunction would stigmatize thinking and censure perceptions that otherwise might politicize the notion of media audiences.

THE SECOND COLD WAR

The sum of a cold war of culture is that market research makes people up into categories of audiences and consumers to extend corporate control over the infrastructure of consumption. Market research companies couldn't do this without getting to know something about personhood and identity, whether marked by class, gender, race, nationality, or local cultural differences. Crucially, as market research's war chest grows so does the capitalization of a vast network of consumer surveillance operations across the planet.

Within the $433 million Kantar Group (number 7 on Table 5.1) there are firms doing advertising pretests and continuous tracking to register people's recognition of brand names and brand loyalty; they build segmentation models that openly rank consumers based on purchasing power, though other variables are used. Kantar is part of the mega-conglomerate WPP, that owns such communications, advertising, and public relations giants as Hill & Knowlton, J. Walter Thompson, and Ogilvy & Mather Worldwide. Within WPP's Kantar Group Ltd. there is a company called Millward Brown International (MBI), which runs a global market research operation out of London. MBI also owns smaller market research firms, one of which is the Spanish company, Alef. I've analyzed the significance of this network in more depth elsewhere (Maxwell, 1996). Among the interviewers working for Alef in Madrid are Enrique Rodriguez and Valle Rodriguez, whose insights into the job of scanning popular tastes for big international commercial clients will help me conclude this chapter.

In today's neo-liberal Spain, Enrique said, "there's a lot more advertising and people act like they're saturated and bored with it"

(Interview January 27, 1995). So when you track preferences for TV programs or the effectiveness of commercial publicity it's better to be cagey. "If you tell them directly, they might lose interest. So you have to be vague; play with them a bit. Instead of saying you're interviewing them to see how well a brand of chewing gum sells, for example, you'd say it's a survey on people's opinions about a food product." When people know they're being asked to confirm a commercial notion about the value of something—brand equity, for instance—their attention wanders, they refuse response, or they argue. If they can say what they value in their own words, and if they feel that their opinion is held in high regard by the interviewer, then they're likely to open up and furnish personal assessments of goods, services, and, more than likely, life in general.

Hence, the distant political economy that brought the interviewer to the door is disavowed. What's displayed is the interviewer's local knowledge, which can foster empathy and solidarity on both sides. This is a key tool used to get people to talk about their personal views of goods and services, a way to extract personal information that can help merchandisers put a familiar face on a strange commodity. For this reason, Enrique and his coworkers have to understand "scores of different types of people in Spain." He added, "it's not the same to do an interview in the Basque Country as it is in Galicia or Catalonia or Madrid or Andalusia. I don't know how to explain it, except to say that a Gallego and an Andalusian have about as much in common as an American and a Korean." The Kantar Group's technicians in London or New York don't need to have direct experience with values and tastes that diverge from their client's, because their global network allows them to benefit from on-the-ground expertise in local cultural differences.

The burden of representing the corporate side in this encounter falls on the shoulders of proxies like Enrique and Valle. They are constantly carrying out cultural translation in order to satisfy their client's demands without exacerbating the tension between corporate and popular value systems. "How do you ask someone to define the personality of a piece of candy?" Valle complained (Interview January 27, 1995). "Is it fun? Does this gum exude confidence? Come on, really, how are you supposed to ask someone that?" These interviewers work hard to encourage people to think about a commodity's human traits, figuring out ways to ask such questions as which detergent is the most maternal, the most sensitive or caring. As Valle said, "we have to adjust the questionnaires to fit the Spanish situation better; they're not the kinds of things you'd ask someone who lives here."

Testing for personal traits embodied in the commodity is, of course, how an enterprise like Kantar puts local surveillance to work for its global clients. It might sound foreign, but the goal of eliciting personal responses is to find out what would make goods and services, especially foreign ones, appear more like something or someone "who lives here." If Valle can find out when and in what ways Spanish shoppers see themselves and their values in commodities, then her bosses can help their clients domesticate their merchandise and socialize the corporate sense of value.

The commodity form cannot, meanwhile, stop people from valorizing things in ways that compete with the corporate view of the world. Thus the research cycle begins again, bringing interviewers like Valle face-to-face with the competition. "When people are aware that there's a cultural invasion taking place," said Valle, "they speak to the interviewer as if we were going to go back and tell the head of the company where to get off." Although she can understand such popular resentment, even be pleased by it, Valle still has a job to do. "You can't encourage that response," she said.

CONCLUSION

Consumer surveillance furnishes one empirical problem in which the skills of political economists and cultural studies professors are best combined. What systemic analysis explains is the general movement of capital toward the intensive capture of informational resources, a move into both the public spaces where people connect and the intimate spheres of personal assessments of value, desire, and taste. In the past, political economists have been documenting and analyzing imperialist extensions of business and military networks, emphasizing that information and communication corporations are the key enablers and primary beneficiaries of capitalist expansion. Propaganda favoring capital has always spearheaded and followed this expansion, and whether or not it finds a receptive public hearing, capital's propagandists persist in their efforts to shape identities that are compatible with the corporate view of life. However, it is also the case that top-down notions of identity are as much the product of surveillance techniques of measurement and classification as they are of socioeconomic pressures to shape life in a way that is congenial with capitalist relations of production and exchange.

Once political economists take surveillance into account, then the old metaphor of the hypodermic injecting dominant ideology into hearts and minds of people around the world can be modified. The hypodermic also represents the techniques by which capital extracts personal information and renders it into a new kind of commodity—one that is bought and sold as marketable knowledge of consumers. As such, this informational commodity gets into public culture in a variety of forms—from product packaging and advertising to words and phrases used by sellers and service providers. In these cultural forms, personal information recirculates as part of a consumerist spectacle of lifestyle components. Whether or not people incorporate these manufactured expressive elements into their lives is a puzzle that market researchers work daily to solve. Finding out how they solve it and what the consequences are for our cultures and societies is easier if we link cultural studies and political economy and remember the common bonds which unite critical left scholarship in communication and cultural studies.

REFERENCES

Garnham, N. (1995) "Political Economy and Cultural Studies: Reconciliation or Divorce?," *Critical Studies in Mass Communication, 12*(1), 62-71.

Grossberg, L. (1995) "Cultural Studies vs. Political Economy: Is Anybody Else Bored with This Debate?," *Critical Studies in Mass Communication, 12*(1), 72-81.

Honomichl, J. and American Marketing Association (1996) "1996 Business Report On The Marketing Research Industry," *Marketing News TM*, June 3, H2.

Mattelart, A., X. Delcourt and M. Mattelart (1984) *International Image Markets*. London: Comedia Publishers.

Maxwell, R. (1996) "Out of Kindness and Into Difference: The Value of Global Market Research," *Media, Culture and Society, 18*(1), January.

McLennan, G. (1996) "Post-Marxism and the 'Four Sins' of Modernist Theorizing," *New Left Review, 218*, July/August, 53-74.

Roach, C. (1997) "Cultural Imperialism and Resistance in Media Theory and Literary Theory," *Media, Culture and Society, 19*, 47-66.

6

The Social Context of Research and Theory

Herbert I. Schiller

In a class-divided society, efforts to explain social or physical phenomena will be heavily influenced by the perspectives and inclinations of the dominating stratum. Karl Marx wrote about this during the 19th century. J.D. Bernal put it this way:

> The existence of class-divided societies does not affect only the material consequences of knowledge, it cuts deep into the root of ideas. The literate and cultured are the ruling class, and the basic ideas that find expression in literature and science are inevitably tinged with ruling-class preconceptions and self-justifications. (Bernal, 1954: 886)

This way of looking at things does not mean that alternative explanations, in any period, are absent. What it generally signifies is that the strongest encouragement—financial support, economic position, and social esteem—invariably will be given to those theorists and researchers who provide findings generally helpful, but at least comforting to the dominant order. No less important, these findings will obtain the widest circulation and attention from the existing communication circuits also at the disposal of the dominating power. The last half century of communication research and theorizing—undertaken in the United States—richly confirms these theses. The overall context may be summarized briefly.

At the end of World War II, the United States was the world's most powerful economy—economically energized by the conflict, politically secure, and culturally poised to capture the international symbolic sphere. Even at that time, the U.S. economy was a corporately organized and highly concentrated system.

The strategic interests of this system were twofold. One was to deny the leftist mass movements in Western Europe and elsewhere their strong claim to move their societies in a new, noncapitalist direction. The other vital goal was to extend U.S. economic and social influence over the newly independent and other Third World nations, while at the same time ensuring their envelopment in the world capitalist system.

A variety of means were employed to achieve these ends, including economic bribery, presented as "aid"—this was the essence of the Marshall Plan—and denial of "aid," if a state proved recalcitrant to American demands. Also, the option of military intervention was always present. Finally, massive persuasion, utilizing the new communication technologies in the hands of the state and commercial (pop cultural) sectors was utilized.

In implementing and explaining theoretically (justifying) these aggressive policies and actions, a new field of inquiry—communication research—was born. Actually, the origins of communication research date back to the pre-World War II years, when it developed mostly as market research for the big consumer goods producers and the broadcasting industry that carried their sponsorship. But it was only after the war that the field of communication research really blossomed. And no wonder! It was organically tied to the power centers of the age—military, corporate, and state. These were the foci vigorously pursuing their designs of U.S. global ascendancy. No less important, the structural changes in the economy then underway made information and persuasion steadily more essential in the operation of an advanced capitalist system, in the beginning at home, and later on, as underpinning for the global market economy. As one historian recently put it:

> As the political climate shifted in the late 1940s from the war against fascism to the crusade against communism, the basic concepts of communication research could be, and were easily redeployed. How communication might build loyalty at home and stable, new, non-

communist nations around the globe became critically important to the field. It was, in large part, the new, cold war use of these concepts that made the field of communication research take off. By the mid-1950s, it was a richly funded area of inquiry. (Cmiel, 1996: 95)

The absorption of the new field of communication into class domination is not a unique example of systemic cooptation. Robert Heilbroner, for example, in a recent work (with William Milberg)notes: ". . . our discipline [economics] . . . is intrinsically embedded in capitalism and to some degree thereby becomes its self-justifying voice, even when it is quite oblivious of serving that purpose . . . (Heilbroner and Milberg, 1995).

We skip over the possibly most class-subservient field of all, political science. Yet the situation in communication research is unique in at least one respect. Its takeover was observable from its inception and the subordination of its practitioners glaringly overt. The aims it served were obvious (at least in retrospect). In other social and physical areas of knowledge, the influence of dominating class power may be more veiled, sometimes nearly invisible to casual observation.

The specific means that were employed to make communication research an adjunct of U.S. power have been masterfully documented by Simpson (1994) who recounts how the "founding fathers" of the new discipline were recruited to work for the Pentagon, the intelligence services, and the foreign policy establishment.

The connection and utility of communication research to American postwar expansive capitalism can be briefly, and only limitedly, reviewed here. The first communication "project" of critical importance to this aggressive expansion was the creation of a hysterical atmosphere at home (quickly transported abroad) that enabled U.S. geopolitical designs to proceed with near total popular support. This was achieved with the launching of a longlasting and pervasive anticommunist crusade. The central argument justifying anticommunism and the overwhelming fear it generated was that the world was threatened by Soviet military aggression. Nonsensical on the face of it—the Russians had just lost more than 20 million people and were economically devastated—the orchestration of the powerful media system and the entire culture made the threat acceptable and frightening.[1]

Anticommunism doctrine served to sanction and purify socially destructive U.S. policies and actions over a 50-year period. Communication scholarship and scholars actively participated in the cre-

---

[1]George Kennan, generally credited with the formulation of the "containment of communism" doctrine published in 1947 in *Foreign Affairs* magazine, in recent years has repudiated the thesis and claims he was "misinterpreted."

ation and maintenance of this Big Lie. Wilbur Schramm, for example, who became the leading figure in U.S. communication research was a dedicated worker in the construction of the anticommunism climate. As early as 1950, in the first months of the Korean War Schramm went to Korea, under the auspices of the U.S. Air Force to survey Koreans who had been in Seoul during the brief Communist occupation.

Ignoring the complicated background to the Korean War—one American historian viewed it more as a civil war—Schramm and John W. Riley, Jr., published "The Reds Take a City: The Communist Occupation of Seoul" in 1951. The book's propagandistic intent was set forth in its introduction, written by Frederick W. Williams:

> As the authors of this book point out, the model of the Communist blueprint for Seoul was Pyongyang, Prague, Bucharest, Moscow. Here, then, is the lesson of Communist intentions, intentions which are being consistently planned for execution in every home—in city and on farm—around the world. In your home, too! (v-vi)

Schramm and Riley's conclusion is no less emotional and demagogic:

> [The study] affirms our observation that the Communist system promises much to many but in fact delivers its rewards to only a few . . . the free people of the world may take heart . . . [but] how many more such accounts must be written? (206)

This was a foretaste of what was to come from communication researchers in the years to follow. Another project, in 1953, was a recipe-for-propaganda book produced under the direction of Schramm for the instruction of the United States Information Agency (USIA). Let it be recalled, that this was an intense period of the cold war during which the USIA was globally engaged in disseminating official interpretations of bitter international disputes. Suggestive of the atmosphere of that era, the study was classified for 20 years. When finally published commercially in 1976, its author, Leo Bogart, explained that the book's reappearance might help to restore the anticommunist perspective of the pre-Vietnam period. He wrote: "A generation of intellectuals—including historians—were conditioned during the Vietnam War to question and oppose American foreign policy and to assume that its Communist opponents were the protagonists of oppressed people longing for redress of long-standing grievances" (Bogart, 1976).

Additional academic contributions to the work of the USIA were also noted: ". . . with the advice of Paul Lazarsfeld and his associates at Columbia University, the Voice of America in New York had built up an impressive research staff of 150, headed by the sociologist Leo Lowenthal and including Ralph White, M. Fiske. Joseph T. Klapper and Harold Mendelsohn" (Bogart, 1976: xx). Whatever the book's "success" in making its 1953 anticommunist premises more credible, it offers additional evidence of the unstinting cooperation communication scholarship supplied to postwar American imperial power.[2]

To be sure, the field of communication was not a unique subject for such efforts. A special issue of *Radical History Review* (1995), entitled "The Cold War and Expert Knowledge," documents similar practices in psychology, operations research, and economics.

SOME THEORETICAL UNDERPINNING

Along with communication scholarship's well paid service to the state machine which was organizing the world economy along lines agreeable to dominant economic interests in the United States, was another, perhaps more important contribution. The new discipline supplied the theoretical models that underpinned and energized a vital segment of postwar American foreign policy. Exemplary here is the work of Daniel Lerner, who, in Jeremy Tunstall's view, was the intellectual leader of a key group of communication scholars that included Schramm and Ithiel DeSola Pool (Tunstall, 1977: 208).

Lerner was among the first to grasp, and articulate, the geopolitical strategy of securing the ex-colonial world for Western-structured "development." In this, he helped found the new field of development communication that incorporated this strategy in its underlying assumptions and practices.

In the many variants of developmental theory, communication played a key role, the most important of which was to instill the modernization idea in what the scholars regarded as hitherto passive peoples. The media were the catalytic force. Here again, Cmiel writes: "By the mid-1950s . . . communication research became a central pillar in what came to be known as 'modernization theory' and a part of the Cold War offensive against communism. Mass communication was now seen as critical to building loyalty to the modern nation-state and as a theme of dozens of 1950s studies, including Lerner's very influential work" (Cmiel, 1996: 96).

---

[2]Another example is a book published by Schramm in 1957, *Responsibility in Mass Communication*, which Cmiel writes, "reeks of Cold War apologetics" (Cmiel, 1996: 95).

Lerner understood that it was the "emergence of the Third World" that constituted the grand prize at stake—as well as being a determining factor in the longterm viability of the world market system. He put the challenge to American postwar expansionist policy this way:

> The long era of imperialism (subordination) is recently ended; the campaign for international development (equalization) has just begun. In the new process, international communication operates in behalf of different policy purposes under different socio-economic conditions by different psychopolitical means. Indeed, in the transition from imperialism to international development, there has been a fundamental change in the role of communication. Under the new conditions of globalism, it has largely replaced the coercive means by which colonial territories were seized and held. . . . *The persuasive transmission of enlightenment is the modern paradigm of international communication.*" (Lerner, 1969: 192. Emphasis added.)

Here, indeed, is the formula of late 20th-century capitalism that has been so effectively applied by United States policymakers and their international counterparts. Lerner's special talent rested in his recognition of the key role communication might (and did) play in the creation of the global market economy, with the United States at the center of the system. In Lerner's prescription, there is a "transition from coercion to communication."

Actually, coercion has by no means been absent in recent decades and Lerner's formulation is applicable only if the ex-colonial area/nation has settled for a market economy and allowed itself to be absorbed in the dominant world business order. Those new or old states that insisted on some measure of autonomy in the social character and operation of their economies have faced unrelenting combinations of economic and military force. The dozens of direct interventions, the organization of military coups, and the economic blockades imposed by Washington over the last 40 years constitute a huge data base of aggression. At the same time, the utilization of international communications once a region has been "stabilized" has provided an essential ingredient for making the operational routines of the world commercial economy effective.

The ratios that American communication specialists calculated to indicate developmental levels—so many movie seats, newspapers, radio sets per capita, and so forth—however trivial, did, in fact, though certainly not intentionally, measure one important condition. It revealed how far a country had been propelled into the global market system, and, relatedly, how deeply it had been penetrated by U.S. media products and services and outlooks. . . . The ratios were (and still are) a measure of the extent to which "the persuasive transmission of enlightenment" had occurred.

BRIEF PERIOD OF CHALLENGE TO THE DOMINANT PARADIGM (1960s-1970s)

A mini- crisis of sorts was experienced by communication scholarship— as it was in most other scientific fields—in the late 1960s and throughout most of the 1970s. It developed as a reaction to the general crisis affecting United States power. Opposition to the the bloody, imperialist war in Vietnam, the civil rights upsurge, and the emergence of the women's movement, for a brief moment, shook Washington's imperial course. These movements encouraged and provided a receptive atmosphere for the work of a small number of researchers who had begun to question both the domestic and international foundations of the dominant communication paradigm.

This critical work largely, though not exclusively, identified with the claims of the disadvantaged majority of states, as well as with domestically voiceless groups, for a new, international information order. It detailed how unilateral and top-down was the flow of information inside and between nations. It sought to reduce the Western monopoly on information flows, to expand the number of voices in the media arena, and to lessen the pervasive commercialism that enveloped the cultural climate in all areas subject to Western, mostly United States, media product.

Cultural imperialism, a term ridiculed when not ignored, by prevailing communications scholarship as well as the industrial media practitioners, emerged for a moment as a discussable concept. For about a decade, the hegemony of Establishment communication theory and scholarship was on the defensive. Indicative of this fleeting period, Everett Rogers, one of the long-standing members, and proponents of orthodoxy, published an essay on "The Passing of the Dominant Paradigm" (1976).

Actually, Rogers' appraisal was mistaken. American domination in theory and practice reasserted itself by the end of the 1970s. It is not a random political development that Ronald Reagan became president of the United States in 1980. His election signalled an offensive, more ferocious than ever, of American capitalism to extend world market share, destroy socialism, and intensify the exploitation of the working classes. In keeping with the thesis of this article, it was to be expected that the field of communication scholarship would quickly get in step with the guardians of systemic power. How it did so is the focus of the next section.

THE NEW AND IMPROVED DOMINANT PARADIGM

To fully appreciate the curious world of communication scholarship over the years since Rogers' acknowledgement of its earlier deficiencies, it is helpful to note, however briefly, the publicly known developments in the private cultural industries in this period. The last 15 years in the United States—and in Western Europe as well—have witnessed an unprecedented increase in the concentration of ownership and control in the communication sector. Publishing, radio, television, film, recording, and telecommunications have been assembled into huge conglomerate enterprises, representing hitherto unimaginable concentrated cultural power. Corporations such as Time Warner, Disney-Capital Cities-ABC, Murdoch's News Corp. Ltd., Viacom, Bertelsman and half a dozen other telecommunications and computer software giants now preside over the global symbolic environment.

Preceding and facilitating this massive transformation in the character of private cultural production have been the twin movements of deregulation and privatization. After being initiated in the United Kingdom (Thatcher) and the United States (circa Reagan) these policies have been carried out in one country after another—wherever the transnational corporate order prevails. (In fact, this means everywhere, with a couple of minor exceptions.)

These two movements, selling off public sector enterprises to private capital and reducing, when not eliminating, social accountability of corporate enterprise, have had an especially baleful impact on the communication industries. In the United States, they have enabled an almost limitless pyramidization of television, film, radio, and publishing properties into what were already powerful corporate hands. They have also, largely stripped away what modest public oversight existed over the cultural industries—television, radio, and press, in particular (Schiller, 1996). Experiences in Europe, West and East, when not identical, are similar, taking national specificities into account. All of this has led to the existing situation wherein a good part of the world's cultural production is corporately manufactured and distributed. Independents and small-scale private producers remain, but they exist on the margins or as feeder tributaries to the big companies.

This is the communication-cultural context that exists, whether it is recognized or not by researchers in the field. Given this condition, one might imagine that the time is propitious for studies of corporate cultural power: for example, comparative studies of how national systems of broadcasting and telecommunications have been privatized; an examination of techniques of subduing, misleading, or pacifying message receivers; accounts and analyses of media subservience or collaboration with corporate and political power; the implications of excessive corporate power for freedom of the press, if not the very principle of a free press; critiquing the introduction of new information technologies, and, assessing what corporate "speech" means for individual speech. Numerous other questions come to mind that, if examined, could illuminate the communication condition in a time of far-reaching monopoly.

Some of these studies may, in fact, already have been undertaken. But the attention of most scholarship has been directed elsewhere. It has centered on audience research, the receivers, not the producers, of the symbolic material. Oliver Boyd-Barrett (1995) opines: "If obliged to define a single distinguishing feature of media study over the past 15 years, many scholars would focus on new approaches to audience or 'reception' analysis" (498). James Curran (1995: 505:11) described this development, nonperjoratively, as "revisionist" theory. This bears a striking resemblance to what occurred half a century earlier. In the late 1930s, "effects research" served to divert attention from the powerful role of persuasion and who the persuaders were (Cmiel, 1996: 92-3).

Actually, audience research could be a fruitful area to study, if it were informed by the context of the current period of media colossi. If it were motivated by a desire to do battle with the controlling corporate cultural forces of the day, some very interesting work could be expected. Perhaps such work is underway. Unfortunately, the bulk of the research, wittingly or not, has a different objective. It serves to *deny* the influence of the prevailing corporate cultural infrastructure. At the same time, it insists that individuals (audiences) are actively and successfully engaged in resisting, *subjectively,* the messages and images of the Disneys, Time Warners, and Viacoms.

This emphasis on audience resistance, and an accompanying indifference, if not denial, of corporate symbolic domination, contributes—whatever the researchers engaged may think or claim—to a grotesque distortion of reality. It weakens, actually undermines, any effort to tangibly resist corporate cultural domination. Boyd-Barrett, noncommittally, notes: "Revisionism undermines the force of the radical critique of mass communication in that it serves the interests of the powerful and contributes to the social reproduction of inequality" (1995: 500).

Graham Murdock (1995) is less distanced. He writes: "The stark vertical structures of inequality have been bulldozed off this [revisionist theory] map and the economic and political dynamics that have built them have slid from view . . . class has become a category that dare not speak its name" (91).

The impact of revisionist theory is not limited to the United States and the United Kingdom's national space. Active audience proponents deny the influence, sometimes even the existence, of global cultural power. The audiences in countries receiving the monopoly cultural flows are claimed by revisionist theorists to be unaffected because each audience makes it own interpretations of the products entering its senses. In effect, if the active audience theorists have it right, the efforts of 130 or so countries in the late 1960s and early 1970s to change their informational environment because it was dominated by external, monopoly forces were misplaced. In revisionist theory, cultural imperialism, like inequality and class, "slide from view."[3]

All the same, the material world of privileged economic interests and class power does not disappear. In fact, it asserts itself regularly in pursuit of its well understood needs. A recent article in *Foreign Affairs,* the foreign policy journal of a powerful section of the American establishment, provides a difficult to ignore perspective to those who discount concentrated cultural power and its beneficiaries. Written by Joseph S. Nye, Jr., the Assistant Secretary of Defense for International Affairs in the Clinton Administration, and William A. Owens, former Vice Chairman of the Joint Chiefs of Staff, also in the Clinton Administration, their article is titled "America's Information Edge," and it is directed to those who don't yet grasp what the authors see as the rich possibilities of assuring U.S. global domination in the next century. Unlike those who deny or minimize the presence of existing U.S. global cultural power, Nye and Owens (1996) affirm it and press to employ the new information technologies—cable, satellites, computer networks—to deepen and consolidate it. These influential contributors argue that the United States should take advantage of "its international business and telecommunications networks," because American popular culture already "dominates film, television and electronic communications." By doing this, they claim, "the 21st century, not the twentieth, will turn out to be the period of America's greatest preeminence. Information is the new coin of the realm, and the United States is better positioned than any other country to multiply the potency of its hard and soft power resources through information" (Nye and Owens, 1996).

How paradoxical that representatives of power have no difficulty with referring to domination, whereas so many communications researchers seem unable to utter the word. Nye and Owens may be overly optimistic about American "preeminence" in the century ahead. What is not in doubt, is that issues of information control and cultural independence will be the battleground in the years ahead.

---

[3]Two researchers acknowledged that the motivation for their audience impact research was to refute cultural domination theory. Tamar Liebes and Elihu Katz (1990) begin their study with this sentence: "Theorists of cultural imperialism assume that hegemony is prepackaged in Los Angeles, shipped out to the global village, and unwrapped in innocent minds. We wanted to see for ourselves. . . ." (v).

This poses a transcendent question. Will those informed in communication theory and research continue to serve systemic power as so many of them dutifully have done over the last half century? Or will they apply their capabilities and talent toward critical assessment of the institutional structures now in place? A field's integrity is at stake.

REFERENCES

Bernal, J. D. (1954) *Science in History.* London: Watts & Co.

Bogart, L. (1976) *Premises for Propaganda: The United States Information Agency's Operating Assumptions in the Cold War.* New York: The Free Press, Macmillan.

Boyd-Barrett, O. (1995) "Approaches to 'New Audience Research.'" In Oliver Boyd-Barrett and Chris Newbold, eds. *Approaches to Media.* London: Arnold.

Cmiel, K. (1996) "On Cynicism, Evil, and the Discovery of Communication in the 1940s," *Journal of Communication, 46*(3), Summer, 95.

Curran, J. (1995) "The New Revisionism in Mass Communication Research: A Reappraisal." In Boyd-Barrett and Chris Newbold, eds. *Approaches to Media.* London: Arnold.

Heilbroner, R. and W. Milberg (1995) *The Crisis of Vision in Modern Economic Thought.* Cambridge: Cambridge University Press.

Lerner, D. (1969) "Managing Communication for Modernization: The Development Construct." In Arnold A. Rogow, ed. *Politics, Personality and Social Science in the Twentieth Century: Essays in Honor of Harold D. Lasswell.* Chicago: University of Chicago Press.

Liebes, T. and E. Katz (1990) *The Export of Meaning, Cross-Cultural Readings of Dallas.* New York: Oxford University Press.

Murdock, G. (1995) "Across the Great Divide: Cultural Analysis and the Condition of Democracy," *Critical Studies in Mass Communication, 12*(1), March, 91.

Nye J. S. Jr. and W. A. Owens (1996) "America's Information Edge," *Foreign Affairs,* March/April, 20-36.

Radical History Review. (1995) "The Cold War and Expert Knowledge," *63,* Fall.

Rogers, E. (1976) "Communication and Development: The Passing of the Dominant Paradigm." In *Communication Research.* New York: Free Press.

Schiller, H. I. (1996) "The United States." In *Media Ownership and Control.* London: International Institute of Communication (IIC): 249-60.

Schramm, W. and J. W. Riley Jr. (1951) *The Reds Take a City: The Communist Occupation of Seoul.* New Brunswick, NJ: Rutgers University Press.

Simpson, C. (1994) *Science of Coercion: Communication Research and Psychological Warfare, 1945-1960.* New York: Oxford University Press.

Tunstall, J. (1977) *The Media Are American.* New York: Columbia University Press.

7

How Can Audience Research Overcome the Divide Between Macro- and Microanalysis, Between Social Structure and Action?

Svein Østerud

HOW DO AUDIENCES CONSUME MEDIA?

With his seminal paper, "Encoding and Decoding in the TV Discourse," first published in 1973, Stuart Hall drove a wedge into the simplistic uni-linear conception of the communication process inherent in both the behaviorist "effects" research and the functionalist "uses and gratifications" research, paradigms which in succession had prevailed in communication studies from its initial stages in the 1920s.[1]

In this paper on the model of Marx´s distinction between separate stages in the circulation of commodities, Hall describes communica-

---

[1]Stuart Hall´s contribution to the development of audience research is also one of the topics of my article, "Toward a Pragmatic Understanding of Television Reception" (Østerud, 1999).

tion as a circulation of messages, a circulation that comprises corresponding stages, namely production, distribution, and consumption. The meaningful content that is produced at one end of the chain of circulation can only be transmitted through a form that consists of linguistic signs and is organized by means of linguistic codes and conventions. Like all other messages of communication, it is given a *discursive form* that is determined not only by the material tools (i.e., the media technology), but also by the conditions of production (i.e., the organization of media practice). It is in this discursive form that the message is transmitted to the receivers at the other end of the chain of circulation. At this stage the discourse will have to be translated again and transformed into social practice if the circulation is to be completed. Until the "meaning" is produced at the receiving end, one cannot, to Hall´s way of thinking, speak of any consumption. And unless the meaning is articulated in practice it can have no effect.

Even though Hall´s great achievement is to have deconstructed communication, dividing into stages what was previously regarded as an integrated and continuous process, he clearly wants to contribute to a holistic understanding of communication. He describes the different stages of the circulation as integral parts of an entirety, each stage being more or less autonomous and unable to prescribe or guarantee the next stage of the circulation. Thus, coding and decoding may be said to have separate modalities and separate conditions of existence. Both are decisive stages, even if they are relatively autonomous in relation to the communication process as a whole. Each stage may constitute an interruption or a disturbance of the efficient flow of discursive forms. Inasmuch as it is *to* the discursive form that the sender encodes a meaningful content and it is *from* the discursive form that the receiver decodes a meaningful content, this occupies a central position in the flow. In short, the transformations to and from the discursive form are related stages without being identical:

> Production and reception of the television message are not, therefore, identical, but they are related: they are differentiated moments within the totality formed by the social relations of the communicative process as a whole. (Hall, 1980: 130)

In separating encoding and decoding as relatively autonomous stages in the process of communication and pointing out that there need not be symmetry between them, Hall paves the way for a novel paradigm of audience or reception research. As suggested, this is a paradigm that dismisses preceding paradigms leaning either on behaviorist psychology or functional sociology. Secondly, it is a paradigm that extends the semiological approach to include not only the encoding but also the decoding; that is, not only the production, but also the reception of messages. Or rather, it is a paradigm that tries to patch together two different frameworks of explanation, one that studies meaning-making in semiotic terms and another that positions readings on an ideological scale. But inasmuch as both these frameworks are in themselves problematic, merely patching them together makes for a loose amalgamation that glosses over theoretical problems. At the sending end of the circuit the message is described partly in terms of "polysemy," which suggests a textual property of openness, partly in terms of "dominant" or "preferred meanings," implying that the dominant social order is imprinted upon it. What is called for here is a more profound discussion of the arbitrariness of the sign; that is, the extent to which the sign is embedded in social reality. Also at the receiving end of the circuit social reality plays a subordinate part, as the three decoding positions, "dominant-hegemonic", "negotiated," and "oppositional" seem to be purely mental or cognitive processes with no direct bearing on the material and social world in which the audiences move (see also Schrøder, 1997).

I have no qualms about endorsing Hall´s dismissal of the behaviorist paradigm that for so long dominated communication research. But it is a question whether this very dismissal may have induced him to leave out important pragmatic aspects of the act of reading or interpreting messages. Surely the interpretative acts of the audience are woven into their everyday social practice and depend upon the discursive socialization that each individual has experienced. When we speak of consuming audiences we are referring to their decodings as instances of social practice and as such consequences of social parameters as class, gender, ethnicity, and so forth. It seems to me that Hall falls into the error of disembedding the act of meaning-making from its social substratum when he establishes a sharp distinction between the decoding of the message and the use of it:

> Before this message can have an "effect" (however defined), satisfy a "need" or be put to a "use", it must first be appropriated as a meaningful discourse and be meaningfully decoded. It is this set of decoded meanings which "have an effect", influence, entertain, instruct or persuade, with very complex perceptual, cognitive, emotional, ideological or behavioural consequences. (Hall, 1980: 130)

Here the aspect of *use* is understood as a secondary phenomenon. It is described as the "perceptual, cognitive, emotional, ideological or behavioral consequences" of a preceding appropriation of the meaning of the message. But in practice it may be difficult to operate with such a sharp distinction between the intellectual appropriation of its meaning and the behavioural use of the message. These processes often merge in such a way that it is impossible to determine what is the prelude and what is the sequel: consumption includes both the appropriation of the meaning of the message and its realization in practical action.

In the following I shall try to demonstrate that Hall's failure to incorporate the more pragmatic aspects of reception when discussing how audiences consume TV messages has provoked a research paradigm that goes to the other extreme, directing its attention almost exclusively to the aspect of use, namely ethnography.

ETHNOGRAPHY: A CHANGE OF FOCUS FROM TEXTUAL IDEOLOGIES TO VIEWING PRACTICES

It is now more than a decade since ethnography was established as a valid method of studying television and its viewers. This represented a shift in emphasis away from the textual and ideological construction of the subject, illustrated by Hall's model, to socially and historically situated people. As early as 1978 Willemen made the following crucial differentiation:

> There remains an unbridgeable gap between "real" readers/authors and "inscribed" ones, constructed and marked in and by the text. Real readers are subjects in history, living in social formations, rather than mere subjects of a single text. The two types of subject are not commensurate. (Willemen, 1978: 48)

David Morley's *The Nationwide Audience,* published two years later, may be seen as an attempt to investigate empirically the difference between reader responses constructed by the researcher on the basis of textual analyses and "real" responses generated by socially and historically situated readers.

However, in his audience study Morley overemphasizes class in relation to other social factors. Accordingly, his audience groups become embodiments of ideological positions rather than subjects in history. It is fair to say that in the *Nationwide* study the level of agency is mechanically grafted upon the level of structure or—to quote Morley's own self-reflective comment, "there is a tendency in the *Nationwide* book to think of deep structures (for instance, class positions) as generating direct effects of the level of cultural practices" (1986: 43). The viewers are understood as positioning themselves in relation to the hegemonic ideology inherent in the text by way of a "dominant," a "negotiated," and an "oppositional" reading, respectively, without any explanatory value being given to possible differences between them in social context. In other words, what Morley fails to explore is the domestic context of television viewing or the varied social uses to which television can be put. The *Nationwide* study tells us very little about how the everyday domestic context influences what the individual viewers choose to view, how they view, or the sense they make of it.

In recognition of some of the shortcomings of his own *Nationwide* study, Morley undertakes a change of focus in his next audience research project, *Family Television: Cultural Power and Domestic Leisure,* which appeared in 1986.[2] Now he wants to pursue the question of how people watch television in its more "natural" setting, at home with their families. *Family Television* must be reckoned among the sociologically oriented "leisure studies," setting out to explore the changing significance of the "box in the corner" in the context of the growing impact of new technology, both in diversifying the nature of the home-based leisure opportunities and in reemphasizing the existence of the home as the principal site of leisure.

This research development, which Morley himself epitomizes in the heading of Chapter 3—"From 'Decoding' to Viewing Context"—is important inasmuch as it retrieves the concept of use or viewing behavior. The severe criticism levelled by critical theory-inspired scholars at the predominant paradigm of the 1960s and 1970s, namely the behaviorist-inclined "uses and gratifications" approach, had to some extent brought the very concept of use into discredit. During the last decade Morley and a host of other advocates of the culturalist and ethnographic approach have restored the behavioral aspect of reception, only this time relieved of its behaviorist legacy. They insist that media use is a significant element in "everyday life"; it is a set of practices that could be understood only in relation to the particular social context and to other practices. The object of these ethnographic studies is the way people live their culture.

A CRITIQUE OF ETHNOGRAPHIC AUDIENCE RESEARCH

If we were to evaluate these studies, however, there are some grounds for concluding that they have been focusing on questions that—unless they are placed in a wider context—may seem rather trivial, such as who

---

[2]Morley formulates his own self-criticism as follows (1986: 43): "This is to stress the point that the Althusserian drift of much early cultural studies work (and it is this which, evidently, underlies much of the *Nationwide* project) would reduce our shop steward to the status of a mere personification of a given structure [...]."

watches which types of television programs, who gets to choose which programs the family will watch, who watches in silence and who talks about what they watch, and how television viewing fits in with domestic work, childcare and leisure interests.

Quite a few of these ethnographically guided empirical studies testify that in audience research, following a period of preoccupation with the process of textual decoding, the pendulum has swung to the other extreme. The development in Morley's audience research, as outlined above, illustrates how the imperative shift of emphasis from textual ideologies to concrete viewing practices, that is, from conditioning structures to human agency, is apt to jettison the structural aspect altogether. As I shall try to substantiate in what follows, there is in this form of ethnographic research a tendency to equate audience studies with studies of people's viewing habits. And this is, no doubt, a reductionist tendency that can hardly be said to represent much of an improvement on its predecessor, the much criticized "uses and gratifications" approach. Furthermore, I shall argue that it is only by extending their sphere of interest to the television content that audience researchers can hope to reveal how television viewing interferes in the structures of society.

To focus, as ethnographic audience research does, on television as a technical apparatus and an integral part of our domestic culture, is a contribution to the revitalization of Marshall McLuhan's "medium theory," epitomized by the catchphrase "the medium is the message." McLuhan's basic idea is that television, indeed any novel medium technology, has the power to change deeply engrained values and habits. Now this idea has—rightly or wrongly—been interpreted as implying a form of technological determinism, a determinism from which ethnographically oriented researchers have been concerned to distance themselves. They do not consider television to be constitutive, but rather incidental to the shaping of domestic culture. In their analyses, television is allowed to define a potential space within which individuals, families, and neighborhoods in different ways can create something of their own culture and their own identities. They demonstrate, for example, how the television set may become the target of conflict over viewing choices, how technologies in general are incorporated into the household as expressions of gender and age differentiation as well as assertions of status, how television may influence perceptions of time and how, together with other technologies like the video and the microwave, it may facilitate control of time.

It is significant that James Lull, one of the initiators of ethnographic audience research and editor of a collection of ethnographic essays on family life with television, entitled *World Families Watch Television*, makes a very emphatic reference to McLuhan's book, *Understanding Media*. In a summary final chapter Lull insists that the media are not merely extensions of human perceptual senses, as McLuhan would have it; indeed the findings reported by the contributors to the collection of essays give occasion to consider the social uses of television as "extensions of the personal and social positions and roles of family members." He proceeds to frame a typology of audience "extensions":

> Thus it is helpful to distinguish three levels of ritualized extension centered on television: the *culture,* characteristics of a social context broader than the family itself, the *household* (defined as the *domestic establishment,* including both family members and the physical location), and the *person.* (Lull, 1988: 239)

It is worth noticing that Lull's typology bears on what he calls "levels of ritualized extension" of our day-to-day behavior. But then, of course, the title of his essay is "Constructing Rituals of Extension through Family Television Viewing." Correspondingly, we find in this book essays about the ways in which different national cultural patterns are constantly extended and amplified in viewing practices. We find essays about how the household is extended through the viewing practices of family members, thereby sustaining traditional patterns of gender-based social roles and sharing of labor. And we find essays about how the interests and activities of individual viewers are extended into television viewing, and how their age-based identities are reinforced through their program preferences and styles of viewing.

As this paraphrase of Lull's synthesizing essay suggests, television is understood by him and the contributing authors as an extension of the viewers' activities at the cultural, household, and personal levels. This is an understanding that tends to reduce audience involvement with television to rituals, routine activities, and habits. Lull uses these three expressions alternately to denote the repetitive and culturally reproductive character of our television involvement. According to Lull many characteristic patterns "can be regarded as *rituals* that are manifestations of microsocial (family) and macrosocial (cultural) *rules.*" He goes on to offer the following definition of the key notions of ritual and rule:

> "Ritual" refers to repeated, regular family activity, elevated to a nearly ceremonial level because of the cultural power of television. "Rules" are socially coordinated understandings that promote patterned behavior, including routine acts of contact with the mass media. (Lull, 1988: 238)

Lull is no doubt right in maintaining that a fair amount of television viewing has a ritual character and should be understood as observance of cultural rules. He and his collaborators deserve credit for having called attention to this fact. But this is surely not the whole truth about audience involvement with television. If it had been so, there would have been no way in which television could have contributed to shape opinions and alter cultural patterns, to increase the political awareness of families, and inform and educate persons. The ethnographic framework for analysis of television viewing, such as it is developed in this book, is too narrow to be able to explain the potential of television for triggering off social and political revolutions and transforming culture.

The concluding paragraph of Lull's essay has the ambitious heading "Extensions and Effects." However, unless one is prepared to endorse the technological determinism attributed to McLuhan, it seems difficult to reconcile the idea of television as an extension of cultural, household, and personal agendas with the idea of television as having a substantial effect on the culture, the household, and the person. The consequence of reducing television to a technological and social device that is more or less frictionlessly integrated with already existing cultural patterns and habits, is that one loses sight of the ideological power that may be inherent in its content. Television is, of course, also a medium of information and communication, and for the individual viewer to be involved with it is also to expose himself or herself to the ideological codes of the transmitted texts.

THE DOUBLE FUNCTION OF TELEVISION

In the midst of the predominantly reductionist reports in the book there is, however, one paragraph that emphasizes this very double function of the TV medium. David Morley starts his essay with a general survey of television audience research in Britain, claiming that:

> Previous work in this area has tended to focus too narrowly on one or another side of a pair of interlinked issues that need, in fact, to be considered together: These are the issues of how viewers make sense of the materials they view, and the social (and primarily familial) relations within which viewing is conducted. (Morley, 1988: 27)

According to Morley these two issues, "how viewers make sense of the materials they view" and "the social relations within which viewing is conducted," have previously been assigned to different research traditions—

one within the realm of literary/semiological perspectives, the other within the field of sociological leisure studies. Morley argues that now is the time to bridge the gulf between these two traditions. But neither Morley himself nor any of the other contributors can be said to live up to such holistic ideals in their empirical reports.

The inadequacy of this form of ethnographic audience research may be highlighted through a notion that Roger Silverstone has brought to bear on television, namely its "double articulation" into the household. This is an expression derived from the French linguist André Martinet, who saw the unique capacity of natural language to convey complex meanings as the result of the articulation of both its phonemic and morphological levels. Sounds carrying no meaning were a prerequisite of words or signs with meaning. The meaningfulness of natural language is made possible by both. Similarly, the meanings of television are articulated both through its status as a technological object and through its function as a medium of communication. Silverstone formulated this:

> Put very simply, television is doubly articulated into a household because its significance as a technology depends on its appropriation by the household both as an object (the machine itself) and as a medium. (Silverstone, 1994: 83)

Television must be regarded both as an object and a medium, or, to put it another way, it consists of both hardware and software. The meaning of television as a technological object is articulated through the practices of its production, marketing, and use; its meaning as a medium, on the other hand, is articulated through its communications—the programs, narratives, rhetorics, and genres. These two articulations are interwoven: the significance of television reception is defined by the consumption of both the technology and its contents.

Against the notion of television as doubly articulated into the household, ethnographic studies of the kind exemplified above may be judged to have simplified matters. In focusing attention on the technological instrument—the appliance itself—and the way in which it is appropriated into the culture of the household, these studies are liable to play down its function as a medium of information and communication. This means that what Silverstone calls television's second articulation, the way in which viewers individually negotiate with it by relating to such components as programs, narratives, rhetorics, and genres, does not take up much space in any of the reports in question.

A CALL FOR A COMBINATION OF AN EMIC AND
AN ETIC PERSPECTIVE

As long as ethnographically oriented audience research tends towards confining its sphere of interest to the one articulation of television, namely that which is based on its status as a technological and social object, this research is bound to remain on the level of sociological microanalysis. This is a level of analysis in which individuals and families and their actions and reactions are the sole ingredients of social explanation. Only by allowing for the double articulation of television—its software as well as its hardware—can audience researchers expect to be able to analyze power and ideology, and to understand the complex ways in which structure and agency intersect in the routine activities of everyday life.

There is no denying that the ethnographic approach has stood television audience research in good stead. But ethnographic approaches can be of different kinds, and it may be that audience research has given preference to an approach that fails to do justice to the complexity of viewers' involvement with television. There is, in anthropological methodology, a well-established distinction between an "emic" or inside perspective and an "etic" or outside perspective. Kenneth Pike, who seems to have coined these terms, states the idea as follows:

> In contrast to the etic approach, an emic one is in essence valid for only one language (or one culture) at a time. . . . It is an attempt to *discover* and to describe the pattern of that particular language or culture in reference to the way in which the various elements of that culture are related to each other in the functioning of the particular pattern, rather than an attempt to describe them in reference to a generalized classification derived in advance of the study of that culture.
>
> An etic analytical standpoint . . . might be called "external" or "alien," since for etic purposes the analyst stands "far enough away" from or "outside" of a particular culture to see its separate events, primarily in relation to their similarities and their differences, as compared to events in other cultures, rather than in reference to the sequences of classes of events within that one particular culture. (Pike, 1954: 8-10)

To summarize: An emic strategy would be "to grasp the native's point of view, his relation to life, to realize *his* vision of *his* world," as was Malinowski's directive. An etic strategy would involve transgressing the native's point of view and studying his behavior in relation to more general theoretical problems. The eticist would seek patterns of behavior as defined by himself in his capacity as observer.

Many research questions require both emic and etic techniques for their solution, and television audience research is replete with questions of this kind. In fact it is impossible for the researcher to understand viewers' involvement with television as an outcome of the dialectical interplay of structure and agency unless he obtains access to knowledge that transcends the perspective of the individual viewer. Since the complex network of dependencies in which actors are entangled are not and cannot be seen from the standpoint of the individual actor's experience, it is the task of the social scientist to test and verify the structure and the figuration of which the actor is a part.

After all, this problem has a history as long as sociology itself. In the past it was discussed in terms of the opposition between "explaining" and "understanding." Pierre Bourdieu has given the opposition a somewhat different shape in making the demands on any social science that it should implement a "double reading." The first reading deals with society in the manner of a *social physics*, that is, as an objective structure, seen from the outside, whose articulations can be materially observed, measured, and mapped out independently of the representations of those who live in that society. In the second reading, which Bourdieu refers to as *social phenomenology,* society appears as the emergent product of the decisions, actions, and cognitions of conscious individuals to whom the world is given as immediately familiar and meaningful. Bourdieu develops the concept of double reading by associating the former with an objectivist or "structural" perspective and the latter with a subjectivist or "constructivist" one.

Apart from being reflections on the nature of social science, Bourdieu's "double reading" represents a call for more epistemological awareness or self-reflection among social scientists. If we were to judge the empirical reports that we have examined above by the standards of social science promoted by Bourdieu, we would have to conclude that in the main they confine themselves to one of the two readings, namely the one that in Bourdieu's writing is referred to as social phenomenology. We do, in fact, encounter a few methodological discussions in the collection of reports, and it is noteworthy that Morley, when epitomizing what has been his goal in the report, adopts a cognate term: "to understand the phenomenology of television viewing" (Morley, 1988: 47). The German contributors to the collection, Jan-Uwe Rogge and Klaus Jensen also offer a description of their empirical method, a description which may be regarded as an amplification of Morley's phenomenology:

> . . . it is necessary to adopt an empathic-interpretive method, an approach that enters into the everyday worlds of families and seeks to understand families within the context of their individual and social

frameworks and then to describe those particular actions. (Lull, 1988, 84f)

Researchers who set themselves to go beyond the cognitive, ideational categories of people in the field and grasp some of the contradictions and dynamics that unfold there, will have to adopt an etic strategy. The condition for establishing what Bourdieu calls the social physics of the field is that the researchers are willing to incorporate etic constructs, that is, theory-derived concepts, at some stage in the research process.

METHODOLOGICAL CONSEQUENCES

It seems imperative to examine in more detail those consequences this line of thought may have for methodological deliberations and choices. Ethnography, as it has been practiced in audience research during the last ten years, normally includes first-hand observations and depth interviewing. Yet there are cases where researchers have chosen to do without first-hand observations on the grounds that this is an approach fraught with validity problems. One may imagine that the presence of an observer who is totally unknown to the families being observed will disturb the setting for their viewing and render communication activities artificial. And even after the family members have accustomed themselves to his presence so that it no longer is felt to be obtrusive, it is hard to see how his living together with the family over several days, in some cases up to a week, can fail to influence the rhythm of the family life.[3]

It has been maintained that this influence is reduced if the observations are effected by means of technical equipment, with video-cameras mounted on the television set to record the viewers´ behavior in front of the screen, and microphones distributed about the sitting-room to tape their conversation and other sounds. But no matter how accurate such technical registration could be practiced it would not have been able to capture the whole context of their viewing behavior.

There is also a more indirect way of exploring a family´s viewing behavior, namely by reconstructing its rituals, routines, and habits solely on the basis of interviews with the family members. But this is also a

---

[3]It seems that such validity problems are played down by Lull, (1990: 32), where he simply contends: "Subsequent research, where observers spent from three to seven days with families, has demonstrated that, in the vast majority of cases (more than 80 percent), families indicated at the conclusion of the observational period that no major behavioral alterations had taken place due to the presence of the investigator."

method with inherent pitfalls and deficiencies. It demands both built-in safeguards in the interviewing technique to discourage respondents from being disingenuous in their reporting, and an analytical capacity on the part of the researcher to detect untruthful accounts that, notwithstanding, may have infiltrated the interview data.[4]

However that may be, ethnographic method, such as it has been employed in the projects examined above, is inadequate for an analysis of the whole context of television viewing. Like all domestic activities, television viewing takes place within a field where ideological structures and discourses are at play. In order to take stock of those transmitted by the TV medium, the researcher will have to undertake a semiotic analysis of the programs to which the viewers are exposed. It means, in other words, that we are in need of a holistic methodological approach to the field, an approach that embraces methods derived from both the social and the human sciences.

If we want to explore the dialectical relations between the ideological structures of television texts and the behavioral competencies of viewers, we shall have to inquire not only about their genre and program preferences but also about their interpretation of particular programs, and even particular episodes within these programs. In consequence it would be preferable, although not necessary, for the researcher to have familiarized himself with and even analyzed the programs he chooses to be the focus of the interviews. Such first-hand knowledge of the programs would enable him to elaborate an interview guide with questions of a more critical and discriminating power. If, on the other hand, the interviews take as their starting point programs that are, in whole or in part, unknown to the researcher the questions will of necessity be less theory-guided. This will make the researcher's analysis more complicated and unpredictable, and it will prevent him from embarking on the analytical work until the transcripts of the interviews are available.

Assuming that audience research aimed at bringing out not only the rituals, routines, and habits of families and family members watching television, but also the dialectical relations between the conditioning structures of the field and the actors who operate there, then what would be the underlying structure of this research? As we have argued above, this research should include components of both the social and the human sciences or, more precisely, of ethnography as well as semiotics. But what can serve as a synoptic and guiding idea for a research project that sets out to disclose the dynamics of the field? Since the dynamics of this field, being manifest in differential patterns of interaction between

---

[4]This method was adopted by David Morley in the research project reported in *Family Television*, 50 ff., where some of these problems are raised in the chapter "Objectives, Methodology and Sample Design."

ideological discourses and interpretive competencies, normally exceeds the scope of the individual viewer, the researcher will have to resort to what we previously has referred to as an etic concept.

THE METAPHOR AS A SENSITIZING CONCEPT

Silverstone's "double articulation" was introduced above and utilized in a critical examination of some ethnographically oriented research projects. Perhaps this concept could serve the purpose? Without working out any denomination of this kind, Jean Baudrillard makes use of the same idea to differentiate between forms of media consumption in different social classes. According to the early Baudrillard writings, television can be bought for two different reasons: as an object itself, and as such an indication of "recognition, of integration, of social legitimacy," and it can be bought not for what it is but for what it can do. These extremes are respectively defined as that of television as the site of a ritual practice, as an object whose value is determined by its exchange value; and that of television as the site of a rational cultural practice, as a medium whose value is determined according to its use value:

> There are those for whom TV is an object, there are those for whom it is a cultural exercise: on this radical opposition a cultural class privilege is established that is registered in an essential social privilege. (Baudrillard, 1981: 57)

The distinction made by Baudrillard and later further developed and denominated by Silverstone as the "double articulation of television" is important for theoretical purposes, but it is far too crude to be of any service in empirical studies. It is, no doubt, an oversimplification to postulate, as Baudrillard does almost without any qualification, that lower-class households consume television as an object, whereas middle- and upper-class households consume it as a medium. It may be assumed that a thoroughgoing empirical investigation would produce the picture of a more differentiated media consumption in all the social classes.

Nevertheless, it was along these lines I was thinking when in 1988 I made plans for an investigation of Norwegian viewers' reception of the television coverage of the summit meeting between Reagan and Gorbachev in Moscow in May-June of that year. At the initial stage of the research project, I was unable to come up with any hypothesis about the relationship between individual viewers' interpretive competencies and their interpretations of the news programs. I was only under the impression that differences of interpretation would show up and that these would somehow correspond to differencies in socioeconomic and cultural position among the viewers.

While I was in the process of finalizing the interview guide, an image from my previous studies into ancient cultures came to mind, namely a metaphor originating from Roman mythology. In ancient Rome, the entrance to the house was believed to be guarded by the god Janus. His name is related to the Latin word for door, *janua*. In the north-western corner of the Forum Romanum there was a double gate that was consecrated to Janus, and in the middle there was a bronze image of the god with the two faces, one looking east and the other looking west. According to popular religion, the vigilant god was able to look both forward and backward, both in space and time. In the same way as Janus was the god of entry in a spatial sense, he was also the god of every beginning in time. The first month of the year, *Januarius,* was named after him, and the first day of each month was consecrated to him. To the Romans, Janus seems to have been a symbol that they used not only to orientate themselves in time and space, but also to signalize their relationship to the outside world. Whenever the Romans were at war with neighboring states, the leaves of the double gate were left open, but in times of peace they were shut.

Throughout the rest of the project the two-faced Janus functioned as a metaphor and a sensitizing concept for my investigation.[5] The TV screen may be compared with the two-faced Janus inasmuch as one side of it faces the sitting room of the viewer, and the other faces the outside world. The actual television box is situated, so to speak, on the door sill—that is, on the threshold between the private and the public sphere. Home is, of course, the site of that part of our lives that we do not want to expose to the public, whereas the space outside is accessible to all, and therefore the arena for affairs that the citizens must deal with jointly. The television box is part of the inventory of our private homes, and the images we receive on the screen are incorporated in the cultural milieu we create in our sitting rooms. On the other hand, the images on the screen point to the public sphere, to the world beyond the private home of the individual viewer, enticing him or her to undertake imaginary journeys to unknown places and countries.

---

[5]Cf. the account of the use of metaphor in field research by Lofland and Lofland (1984: 122f), and Blumer (1954) gives a definition of the related analytical instrument, i.e., "sensitizing concepts," where he contrasts it with "definitive concepts" (3-10): "Instead, it gives the user a general sense of reference and guidance in approaching empirical instances. Where definitive concepts provide prescriptions of what to see, sensitizing concepts merely suggest directions along which to look" (7).

The location of television on the threshold between interior and exterior, between the private and the public sphere gives rise to a fundamental ambiguity in its way of functioning. Like Janus´ double gate on the Forum Romanum, television can shut the outside world out, with the consequence that the images on the screen are reduced to decorative and entertaining elements in the home environment. On the other hand, it can also be kept open to the outside world, giving the viewers the feeling of being transported to arenas where the political discussions take place in the case of both domestic and foreign affairs. However, the recent modernization of program production involves a blurring of the boundaries between these two spheres. This leads to an interweaving of the two functions of television, counteracting any attempt made by viewer(s) to keep the private and the public spheres strictly apart.

As already suggested, Silverstone proposes a similar understanding of the functions of television inasmuch as he places television in an intermediary position between opposing tendencies, represented by "home" and "reach":

> Television and other media are part of home—part of its idealisation, part of its reality. The dimension of home that involves positive feelings of security and belonging are both challenged and reinforced by a medium that brings the world into the interior. New media or unacceptable images are threatening, and television is something that has to be controlled, if only on behalf of the children. Yet the "box in the corner" is, in our dependence on it, a crucial link to a shared or shareable world of community and nation, and, as such, acts to extend the boundaries of home beyond the front door. (Silverstone, 1994: 29)

This is an elaboration of Joshua Meyrowitz´s (1985) seminal discussion of television´s contribution to changing the relationship between home and reach.[6] Both set out to diagnose the sociocultural change we all experience in the wake of the advent of modern communication technology. What they both underemphasize, however, is the fact that different viewers meet this new challenge with different strategies.

CAN AUDIENCE RESEARCH DERIVE INSPIRATION FROM LIFE-WORLD PHENOMENOLOGY AND STRUCTURATION THEORY?

Today, television has become integrated into our daily lives and our experience of television is a piece of our experience with the world

---

[6]Meyrowitz (1985) spells out the cultural consequences of the fact that television perforates the boundary between the private and the public.

(Heath, 1990).[7] Even while watching television, we constitute what Alfred Schutz and Thomas Luckmann in their so-called life-world phenomenology refer to as the "spatial arrangement of the everyday life" (Schutz and Luckmann, 1974). So the above distinction between the inside and the outside world, between home and reach, may be regarded as analogical to the distinction made in life-world phenomenology between the primary and the secondary zone of operation. These are defined precisely as "the province of non-mediated action or the primary world within reach" and "the world within potential reach." About the latter Schutz and Luckmann state that it "finds its limits in the prevailing technical conditions of a society."

Considering the highly advanced level of modern communication technology, there seems to be practically no limit to what can be brought within the potential reach of viewers. The limits are rather to be found in the attitudes of viewers, or, more precisely, in the varying degree of disposition encountered among them to make the most of this opportunity. But here we are up against a sociological theme that cannot be addressed by an argument developed in the vocabulary of constitutive phenomenology. It raises the issue of differences in viewing strategies and these differences are ultimately expressions of cultural power or class position.

Researchers setting themselves the task to investigate how social life is reproduced through communication will be better served by a sociological theory that combines the space-time argument with a theory of power and class structure. That is precisely what we have in Anthony Giddens' theory of *structuration.* This is a theory that explains the reproduction of social life in terms of an interchange between *social integration* and *system integration.* The same pair of concepts occurs in Habermas' theory of communication, but Habermas fails to become engaged with the spatiality of social life, with what Giddens calls "time-space routinization" and "time-space distanciation" (cf. Giddens, 1984: 28ff, 64ff, 111ff, 258ff).

Giddens maintains that the continuity of everyday life still depends, in large measure, on routinized interactions between people who are *copresent* in time and space. In traditional societies, relations of copresence tended to dominate influences of a more remote kind. As a consequence of the advent of modern communication technology, social life increasingly depends on interactions with others who are *absent* in time and space. One of the objectives of structuration theory is—to quote Giddens—to show how the "limitations of individual 'presence' are

---

[7]Heath (1990: 267) speaks of television's "seamless equivalence with social life."

transcended by the 'stretching' of social relations across time and space"
(1984: 35). This could be done through empirical research that examines
how modernity has altered the conditions of social and system integration and thereby changed the nature of the connections between the
proximate and the remote in time and space. Giddens suggests that we
should study individual lifetime biographies, analyzing them as life-paths
in time and space.

This is more or less what I tried to do in my own research once
the interview data had been collected and was available in transcript. At
this stage the focusing of my analytical work was motivated just as much
by my increasing familiarity with these theories as by the sensitizing concept of the two-faced Janus. What I singled out in my first perusal of the
data was the very themes of time and space, themes on which all my
respondents had pronounced. In fact, the way in which they had
described their own involvement with television encouraged me to construe it as individual attempts to organize space and time through the
medium.

As is well known, we all move in physical contexts whose properties interact with our capabilities, at the same time as we interact with
one another. For some individuals, as I also encountered in my sample,
their life-path can be represented as the repetition of routine activities
across days or longer spans of time. Their relation to television is not
excepted from this pattern: the timetable of the programs is without
much ado made to fit in with their daily routine, or is simply allowed to
determine the daily routine of their domestic life. Figuratively speaking,
these people shut themselves in with their TV set, engaging in a face-to-
face communication with the talking heads on the screen.

At the opposite end of the scale there are individuals, also
included in my sample, who are more disposed to undertaking imaginary
long-distance "travels" by way of television in order to stretch their horizon beyond the one at hand. This means breaking away from the routinized path of everyday life, or—to put it differently—allowing the time of
transmission of selected programs to interfere with their daily habits.
Time-space distanciation of this kind requires a high degree of coordina-
tion of daily activities and spells of TV viewing. It also involves a more
reflexive, discursive consciousness on the part of the acting self.

However, life-path in time and space was not the only theme
that made it possible for me to differentiate between viewing strategies
among the respondents. The taxonomy that I was able to establish was
based on another two themes, namely the viewers´ relation to authority
and their relation to the medium itself. It may be said about these
themes that they verge more on the cognitive than the behavioral aspect
of their viewing strategies. However, the whole project is characterized
by a pragmatic way of thinking that repudiates any attempt to discrimi-

nate between cognitive and behavioral aspects, and by a terminology that strives to overcome this dichotomy. Such a term is Bourdieu's *habitus,* of which I took advantage when diagnosing the viewing strategies of the respondents on the basis of their relation to the above-mentioned four themes. Leaning on Bourdieu's theory of practice, I extracted from the data four different class-specific viewing strategies which I named "habitus profiles."

There was in my data a close correlation between the respondents' organization of time and space and their understanding of and their placing of themselves in the political order. Individuals whose daily trajectory hardly overstepped the domestic sphere were liable to disclaim responsibility for what happens in the world of high politics. They regarded themselves as incompetent to perform in the public sphere and left it to those in power to make decisions for them on their behalf. If they took an active part in politics at all it was within the confines of their own local community. Other individuals who made their way to distant areas via modern media technology were already political participants of a sort and did not refrain from taking part in political discussion(s).

A corresponding pattern of variation was to be found in the respondents' understanding of television as a medium. For some individuals television was a "window on the world," as if the glass on the screen provided an innocent vision of the world uncontaminated by the politics of representation. They quite naively believed that television enables us to see for ourselves what is going on without interference from others. At the opposite end of the scale, there were individuals who were fully aware of the complexities involved in the process of technically mediating reality. Even if they were able to see that reality, as it is rendered by television, is a construction, that is, a joint product of human and technical intervention, they knew how to make use of television both to orientate themselves in reality and to assert themselves in that reality.

SUPER-THEMES OF NEWS RECEPTION

My findings bear a certain resemblance to those reported by Klaus Bruhn Jensen from a study of Danish viewers' reception of television news. In the interview data Jensen detected some generalized concepts that he found served as "a common denominator for the universe of television news and the respondents' universe of everyday experience":

> Specifically, a number of the respondents relied on certain highly generalized concepts in order to construct any coherence at all in several stories. These super-themes apparently served as a com-

mon denominator for the universe of television news and the respondents' universe of everyday experience. (Jensen, 1995: 156)

In his theoretical discussion, Jensen argues that his own "findings suggest a revision of the frameworks of cognitive psychology as applied in studies of how audiences arrive at a coherent understanding of media discourses" (1995: 155). Whereas these studies are criticized for their preference for formal analysis, Jensen proposes that we should look for "particular content themes or the interpretive constructs that audiences derive from stories in their particular context of reception" (Ibid.: 155). These are referred to as super-themes and described as follows:

> Super-themes are simultaneously very general and very concrete categories of understanding, simultaneously a strength and a weakness of reception. They are general, or flexible, to the extent that they accommodate a variety of perspectives on, domains of, and propositions about social reality; they are specific to the extent that they relate to details of the news event, as represented in visuals or commentary, and perhaps to viewers' concrete life experiences. Super-themes are a strength in that they allow viewers to make personally relevant sense of the news, but a weakness in that they do not empower viewers to act on that sense in political contexts. (Jensen, 1995: 156f)

In the same breath Jensen calls for a typology of super-themes, but the examples he adduces from his own and other research confirm what can be inferred from this quotation, namely that these super-themes, are conceived within a cognitive paradigm. They may be such components as time, space, and authority, as they indeed are in my own research, but in his representation they are depleted of their behavioral component. In the pragmatic tradition to which my research is indebted, time, space, and authority are themes that we relate to not only in our mind but also in our action.

REFERENCES

Baudrillard, J. (1981) *For a Critique of the Political Economy of the Sign*. St. Louis: Telos Press.

Blumer, H. (1954) "What is Wrong with Social Theory?" *American Sociological Review, 19*, 3-10.

Giddens, A. (1984) *The Constitution of Society. Outline of the Theory of Structuration*. Cambridge: Polity Press.

Hall, S. (1980) "Encoding and Decoding." In Stuart Hall, Dorothy Hobson, Andrew Lowe and Paul Willis, eds. *Culture, Media, Language*. London: Hutchinson: 128-38.

Heath, S. (1990) "Representing Television." In Patricia Mellencamp, ed. *Logics of Television*. Bloomington: Indiana University Press: 267-302.

Jensen, K. B. (1988) "News as Social Resource," *European Journal of Communication, 3*(3), 275-301

Jensen, K. B. (1995) *The Social Semiotics of Mass Communication*. London: Sage.

Lofland, J. and L. H. Lofland (1984) *Analyzing Social Settings. A Guide to Qualitative Observation and Analysis*. Belmont, CA: Wadsworth Publishing.

Lull, J., ed. (1988) *World Families Watch Television*. Newbury Park, CA: Sage.

Lull, J. (1990) *Inside Family Viewing. Ethnographic Research on Television's Audiences*. London: Routledge.

McLuhan, M. (1964) *Understanding Media: The Extensions of Man*. London: Routledge.

Meyrowitz, J. (1985) *No Sense of Place. The Impact of Electronic Media on Social Behavior*. Oxford: Oxford University Press.

Morley, D. (1980) *The Nationwide Audience*. London: British Film Institute.

Morley, D. (1986) *Family Television. Cultural Power and Domestic Leisure*. London: Comedia Publishing Group.

Morley, D. (1988) "Domestic Relations: The Framework of Family Viewing in Great Britain." In James Lull, ed. *World Families Watch Television*. Newbury Park, CA: Sage: 22-48.

Østerud, S. (1999) "Towards a Pragmatic Understanding of TV Reception: Norwegian Coverage of the Summit Meeting between Reagan and Gorbachev in Moscow, 1988." In Mary Mander, ed. *Framing Friction. Media and Social Conflict*. Urbana: University of Illinois Press: 215-55.

Pike, K. (1954) *Language in Relation to a Unified Theory of the Structure of Human Behavior*. Glendale, CA: Summer Institute of Linguistics.

Rogge, J.-U. and K. Jensen (1988) "Everyday Life and Television in West Germany: An Empathic-Interpretive Perspective on the Family as a System." In James Lull, ed. *World Families Watch Television*. Newbury Park, CA: Sage: 80-115.

Schrøder, K. (1997) *Audience Discourses and Social Change. A Critical Reappraisal of the Encoding/Decoding Model*. Paper presented the th 13th Nordic Conference for Mass Communication Research.

Schutz, A. and T. Luckmann (1974) *The Structures of the Life-World*. London: Heinemann.

Silverstone, R. (1994) *Television and Everyday Life*. London: Routledge.

Willemen, P. (1978) "Notes on Subjectivity," *Screen, 19*(1), 41-69.

8

The Cultural Mediations of
Television Consumption*

Jesús Martín-Barbero

In Latin America the space occupied by culture has become, over the last 100 years, the fundamental arena for debate and questioning of the transformations implied by the modernization of our societies. And within the space of culture, television has emerged as the strategic medium for a process of modernization with a logic that both expresses and comes into conflict with the cultural logics of each society. Television is the medium that opens the way in Latin America for a process of technological innovation and for a series of basic changes in the way people live. It is television that poses for research on communication a very particular kind of challenge: to comprehend that aspect of its influence that enables this medium to incorporate into the discourse of modernity the genres and narrative processes at once both postmodern and traditional.

Unfortunately, until now most of the studies of television in Latin America have been carried out from the limited perspective of legal and

*Translated from the Spanish by Robert A. White, The Gregorian University, Rome.

economic questions or have been too narrowly concerned with its ideological influences. Although these are necessary and valuable studies, they often provide little explanation of the processes of modernization and the new configurations of taste preferences and social uses.

What is necessary now is to take up a very concrete product of the television industry that has been an enormous success in Latin America: the *telenovela*. This genre offers a key site for studying how the commercial logics of production are linked with the cultural logics of consumption. This approach to the *telenovela* makes it possible to enrich and to make more concrete the current debates about the cultural development of Latin America. Culture, in this case, is not understood simply as a body of products but as the organizing matrix of everyday knowledge and behavior. The *telenovela* helps to bring into existence and operation a set of popular cultural competencies quite different from hegemonic culture. The melodrama of the *telenovela* becomes the expression of the living tradition of an "alternative" and "anachronistic" narrative matrix.

The *telenovela* also seems to provide a space for the daily confrontation between the experience of the national—the national tradition of cultural sensibilities, cultural archetypes and classical dramatic characters of literature and popular culture—and the transnational. That is, the *telenovela* provides models of television formats that transcend national frontiers.

In this approach to the analysis of the media, the general objective is to investigate the "mediations" through which are materialized the constraints emerging from the economic and industrial logics of television and which provide a point of articulation with the expectations and modes of perception of different social groups using the media.

The social, cultural, and interpersonal "mediations" of television and specifically the *telenovela* are the "place" where it is possible to understand the interaction of the space of production and the space of reception. What is produced in television is not simply a result of the demands of the industrial system and its marketing strategies but is also a result of the exigencies of cultural patterns, routines of everyday life, and the way of perceiving the world in different subcultures. We are asserting that television, in order to have an audience, must respond to the expectations coming from groups of consumers and it must see these expectations to be legitimate. We would argue, however, that television cannot legitimate these demands unless it resignifies them in terms of the hegemonic discourse of the society.

Thus, the analysis of media requires different types of research projects:

1. The study of the stages of design and realization of *telenove-las* both in the economic context of their production and distribution and in the dynamics of the institutional and professional organization that regulate the relation of television with culture.
2. The analysis of the ways in which general cultural ideologies are translated into particular narrative structures of *telenovelas* and the ways these television formats adapt archaic story forms to the modernizing themes of *telenovelas.*
3. The analysis of the modes of appropriation by different social and cultural subgroups and how these class-based differences of appropriation indicate the linkage of the cultural industry with daily life.

Research dealing with these characteristics of the media goes beyond the limits of academic interest and involves as interlocutors those working in the field of education and cultural promotion. From this kind of research comes materials for understanding the cultural space and cultural conflicts that they have to deal with. Also touched by these issues are those who have some responsibility for designing cultural policies and carrying out projects in the area of communication and culture. Television producers are also challenged by studies of the relation of their work with the social and cultural expectations in their countries.

THE CONCEPTUAL FRAMEWORK: EVERYDAY LIFE, TELEVISION, AND MELODRAMA

To understand the *telenovela* requires that we see both the space of production and the moment of consumption as one interrelated reality. We must conceptualize both from the perspective of everyday life and the characteristics that are shaped by the conditions of the culture industry and the discursive system of a medium. This means that we must look at television not only from the perspective of the products of the industry but also from the perspective of the uses, formats, genres, and different ways of recognizing identity in the media.

Everyday Life as Consumption and Uses

What we are analyzing is how the violence of order becomes a disciplining technology but, at the same time, a network of antidiscipline, a space for play, and an opportunity for resistance and change. (Michel de Certeau, 1980: 70)

In various recent publications Nestor Garcia Canclini has been bringing together elements for a theory of consumption that is not based on reproduction or culturalist conceptions. Following the ideas of Bourdieu, but going beyond them in order to bring in the issues of transformation and forms of production of the popular cultures of Latin America, Canclini states, "It is not a question simply of measuring the distance between the messages and their effects, but constructing an integral analysis of consumption, understood as the set of social processes for appropriating products" (Canclini, 1985: 25). We are not dealing, then, with the repertoire of attitudes and tastes that the marketing studies collect and classify, nor are we moving in the hazy world of simulation and simulacro suggested by Baudrillard. The space of reflection on consumption is a space of daily practices in so far as these are a "a site of silent interiorization of social inequality" (Canclini, 1984: 74), ranging from practices of relation to one's own body, to practices in the use of time, to one's habitat, to consciousness of what is possible and realizable or unrealizable in one's life.

Consumption is also the site of struggle with the permitted limits for the expression of desire and for subversion of the codes and rhythms of pulsation and enjoyment. Consumption is not simply reproduction of social forces, but a site for the production of meaning, a place for a struggle that is not exhausted in the possession of objects but includes the uses that construct a social world making possible the conditions of action for different cultural competencies. De Certeau has elaborated a theory of social use as active agents of appropriation that operate in relation to a received system of practices, but that define their own time and place and construct relationships between one subject and another. This is the other face of everyday life: scattered and secretive creative actions, autonomous production of meaning inserted into the processes of consumption. These social uses may be marginal to the dominant rationality and resistant to any statistical measurement, but they are modes of action that elude hegemony and draw their logic from a popular culture which is a relic from the past and a style of life (de Certeau, 1980: 70ff). This relic is a memory of an experience without discourse, which resists the discourse of reason and allows itself to be expressed only in popular story telling. This relic of the past is made up of knowledge useless for technological colonization, but, even though it is marginal, it charges everyday life with meaning and is converted into a space for silent creativity. What is left over and abandoned becomes a style that is a tactic for action, a way of walking through the city, a form of living in one's house, and of seeing television. This becomes a style created from technical inventiveness and moral resistance.

The logics that regulate practices are not fully occupied in creating social class identities, but, in defining these identities, create a series of new cultural competencies. The *habitus* of a social class[1] cuts across the different class-based uses of television and modes of perception and become evident—ethnographically observable—in the organization of time and space in daily life. What spaces do people create for television and to what extent does television occupy a marginal or central place in the home? Does television preside over the living room, which is the center of social life in the house, or does it take refuge in the bedroom? Is the television hidden in a cupboard and taken out only to see something very special? The reading of this topography of media space makes possible the organization of a symbolic topography shaped by the practices of social class. In the same way, it is possible to trace out a typology of time of the media: from the practice of keeping the television screen lit up all day to a practice of only watching news or the BBC series. This temporal spacing can establish a range of uses related not just to the quantity of time used but to the quality of time and to the social meaning of that time (see Thiolent et al., 1982) or to the type of demands that different social classes require of television.

In the practices of daily life, we hear not only the discourse of social class but also the cultural competencies that are diffused through social class and through formal education in its different modalities. Especially noteworthy are the competencies that are shaped by ethnic background, the regional dialects and the various urban cultural mixtures (*mestizajes*). There are competencies based on specialized knowledge and on narrative or gestural memory. Likewise the conditions of age and gender help to create different worlds of imagination.

Television as Repetition and Fragmentation

> Repetition is the beginning of the organization of a poetics, but on the condition that one knows how to recognize what is its order. (Calabrese, 1984: 70)

In our society the time that is seen to "run on" and that can be measured is productive time valued for its capital. The other time, which is created in the practices of everyday life, simply repeats itself and is made up of fragments, not units accumulated and entered into an accounting system (Pires do Rio Caldeira, 1984: 114ff). But isn't the cultural matrix that organizes the time of television precisely that of repetition and fragments? And is it not true that television, by inserting itself into the daily

---

[1]The term *habitus* is defined by Bourdieu as "a system of enduring conditions which integrate all past experiences and function as a matrix of perception, of appreciation and of action. The habitus makes it possible to carry out a series of continually new and differentiated tasks" (Bourdieu, 1972: 178).

routines, incorporates daily life into the commercial world? The time process organized by the order of television programming brings together, simultaneously, the form of profitability and the form of the scheduling. That is, the value of every program is established by the matching of the genre with the proper time of the day. Every genre belongs to a family of texts that are replicated and substituted according to the different time slots of the day and of the week. As a time "utilized," each text follows an hourly sequence that "makes up" the programming in the different days and in the different cadence of weeks and seasons.

Seen from the perspective of television, leisure time hides but also reveals the form of time of work; the *telenovela,* for example, articulates fragmented leisure time with an ordered series of time established by work. Foucault says that power is articulated directly with time because it is in the organization of time that one can see most clearly movement toward uniformity cutting across the diversity of social origins (1986: 164). The temporal movement of television, however, is not simply the language of the productive system—the language of standardization--because underlying productive time one can hear other voices: the voice of popular story telling, the account of adventures, the repetitive refrain of popular song. This serial process represents an aesthetics "where recognition is the foundation for an important part of the pleasure, and, as a consequence, time becomes the criteria of the value of symbolic goods" (Sarlo, 1987: 155). These voices are now integrated into the new language which, according to Benjamin, the technology of reproducible art has made possible. This language articulates the sensorium of the new publics that emerge with the formation of the urban masses (Benjamin, 1982: 15ff).

What we have then is an aesthetic of repetition which, working with the variation of an identity or the identity of diverse things, "links the discontinuity of the time of the narrative with the continuities of the time narrated" (Calabrese, 1984: 70). This goes back to the sense of duration created in the serial novels, published in weekly "chapters" in the 19th-century newspapers. The structure of seriality enabled the reader from the popular classes to make the transition from the oral story telling to the novel. The *telenovela,* produced in series, plays the same role: the mediation between the demands of the television format, arising from the productive system and the modes of seeing, and the cultural matrices and uses of the public.

It is quite clear that the notion of genre with which we are working has little relationship to the literary notion of genre as a property of the text and still less relation with the taxonomies created by structuralism (Todorov, 1978). We are taking our concept of genre from the team of Italian researchers who refer to a genre as above all a strategy of communicability, that is, "the forms in which both producers and receivers make their intentions mutually recognizable and organize the communicative competence of each other" (Casseti, Lumbelli and Wolf, 1980, 1983). Two factors, in my estimation, have impeded our ability to understand the real function of genre not only in production but also in reception, that is, in the narrative competence of the spectators: the tendency to consider genres as largely a literary invention and a contrary tendency to reduce genres to a simple recipe for construction of a narrative or as a label to promote marketing with certain publics. Any television viewer knows when a story line has been interrupted and how it can be completed. Viewers are capable of summarizing a narrative, giving it a title, comparing it with other stories and classifying it according to standard criteria. Those who who know well the genres, insofar as they are natives of that television textual culture,[2] can speak the language of genre even though they cannot explain analytically the grammar of genres.

Melodrama as Recognition and as an Anachronism

> The narrative of exaggeration, of paradox, and the moralistic record of social difference or political inequality—like the sadness of love—have the appearance of exemplar expressions of situations which reveal virtues and vices. (Meyer, 1984: 49)

Melodrama and everyday life: what is the meaning of the interlinking of these experiences? Isn't melodrama the narrative most distant from life, the most dreamlike experience? And yet melodrama touches everyday life, plugged into it not only as the counterpart or substitute for life, but as something that is constructed, like everyday life, with the organization of time in terms of repetitions, with odd juxtapositions of the anachronistic and the modern and with a temporal space for the constitution of primordial identities.

   Of the two levels of meaning in which the notion of recognition moves, the dominant rationalism gives it only a negative interpretation: on the level of knowing and recognition, it is a purely redundant operation, useless expenditure. And if this conception is projected onto the issue of ideology, the outcome is even more radically negative: in the realm of ideological alienation to recognize means to be deceived and to remain unknown. There exists, however, another theoretical matrix that attributes to recognition quite a different sense. To recognize means to interpellate and to be addressed: it is a question of being treated as a subject, and recognized not just as an individual author of action but as

---

[2]Regarding the notion textualized culture and its difference from "grammaticized" culture, see Lotman and Uspenskij, 1972.

social actors. Whether as a social class or as a political movement people are constituted and reconstituted in the symbolic narrative of interpellations and recognitions. This subjective dimension cuts across the social cohesion, sustaining the institution of the social contract.

This question of recognition has to be introduced because what melodrama brings into play is precisely the drama of recognition[3]—The recognition of the long-lost son by a father or the mother by a son. What moves forward the plot in melodrama is always the misrecognition of one identity and the struggle against all of the evil destinies, the false appearances, and against all that hides and disguises: the plot is a struggle to recognize and be recognized. Perhaps there lies the secret connection of melodrama with the history of the Latin American subcontinent. Could this not be the reason why this popular genre has achieved the success never touched by genres such as comedy, action-adventure, or terror. Whether the form is the tango, the classical popular Mexican film, the *telenovela,* or newspapers of sensationalist crime, melodrama is working as the deep vitalizing current and the collective imagination. It seems that there is no access to the historical memory of Latin America except through the melodramatic imagination. In any case the element of misrecognition that runs through so many of the social interactions of melodrama speaks to many people who search for their identity in the primordial sociability of family relations and in the social solidarity of the neighborhood, region, and friend networks.

Would it be out of place to ask to what degree the success of melodrama in these countries is in proportion to the failure of those social and political institutions that have developed unaware of the weight of that "other" social contract and are incapable of creating the same sociocultural density? These institutions seem to lack the sociability that finds its roots in the popular cultures. "There the rhythm of family relations is the time defining the meaning of the social. A person is first of all a member of one's kinship. From the temporal framework of family one links up with the time of the societal collectivity" (Zonabend, 1980: 308). How is the time of "history"—which is the time of the nation and of the world, the time of the great events which occasionally break into the rhythm of personal and community life—linked to the basic time of life? In this time of life we move in unbroken fashion from birth to death, a road in which the only signposts are the rites of passage that indicate that we are passing from one age to another. Indeed, it is this time of family that makes possible communication between "history" and "life."

Hoggart comments that in the life of the working class in the city—note that he is not speaking of rural folk, who may be marginal to

---

[3]A significant study of melodrama from this perspective is found in Brooks, 1974.

history and progress—historical events go unperceived except when they affect the rhythm of life of family groups (1972: 308). A war is perceived as "the time when my uncle died" and the national capital is "where my sister-in-law lives." In the world of the popular classes the areas of sociability with the greatest cultural authenticity are the family and the neighborhood—in spite of all the conflicts and ambiguities they may imply. Increasingly with the great migrations to the city, the neighborhoods are a form of extended family for the rootless and economically insecure.

It might seem that this world of family forms of existence has been abolished by the great transformations brought about by capitalistic progress in the areas of work and leisure, and in the commercial organization of life in the home and of work. In fact, industrialization and urbanization have not eliminated these elemental relations but only made them a picturesque anachronism. These anachronisms, however, are precious because this is, finally, what makes sense out of melodrama in Latin America. It is the relation based in family that mediates between the time of everyday life—a sociability that is repudiated and devalued by public economic and political institutions but that is culturally alive—and the time of the story. The memory of the family makes it possible for people to recognize their identities in melodrama. Anchored in this experience, people can transform everything into melodrama and take revenge, secretly, on that abstract sociability imposed by the commercialization of life and by cultural dispossession.

The Strategies of Analysis

Let us now map out both the diverse conceptualizations required by the different aspects of *telenovelas* to be studied and the diverse operative modes of analysis of narrative fiction.

THE STRUCTURE AND DYNAMICS OF PRODUCTION

Here we are dealing with the conditions of the production of telenovelas as a process of work (Casullo, 1985: 12ff)—a realm of ideologies incorporated into everyday practices, technique, and procedures, hierarchies of command in an organization, moving through production phases, and facing budget restrictions. This implies the differentiation of two operations. One is the ethnographic and sociological reconstruction of the practices and conditions of productions, a description of routines and divisions of labor as these are typically carried on in telenovela realization at the present time. The other operation is the construction of the history of the changes in these conditions of production and the cultural models that these changes are following. These are the conditions and concrete instances that we now want to specify in greater detail.

- The context of industrial competition, understood as the productive capacity of an enterprise expressed in terms of the degree of technological development, the readiness for innovative risk and the degree of professional diversification and specialization.
- The communicative competence realized in terms of the recognition by the publics, but not necessarily limited to what is measurable by the audience ratings, as this communicative competence can also be qualitative; that is, expressed more in the intensity of audience loyalty rather than in the size of audience.
- The levels and stages of decision making in the production of different genres. For example, who, in what moments, and with what criteria can something be included in a *telenovela*.
- Professional ideologies as a field of tension between different conceptions of the *telenovela*: the demands of the productive system with its industrial and commercial logics, the rules of the genre, the social expectations of producers, the initiative and creativity of the members of the production team including the directors, script writers, actors, cameramen, those in charge of studio settings, and so forth.
- The production routines necessary to keep daily series on the air: the habits of work that this demands, the limitations imposed on production and creativity by the profit expectations, but also the openings that permit experimentation and personal style to be incorporated into the work patterns.
- The strategies of marketing not as something that is added on when the production is finished, but as the planning that leaves its mark on the content: the structure of the format, the models of narrative development, the advertising promotion of the new series, the place that this *telenovela* will have in the programming schedule, and the differentiating elements that are introduced for a product aimed primarily at a domestic market or one that is also going to be aimed at an international market.

THE SOCIAL USES AND DIFFERENT WAYS OF
WATCHING TELEVISION

Here our research operations focus more on the processes of appropriation of the *telenovela* by different audience groups; that is, the diversity of social and cultural conditions that influence the way the *telenovela* is seen and enjoyed. There are three major aspects of social uses that need to be taken up, each with its particular methodologies.

Habits of Consumption of Television and Domestic Routines

If we take the family as the basic unit of the audience and the primordial context of recognition, this stage is operationalized through a questionnaire directed toward the mother of the family or whoever holds her position. The universe of the survey is defined by the social stratification established by a national department of statistics and the adaptations of this schema to different regions. This questionnaire touches on the following areas:

- Basic data regarding the type of housing and composition of the family;
- The degree of use of television by different members of the family;
- The way that television viewing is integrated with the household routines;
- How decisions are made in the household regarding what is to be watched and the relations of family power that underlie these decisions;
- The programming habitually selected;
- The interrelation of television use with other communications media.

The application of the questionnaire is accompanied by an ethnographic study regarding the living space of the family in order get a photographic image of the organization of the place occupied by the television and the relation of television to the system of functional and decorative objects in the house and to the aesthetic design and rituals of the home.

The Spatial Networks of Conversation and Resemantization of the *Telenovela*

The *telenovela* is "a unique genre in that it is lived outside of the immediate textual experience" (Muñoz, 1985: 294). The full meaning and pleasure are found not just in the text but more in the discussions of the family, the neighborhood, work place, and friend networks. The *telenovela* is a subject of discussion that is constantly reappearing in the daily communication, and it is the object of different readings within and outside of the home.

This dimension of the research inquires about what spatial contexts and which social actors are influential in the "circulation" of meaning and resemantization of the *telenovela*. On which aspects of the drama is the attention and reading of the audience focused? Around what human concerns is the reading anchored? What kind of characters catalyze the desire and phobias of the public? Thus the principal spaces to be studied are the following:

- Are the social actors of the network centered in one household primarily members of this family or—typical of neighborhoods of the popular class—are they also neighbors and friends.
- The relation of this house to the neighborhood; that is, the space from the door of this house to the corner store, the bar, or pub.
- The place of work and the actors who are discussion companions in the moments of coffee break, moments of rest, or at meals.
- Other places, such as the market or meeting points of friends and associates in community activities or social movements.

Cultural Competence and the Collective Imagination

We refer here to the cultural capital, the knowledge and interpretative grammars that are stored in memories and that mediate the readings of the *telenovela* by groups of different social, ethnic, racial, or regional origin. What are the collective imaginations through which different groups project their identity: youth, women, peasants, people of the city? From what perspective do these different subjects look at the *telenovela*? From what fabric of codes and inflections, grammars, and deviant perceptions are the interpretative readings constructed? Access to these cultural competencies and collective imaginations passes through the story telling modes of people, because it is in these narrative patterns that the conditions of recognition are activated and from which are "cited" the personal texts that the diverse readings go back to.

The methodological trajectory, therefore, begins with the mode of perception of the members of the audience and moves toward the ways of letting them tell the story of what they see. The only path of access to their experience of seeing the *telenovela* passes through the activation of their narrative competencies. It is through these narratives that the diverse social groups reveal what they, as a public of television, hold regarding the meaning of the text.

Some of the strategies for activating the narrative competency of the television viewers are the following:

- The narration of interpretations by a group of devoted fans of the *telenovela* that evidently find great pleasure in this.
- The individual narration of chapters of a *telenovela* presently being shown on television.
- Organize the viewing by a group of a recording of an episode of a *telenovela* in a way that permits the group to stop the viewing and to enter into a discussion of different continuations of the story, especially when there are tense moments that allow for different solutions of dilemmas in the plot.
- Gather oral or written summaries of what a person thinks has been the narrative development of the *telenovela*.
- Histories of a person's life that have as a focal point the relation between the *telenovela* and daily routines.
- Workshops for the production of stories, cartoon narratives, or photonovelas constructed with characters, situations, and conflicts from a *telenovela*.
- Workshops to create, from photos published in newspapers and magazines, a story about events in their own lives that are similar to the story of a *telenovela*.

The Textual Composition

The analysis of the text of a *telenovela* that we propose is focused on the movement which oscillates back and forth between the distinctiveness of the *telenovela* as a genre of fiction narrative, a textual world closed in upon itself, and how members of the audience perceive the references by the telenovela text to their world. Regarding the analysis of the fictive world of the *telenovela*, the methodology revolves around the fact that the construction of the genre is usually in contradiction to the world of "high culture," but is close to the aesthetic tone of mass culture. One can argue that the genre is precisely the smallest unit of the content of mass communication (especially at the level of fiction, but not exclusively), and the market expectations of the public placed on producers are voiced in terms of the genre. If researchers wish to gain an under-standing of the latent meaning of the mass media texts, the best means is access to the perception of the genre (Fabri, 1973: 77).

Regarding the relation of the *telenovela* to the world of the audi-ence groups, one must keep in mind that references to the life of televi-sion viewers is not in terms of direct reproductions of elements of peo-ple's daily life transplanted directly into the *telenovela*. As Magnani notes, "It is not the representation of the concrete and particular which gives to a fictive account the appearance of reality but a certain generali-ty which looks simultaneously to the fictive and the real and creates a consistency between the facts of the real world and the world of fiction" (1984: 175). In the movement between the world of the genre and the world of real life, melodrama functions as the narrative matrix and setting that permits one to analyze more deeply the movement of transformation of a narrative. Between fidelity to one's memory and the close following of a format, there is innovation and adaptation going on. We are dealing here with an analysis that seeks the construction of a typology of the *telenovela* in Latin America, taking as the parameter the local transfor-mations both of the genre and of the medium. We would propose the fol-lowing levels of analysis to get at this:

- The subject matter of representation: How does the text take material from life and from this create a fictional dramatization?

  What social actors appear as the protagonists in a certain type of *telenovela*? To what social class do they belong? To what occupations or professions? What gender? What ages? Are they rural *campesinos* or urban dwellers? Rich or poor?

  What kind of conflicts are the plots centered around: kinship or family? Affective relationships? Work? Social climbing?

  In what meeting places is the action centered? The home? The street? Workplaces? Places of leisure? And so forth.

  What daily routines does the *telenovela* construct? Out of what patterns of behavior is the daily life of the protagonists made up?

- The structure of the imagery: What do we see in the system of images?

  The spaces and objects that are "placed in images" to produce an atmosphere and a dramatic ambiance for identification.

  The times referred to (or avoided) in the production of different imagined sequences: the time of the remote past, the time of the "timeless," present time, and so forth.

The images that create opposing symbolizations between the noble and the vulgar, the modern and the traditional, the rural and the urban, masculine and feminine, people of one's own country and foreigners, and so forth.

- The structure of story: With what narrative pattern and with what conditions is a history created?

  The identifying name: is the *telenovela* identified through its title, the credits, the musical themes, the types of characters, and so forth?

  The breaking up of the story line as a mode of organizing the time duration (by episodes, inside of a particular episode, etc.) and to facilitate the following of the story line.

  The composition or construction of the continuity: the different types of connections within the story, the syntax that supports the unity over a period of months or even years.

  Whether a story line is closed in on itself or more open to current events and to the events surrounding its production.

  The degree of effectiveness of the story through the quality of the acting or by giving it a sensational or spectacular dimension.

  The degree of verbal rhetoric and the differentiation of language in terms of a more refined terminology, more colloquial, more standard, regional, proverbial, and so forth.

- The use of the language of the medium: To what extent is the inherited language of television used?

  Does the production borrow the language of theater or of film or some experimentation with the expressive possibilities of video?

  Is there a language of uninterrupted camera shots of scenes or are there frequent cuts? What is the treatment of interiors or open spaces?

  Is the editing purely functional or is it more subjective and expressive?

  Are the sets spare and implicit or are they richly decorative and explicit?

CONCLUDING REMARKS

The combination of strategies of analysis that this research approach proposes is an attempt to get beyond the level of contents and the semiotic codes of meaning to the level of *cultural matrices*. Semiotic analysis has never been sufficient to understand the interweaving of different levels of real and mythical time and the crossings from fiction to real life that make up the complex narrative structure of the *telenovela*.[4] Also too limited is an anthropology which, in order to conceive of the interconnections must dissolve the conflicts or, to reconstruct the differences, must isolate them from the dynamics that gives them life.[5] To speak of cultural matrices is not a return to the archaic, but rather to make explicit the different levels of meaning construction that are operating in the *telenovela*. That is, we are not speaking of the remnants of a cultural past when the narratives and popular gestures were authentic lived expressions, but why certain types of narrative matrices and settings of the *telenovela* continue to be part of living contemporary culture, because they are secretly, and in an unnoticed way, articulating the life, fears, and hopes of people today.

REFERENCES

Benjamin, W. (1982) "La obra de arte en la época de su reproducibilidad técnica," *Discursos interrumpidos*. Madrid: I. Taurus: 15ff.

Bourdieu, P. (1972) *Esquisse d'une théorie de la practique*. Gineve: Groz.

Brooks, P. (1974) "Une esthétique de l'etonnement: Le mélodrame," *Poêtique, 19*.

Calabrese, O. (1984) "Los replicantes," *Analisi, 9*, 70.

Canclini, N. G. (1984) "Gramsci with Bourdieu: Hegemony, Consumption and New Forms of Popular Organization," *Nueva Sociedad, 71*, 74.

Canclini, N. G. (1985) *Cultura y poder: donde está la investigación*. Mexico: Mimeo.

Casseti, F., M. Lumbelli and M. Wolf (1980, 1983) "Indagine su alcune regole di genere televise," *Richerche sulla comunicazioni, 2 & 3*.

Casullo, N. (1985) "Comunicación y democracia: de la maquinaria cotidiana al debate mundial," *Comunicación la democracia difícil*, 12ff.

de Certeau, M. (1980) *Invention du quotidien* Col 10118 Paris.

---

[4]For an analysis of the overlapping layers of time in the Brazilian *telenovela*, the contrast of the "extended time" of the popular narrative with the short, fragmented, rapid time of television discourse, see A. and M. Mattelart, *Le carnival des images*, pp. 55ff.

[5]Regarding the limits of anthropology, see the debate surrounding urban anthropology (Durham, 1986: 210ff).

Durham, E. (1986) "A pequiisa antropologica con populaçoes urbanas: problemas e perspectivas." *A aventura antropologica*. Sao Paulo: Paz e terra: 210ff.

Fabri, P. (1973) "Le comunicazioni di massa in Italia: Sguardo semiotico e malocchio de la sociologia," *Versus, 5*, 77.

Foucault, M. (1986) *Vigilar y castigar*. Madrid: Ed. Siglo XXI.

Hoggart, R. (1972) *The Uses of Literacy*. London: Penguin Books.

Lotman, J. and B. Uspenskij (1972) *Semiotica de la cultura*, 67ff.

Magnani, J. G. (1984) *Festa no pedaço: Cultura popular e lazer na cidade*.

Mattelart, A. and M. Mattelart (1987) *Le carnival des images*.

Meyer, M. (1984) "Pagina virada de meu folhetin." In Ligia Averbuc, ed. *Literatura en tempo de cultura de massa*. Sao Paolo: Nobel: 33-57.

Muñoz, S. (1985) *El sistema de comunicación cotidiana de la mujer pobre*. Cali: Mimeo: 294.

Pires di Rio Caldeira, T. (1984) "A noçao de tempo e nocotidiano." In *A politica dos outros*. Sao Paulo: Editora Brasiliense: 114ff.

Sarlo, B. (1987) "Lo popular como dimensión tópica retórica y problematica de la recepción," *Comunicación y culturas populares in Latinamérica*. Mexico: Ed. Gustavo Gili: 155.

Thiolent, M. et al. (1982) "Televisao, poder e classes trabalhadoras," *Cuadernos Intercom, 2*.

Todorov, T. (1978) "Tipologie du roman policier," *Poêtique de la presse*. Paris.

Zonabend, F. (1980) *La mémoire longue*. Paris: PUF: 308.

IV

CONSIDERING METHODOLOGICAL APPROACHES/QUESTIONING THEORY AND METHOD

9

*Less is More: Media Ethnography and Its Limits**

Kristen Drotner

To generalise is to be an idiot.
—William Blake

Through the 1980s, international media research became deeply influenced by the so-called "interpretive paradigm" (Lindlof and Meyer, 1987: 4), a development that was also named "new audience research" (Ang, 1991), "reception theory" (Jauss, 1970; Jensen, 1991) and "new revisionism" (Curran, 1990). Together, these terms denote some of the main characteristics of the paradigm, namely that attention is being paid to the various ways in which the media produces social meaning, particularly through television, and the various ways in which these meanings enter people's everyday lives, particularly through media use. However, the

*This is a revised version of an article published in Peter I. Crawford and Sigurjon B. Hafsteinsson, eds. *The Construction of the Viewer: Media Ethnography and the Anthropology of Audiences.* Højbjerg: Intervention Press, 1996.

different terms also denote some basic controversies that were thrown into relief by the increasing influence of interpretive studies. How new are these approaches really? What are their scientific relevance and political acumen?

Judging by trends in the international literature of mass communication, the term "media ethnography" has become an equally controversial catch phrase of the 1990s. Already in 1988 the U.S. media researcher James Lull, himself a pioneer of media ethnography, called the term "an abused buzzword in our field" (Lull, 1988: 242). Whether abused or not, media ethnography radicalizes the fundamental questions already addressed by interpretive studies of the 1980s. But the prevalence of the term also tends to defuse the answers to be gained from the discussion. In my view, we need to define much more precisely what we mean by media ethnography.

In the following, I offer such a definition drawing on my own and other Nordic media ethnographies. It is my main contention that media ethnography is most fruitfully defined as an epistemological alternative to current reception studies and not, as is usual, as its continuation or supplement. Moreover, I situate the recent and rapid popularity of ethnographic approaches to media studies within the wider framework of cultural and social realignments of modernity. The ethnographic approach, I propose, may be seen as one of the more useful attempts to overcome the impasse created by the dualist paradigms on which most classic disciplines are based. Hence the popularity of ethnography may be interpreted as an acknowledgment of the necessity to bridge internal and external borders in academia that have traditionally been deemed natural or inevitable.

BETWEEN TALK AND ACTION

My own path to media ethnography is empirical rather than theoretical. Like many researchers I have needed a certain distance of time to clarify the routes I took and the ones I escaped. Thus, the following description is a necessary post-festum reflection that I could not make during the research process, although naturally it produced its own forms of afterthought.

Some years ago, I followed a group of Danish 14-17-year-olds who were making videos in their leisure time (Drotner, 1989, 1995). The investigation took place in a largely middle-class suburb of Copenhagen and it formed part of a larger study I undertook that also included quantitative analysis of questionnaires ($N =162$). I was interested in seeing how visual genres are negotiated and made meaningful in gender terms and my assumption was that this negotiation is highlighted with particular clarity in media production: the very process of video-making draws on—and is a tangible articulation of—the producers' tacit knowledge of genres, codes and conventions culled from their reception of media through the years. This assumption led me to adopt a broad research design and employ traditional ethnographic methods. For a year, I made participant observation of the group, I had informal discussions when we met, and I also made in-depth interviews with each of the participants in their homes. In addition, I analyzed the group's videos as well as a selection of their media products (books, magazines, films—they watch very little television). During the first interview, which I conducted quite early on, I tried to probe into the importance of their video-making by asking each of them what they thought they learned from it. The response given by 16-year-old Peter, doing his ACE (*gymnasium*), is entirely typical of the answers I received:

> I don't know if I will ever use it [video-making]. Well, I don't know if you could say I have learned anything. It has been a hobby, of course, a nice hobby . . . but apart from that I don't know.

Like the majority of my informants, Peter here dismisses his leisure activities by writing them off as mere hobbies. Was video-making really of no special significance to them? Or did they answer what they thought I wanted to hear? How could I find out about the relations between their genre priorities of reception and then the attention they paid to video production? As it turned out during my observation of their activities, most of my informants were, in fact intensely preoccupied with the production process; they drew on their media competences and preferences, and would cancel parties and important sports matches in order to be with the video group. I grasped this enthusiasm also in my final interview made at the end of my year's observation. Here, I asked them to tell me *how* they got their ideas for various scenes and how they made these, but not why they made video or what they learned from it. Their radiant eyes and eager voices as they filled me in were a clear confirmation that the process was indeed profoundly important to them.

The triangulation method proved a key to my analysis: it was the very discrepancy between what they said and what they did that formed a core of significance. For although Peter like the others clearly identifies "learning something" with serious schooling and hence writes off his video-making as unimportant, his actions prove that he does, indeed, learn a lot. But the attraction of video to young people of both sexes, in aspects of reception and production, lies in its being regarded as non-schooling: it is self-defined, fun, and rarely planned ahead. Watching videos as well as making them are processes lodged outside the realm of regularity: hence they are deemed insignificant, and in that lies precisely their attraction. Through their appropriation of videos, these middle-class adolescents may be seen to negotiate the contradictory demands made on them to have fun without forfeiting their academic aspirations.

Moreover, my different approaches to the two interviews demonstrate that the problem of asking the right questions cannot be reduced to a matter of substance—it is as much a matter of form. Some informants, including mine, are unused—or unwilling—to analyze and hence discuss motives and moods, although they are brilliant storytellers. Story telling is constitutive to our perception of ourselves and the world (Bruner, 1990; Johnson, 1987; Shotter and Gergen, 1989), and hence it is the analytical endeavor of the researcher, not an empirical endeavor of most informants, to unravel the motives hidden behind gestures, silences, or an excited tone of voice (Corradi, 1991; Fornäs et al.,1990).

Finally, it was only because I spent such a long time with "my" group that I became able to see the discrepancies between talk and action. Crucially, the process facilitated my realization that the contradiction between form and substance was an epistemological discrepancy more than an empirical one: whereas I initially sought to explain the group's negative attitudes in terms of their ambivalent relations to schooling, I ended up by realizing that the discrepancies were equally rooted in my own ways of asking. Because ethnography is an interpretive science, what we look for depends fundamentally on what we can see.

TRADITIONS OF MEDIA ETHNOGRAPHY

Without realizing it at the time, my own study formed part of an ethnographic trend in media studies. Having previously worked on historical reception analysis (Drotner, 1983, 1988), I felt a need to get a more complete picture of the intricate processes of media use in addition to a more personal need to get out of archives and libraries into what I— rather naively as it turned out—perceived as "the real world."

My own trajectory mirrored contemporary moves. Media ethnography was born out of a general interest in qualitative media studies and a particular interest in what Stuart Hall has termed "the decoding" part of the mass-communicative process (Hall, 1973). Although these interests are rooted in divergent traditions of research, they all stress that viewing, listening, and reading are active processes of meaning making. Also, it is vital to note that a resurging interest in the receivers is far from limited to mass-communication research. Within literary studies, Hans Robert Jauss, a German, coined the term "reception theory" in 1967, and his ideas gave rise to both historical and contemporary studies of literary reception (Holub, 1984; Jauss, 1970), an interest that surfaced in North America as "reader-response theory" (Fish, 1980; Suleiman and Crosman, 1980; Tompkins, 1980). Also in the 1970s, film research was heavily influenced by Christian Metz, a Frenchman, and his psychosemiotic theories of the spectator as a textual construction (Metz, 1977). Already at that time, one noted that the receiver is no simple or self-evident term (Brunsdon, 1981; Kuhn, 1984): Receivers may be located in the past or they may be found just outside the researcher's office. In film theory and reader-response criticism the terms "spectator" and "reader" denote textual positions, whereas in literary and visual reception analysis an "audience" consists of actual people. Partly as a result of these theoretical differences, audience researchers tend to stress diversities of reception more than is the case with text-based spectator criticism.

A specific interest in ethnographic approaches appear at roughly the same time in several research milieus in countries as diverse as Australia (Hodge and Tripp, 1986), Brazil (Leal, 1986, 1990), Sweden (Fornäs et al., 1988/1995), and Germany (Baacke et al., 1990; Rogge, 1991). Obviously, English publication dates are a poor guide to authors' publications in their own languages and their influences on a national level. I mention this diversity because the current debate on media ethnography harbors an inherent Anglo-American perspective (Jankowski and Wester, 1991; Jensen, 1991; Lindlof, 1987; Morley, 1992: 173-97) that severely restricts an understanding of the broader sociopolitical contexts in which scientific discourses emerge and circulate. Thus, while the interest in media ethnography in Britain is rooted in the cultural studies tradition that developed as an interdisciplinary perspective in the 1970s under the combined influences of marxism, structuralism, and feminism, media ethnography in North America is shaped in opposition to the positivist paradigm and quantitative methodology dominating the social sciences, including media studies. Conversely, in Brazil media ethnography is deeply embedded in wider discussions of the political role played by the media (Canclini, 1988; Martin-Barbero, 1993), a perspective that also resonates in the Nordic countries, where the humanities form an important institutional frame and German critical theory forms an equally important theoretical frame for the development of media research from the early 1970s on.

KEY PROBLEMS: TEXT AND CONTEXT

Irrespective of theoretical and national differences, the growing interest in the receiving end of communication has recurrently faced two fundamental questions: is meaning made by the producers, the text, or the audience? Should our analytical context be the actual situation of decoding or include its wider ramifications? Media ethnography has developed as one of several attempts to answer these questions. The ethnographic perspective is often applied as a means to bridge the empirical gap between text and audience (texts are used as part of our everyday interactions). Similarly, many of us hope to close the theoretical gap between semiological approaches and more sociological approaches to the media (texts are only texts when used—and they are used as part of everyday life). Although anthropologists have a long tradition of studying interpersonal forms of communication, it is only in 1980 that an ethnographic perspective enters media research (Bryce 1980; Lull, 1980), and it takes another few years before that perspective surfaces as a significant discursive stance. In 1988 the U.S. media researcher, Janice Radway, herself a pioneer of reception analysis, addressed the fundamental problems of reception analysis in this way:

> No matter how extensive the effort to dissolve the boundaries of the textual object or the audience, most recent studies of reception, including my own, continue to begin with the "factual" existence of a particular kind of text which is understood to be received by some set of individuals. (Radway, 1988: 363)

The problem, as Radway sees it, is that the relation between text and context remains an external relation in reception studies. As a remedy she urges her fellow researchers to focus upon "the endlessly shifting, ever-evolving kaleidoscope of daily life and the way in which the media are integrated and implicated within it. . . . Ethnography may still be the most effective method for organizing such an expedition because it makes a concerted effort to note the range of daily practice and to understand how historical subjects articulate their cultural universe" (Radway, 1988: 366). In a similar vein, David Morley and Roger Silverstone, pioneers in British reception analyses of television, call for a more encompassing perspective on the media and advance an ethnographic approach that they define as "the analysis of multiply structured contexts of action, aiming to produce a rich descriptive and interpretive account of the lives and values of those subject to investigation" (Morley and Silverstone, 1991: 149-50; see also Morley, 1992: 183).

Unlike Jennifer Bryce and James Lull, Radway as well as Morley and Silverstone retain an interest in the textual dimensions of analysis just as they stress the importance of locating and analyzing contradictions in the various forms of data. The Dutch media researcher Ien Ang supports a similar stance in her important critique of the positivist tradition in audience research (Ang, 1991). In doing so, she radicalizes the demands made on media ethnography:

> [Ethnographic understandings] cannot—and should not—give rise to prescriptive and legislative solutions to established policy problems, precisely because the ironic thrust of ethnography fundamentally goes against the fixities of the institutional point of view. (Ang, 1991: 166)

Here, Ang's distinction between institutional and reception analyses of the media is made into a distinction between structural and ethnographic approaches to those analyses. Such conclusions would imply that one cannot make ethnographic studies of media production, which is incorrect (Gans, 1979; Helland, 1993; Tuchman, 1978). More importantly and perhaps inadvertently, her form of argumentation serves to prioritize an ethnographic perspective over more structural approaches. In my view, Ang hereby lends herself to what one might term an ethnographic fundamentalism, a moral belief that ethnography is a superior approach to media studies and hence ought to be promoted in favor of other traditions in the field. Such conclusions are neither feasible nor desirable: naturally we cannot and should not make ethnographic analyses of all media users (or media producers for that matter). Media ethnography neither can nor should become a substitute for other procedures of analysis. But because Ang's conclusions resonate widely within the debate on media ethnography today, it seems vital that we begin to define much more precisely—and within the interpretive paradigm itself—what we mean by the concept.

DEFINING MEDIA ETHNOGRAPHY

As indicated by the above quotations, there exist important theoretical and national differences within media ethnography. Still, the dominant Anglo-American discussion is united in its perspective on media ethnography: it is regarded as an extension of or supplement to reception studies or the new audience research. This extension is seen in both empirical and methodological dimensions of research. In empirical terms, media ethnography is defined as an extension of the contextual field within which the messages of a particular medium are appropriated. Whereas reception researchers concentrate upon the immediate situation of decoding (possibly with a dose of sociological information about the audiences), media ethnographers situate their analysis within the broader framework of the recipients' everyday lives (Drotner, 1994). In methodological terms, most Anglo-American media ethnographers make participant observation for a short period of time (from a day to some weeks) and regularly combine this with in-depth interviews and possibly diaries kept by the informants. More sources of data make up a more multifaceted picture, as Morley and Silverstone call for.

However, in epistemological terms studies such as those performed by Lull (1980), Morley and Silverstone (1990) and Gray (1992) mark a continuation of the perspective already found in qualitative audience research: they take as their point of analytical departure a specific medium, primarily television, and they concentrate upon deciphering the often intricate relations of decoding within a specific context, primarily the home. Hence, this type of media ethnography, as I see it, by necessity continues to struggle with the recurrent problems besetting reception analysis without developing new means by which these problems may be tackled or overcome.

I suggest that we define media ethnography much more narrowly in order that we may sharpen our analytical tools and get a clearer perspective on its pitfalls and possibilities. My proposition is this: *media ethnography may be defined as an epistemological alternative to other forms of qualitative media studies and not as their extension.* Such a "narrow" or specific definition marks itself off from the broader or more encompassing definitions in at least four respects. Firstly, and most importantly, the analytical point of departure is a particular group of people, not a particular type of medium. If the group chosen consists of media recipients, one may study how various forms of mass media enter their everyday lives and are appropriated as material and symbolic cultural resources. If the group chosen consists of media producers, one may, for example, study how various program formats and genre schemes enter their creative processes and how tacit and explicit norms of production underly their professional backgrounds, work relations, and routines.

Secondly, one defines the group as media users, that is, one studies the informants as recipients as well as producers of mediated communication, if with varying emphasis. This perspective gives a richer and, in my own experience, more accurate basis for evaluating the social and political implications of media use because it facilitates analyses of mediated communication across a wide range of cultural registers. Thirdly, one follows the group of informants in different locations, accompanying them to school or work, going shopping, or attending the sports center with them. Finally, the researcher stays so long with the group that one's preconceptions are not only denaturalized but also reframed as new cultural patterns.

Following the dictum of the Bauhaus architect Mies van der Rohe that "less is more," I think my narrow definition of media ethnography has several assets. It facilitates a more precise distinction between different qualitative approaches to media studies and hence serves to sharpen our methodological awareness in whose absence recurring problems turn into repetitive discussions. Moreover, by approaching media use from a different angle my definition may help illuminate different aspects of media use from the ones usually found in qualitative studies and hence nuance conclusions drawn from more traditional forms of institutional and reception analyses. Finally, and perhaps most centrally, such an approach to the media minimizes the often acknowledged danger of overemphasizing certain patterns of production or reception culled from analyses of a specific medium (Morley and Silverstone, 1991).

As is evident, this definition of media ethnography corresponds to the one adopted in my own study of adolescents' video use. Only by reflecting upon my empirical findings has it been possible for me to clarify the more general principles of selection that underlie my own approach. More to the point, these principles also inform a number of other media ethnographies in, for example, Germany (Baacke et al.,1990; Rogge and Jensen, 1988) and the Nordic countries (Berkaak and Ruud 1994; Fornäs et al. 1988/1995; Fuglesang, 1993; Rasmussen 1990; Ruud 1995). These studies seldom figure in the international literature of mass communication, an invisibility that seems less a result of language barriers, as some of these studies are, indeed, published or reported on in English. Perhaps more important is that these studies fall outside the reigning discourse on media ethnography and hence tend to be defined as, for example, urban studies, social anthropology, or youth research. Still, studies such as these serve to nuance Lull's rather scathing remark that Radway and Morley "seem to be the only ones in cultural studies who have made systematic, face-to-face contact with audience members in order to construct descriptions and theoretical accounts of the audience's feelings and activities" (Lull, 1988: 240).

Crucially, the results of these studies indicate what may constitute the main strengths of media ethnography: theoretical complexity, methodological processuality and epistemological reflexivity. This is not to say that such strengths cannot be found in other approaches to the media, but rather to stress that it is the combination of such strengths that marks off media ethnography. Let me give some examples of this, relating my discussion to current problematics facing media-ethnographic debate.

CROSSING DISCIPLINES AND DISCOURSES

As already mentioned, it is a main ambition of much media ethnography to offer encompassing theoretical and empirical analyses of mediated meaning processes. As a result media ethnographers are often analytical octopuses reaching out to a range of disciplines and fields. For some the ambition is to form new and more complete "super-theories," whereas others thrive on a "unity in diversity." Although such eclecticism naturally runs the risk of making an ideal of uncritical sampling, it also enforces a constant discursive awareness, an uncoupling of theoretical taken-for-grantedness that in the final analysis may be more useful: in today's integrated media cultures it is a difficult—and distinctive—challenge to prise open for analysis how various forms of media intertwine, creating new codes of understanding and experience on public agendas and in our private lives. Media ethnography offers analytical tools with which we may grasp these various forms of intertextuality be it on the level of text, genre, medium, or locations of use.

For example, applying a broad definition of media ethography and hence taking a particular medium as analytical point of departure, one may investigate how various *genres* talk to us and to one another as intertextual memories: TV commercials for cereals often call upon cartoon universes (including the music) that even young children recognize and most appreciate, and certain catch phrases enter our daily conversation as beloved or bemused elements in our stock of cultural references. Applying a more narrow definition of media ethnography and taking a particular group as analytical point of departure, one may in addition follow how different *types of media* constitute intertextual registers of meaning. In my own study, it was quite obvious that my young informants in making their various videos not only drew on their accumulated knowledge of films and television programs they had seen over the years, but that they equally and imperceptively included plot elements and character traits culled from books or cartoons they had read. Not unexpectedly, the boys favored action elements and the more sleazy figures, whereas most of the girls would hanker after romance and psychological introspection, so that the video group often faced prolonged negotiations before shooting a particular scene (Drotner, 1989). What is important here is that these negotiations were formed as covert exercises in genre and media intertextualities. If it is true, as I stated above, that media production highlights how we also as recipients form our cultural identities with the media as important props, then the intertextual sensitivity found in media ethnography offers a rich analytical resource for modern media research.

However, the theoretical diversity of media ethnography has also proved a bone of contention. Below, I shall just touch on two recurring allegations: First, can media ethnographic findings be generalized? This question focuses on how theory is constituted. Second, can media ethnography be related to other types of media research and with what political implications? This question focuses on what theories may be formed at all.

THE PARTICULAR AND THE GENERAL

The theoretical complexity of media ethnography opens for studies of variation in media production and media reception. Some researchers apply a discourse of political correctness and like Ang argue for specific media ethnographies in favor of more general approaches such as may be found in statistical samplings. Others, particularly in the United States, abandon any notion of explicit hierarchy by equalling variety of use with willful use if not directly subversive use (Fiske, 1986; Jenkins, 1991; Lewis, 1991; Schwichtenberg, 1993). Notions such as these have caused much and in my opinion rightful criticism of media ethnography particularly from researchers whose work is based on more traditional institutional approaches.

For example, the British media researcher John Fiske's findings that a group of Australian teenagers make oppositional readings of a certain program naturally does not warrant his general conclusion of television as promoter of a "semiotic democracy" (Fiske, 1986). These teenagers may in more general terms constitute their cultural identities through registers of opposition and if they do, their reception may be termed preferred readings (Hall, 1973). And, self-evidently, such findings cannot be directly transferred to include all other (teenage) groups nor endorse relativist interpretations of "anything goes." On the other hand, particular findings may reach beyond themselves, and all researchers start with inklings and informed guesses made on the basis of former experiences and knowledge. The interesting question here is not whether or not we may generalize media-ethnographic findings but how we do so.

These questions are basic to any qualitative study and may caution media ethnographers to learn from pioneers in qualitative methodology. My own reflections are inspired by the American sociologists Barney Glaser and Anselm Strauss, who make an important distinction between formal and substantive categories in which the former subsumes the latter (Glaser and Strauss, 1967). In my own study I started making substantive categories dividing my informants into the "romantic girls" and the "action-oriented boys." Only later did I come to see these oppositions as part of a formal category of gender that is established processually through articulations played out against negations of other-ness: favoring romantic schemata, for example, was an attempt to make invisible the violence inherent in an action plot and to keep its corollary of aggression at bay. But it was an abortive attempt because the boys were constantly opposing and undermining such attempts—and vice versa. It was precisely the drawn-out character of observation that allowed me to gradually perceive this process of genre play as a process of mutual articulation and negotiation of gendered otherness whose implications, of course, reach beyond the making of amateur videos.

"To generalise is to be an idiot," said the poet William Blake almost 200 years ago—maybe in an ironic attempt to address the con-tradictions inherent in his own dictum. The same could be said today about many qualitative studies in general and ethnographic studies in particular. Because we cannot make complete generalizations we do not have to abandon categorization beyond the particular case—incomplete generalization is a useful, and indeed necessary, part of interpretation.

MICRO AND MACRO ANALYSES

How can media ethnography be related to other types of media research and with what political implications? As noted above, this question points to another thorny issue in media ethnography that focuses on what theo-ries may be formed at all.

As we saw, Ang argues for a prioritization of media ethnogra-phies as much-needed alternatives to positivist theorizing and quantita-tive methodologies. Conversely, the British media researcher John Corner is among the growing number of people who equal an ethno-graphic microperspective with myopic politics. Corner makes a tradition-al sociological distinction between micro- and macroanalysis, a distinc-tion, which he specifies as a division in media research between what he terms "the public knowledge project" and "the popular culture project," information versus entertainment. According to Corner certain unspeci-fied colleagues working on fictional genres demonstrate a "loss of critical energy, in which increasing emphasis on the micro-processes of viewing relations displaces (though rarely explicitly so) an engagement with the macro-structures of media and society" (Corner, 1991: 269).

With all due respect for Corner's political engagement, I find his form of argumentation misplaced: he uncritically equals a question of analytical scale (micro-macro) with a question of empirical hierarchy ("viewing relations" versus "media and society") and political relevance ("loss of critical energy"). Hereby he overlooks or chooses to ignore a long tradition of feminist critique made of those hierarchies as gendered power relations, just as he fails to address more recent sociological discussions of the micro-macro distinction as a processual relation rather than a static opposition (e.g., Giddens, 1984). Because the political questions raised by Corner are central and because his simplified answers are shared by a number of researchers, it is vital to stress that the analytical scale of an investigation says nothing of its political implications. It all depends on the issues raised and the thoroughness and thoughtfulness with which explanations are given.[1]

MEDIA PROCESSES

Too little too late or too much too soon. Media ethnographers are variously accused of doing both, and the accusations touch upon the second of the strengths I see in media ethnography: its methodological processuality. Following Clifford Geertz' dictum of thick description and opting for a variety of data culled over time, I got a more nuanced picture of my informants and it was only because I stayed with them so long that my empirical obstacles could turn into analytical insights. I do not claim to have come up with a truer analysis than colleagues following other methodological paths, but my analysis stresses different aspects.

The crucial element here is time (Drotner, 1993a). Most Nordic media ethnographers have been very persistent: In Norway a musicologist, Ewen Ruud, and an anthropologist, Odd Are Berkaak, have been following a music group for almost three years (Berkaak and Ruud, 1994; Ruud 1995), and in Sweden musicologist Johan Fornäs and his colleagues followed three groups of rock musicians for two years and made reinterviews on publication of their results (Fornäs et al.,1988/1995, 1990). At the other end of the scale, Lull's assistants stayed one week at the respective informant families (Lull, 1980). Although it may not be possible or necessary to specify precisely how long it takes to do media ethnography, I find it vital that processes of signification are at the core of investigation for it to be media ethnography at all. The processual character not only relates to the empirical investigation of how mediated meaning making is formed and integrated into people's daily lives. It is also a methodological issue. As stated in my above definition I think that the researcher should stay with his or her

---

[1]Corner's mode of argumentation is but one example of the detrimental results of many media researchers' ignorance of fundamental insights gained in feminist research. This tradition underlies media ethnography as a stream of inspiration that is forgotten as ethnographic approaches gain acceptance by the academic establishment. See Drotner, 1993b.

informants so long that one not only questions immediate evaluations but also come to see these within new cultural frameworks. If one can do this in a day or a week, then fine. Most of us need rather more time.

In methodological terms, the ethnographer is situated between the familiar and the unfamiliar. In his famous essay "The Stranger" the Austrian sociologist Alfred Schutz notes how the stranger coming to a new location is "a marginal man" [sic], and because of this marginality:

> the cultural pattern of the approached group is to the stranger not a shelter but a field of adventure, not a matter of course but a questionable topic of investigation, not an instrument for disentangling problematic situations but a problematic situation itself and one hard to master. (Schutz, 1964: 104)

Social and cultural marginality sharpen our senses and dislodge the obvious so that we simultaneously perceive our surroundings and ourselves in new ways. As stressed by the British sociologists Martyn Hammersley and Paul Atkinson, an ethnographic study should stop when the researcher feels at home, because then one is integrated either as a person or as a researcher. In both cases the sensitivity of marginality is lost (Hammersley and Atkinson, 1989: 103-04).

Several media researchers (e.g. Corner, 1991; Schrøder, 1994) caution against such immersion because, so the argument goes, one loses sight of the media in a maze of contextual information. Again, such arguments are based on selective evidence of actual ethnographic studies of the media. Although it is true that on reading Lull (1980), Katz and Liebes (1984) and Gray (1992), for example, we remain rather ignorant of what goes on at the television screen, other investigations integrate textual analysis into the ethnographic account (Drotner, 1995; Fornäs et al.,1988/1995; Rasmussen, 1990). But the function of textual analysis often differs from what we see in, for example, reception analyses focusing on single programs or genres and applying in-depth interviews. Given the processual character of an ethnographic account and the emphasis laid on media use, one may pay more attention to the discursive schemata and formats that get taken up, appropriated, or transformed by informants while neglecting more encompassing analyses of textual structures. Despite ideals of more complete accounts, the ethnographic perspective harbors partialities of its own, and we may heed Jan-Uwe Rogge's perceptive remark that when we look at the media from the perspective of the families using them, then "the media not only appear different from how they do to the researcher or the educator, they actually are different" (Rogge, 1991: 173). But then perhaps the aim of scholarship should not be the creation of only one picture.

The question of context may, indeed, be tackled by combining a "narrow media ethnography" with more traditional forms of reception analysis. One may use, for example, observation as an entry into and patterning of the media uses and/or media production of a particular group followed by selecting particular media or genres for closer textual analysis and particular informants for in-depth interviews. This may be a feasible approach when studying complex media settings such as families comprising several generations and occupying a variety of physical places and textual spaces. In such settings a "full" ethnography over an extended period of time may prove too unmanageable for an individual scholar. Still, in order to be of any use the ethnographic phase should be long enough to allow for patterning formation to emerge.

REFLEXIVE REALITIES

Obviously, notions of research as an exercise in partial truths is fundamental to all qualitative studies. Even so, I take reflexivity of this partiality to be a particular strength of ethnography, and my reasons to do so are these: reflexivity becomes an acute necessity when one applies several methods such as is the case in media ethnography, because different types of data will inevitably contradict one another, leaving the researcher with a burden of validation that in my experience is heavier than in most other types of research. Perhaps for this reason the debates on reflexivity have been most active over the last few years in disciplines and research fields inspired by ethnography, and this offers an added reason to engage in the debate.

The so-called postmodern ethnography heralded by the publications of American male anthropologists such as George Marcus, James Clifford, and Michael Fischer (Clifford and Marcus, 1986; Marcus and Fischer, 1986) and followed by a spate of conferences, debates, and rejoinders (e.g., Geertz, 1989) is perhaps more significant as a sign of the times than as an element in an ongoing academic debate. The insistence that partiality is not only a methodological issue but also an epistemological and discursive power struggle was forcefully made from the late 1970s on by feminist and ethnic researchers entering the academic establishment (e.g. *Cultural Studies*, 1990; Moore, 1994; Ortner, 1984; Rosaldo, 1980; Stacey, 1988), just as the focus on the receiver as implied in the process of creation was heeded by visual anthropologists very early on (Crawford, 1996).

Judged narrowly from within media studies, the popularity of postmodern ethnography must be seen as a result of two recent developments, namely the growing academic acceptance of qualitative approaches and the concomitant added experience that many male researchers now have in conducting empirical studies based on, for example, in-depth interviews, participant observation, and discourse analysis. Few of the media researchers who actually perform research and not only write about it, endorse radical deconstructivist views, whereas most heed what Hammersley call a "subtle realism" (Hammersley, 1992: 50-4), a research position that traverses the field opened between a traditional and unquestioned belief in the realism of going natural and the more populist versions of postmodern relativism. In my own experience, this subtle realism draws us in two directions: if the position is to have any realism in it, it calls for humbler or perhaps more pragmatic forms of reflexivity that are borne by actual investigations. Some of my own reflections along this line are given above. Conversely, if a reflexive realism is to have any reflexivity in it, it calls for relating one's concrete studies to wider social and cultural developments. By way of conclusion, I would like to reflect upon those developments.

BEYOND DUALISM

The growth in media ethnography must be seen as part of changes in international media structures and in the everyday cultures that the media both feeds on and helps to nurture. The combined internationalization and commodification of media output brought about by technologies such as cable and satellite television means that old media formats are made obsolete whereas new formats rapidly gain ground. For example, pay television and narrow casting facilitate more individual forms of reception, whereas the production systems become more and more integrated on a global scale. As a result, media researchers need to redefine traditional production and genre concepts.

Audiences change, too. The mere fact that potential access is opened to an increasing range of media makes for polarization between the haves and the have-nots in media cultures, and this polarization is seen between regions as well as within them. As for those who do employ these potentials, the more flexible media structures make for more dispersed media use. Again, media researchers need to redefine traditional conceptions of audiences as a unified and generalizable mass of people that may be analyzed in terms of sociodemographic variables (Ang, 1991). The new audience research in general, and media ethnography in particular, is one of the routes that researchers embark upon in order to make more nuanced concepts of audiences and their contradictory cultures.

The phenomenal growth if uneven distribution of interactive computing and internet services has radicalized the demands made for reshuffling received notions of media technologies, applications, and texts. Interactive computers rarely operate as mass media, nor are they ordinary forms of interpersonal communication that presuppose a shared place, and often their users are as much producers as audiences/receivers. Moreover, the multidimensionality of computer texts challenge traditional theories of semiology based on print media and linear plot structures. Perhaps more than any other recent developments in contemporary media culture, computers challenge researchers to reach beyond traditional theories and methodologies. Evidently, media ethography with its comprehensive definition of texts and users offer one way to go.

But we have to look beyond the internal developments in contemporary media cultures in order to understand the booming interest in media ethnography. Throughout modernity we have seen a discursive opposition between "high" and "low" in cultural discourse. This opposition has been sustained in the face of repeated intertextual dialogues made between the two discursive registers. Thus, the collage techniques applied by the cubist movement of the 1920s drew on a mediated aesthetic of posters and newspapers. Early animation film was often inspired by classical music and started production with the sound tracks, and one cannot think of Roy Lichtenstein and pop-art of the 1960s without Mickey Mouse, Batman, and other cartoon figures (Drotner, 1996). Even so, only with postmodernist and deconstructivist cultural criticism— both often directly inspired by media developments—has the discursive divide between "high" and "low" culture been broken down. Today even old intertextual interfaces are being discovered in light of more recent theoretical developments, although the cultural crossovers are variously hailed as harbingers of multicultural innovation and deplored as catalysts for a dissolution of all distinctions of quality. Irrespective of evaluations, however, the increased awareness of cultural and discursive crossovers enforce cultural critics, including media researchers, to sensitize cultural concepts to a new set of realities: we must also be able to understand and interpret a wider spectrum of (inter)cultural signs, and we can no longer safely define ourselves as experts trained in judging immutable cultural qualities when we see them. Media ethnography can be seen as one of several attempts to nuance our cultural perspectives.

The media has become more commodified, the audiences more dispersed, media technologies more diversified, and cultural criticism more heterogeneous—these combined developments go some way to explain the recent and rapid increase in media ethnography. Still, it is vital to note that what one may call "the ethnographic turn" is not limited to media studies. In recent years we have seen similar turns in sociology (e.g. Alexander and Seidman, 1990; Bertaux, 1981; Smith, 1987), education (Malmgren, 1992; Nielsen and Larsen, 1985) and interdisciplinary fields such as cultural studies, women's studies and youth research (Kleven, 1992; Nissen, 1993; Willis et al., 1990). In my view, the widespread popularity of ethnography is fundamentally related to social changes, to what one might call the ethnification of modern societies where established physical and mental borders are broken down and new frontiers established.

The discursive popularity of ethnography, then, must be seen within the wider ramifications of social realignments and cultural diversification, developments that have been pertinent to public agendas since the 1970s. From then on, many countries have faced new challenges of adapting themselves to becoming multicultural societies with a more international political outlook and less economic independence. Because ethnography originated as a systematic means to understand and explain cultural meanings that are unknown to the investigator, an increasing number of social and cultural researchers not unnaturally looked towards the ethnographic tradition in their attempts to analyze new and complex developments closer to home. Beyond anthropology and ethnology, the research milieus first adopting ethnographic methodologies were often those that, for better or worse, were least bound by established institutional frameworks: women's studies, ethnic studies, studies on youth.

Moreover, it could be argued that over the last 20 years it is precisely women, ethnic groups, and young people who have spearheaded more general developments within modernity towards internationalization and multiculturalism. When women, Chicanos, and blacks entered the academy in larger numbers during the 1970s, their positions fundamentally served to politicize and dislocate established discursive hierarchies. So researchers, men and women, whites and blacks, simply had to sensitize their theories and methodologies to a changing set of realities. Beyond the early application and development of ethnographic methodologies, these new groups have enriched the development of interpretive research in general and media ethnography in particular with their epistemological insistence on otherness and its theoretical corollary of power relations and negotiations, just as in empirical terms they have diversified studies of genre and context by foregrounding for example, soaps and melodrama and their domestic sites of appropriation (Drotner, 1993b).

Of more principal importance, ethnographic perspectives offer an alternative to two paradigms dominating the arts and social sciences, namely what the British sociologist Anthony Giddens terms the structure and the action paradigms. This dichotomy, with varying political inflections, has materialized under theoretical headings such as positivism versus naturalism (Hammersley and Atkinson, 1989: 2), administrative versus critical science (Gitlin, 1978; Lazarsfeld, 1941), structuralism versus culturalism (Hall, 1980). The dichotomy has also resonated as empirical oppositions between subject and object in psychology, individual and society in sociology, signifier and signified in semiology. The contradictory and multifaceted social and cultural developments have made such theoretical dichotomies increasingly untenable, and today we witness a number of attempts to overcome the intellectual impasse of dualist thinking: feminist psychologists have sought to undermine the notion of subjectivity as a unified entity, the American philosopher and linguist C. S. Peirce enjoys a renaissance with his theories on semiotic processes of signification, and Giddens with his structuration theory seeks to bridge traditional sociological gaps (Giddens, 1984).

But perhaps the answer lies not in establishing new grand theories. Analyzing complicated modern societies—and few societies are untouched by modernization—require that we apply increasingly complex theories. The turn towards ethnography must be regarded as an important attempt to overcome traditional dichotomies without forfeiting the insights gained by concrete empirical studies. For some researchers ethnography more or less equals qualitative sociology. Others see it as a specific methodology based on participant observation. To me, the contemporary popularity of ethnography across the academic board can only be explained if we consider the concept as something other than qualitative sociology and more than a technique of investigation. As I have sought to argue, we must also consider ethnography as an epistemology, an approach to research that includes a view upon the world. Rooted in international trends towards ethnification and hybridization, interdisciplinary in its approach and often critical in its aims, ethnography offers a powerful resource for future cultural research that increasingly includes the media.

REFERENCES

Alexander, J. C. and S. Seidman, eds. (1990) *Culture and Society: Contemporary Debates.* Cambridge: Cambridge University Press.

Ang, I. (1990) "Culture and Communication: Towards an Ethnographic Critique of Media Consumption in the Transnational Media System," *European Journal of Communication, 5*(2-3), 239-60.

——— (1991) *Desperately Seeking the Audience.* London, New York: Routledge.

Baacke, D. et al. (1990) *Lebenswelten sind Medienwelten: Medienwelten Jugendlicher, Vol. I. Lebensgeschichten sind Mediengeschichten: Medienwelten Jugendlicher, Vol. II.* Leverkusen: Leske und Budrich.

Berkaak, O. A. and E. Ruud (1994) *Sunwheels: Fortellinger om et rocke-band* [*Sunwheels: Narratives of a Rock Band*]. Oslo: Universitetsforlaget.

Bertaux, D., eds. (1981) *Biography and Society: The Life History Approach in the Social Sciences.* Beverly Hills, CA: Sage.

Bruner, J. (1990) *Acts of Meaning.* London, Cambridge, MA: Harvard University Press.

Brunsdon, C. (1981) "Crossroads: Notes on Soap Opera," *Screen, 22*, 32-7.

Bryce, J. W. (1980) *Television and the Family: An Ethnographic Approach.* Ph.D. dissertation, Columbia University, Teachers College.

Canclini, N. G. (1988) "'Culture and Power: the State of Research," *Media, Culture and Society*, 10.

Clifford, J. and G. E. Marcus, eds. (1986) *Writing Culture: The Poetics and Politics of Ethnography.* Berkeley: University of California Press.

Corradi, C. (1991) "Text, Context and Individual Meaning: Rethinking Life Stories in a Hermeneutic Framework," *Discourse and Society, 1*, 105-18.

Corner, J. (1991) "Meaning, Genre and Context: The Problematics of 'Public Knowledge' in the New Audience Studies." In James Curran and Michael Gurevitch, eds. *Mass Media and Society.* London, New York, Melbourne, Auckland: Edward Arnold: 267-84.

Crawford, P. I. (1996) "Text and Context in Ethnographic Films: Or 'To Whom It May Concern.'" In Peter I. Crawford and Sigurjon B. Hafsteinsson, eds. *The Construction of the Viewer: Media Ethnography and the Anthropology of Audiences.* Højbjerg: Intervention Press: 135-49.

Cultural Studies 4, 3 (1990) Special issue on "Chicana/o Cultural Representations: Reframing Alternative Critical Discourses."

Curran, J. (1990) "The 'New Revisionism' in Mass Communications Research," *Critical Studies in Mass Communication, 7*(2), 145-68.

Drotner, K. (1983) "Schoolgirls, Madcaps and Air Aces: English Girls and Their Magazine Reading Between the Wars," *Feminist Studies, 9*(1), 33-52.

—— (1988) *English Children and Their Magazines, 1751-1945.* New Haven, MA.: Yale University Press. Orig. 1985.

—— (1989), "Girl Meets Boy: Aesthetic Production, Reception, and Gender Identity," *Cultural Studies, 2*, 208-25.

—— (1995) *At skabe sig - selv: ungdom, æstetik, pædagogik.* Copenhagen: Gyldendal. (Original work published 1991)

—— (1993a) "Medieetnografiske problemstillinger: En oversigt," *Mediekultur, 21*, 5-22.

———— (1993b) "Media Ethnography: An Other Story?" In U. Carlsson, ed. *Nordisk forskning om kvinnor och medier.* Gothenberg: Nordicom: 25-40.

———— (1994) "Ethnographic Enigmas: 'The Everyday' in Recent Media Studies," *Cultural Studies, 8*(2), 341-57.

———— (1996) "Cross-Over Culture and Cultural Identities," *Young: Nordic Journal of Youth Research, 4*(7), 4-17.

Fish, S. (1980) *Is there a Text in this Class? The Authority of Interpretive Communities.* Cambridge, MA: Harvard University Press.

Fiske, J. (1986) "Television: Polysemy and Popularity," *Critical Studies in Mass Communication, 3*(2), 391-408.

Fornäs, J., et al. (1995) *In Garageland: Rock, Youth and Modernity.* London: Routledge. (Original work published 1988)

———— (1990) *Speglad ungdom: Forskningsreception i tre rockband.* Stockholm, Stehag: Symposion.

Fuglesang, M. (1993) *Veils and Videos: Female Youth Culture on the Kenyan Coast.* Stockholm: Almqvist and Wicksell, Dissertation.

Gans, H. (1979) *Deciding What's News.* New York: Pantheon.

Geertz, C. (1989) *Works and Lives: The Anthropologist as Author.* Cambridge: Polity Press. (Original work published 1988)

Giddens, A. (1984) *The Constitution of Society.* Berkeley: University of California Press.

Gitlin, T. (1978) "Media Sociology: The Dominant Paradigm," *Theory and Society, 6,* 205-53.

Glaser, B. G. and A. L. Strauss (1967) *The Discovery of Grounded Theory: Strategies for Qualitative Research.* Chicago: Aldine.

Gray, A. (1992) *Video Playtime: The Gendering of a Leisure Technology.* London: Routledge.

Hall, S. (1973) "Encoding and Decoding in the Television Discourse," *Occasional Paper, 7.* Birmingham: CCCS.

———— (1980) "Cultural Studies: Two Paradigms," *Media, Culture and Society, 2,* 57-72.

Hammersley, M. (1992) *What's Wrong with Ethnography? Methodological Explorations.* London: Routledge.

Hammersley, M. and P. Atkinson (1989) *Ethnography: Principles in Practice.* London, New York: Routledge. (Original work published 1983)

Helland, K. (1993) *Public Service and Commercial News: Contexts of Production, Genre Conventions and Textual Claims in Television.* University of Bergen: Department for Media Studies, Report no. 18.

Hodge, R. and D. Tripp (1986) *Children and Television.* Cambridge: Polity Press.

Holub, R. C. (1984) *Reception Theory: A Critical Introduction.* London: Methuen.

Jankowski, N. W. and F. Wester (1991) "The Qualitative Tradition in Social Science Inquiry: Contributions to Mass Communication Research." In Jensen and Jankowski, eds. (1991): 44-74.

Jauss, H. R. (1970) *Litteraturgeschichte als Provokation.* Frankfurt: Suhrkamp.

Jenkins, H. (1991) *Textual Poachers: Television Fans and Participatory Culture.* London: Routledge.

Jensen, K. B. (1991) "Reception Analysis: Mass Communication as the Social Production of Meaning." In Jensen and Jankowski, eds. (1991): 135-48.

Jensen, K. B. and N. W. Jankowski, eds. (1991) *A Handbook of Qualitative Methodologies for Mass Communication Research.* London, New York: Routledge.

Johnson, M. (1987) *The Body and the Mind: The Bodily Basis of Meaning, Imagination, and Reason.* Chicago, London: University of Chicago Press.

Katz, E. and T. Liebes (1984) "Once Upon a Time in Dallas," *Intermedia, 12,* 3.

Kleven, K. V. (1992) *Jentekultur som kyskhetsbelte: om kulturelle, samfunnsmessige og psykologiske endringer i unge jenters verden.* Oslo: Universitetsforlaget.

Kuhn, A. (1984) "Women's Genres," *Screen, 25*(1), 18-28.

Lazarsfeld, P. F. (1941) "Remarks on Administrative and Critical Communications Research," *Zeitschrift für Sozialforschung/Studies in Philosophy and Social Science,* 9.

Leal, O. F. (1986) *A leitura Social da Novela das Oito.* Petropolis: Vozes.

—— (1990) "Popular Taste and Erudite Repertoire: The Place and Space of Television in Brazil," *Cultural Studies, 1,* 19-29.

Lewis, L. A., ed. (1991) *The Adoring Audience: Fan Culture and Popular Media.* London, New York: Routledge.

Lindlof, T. R., ed. (1987), *Natural Audiences: Qualitative Research of Media Uses and Effects.* Norwood, NJ: Ablex.

Lindlof, T. R. and T. P. Meyer (1987) "Mediated Communication as Ways of Seeing, Acting, and Constructing Culture: The Tools and Foundations of Qualitative Research." In Lindlof, ed. (1987): 1-30.

Lull, J. (1980) "The Social Uses of Television," *Human Communication Research, 6*(3), 195-209.

—— (1988) "Critical Response: The Audience as Nuisance," *Critical Studies in Mass Communication, 5,* 239-43.

Malmgren, G. (1992), *Gymnasiekulturer: lärere och elever om svenska och kultur.* Lund: University of Lund 92: 188. Dissertation.

Marcus, J. and M. Fischer (1986) *Anthropology as Critique.* Chicago: University of Chicago Press.

Martin-Barbero, J. (1993) *Communication, Culture and Hegemony: From the Media to Mediations.* Trans. Elizabeth Fox and Robert A. White. Mexico City: Gustavo Gili.

Metz, C. (1977) *Le signifiant imaginaire.* Paris: Union Générale d'Editions.

Moore, H. (1994) *A Passion for Difference: Essays in Anthropology and Gender.* Cambridge: Polity Press.

Morley, D. (1992) *Television, Audiences & Cultural Studies.* London: Routledge.

Morley, D. and R. Silverstone (1990), "Domestic Communication: Technologies and Meanings," *Media, Culture and Society, 1*, 31-55.

——— (1991) "Communication and Context: Ethnographic Perspectives on the Media Audience," In Jensen and Jankowski, eds. (1991): 149-62.

Nielsen, H. B. and K. Larsen (1985) *Piger og drenge i klasseoffentligheden.* Oslo: Pedagogical Research Institute, Oslo University.

Nissen, J. (1993) *Pojkarna vid datorn: unga entusiaster i datateknikens värld.* Stockholm: Symposion. Dissertation.

Ortner, S. (1984) "Theory in Anthropology since the Sixties," *Comparative Studies in Society and History, 26*(1), 126-66.

Radway, J. (1988) "Reception Study: Ethnography and the Problems of Dispersed Audiences and Nomadic Subjects," *Cultural Studies, 3*, 359-76.

Rasmussen, T. A. (1990) *"Tror du kun det er dig der har øjne": Actionfilm og drengekultur.* Aalborg: Department of Communication, Aalborg University Center.

Rogge, J.-U. (1991) "The Media in Everyday Family Life: Some Biographical and Typological Aspects." In E. Seiter et al., eds. *Remote Control: Television, Audiences and Cultural Power.* London: Routledge: 168-79.

Rogge, J.-U. and K. Jensen (1988) "Everyday Life and Television in West Germany: An Empathic-Interpretive Perspective on the Family as a System." In J. Lull, ed. *World Families Watch Television.* Newbury Park, London, New Dehli: Sage: 80-115.

Rosaldo, M. (1980) "The Use and Abuse of Anthropology: Reflections on Feminism and Cross-Cultural Understanding," *Signs, 5*(3), 389-417.

Ruud, E. (1995) Music in the Media: The Soundtrack Behind the Construction of Identity," *Young: Nordic Journal of Youth Research, 3*(2), 34-45.

Schrøder, K. (1994) "Audience Semiotics, Interpretive Communities and the 'Ethnographic Turn' in Media Research," *Media, Culture and Society.*

Schutz, A. (1964) "The Stranger: An Essay in Social Psychology," In *Collected Papers. Vol. II.* The Hague: Martinus Nijhoff.

Schwichtenberg, C., ed. (1993) *The Madonna Connection: Representational Politics, Subcultural Identities, and Cultural Theory.* Boulder, San Francisco, Oxford: Westview Press.

Shotter, J. and K. J. Gergen, eds. (1989) *Texts of Identity.* London: Sage.

Smith, D. (1987) *The Everyday World as Problematic: A Feminist Sociology.* Boston, MA: New England University Press.

Stacey, J. (1988) "Can There be a Feminist Ethnography? *Women's Studies International Forum, 11*(1), 21-7.

Suleiman, S. R. and I. Crosman, eds. (1980) *The Reader in the Text: Essays on Audience and Interpretation.* Princeton: Princeton University Press.

Tompkins, J. P., ed. (1980) *Reader-Response Criticism: From Formalism to Post-Structuralism.* Baltimore: Johns Hopkins University Press.

Tuchman, G. (1978) *Making News: A Study in the Construction of Reality.* New York: Free Press.

Willis, P. et al. (1990) *Common Culture: Symbolic Work at Play in the Everyday Cultures of the Young.* Milton Keynes: Open University Press.

10

Audiences' Expectations and Interpretations of Different Television Genres: A Sociocognitive Approach

Birgitta Höijer

Television is the most popular story teller in modern time. In documentary and fictional accounts television narrates about human destinies, about societies, and about the world. Television mediates reality and imagination. Human beings have always taken part in such narratives, but never before in history has this been possible to such an extent. Over time, television has also extended visual narrative modes and developed specific genres of its own.

Studies within the uses and gratifications tradition have shown how different needs might be satisfied by television viewing, such as surveillance, reality exploration, excitement, entertainment, escapism, and companionship (e.g., Rosengren, Wenner and Palmgreen, 1985). Reception studies have shown how audiences experience television and actively decode television programs (e.g., Ang, 1985; Hagen, 1994; Höijer, 1992a; Jensen, 1988; Liebes and Katz, 1993; Livingstone, 1990; Morley, 1980; Schrøder, 1988). Cultivation studies (e.g., Signorielli and

Morgan, 1990) point out long-term effects of television viewing on conceptualizations of social phenomena, and other effect studies focus on, for instance, aggression (for a review, see von Feilitzen, 1994), distribution of knowledge, or other aspects of learning (see McQuail, 1994). Results within all traditions show individual and social differences in audiences' responses to television.

Rather than regarding these approaches in opposition to one other, they may be seen as focusing on different aspects in the very complex interplay between television and audiences. Most studies of audiences' uses, reactions to, and receptions of television, however, either focus on a single genre within television, such as news or soap opera, or treat television as a general phenomenon without considering the question of genres at all. These tendencies have been criticized by Corner (1991), who argues that thorough studies and comparisons of genres are missing in audience research. All too easily we may be caught in extreme positions, either in essentialism (forget about the reader), which Corner (1991) warns against, or in its opposite, antiessentialism (total freedom for the reader or forget the text), which Fetveit (1996) warns against.

Television is, as Attallah emphasizes, organized around genres:

> . . . the entire television industry is organised around the production of specific genres. Everything that appears on television effectively fits into one genre or another. Television could be said not to exist outside of its genres. There is nothing that is just "television." It is always a specific type of television: police show, soap opera, and sports casts. (1984: 227)

At the same time it is important to note that most audiences like to watch a whole set of different genres. People, of course, have somewhat different preferences, and some have very specific ones, but mostly television genres do not have very different audiences:

> . . . in more than thirty years there have been no reports, as far as we know, of any dramatic and consistent examples of segmentation for different programmes. (Barwise and Ehrenberg, 1988: 30)

As viewers we usually are somewhat omnivorous beings. We watch both news and other factual programs, different types of fiction, and all sorts of entertainment programs. Barwise and Ehrenberg (1988) conclude that television makes it possible for people to concentrate their viewing around one or two single genres, but most people do not. Instead, they prefer variation. This is not to say that there are no viewers or no demographic groups with more specific preferences. Young people, for instance, watch news and factual programs less than others, young and middle-aged women do not watch sports programs as much as others, male viewers watch action series more than female viewers who, in their turn, watch romantic series more, and so forth (Abrahamsson, 1993). Nevertheless, most of us see a little of everything.

Another shortcoming in most audience studies is the theoretical gap between the discourse level and the level at which audiences process and interpret discourses; that is, between culture as an "outside" phenomenon and as an "internal" process in the mind. In relation to cultivation analysis, for instance, this problem has been pointed out by Hawkins and Pingree (1990: 35): "What are the psychological processes that lead individuals to construct their own social reality in ways that mirror both the facts and the ostensible meaning of television's social reality?" Others have expressed this by emphasizing a need for cognitive perspectives, for example, in relation to reception studies (e.g., Höijer, 1992b; Livingstone, 1989), or in relation to communication studies in general (Cappella and Street, 1989; Mendelsohn, 1989).

Applying a cognitive perspective and keeping in mind the concept of genre and the note of the omnivorous viewer suggest a need to carry out comparative studies of the same viewers´ receptions of different television genres. In the following section, studies will be presented that focus on audiences´ receptions and conceptualizations of three popular narrative forms in television: news, social-realistic fiction, and prime-time soap opera. If we find large differences among receptions of these genres we might conclude that texts are powerful. Small differences, on the other hand, would indicate that the influence of the text is limited. However, first a few words about narratives in a cognitive view.

NARRATION AND MIND

According to Bruner (1990) the narrative form is a general form for cognitively organizing experiences in mind, and Stern (1985) shows how we as individuals already early in childhood develop a narrated self. Thus, narration is not only connected to texts, but to a more basic psychological and mental form. Narration is important in our identity building and in our never-ending interpretation and understanding of the world.

Bruner emphasizes that narratives are concrete. They tell about a world in which individual destinies are depicted in concrete, space- and time-bound situations. This is the way we also structure and tell others the stories of our own lives and things we experience: "Yesterday when I was on the train on my way to work I met NN and he told me that. . . ."

Applied to television genres, Bruner's narrative characteristics seem to fit best into television fiction. The news genre is not as firmly rooted in the concrete as the narrative form prescribes. Individual destinies are not depicted to the same extent as in fiction, and so forth. Although there is a tendency that news is becoming more and more fictionalized (e.g., Dahlgren, 1995; Fiske, 1987), news usually also focuses more on abstract themes, such as the social and political course of events. News also relates facts and figures, and all kinds of propositions and arguments, which are rarely part of fiction. News apparently is a genre somewhere in between the two modes of mind that Bruner (1986) claims are two fundamentally different modes of cognitive functioning: the narrative mode and the argumentative, or paradigmatic, mode. The latter is based on a more "scientific" way of thinking in which logical reasoning and concept formation play important roles. Piaget (1926/1955) and Vygotsky (1934/1986) describe the development of this kind of thinking in young people. The narrative mode is, however, a more basic mode developed very early in childhood and used in our everyday interaction with the world.

Below I present some results from comparative reception studies in which viewers have been interviewed or have answered a survey about their conceptualizations and interpretations of different narratives, or genres, in television (Höijer, 1991; 1995).

METHOD

Reception interviews were conducted immediately after viewers had watched specific programs. The narrative syntagm, that is, the succession of scenes in the fiction narratives and sequences in the news stories, was used as the basis for the disposition of the reception interviews. Such textual segments constitute basic elements in television aesthetics (Ellis, 1982; Fiske, 1987), and are good starting points for reception interviews. By interviewing viewers about a succession of scenes or sequences the interpretations may be uncovered and communicated step by step by way of a cognitive unravelling process that is concrete and close to the viewers´ interpretation perspectives as they have developed during watching the program.[1] Open questions were

[1]There was, of course, some individual variation in relation to the order of the scenes/sequences the informants talked about. Mostly however, and especially in relation to the fiction stories, the informants preferred to keep to the same order as the scenes appeared in the program. Questions about the stories as wholes were also asked, but these questions usually received very brief answers.

asked in relation to the scenes/sequences, such as, "Tell me about your impression of that scene"; "Did you take particular note of anything they said, or anything in the picture? What?"; "Did you think about anything during this part? What?" Each viewer was encouraged to elaborate her/his answers by "open" follow-up questions, such as, "Tell me more about that" or "Did you notice anything else?"

Individual interviews were also carried out so as to obtain data on the viewers' personal history, sociocultural activities and certain orientations or frames of reference, such as conceptions of gender and social class and conceptions of genres. Here I only present conceptions of genres.[2]

In order to create an interview situation in which a viewer's conceptual frameworks and reception can be brought to the fore and rendered conscious and communicable, we need a sensitive interview method. The interview technique used is based on ethnographic and psychotherapeutic techniques, and has been developed in earlier studies (cf. Höijer, 1986, 1990).

The informants were recruited with the assistance of the Audience and Program Research Department of the Swedish Broadcasting Corporation. They were men and women between 30 and 50 years old in unskilled and semiskilled occupations (working class) and in upper-level white-collar occupations (middle class). The two qualitative studies that I draw on included 16 and 23 informants, respectively (Höijer, 1991, 1995). In the survey study a random sample of more than 1,000 persons answered a questionnaire about television viewing and their ideas and receptions of different types of programs (Höijer, 1995).

AUDIENCES' EXPECTATIONS ON FICTION AND NEWS

Genres are not only connected with textual characteristics but also with our expectations of texts.[3] Neale (1990) talks about systems of orientations, expectations, and conventions that circulate between industry, text and subject. With the help of our ideas about genres we generate expectations about programs, be they news or fiction:

---

[2]Social class perspectives are analyzed by Ross (1993). For an overview of the project, see Höijer, Nowak and Ross (1992).

[3]According to cognitive theory expectation is seen as "a mental set with a good deal of conscious cognitive processing involved and is assessed phenomenologically" (Reber, 1985: 256).

They offer a way of working out the significance of what is happening on the screen: a way of working out why particular events and
actions are taking place, why the characters are dressed the way
they are, why they look, speak and behave the way they do, and so
on. (Neale, 1990: 46)

The ideas about genres that the audience express separate very clearly
between news and fiction on the one hand, and between different types
of fiction on the other hand.

Expectations on Fiction

The audience expects that fiction narrated in social-realistic mode[4] will
be meaningful as imaginary but materialized accounts of some social
reality. They expect that such fiction can be interpreted in relation to cultural and personal experiences and cognitions from everyday life, that is,
the social world outside the textual world or the genre. The viewers do
not use the concept social-realistic fiction, however. Instead they mention different television series they have watched, or they sometimes
quite generally talk about Swedish series and contrast them with
American series. The latter is an overstated generalization, because
there are different types of domestic as well as foreign fiction on television. The viewers know that very well, but since we often generalize
quite roughly about social phenomena in everyday language, many
viewers do it also when talking about genres. The answers reflect the
fact that there is a long tradition of social-realistic fiction in Swedish television, and that many soap opera series are U.S. productions. Extracts
from the answers are given below:

"Three Loves" seemed to be much closer to real life. Many things
that happened there seemed quite familiar. It's more down to earth.
In a way it was just like real life. It feels as if things really were that
way. (male, janitor)

Swedish TV series are often more involving, they are about everyday life, sort of. It feels as if they are rather close to the truth, or the
facts. (female, bookbinder).

---

[4]Realism certainly is a problematic concept, and there are many forms of realism
which, for instance, are discussed in film theory. I use the term social-realism to
refer to an intention to narrate a historical and social reality and give it some
form of empirical authencity.

> Sometimes you can see yourself. But really not in "Falcon Crest." I
> feel more at home in the Swedish series than in the American ones.
> I can't step into reality in such series. But in "Three Loves" I can—I
> could just blend into it. (female, caretaker)

If we turn to popular fiction, especially American prime-time soap opera,
it would be reasonable to say that the audience does not expect the
genre to be meaningful in view of their everyday cultural and social
experiences and cognitions. On the contrary, this genre is expected to
be interpretable as an universe of its own, as an intertextual discourse
characterized by depicting an unreal and exaggerated world:

> It's so far removed from reality. There's nothing else you can com-
> pare it with. It is as if you just closed your eyes and entered a world
> of dreams. I don't think it is possible at all to make any associations
> to the real world. (female, M.B.A.)

> "Dallas" and "Falcon Crest" are just somewhat exaggerated. Strange
> things happen. They are exaggerated and you can't identify with
> them. There are just incredibly many plots going on all the time and
> they are so treacherous to each other. They are just not real people"
> (female, shop assistant)

> "Dallas" is just hard to believe. "Dynasty" too. It hasn't much to do
> with real life. Being flashy is all that matters. They are untrue to each
> other and many other things. . . .Well, they do show a drilling rig and
> a fist fight once in a while. But that doesn't make it a story. (male,
> prison warden)

The last quotation may be a little hard to interpret, but knowing that this
viewer emphasizes the almost documentary character of some domestic
series (in the social-realistic genre)—"I would like to call them social features"—we may interpret what he says. Although he finds some realistic
details in "Dallas" and "Dynasty" (drilling rigs and fist fights), it is not
enough to relate the genre to social reality: "But that doesn't make it a
story." The realism does not have the overall narrative role that is
required in order for the audience to conceive this genre anchored not
only in fantasy but also in reality.

    In relation to social-realistic fiction, however, almost every view-
er explicitly or implicitly formulates the double nature that characterizes
many fiction genres, that is, its anchoring both in fantasy and reality, or
as Bogart (1980: 238) has put it: "Fiction evokes the uniquely human
ability to imagine things other than as they are . . . fantasy represents a
reconstruction of reality." Viewers express this in formulations like "Well,
of course, it is all made up, but it could have happened in just about any

town in northern Sweden," or "You get a feeling of reality. Anyway, even though it isn't a true story, it is close to one."

Expectations on News

The news genre is even more connected to reality, according to the audience. News is perceived as "reality," "facts," "things that have happened," "information," "the grim truth." News is a very serious matter for the audience, expressed in formulations like, "We need the news. We have to watch what's going on on earth," or "The most important thing on TV is the news, the rest you can live without," or "You are much more serious about the news." According to Hagen (1994), watching news is mainly perceived as part of a general citizen's obligation to be an informed person; it is a duty to keep up with the news. This tendency was also very clear in my studies, although there also was a weak tendency to connect news viewing with entertainment, a result already demonstrated by Schramm (1949) and later supported in uses and gratifications studies (e.g., Wenner, 1985) and reception studies (Hagen, 1994; Jensen, 1986). Anyway, in audience cognitions the news genre is firmly anchored in reality and almost nobody sees any relation to fantasy or fiction genres. Only two persons saw tendencies to genre similarities between news and fiction, a phenomenon that is documented and discussed in mass communication research (e.g., Fiske, 1987). A large majority strongly rejected any similarities when asked about that: "I can't see any similarity." The genre expectations focus information, knowledge, and learning, and are in concordance with the worn cliché, "a window on the world":

> In a way the (television) news is some means of information, channel of knowledge or distributor of news. (male, consultant)

> You can see what's going on on earth. Watch what is happening on the other side of the earth and get a view into how things work in other cultures. It's your lookout to the world. (female, bookbinder)

News is expected to be interpretable as a meaningful reporting about reality, about ongoing events, and courses of events in the world.

Conceptions about genres are quite unanimous among viewers, at least the adult ones. Audience's genre codes are rarely oppositional. Instead, they are dominant codes with a high degree of correspondence with the official institutional ideology. As generic distinctions between news and fiction, and between different types of fiction are crucial for television companies, they also are for the audiences. Audiences meet the different genres with different expectations on how to find meaning in them, and which type of pleasures and type of knowledge they can expect.

Audiences' genre expectations relate very well to the concept of narrative verisimilitude within genre theory (see Neale, 1990). Expectations about popular fiction (especially American prime-time soap opera) is characterized by generic verisimilitude, that is, how things use to be narrated within the genre or what is believed to be plausible within the universe of the genre itself. Expectations about social–realistic fiction is characterized by sociocultural verisimilitude, that is, cognitions about what is believed to be plausible in different sociocultural contexts in the real world. Expectations about news are also characterized by sociocultural verisimilitude, although they more often are based on mediated cognitions rather than on personal everyday experiences. I therefore suggest that we add a third type of verisimilitude to the other two emanating from Todorov and discussed by Neale. We may talk about mediated sociocultural verisimilitude based on audience's vicarious "knowledge" about social phenomena, events, and courses of events in the world.

How, then, do we acquire genre expectations? The most important source are the texts themselves. By watching similar types of programs over and over again we build up cognitive schemas about genres. Other sources are different discourses on television; for example, conversations we take part in and magazine articles we read.

AUDIENCES´ INTERPRETATIONS OF GENRES

The reception interviews show how genre expectations usually are redeemed when viewers meet different texts, but there also are examples of how deviations in the texts from the typical of the genre override the expectations and activate other interpretation schemas.[5]

Stories within the American popular fiction[6] genre are interpreted as fabrications that bear very little relation to reality. The plots, the events, and the protagonists are given meaning in light of what the audience knows from earlier episodes or ideas about genre conventions, that is; how they perceive that things use to be within this narrative tradition:

---

[5]Examples of how textual deviations from the genre typical override audience´s expectations are given in Höijer (1995).

[6]Programs included in the qualitative studies have been an episode of "Falcon Crest" and the television film "Against all Odds," and in the survey "Falcon Crest" and "Dallas."

> I suppose it's a common trait for this kind of series. New plots emerge and then it all starts again from somewhere else. It's so typically American. You could see how she taught that guy a lesson. And then you could see in his eyes, and hear from the music, that he would go for a revenge. (male, senior civil servant)

> After all, she is disgusting, spoiled. But that's the part she has had all the time. Her thing is to be disgusting. After all, in this series all women are supposed to be very female and all men very male. (female, M.B.A.)

The interpretations focus on the plot and on the protagonists, who are attributed quite stereotypical characters, as indicated in the quotation above. It is rare that viewers´ own experiences are used as frames of reference for the interpretations, and viewers also rarely draw conclusions or generalize about social or human phenomena from the programs. Instead, intertextuality is the basis for the interpretations and the viewers devote themselves to the actions and events in the story. Below is a typical example on how viewers' thoughts revolve round the plot.

> He just keeps winning. That's how I thought. Everything is in his favor. I was surprised since I thought things would be rougher. But he just shoved him aside and then they became friends. Later the idea of blackmail struck me. At least that he would be able to consider it. And I never thought they would win those 25,000. That's what I thought. I thought something would happen. I also thought they might replace her or that he would report that NN was cheating. (male, blue collar worker)

The frames of reference used as interpreting schemas for narratives within the social-realistic genre[7] emanate from viewers´ personal spheres of experiences. The protagonists are perceived as socioculturally believable and they are interpreted in the light of everyday knowledge about human beings: "He was an unkind farmer, just like my grandfather," or "That terrible stubbornness. I started to think of a person I know." Similarly, the social setting, the events, and the plot are interpreted with reference to life itself and the audience also generalize from the program back to reality: "I recognise parts of the way they showed family relations. You can bring parts of it with you in real life." The audience gets involved in the narration in many ways, through identification and

---

[7]Programs included in the qualitative studies have been an episode from "Three Loves" and the television film "Ångslans boningar," both Swedish productions. The first one has been broadcasted in several other European countries. The survey included "Three Loves" and "Den goda viljan" (a Swedish series based on Ingmar Bergman's book about his parents).

recognition, through reading the persons and the social settings in depth, and through activation of oneself in the form of personal memories. On the whole, the interpretations are rich and deep and show personal involvement and generalizations. Below are two examples, one on how viewers read persons and another on how memories are activated:

> Well, when he (Anders) sat in the bus I thought, well, this is a thinking man. He could be, well, a Bohemian or such. He looked as if he was a thinking person, Bohemian. After all, he could have been an alcoholic or whatever. He could have been an odd person, the way he was sitting. Those thoughts remained but then he had done some more talking so I thought he became more and more of a normal person as he was walking along the road. Then Henry came out from the house. I asked myself what does he (Henry) want? I had the feeling that he was going to exploit him (Anders) in some way. This was my second thought, the first one was that he (Henry) was an alcoholic. That was an association from the beer can. When he appeared with it, I thought that he was somebody who was a drinker. (male, blue collar worker)

> This is my childhood. It's pieces of it. The whole '50s when I was a kid. The cars and the motor bikes and the cycles and the clothes. And the womens' hairdos. They were my aunts and my mother and father. They were those people. I remember the machines in the bakery. We lived next to a bakery. We kids ran around the bakery and they gave us bread crumbs and cookies and biscuits. I could feel the smell when I watched those scenes from the bakery. (male, senior civil servant)

In the interpretation of news, the audience also uses reality-based cognitive schemas, partly in the form of cultural schemas about human dramas and people from the private sphere, but mainly referring to cognitions about public persons and social and political phenomena in the public sphere. A specific characteristic of news reception is that it often is quite brief and sketchy, sometimes fragmentary, and not at all as coherent and elaborated as the reception of fiction. One reason could be that news is harder to interpret than fiction. Many studies have pointed at comprehension problems in the news (e.g. Findahl and Höijer, 1981; Gunter, 1987; Lewis, 1991).[8]

Viewers usually focus the events when interpreting news, but also persons, although they are not read as thoroughly as the persons in

---

[8]There are many factors involved here, for example, factors concerning structural, semantic and visual dimensions, and not least the fact that news generally addresses itself to well-informed and well-educated citizens.

social-realistic fiction. Generalizations are typical in relation to news, that is, in their minds viewers move from the program to the external world and draw some conclusion. The specific becomes generalized, sometimes in very concise or metaphoric form: "After all, you become disappointed with politicians. You really don't expect them to accomplish anything." "He was such a rolling stone. Cream of the cream." Other times the generalizations are more elaborate:

> I sat there thinking about the companies that Electrolux bought during several years. I thought this might be the reaction to it. They have expanded quite vigorously. I thought at least parts of this are repercussions from it. And then you start thinking about Sweden and the state of economics in it. It's a consumer goods industry. Refrigerators and consumer goods. Capital goods and such. That's certainly affected when the economy is going down. (male, M.B.A.)

Interestingly, not a single viewer questions the reality status of the news. Viewers can be critical and perceive news items as biased, but there is no doubt that news is considered as representations of reality.

As shown, there are large differences in both expectations and interpretations of different genres. The survey confirms this. The survey further shows that domestic—in this case Swedish—popular fiction places itself in between domestic social-realistic fiction and American popular fiction, but in many instances closer to the latter. For instance, in the survey 69% of the respondents reported that the statement "It's interesting to watch stories that could be real life" very often or most often is true in relation to social-realistic fiction. The corresponding figure for American popular fiction was only 18%, for Swedish popular fiction 30%, and for news a total of 85%. Another result is that 46% reported a high level of learning about human beings (a form of generalization) in relation to social-realistic fiction, 18% in relation to Swedish popular fiction, 8% in relation to American popular fiction and 59% in relation to news. 49% reported becoming greatly involved in social-realistic fiction, 20% in Swedish popular fiction, 12% in American popular fiction, and 57% in news.

If we compare the figures, these results show that there are smaller differences between domestic and American popular fiction than between domestic social-realistic and popular fiction. A conclusion is that cultural origin of the program plays a role in the reception but the narrative form, especially the dimension of realism, plays a more dominant role.

ON MEDIATING IN EXISTENTIAL DILEMMAS

According to Bruner (1990), good narratives may mediate between the norms of the culture and more idiosyncratic wishes, hopes, and conceptions of an individual. We are all part of inherited historical and cultural contexts, but we also take part in this social process as individuals carrying within us our subjective private identities. Processes of identification are important, but at the same time we experience ourselves and others as special, unique, different. Practically all human beings struggle with the dilemma to unite cultural and individual identities, and feelings of belongings go hand in hand with feelings of being an outsider. Most probably many, at least in Western societies, carry strong feelings of alienation within them. After all, Freud in his old age wrote the book *Das Unbehagen in der Kultur* (*Civilization and its Discontents*).

The contradiction between culture and individual exists in all human beings and, according to Lévi–Strauss (1967), in all narratives.

Television narratives within the social-realistic genre invite the audience to learn something about being a human being, that is, being an individual in a culture. The viewers find connections between the narratives and their own experiences, processes of recognition and identification are activated, and generalizations turn up in their minds. We may call this a process of *creative illusion*; that is, an imaginative impression of reality (Höijer, 1991). In this way the narrative may mediate between the individual and the cultural identity of the viewer, and work on the personal dilemma of uniting these contradictory identities. By interpreting others and taking part in how they solve their dilemmas, we may enrich our own lives.

More glamorous popular fiction is a more closing narrative form. The viewers' own social realities are rarely brought into the interpretation process, and in their minds the viewers do not move from the narratives to the external world. Intertextuality dominates and makes the narrative meaningful. Elsewhere I have called this process *pleasurable forgetfulness* (Höijer, 1991). As viewers we may for a while forget our own identities and struggles in life and devote ourselves to the story: "I wondered if he was going to report him. Was he never going to be able to get that amount?" The genre can hardly mediate the dilemma between the individual and culture. In Eco´s sense, they are closed texts that pull "the reader along a predetermined path, carefully displaying their effects so as to arouse pity or fear, excitement or depression at the due place and at the right moment" (1984: 8).

The news genre also quite seldom mediates in our personal identity building. We rarely start to remember experiences from the present and past. We usually keep ourselves outside. But contrary to popular fiction, news opens the mind for learning and generalizations about the sociopolitical world. In our minds we immediately start to think about social phenomena in reality, we draw conclusions, and we build opinions—"You can't trust politicians." According to Jensen (1988), we build super-themes. The whole process is directed towards *reality testing* in the public sphere. There is a large variation, however, among news items. We can always find examples on news stories that are closer to everyday life and of more personal concern to the audience. In such cases our personal identities may very well be involved in the reception process.

ON TEXT AND GENRE

The different processes characterized above run spontaneously in our minds when we meet the genre in question, and a change of genre will inevitably change the direction of the reception process. Interpretation and thought processes are hard to rule by the subject, that is, consciously. They just happen as a result of the interaction between the text and the viewers' collected, self-witnessed and vicarious experiences in the form they are given. Every experience is interpreted and each can only work via our conscious and unconscious cognitive-affective structures. Attitudes and emotions are always part of both our inner world and of our interpretations of the world.

Interestingly, the reality status of a genre seems to increase its emotional power. The viewers became much more emotionally involved in the social-realistic fiction compared to glamorous nonrealistic prime-time soap opera, a result that is confirmed by other studies (Livingstone, 1988; Silj et al., 1988). The reception study further showed that viewers also became emotionally engaged in the news. In fact, in the representative survey study, a majority of the audience (57%) claim that they usually become very much concerned when they watch the news, closely followed by social-realistic fiction (49% usually become very much involved), and that they are much less engaged by both domestic and American popular fiction (only 20% and 12% respectively report that they usually get emotionally engaged). In other studies viewers have reported very strong feelings evoked by violent news, such as stories about innocent victims in Bosnia. There are, however, large differences in reactions; for example, between men and women and between older and younger viewers (Höijer, 1994). Among the viewers I have also often met a high degree of emotional involvement in relation to expository and documentary genres (Höijer, 1986; 1992a). Similarly, Bondebjerg argues for a close connection between realism and emotional involvement:

To say that fiction appeals to imagination and emotion through a direct identification with the story and the characters, and that non-fiction mainly addresses the rational side of reality, truth and arguments is only partly true. In fact documentaries may possess strong emotional identification possibilities, and strong narrative structure, and the reality-status may even increase the emotional impact. (1994: 77)

Apparently, realism invites the audiences to open their minds for emotional involvement, whether it is in fiction or nonfiction genres. When we interpret something as real or socioculturally trustworthy, we also activate our attitudes towards the social world, our emotions and moral standpoints that are inseparable parts of our cognitions. As adults we are without doubt personally involved in social reality, in which we struggle to find meaning, and our wishes and pipe dreams usually have some relation to reality as well. As a child our fantasies may be occupied with having wings so we can fly, but as grown-ups our daydreams bear a more realistic signature. We think about having a good life in terms of inspiring or well-paid work, we dream of a summer house, an interesting journey, that our children will be healthy and happy, and so forth.

Thus, the studies very clearly show a strong influence of the text on audiences' receptions, and texts can be seen as quite powerful in the interaction with audiences. I would, however, warn against textual determinism. A text invites the audience to take a certain spectator position. It invites the audience to interpret it within specific areas of cognitive experiential schemas, and invites the audience to think and associate in certain directions, to get emotionally involved or keep a more distant viewer position. The viewer, on the other hand, meets the text with preconceptions or expectations about how to find meaning in the text as genre, and with all his/her personal and cultural experiences, which also may include some specific knowledge about the text in question. Since genre conventions are quite firm structures and different genres narrate differently, audience expectations usually fit the text quite well, and we will find general patterns in viewers receptions that differentiate between genres.

At the same time, there are social and individual differences in viewers receptions due to variations in personal and cultural experiences. Not all viewers will, of course, remember their childhood when watching "Three Loves" and recognize their aunts and uncles; viewers will notice different parts of the story, interpret persons differently, and so forth. The point is, however, that the overall frame of reference on an abstract level will be similar. It will, for instance, be much more common to build one's interpretations on private sphere experiences in relation to social-realistic fiction, on textual experiences in relation to popular fiction, and on mediated knowledge on public sphere in relation to news. These differences are results of the influence of the texts. However, this is not to see these texts in isolation. Texts are cultural products and bear relations to other texts, as well as to the social world and the audience. They belong to genres. A text both puts constraints on which meanings viewers will find and invites viewers to make different cultural and individual interpretations.

We obviously need a concept of meaning that takes both "the presented meaning" and "the constructed meaning" into account (Lindlof, 1988). Among philosophers, Schaff´s (1962) account of meaning offers a possibility to avoid the pitfalls in both textual determinism and extreme constructivism. Schaff conceives of meaning as consisting of a web of complex social relations and stresses that meaning is inextricably bound up with both signs and the people who use them.

It is a challenge for mass media research to learn a new paradigm of "both/and" rather than the old conflict paradigm "either/or," which will not lift academic research to a higher level. We need research that at the same time recognizes levels and aspects in which texts as genres are powerful and put constraints on the audience and levels and aspects in which audiences themselves are powerful and work on the text.

REFERENCES

Abrahamsson, U. B. (1993) "När kvinnor ser på TV" (When Women Watch Television). In U. Carlsson, ed. *Nordisk forskning om kvinnor och medier.* Gothenburg: Nordicom–Sverige, No. 3: 93-110.

Ang, I. (1985) *Watching "Dallas."* London: Routledge.

Attallah, P. (1984) "The Unworthy Discourse. Situation Comedy in Television." In W.D. Rowland, Jr. and B. Watkins, eds. *Interpreting Television: Current Research Perspectives.* Beverly Hills: Sage: 223-49

Barwise, P. and A. Ehrenberg (1988) *Television and its Audience.* London: Sage.

Bondebjerg, I. (1994) "Narratives of Reality. Documentary Film and Television in a Cognitive and Pragmatic Perspective," *Nordicom Review, 1,* 65-87.

Bogart, L. (1980) "Television News as Entertainment." In P. H. Tannenbaum, ed. *The Entertainment Functions of Television.* Hillsdale, NJ: Erlbaum: 209-49.

Bruner, J. (1986) *Actual Minds, Possible Worlds.* Cambridge, MA: Harvard University Press

——— (1990) *Acts of Meaning.* Cambridge, MA: Harvard University Press.

Cappella, J.N. and R.L. Street Jr. (1989). "Message Effects. Theory and Research on Mental Models of Messages." In J. J. Bradac, ed. *Message Effects in Communication Science.* Newbury Park, CA: Sage: 24-51.

Corner, J. (1991) "Meaning, Genre and Context: The Problematics of 'Public Knowledge' in the New Audience Studies." In J. Curran and M. Gurevitch, eds. *Mass Media and Society.* London: Edward Arnold: 267-84.

Dahlgren, P. (1995) *Television and the Public Sphere. Citizenship, Democracy and the Media.* London: Sage

Eco, U. (1984). *The Role of the Reader. Explorations in the Semiotics of Texts.* Bloomington: Indiana University Press.

Ellis, J. (1982). *Visible Fictions.* London: Routledge.

von Feilitzen, C. (1994). "Media Violence—Research Perspectives in the 1980s." In C. J. Hamelink and O. Linné, eds. *Mass Communication Research: On Problems and Policies. The Art of Asking the Right Questions.* Norwood, NJ: Ablex: 147-70.

Fetveit, A. (1996) "Anti-essentialisme og receptionsforskning: Ett forsvar for teksten (Anti-Essentialism and Reception Research)," *Mediekultur, 24,* 61-73.

Findahl, O. and B. Höijer (1981) "Studies of News from the Perspective of Human Comprehension," *Mass Communication Review Yearbook, 2,* 393-403.

Fiske, J. (1987) *Television Culture.* London: Methuen.

Gunter, B. (1987) *Poor Reception. Misunderstanding and Forgetting Broadcast News.* Hillsdale, NJ: LEA.

Hagen, I. (1994) "The Ambivalence of TV News Viewing: Between Ideals and Everyday Practices," *European Journal of Communication, 9,* 193-220.

Hawkins, R. and S. Pingree (1990) "Divergent Psychological Processes in Constructing Social Reality from Mass Media Content." In N. Signorielli and M. Morgan, eds. *Cultivation Analysis. New Directions in Media Effects Research.* Newbury Park, CA: Sage: 35-50.

Höijer, B. (1986) *The In-Depth Interview as a Method for Studying Programme Comprehension and Audience Response.* Stockholm: Swedish Broadcasting Corporation, Audience and Programme Research Department, Rep. No. 5.

——— (1990) "Studying Viewers' Reception of Television Programmes: Theoretical and Methodological Considerations," *European Journal of Communication, 5*(1), 29-56.

——— (1991) *Lustfylld glömska, kreativ illusion och realitetsprövning. Om publikens tankeprocesser vid tittandet på fiktion och fakta (Pleasurable Forgetfulness, Creative Illusion and Reality-Testing.*

About Viewers 'Thought Processes in Relation to Different Genres). Stockholm: Swedish Broadcasting Corporation, Audience and Programme Research Department, Rep. No. 15.

—— (1992a) "Socio-Cognitive Structures and Television Reception," *Media, Culture and Society, 14*, 583-603.

—— (1992b) "Reception of Television Narration as a Socio-Cognitive Process: A Schema-Theoretical Outline," *Poetics, 21*, 283-304.

—— (1994) *Våldsskildringar i TV-nyheter (Depictions of Violence on Television News)*. University of Stockholm: Department of Journalism, Media and Communication, Rep. No. 5.

—— (1995) *Genreföreställningar och tolkningar av berättande i TV (Genre Expectations and Interpretations of Television Narration)*. University of Stockholm: Department of Journalism, Media and Communication, Rep. No. 1.

Höijer, B., K. Nowak and S. Ross (1992) "Reception of Television as a Cognitive and Cultural Process," *Nordicom Information, 2*, 9-22.

Jensen, K.B. (1986). *Making Sense of the News*. Aarhus: Aarhus University Press.

—— (1988) "News as Social Research: A Qualitative Empirical Study of the Reception of Danish Television News," *European Journal of Communication, 3*(3), 275-301.

Lévi-Strauss, C. (1967) *Structural Anthropology*. New York: Doubleday/Anchor.

Lewis, J. (1991) *The Ideological Octopus. An Exploration of Television and Its Audience*. London: Routledge.

Liebes, T. and E. Katz (1993) *The Export of Meaning. Cross-Cultural Readings of "Dallas."* Cambridge, UK: Polity Press.

Lindlof, T.R. (1988) "Media Audiences as Interpretive Communities." In J.A. Anderson, ed. *Communication Yearbook, 11*, 81-107.

Livingstone, S.M. (1988) "Why People Watch Soap Opera: An Analysis of the Explanations of British Viewers," *European Journal of Communication, 3*(1), 55-80.

—— (1989) "Interpretive Viewers and Structured Programs," *Communication Research, 16*, 25-57.

—— (1990) *Making Sense of Television. The Psychology of Audience Interpretation*. Oxford: Pergamon Press.

McQuail, D. (1994) *Mass Communication Theory*. London: Sage.

Mendelsohn, H. (1989) "Socio-Psychological Construction and the Mass Communication Effects Dialectic," *Communication Research, 16*, 813-823.

Morley, D. (1980) The "Nationwide" Audience. *Television Monograph, 11*, British Film Institute.

Neale, S. (1990). "Questions of Genre," *Screen, 31*(1), 45-66.

Piaget, J. (1926/1955) *The Language and Thought of the Child.* Cleveland: Meridian Books.

Reber, A. S. (1985) *Dictionary of Psychology.* London: Penguin Books.

Rosengren, K. E., L. A. Wenner and P. Palmgreen, eds. (1985) *Media Gratifications Research: Current Perspectives.* Beverly Hills, CA: Sage.

Ross, S. (1993) *Television and Interpretations of Class: Some Preliminary Findings.* Paper presented at the XI Nordic Conference in Mass Communication, Trondheim, 8-11 August.

Schaff, A. (1962) *Introduction to Semantics.* New York: Pergamon.

Schramm, W. (1949) "The Nature of News," *Journalism Quarterly, 26,* 259-69.

Schrøder, K. (1988) "The Pleasure of Dynasty." In P. Drummond and R. Paterson, eds. *Television and Its Audiences: International Research Perspectives.* London: British Film Institute.

Signorielli, N. and M. Morgan, eds. (1990) *Cultivation Analysis. New Directions in Media Effects Research.* Newbury Park, CA: Sage.

Silj, A. et. al. (1988) *East of "Dallas." The European Challenge to American Television.* London: British Film Institute.

Stern, D. N. (1985) *The Interpersonal World of the Infant. A View from Psychoanalysis and Developmental Psychology.* New York: Basic Books.

Vygotsky, L. (1934/1986) *Thought and Language.* Cambridge, MA: The MIT Press.

Wenner, L.A. (1985) "The Nature of News Gratifications." In K. E. Rosengren, L. A. Wenner and P. Palmgreen, eds. *Media Gratifications Research: Current Perspectives.* Beverly Hills, CA: Sage: 171-93.

11

The Role of Media in Generating Alternative Political Projects

Robert A. White

Over the last 10 to 15 years much of the discussion regarding the relative independence of audience interpretations of the mass media text has tended to take an either-or perspective: either the text is capable of controlling interpretations or the audience is quite free to reject, reinterpret, or willingly accept the preferred reading. The same dichotomous perspective is present in other debates. Is the audience made up of isolated, more easily manipulated individuals or are audiences (or publics) constituted by interactive networks developed around genres. Is the audience typically grazing across channels to pick up spot impressions or do most members of the audiences have at least some programs that they become emotionally attached to and involved with (Jenkins, 1992: 54-60)?

Most of these contrasting approaches emerge out of the tradition of critical media research and are concerned with the question of how the media affect the political autonomy of individuals or groups and how the media affect the process of democratization of social structures that make autonomous movements for social equity possible. The "pow-erful-ideology" line of research has showed how the media is part of a political-economic hegemony that restricts the range of opposition opin-ion and gains public consent through the institutions that are supposed to promote public debate and dissent (Hall, 1977). This tradition has made less clear how either mainstream or alternative media can con-tribute to the formation of autonomous alternative political projects. The "powerful-audience" tradition of research has argued that the audience, taking advantage of the open and questioning text of the media, gener-ates opinions in opposition to the preferred hegemonic reading and that this opposition is already a form of political action (Fiske, 1987). An extension of the oppositional reception thesis argues that audiences of genres such as women's daytime soap opera form interactive networks and articulate a critical, dissident subculture that is a form of autonomous political action. At least, the dissident subculture is a form of domestic politics that provides a basis for social and political change (Brown, 1994).

Colleagues have rightly questioned whether oppositional read-ings constitute a form of political autonomy even when this is articulated by discussion networks into a dissident subculture. There is very little evidence that the oppositional readings generate an alternative political project and that this contributes to political change (Morley, 1992: 22-32).

There has been relatively little progress in seeing the relation-ships of the poles, in part, I would suggest, because research has tend-ed to isolate the focus upon one factor: the political-economic structure of broadcasting, the text, the audience interpretation, or small interper-sonal networks in relative isolation (Livingstone, 1998: 245). Reception studies have become a kind of ritual of in depth interviewing of 25 fami-lies or individuals in isolation from other individuals regarding interpreta-tions and uses of particular genres.

There are significant instances, I would argue, when mass media have stimulated oppositional readings of the culture that have contributed to an alternative political project. One of the noteworthy examples is the role of popular music in articulating a political opposition to the Vietnam War and to hegemonic ideologies. Ironically, another case, at the opposite end of the cultural-political spectrum, is the role of the electronic church in articulating a movement among largely rural, lower-status, less educated people who feel marginalized in American society (Horsfield, 1984; Hoover, 1988). In these and similar cases, the media influence is only one factor among many. If we are to understand under what conditions the media are likely to be a factor in articulating oppositional readings of the culture and helping to transform this dissi-dence into an alternative political project and movement, we need to locate media and audience reception within a broader theory of sociopolitical change.

In the present analysis, I would like to sketch out a more comprehensive framework of interrelated factors that constitute a dynamic, continually changing construction of culture.

Within this more comprehensive perspective, I have chosen to focus more on the current research dealing with interactive networks around particular genres and how these networks begin to move from a dissident discourse based on a sense of dissident personal and cultural identity to a reconstructed text that presents an alternative social ideal. The crucial point of the move out of an oppositional discourse that simply "celebrates our suffering" to a discourse that proposes a social and, implicitly, a political organization that respects an identity is the moment when the discourse networks around media such as fan clubs begin to produce their own alternative media (Jenkins, 1992). The degree of impact of the alternative text depends on how much the culture industries see the alternatives as a significant market.

In developing this framework, I have found the theory and practice of Freire's education for liberation to be helpful in understand the role of media discussion groups and networks in political projects.

A THEORETICAL FRAMEWORK FOR EXPLAINING THE CONTRIBUTION OF MEDIA TO ALTERNATIVE POLITICAL MOVEMENTS

In the limited space of this chapter, I would like to outline eight major sets of factors that explain conditions under which the media are more likely to articulate the dissident feelings of groups suffering social injustice into an alternative political project and motivate a movement to bring about social change.

1. Political-economic factors: The degree of concentration of hegemonic and ideological power.
2. Strategies of attracting audiences that invite audiences to take possession of the text.
3. The degree to which media genres present the symbols and narratives from the "inside" perspective of audiences.
4. The degree to which the media text "invites" audiences to become aware of their subjective identities and to appropriate that identity positively.
5. The degree to which members of the audience are part of a marginal social group that has its own alternative social mediations.

6. The conditions in which audiences are more likely to habitually deconstruct the media text in terms of their own personal and cultural identities and create an alternative discourse in their network.
7. The creation of alternative media to express identities and the degree to which this alternative media becomes more widely distributed in the subcultural network and in the mass media
8. Factors in the formation of an alternative sociopolitical movement.

THE DEGREE OF CONCENTRATION OF POLITICAL-ECONOMIC AND CULTURAL HEGEMONY

Cultural hegemony is a shifting set of alliances among major cultural fronts that gives this alliance the power to impose agreement and unity regarding the kind of society the allied groups wish to construct (González, 1994). The hegemonic unity, with the implied patriotism and sacrifice for the community, is maintained as long as the cultural fronts feel that their cultural capital based on their cultural identity is given equity. The problematic that cultural hegemony faces is the continual changes in cultural identity and the appearance of new major cultural actors. The agents of cultural hegemony attempt to bring the new actors into the alliance by recognizing enough of their cultural capital in order to gain their support of the alliance.

Various social conditions may make it difficult to admit new cultural fronts to a hegemonic alliance and adapt the dominant cultural myth to recognize the value of diverse cultural capital. A society may be faced with deeply conflicting cultural, religious, and linguistic groups so that one group or a small set of dominant interests gains control and permanently excludes other groups. In the face of rapid social change, a society may not have the fluid communication to adapt and change its cultural myth, especially the narrative texts that redefine heroes, intermediaries, and the images of community reintegration. Minority social groups may not be able to mount a communication system to define and project its cultural capital as valuable for the society and thus make a bid for entry.

Recent studies have shown that virtually all of the above factors were acting in South Africa to open the hegemonic cultural dominance of white Afrikaners to the cultural capital of black Africans: diversity and conflict among the Afrikaners, non-Afrikaner, and Asian members of the hegemonic alliance; a long period of rigid exclusion of the blacks that forced them to mount an alternative movement and define clearly their cultural identity and cultural capital; the good alternative communication of Black Africans and the ability of South African writers and film makers to project the cause internationally; the breakdown of the belief in apartheid myth among Afrikaners; the process of industrialization and rapid modernization in South Africa; and, more recently, a media system that projects a narrative text of multiracial South Africa (Louw, 1994).

STRATEGIES OF ATTRACTING AUDIENCES

Certain genres of popular culture such as women's daytime soap opera, pop music aimed at a specific age group, and science fiction are designed to attract audience identification. Soap opera, for example, tends to incorporate women's discourse and to be oriented in the plot lines, character construction and emotional tone to the subculture of the women who follow this programming. It is well known that the producers of soap opera pay great attention to audience reaction to character, plot line, and the attractiveness of certain episodes (Cantor and Pingree, 1983; Harrington and Bielby, 1995).

To understand audience loyalty to genres, I have found useful Stuart Hall's recent discussion of identity.

> I use "identity" (states Hall) to refer to the meeting point, the point of suture, between, on the one hand, the discourses and practices which attempt to "interpellate," speak to us or hail us into place as the social subjects of particular discourses, and, on the other hand, the processes which produce subjectivities, which construct as subjects which can be "spoken." . . . Identities are, as it were, the positions which the subject is obliged to take up while always "knowing" (the language of consciousness here betrays us) that they are representations, that representation is always constructed across a "lack," across a division, from the place of the Other, and thus can never be adequate—identical—to the subjective processes which are invested in them. (Hall, 1996: 5-6)

Thus, identities are always being explored, always being constructed, and always being questioned in terms of the texts, the patterns of significance in the popular culture around us. The mass media are only the more concentrated, more explicitly narrative, and more symbolically powerful instances of this addressing of subjects.

The most avid fan networks generally build up around that programming that is oriented toward specific audience subcultural identities, and the audience often "takes possession" of the programming. In general, the stronger the subculture sees its identity reflected in the text, the more likely that the fans will form groups to "rewrite" the text from the perspective of their own identities. The most evident cases are the followers of specific youth music genres who form their own musical producing groups. These genres receive far more fan mail commenting on the text and requesting specific changes or even engaging in battles with the producers about how the program should be developed (Jenkins, 1992). When the producers of the program *The Beauty and the Beast* tried to change the plot line and main characters to broaden the appeal of the program to a larger and more diverse audience (demands of the advertisers), the fans staged demonstrations and did everything possible to block this.

What is significant in these cases is that audiences do not only form alternative interpretations in a passive way, but they become producers of alternative media to represent their identities.

A MEDIA TEXT PRESENTING THE "INSIDE" PERSPECTIVE OF AUDIENCES

The commercial media industry is primarily concerned to ensure profits by delivering audiences to advertisers and is interested in audience preferences only to the extent that this is profitable. Although public media claims that its primary motive is service to the needs and interests of the audience, historically the priority is national cultural unity. Most media is aimed at as broad an audience as possible and no one cultural identity is served. It serves the interests of mass media to be politically, religiously, ethnically, regionally, and socially neutral. Mass media is entertaining, but it is designed not to articulate and rouse up identities and resentments with political implications—unless it is profitable.

The popular "youth music" industry is an example where it has paid the media to present music from the inside perspective of youth culture, no matter how outrageous this might seem. Singers are young people who live in youth culture and have a large degree of freedom to follow young people's sensibilities. This representation of youth culture has political implications that one can understand better by examining the Freirian media theory.

Paulo Freire observed that the use of manuals and reading materials designed for urban children left workers and farmers uninspired and dulled (Freire, 1990). The literacy education necessary to vote did not awaken the necessary critical thinking in terms of their own interests, but, instead, left them apathetic and easily manipulated. Freire decided to design educational materials built around the deep personal and social interests of these poor farmers. He first did a survey of what themes and words were closest to their emotional world, and these were used in the literacy process. Words like "terra" (land) that the peasants have worked with daily all of their lives tapped into a rich vein of feeling and imagination. To mention the word "land" in a friendly context would quickly spark off a lively discussion.

Likewise, rock music, with its beat and its lyrics, seems to tap into deep veins of adolescent feeling of celebration but also resentment, rebellion, confusion, and discouragement. Not only does the music give young people a sense of expansive liberation where they can be what they feel like being, but it articulates a level of firm defense of the right to chart one's own life.

MEDIA THAT "INVITES" AUDIENCES TO BECOME AWARE OF THEIR SUBJECTIVE IDENTITIES AND TO AFFIRM THOSE IDENTITIES

Rock music culture not only taps into deep adolescent feelings, but it creates a "friendly space of freedom" in discos and other youth meeting places, in massive rock concerts that are for youth, or in "my" room with my friends. Here, away from adults and other socialization agents, young people can bring their feelings to the surface and let themselves feel them.

Paulo Freire's "pedagogy of the oppressed" is pertinent because it is built around an assumption of identities that are unarticulated because any open expression will bring punishment (Freire, 1989). Generally the educational text is designed not only to warn students not to express their identities, but rather to internalize the dominant hegemonic cultural identity. Many subordinate groups have so deeply repressed the affirmation of the value of their identity that they take for granted the negative image of their own social identities. One of the classic cases are the lower castes of India, who internalize as natural their position in society. Underlying this education for repression is the ideology that only dominant groups are capable of participation in the creation of the national culture. The objective of the Freirian pedagogy is to bring subordinate groups to the conviction that all social identities are important in the creation of a highly pluralistic culture and that all identities have a right to be expressed in cultures.

In this context of deep repression and deep internalization of the negative value of identity, the Freirian method works with assumptions that are relevant for understanding the role of oppositional readings of media: That agents of hegemony design texts—the educational text and virtually all the signification of popular culture—that try to avoid signification that touches on areas of identity and that might bring subjects to reflect on their identity. In part this is due to the fact that subordinate groups have no control over the design of these texts.

An important step in the Freirian approach is to create a space of freedom in which small groups of like-minded friends can express themselves without fear of repression. The starting point for a discussion might be a collectively felt problem, but eventually the group uses a text that they have designed as a representation of the situation in which the problem exists. The discussion focuses on the meaning of the text as each honestly sees it. The discussion encourages each of the participants to speak from feelings and from personal experience so that deep identities are allowed to come into play. If the group shares a common identity, this will come forward.

The group may begin with one text (group media), but then continually reformulate this until they feel that it represents the situation as they see it through their identities. What emerges is not just negative feelings, but the inchoative formulation of a community and a society as they ideally would like to see it.

One of the main reasons why the Freirian method encourages its participants to desire a different kind of social scenario is that they experience profoundly a different kind of social relation. The Freirian pedagogy very much stresses the procedures of equal participation—horizontal communication—but especially dialogue; that is, response to the expression of identity by others. Even if there is disagreement, at least the identity is responded to. The Freirian pedagogy seeks to develop such a profound sense of the dignity, freedom, and creativity of other persons that exploitation of others would be unthinkable. The goal is not simply to get power, but to seek a distribution of various sources of power, especially cultural capital.

Some of the best analyses of the experience of discovering subjectivities are in the descriptions of popular music and identifications (Frith, 1996; Simpson, 1996). Simpson, a young white male, affirms that he has discovered himself and feels most at home with himself when listening to rap music (Simpson, 1996). Frith quotes the British music critic, Frank Kogan, talking about an American rap musician: "Spoonie Gee is not one of us. He has nothing to do with punk culture or post-punk culture . . . (but) listening to Spoonie Gee is like listening to my own feelings, and I have to confront my own fear. This maybe means that I'm not really unlike him. Maybe I'm more like him than I am like you" (Kogan in Frith, 1996: 112-13).

CREATING SOCIAL NETWORKS AROUND MEDIA LOYALTIES

Recent research confirms the development of informal interacting discussion networks among media users, especially in the minority genres mentioned above (Brown, 1994; Lull, 1988, 1990). Like the Freirian discussion groups developed around an alternative text, these networks of like-minded friends provide a space of freedom apart from threatening dissenters or punishing authority figures. Women talking about their favorite soap opera or young people enjoying the music that their parents or school teachers dislike so much can "let down their hair" and let their feelings and identities come to the surface. Fan networks are often groups of people that "straight" people would consider batty or deviant (Jenkins, 1992).

From the research on audience fans, these discussion networks could best be described as being prepolitical; that is, that they create the social conditions that could link these media users into active political movements:

- The discussion networks deal with present social, cultural or political issues, and often represent minority opposition groups. If the media articulates an affirmation of identity, the discussion groups link a sense of identity to their social conditions.
- The discussion networks set up a structure for exchange of information and for opinion formation that can be nationwide.
- The discussion networks are built around common cultural identity symbols and form the basis for mass movements and for projecting identity symbols into the public sphere.
- The discussion networks develop a media-wise people, who gain media literacy, greater knowledge of how the media work, an affirmation of identifications in media use, critical analysis of media, and the ability to create alternative media. The networks develop people who know how to use media and how to influence media or how to use media for influence (Melucci, 1989).
- In some cases the discussion networks may create a leadership and decision-making structure.
- If these networks exist before the common media interest and have a long-established interpretative discourse and independence strategies, then the subculture and solidarity will enable the group to use the media text to generate oppositional interpretations. For example, women's networks around soap opera emerged out of networks of socioemotional support and with an inside language and knowledge kept from the male members of family and community (Brown, 1994).

It is important to stress, however, that these discussion networks are prepolitical, because rarely are they organized to bring about social change and they rarely enter into the public political arena. If, however, these media activated networks are made up of people who are part of a political movement or a movement that has political changes as one of its goals, then the interaction of the media network with the underlying sociopolitical network can provide explosive energy and link the political network into the center of media attention. The counterculture movements in the 1960s and 1970s had roots in a long-standing literary cultural Romantic movement stretching back into the 19th century, and became a dissident political movement in the 1950s. The counterculture movement fed upon issues such as opposition to the Vietnam War among young people, but the rock music network was a major factor in transforming this into a mass movement (Martin, 1981).

Likewise the neo-evangelical fundamentalist movement in the United States was relatively unimportant and lacked energy until people such as Billy Graham and the other televangelists built up the media-connected network. The media network with organizations such as the "700 Club" fed an immense multimedia infrastructure of local charitable action groups, counseling groups, schools, and then political action groups directly mobilized through the media. The power of the movement lies in this infrastructure of local groups and these are the force for "converts", but the public identity symbols giving force and unity are the televangelists (Hoover, 1988; Horsfield, 1984).

One of the reasons that certain sociopolitical movements blossom into a media-related movement is that there is an underlying orientation toward the media in the movement. The counterculture movement was rooted in a literary, poetic mystique that found a new form of popular music a congenial form of public and popular manifestation (Martin, 1981). The theology of the evangelical movement is to preach the gospel to the whole world, and this theology orients the movement toward the mass media (Hoover, 1988).

DECONSTRUCTING THE MEDIA TEXT IN TERMS OF PERSONAL AND CULTURAL IDENTITIES.

Much of the recent research on audience reception has outlined the various deconstruction strategies that audiences, especially loyal fans, use to enjoy a genre or program. This research has established that most audience members are interacting to some degree in their interpretation of the media and that deconstruction and reconstruction is the work of networks of media users. By *deconstruction* I mean the various collective interactive hermeneutical strategies that audience networks use to understand (1) the constructed meaning supposedly built into the text, (2) what the text expects from the audience, (3) what the audience expects from the text in terms of its own identities and experience, and (4) the exploration and recognition of identities through the text. In other words, *deconstruction* centers around recognition and exploration of personal and collective identities through the text, but there is little proactive projection of identities except perhaps to recognize that we are a subordinate group and we are not happy with being a subordinate group.

I would argue that the way audiences deconstruct and reconstruct mass media texts is of crucial importance in using media for sociopolitical change, because in this process audiences begin to individually and collectively elaborate an alternative social project. Indeed, this kind of deconstruction and reconstruction to formulate an alternative vision of society in terms of one's own cultural identity is the heart of the Freirian education for liberation. At the point in the process of the Freirian approach where student participants typically begin to go more deeply into the *causes* of the problems they are experiencing, the participants produce a visual representation of the situation in which they live and the obstacles to resolving the problems they face. This may be sociodrama, sound-slides, a video, an audio cassette, or posters. A nondirective animator simply asks the the small group to look carefully at what they see and what they see as the causes of the problems portrayed. All who have worked with the Freiran process know that this moment of decoding the meaning of the life context is electric—an explosion of insight and emotion, but also joy of discovery. At this point the interrelations and causes began to be clear. Participants no longer have a vague "magical" understanding (to use the Freirian term) of the causes and solutions to their problems—as if some incantation could help—but a critical understanding of the problem and the beginning of clear idea of what to do.

Reception studies, especially in connection with efforts of media education for critical use of the media, are beginning to reveal a process of deconstruction by audiences very similar to that suggested in the Freirian method. Obviously, the use of media in leisure time is less intentional—without the benefit of a group animator—but the fact that audiences tend to follow their favorite genres very closely and very faithfully with very considerable discussion in the fan networks about the media text suggests that the network discussions are a reasonable substitute for the focused discussions. The crucial part of the deconstruction is learning to read the media in terms of one's own personal and cultural identity. The role of the focus group animator and of the discussion network is to help media users to read media in terms of their identity. An important element in the formulation of an alternative sociopolitical project is a thorough exploration of personal and cultural identities, a firm appropriation of that identity, and a carefully constructed new vision in harmony with social identities in a way that respects the rights of others.

There are a number of dimensions in this deconstruction that seem particularly important.

Decoding

A first strategy is simply interpreting the various cultural codes employed. This brings into play not only the considerable knowledge of the genre but can also build upon virtually all of the knowledge of popular culture. What is particularly interesting to audiences is the introduction of new languages and expansion of the conventions of the genre. Some of the analyses of the very open, so-called "postmodern" programming such as *Twin Peaks* becomes particularly intriguing to audiences because the pattern of the culture is itself being questioned. This aspect of decoding is not simply an exploration of the innovations of the media, but a scanning of the innovations in the culture (Brown, 1996)

Reception analysis reveals that the most salient aspect of decoding is the testing of the narrative structure against various dimensions of personal and collective identity to get the "emotional correctness" of the text (Jenkins, 1992), the moral sense of the text (Livingstone, 1990), the consistency in terms of cause-effect, and the "real-world" plausibility in terms of what my identities say is "real" (Brown, 1994). Audiences are aware that all media is a selective construction; what they are testing is whether the selectivity and the construction is what it "should be." Audiences of particular genres are aware that the program is aimed at them, so they have a right to enjoy and agree with what is presented. They are also judging which way the culture should go and want it to open a space for their identities, too. Much of the reconstruction by fan groups emerges from a disagreement with the construction that is perceived.

Knowledge About the Production Processes

Apart from the textual discourse, audiences are bringing to bear all of their knowledge of the construction outside of the textual discourse: casting decisions, private lives of the actors, production quality, ratings, internal disagreements within production and broadcasting organizations, public media policy and virtually anything else about the industry deemed pertinent. Audiences get this information from all of what Fiske (1987) has called the secondary text, but one of the main functions of the social network is to pool the available knowledge. Audiences are quite aware of the arguments that they are being manipulated through the media, so they want to gather all possible information about the decisions in order to situate themselves to judge the actions of the culture industry. For many people, of course, it is not all that important to know if there is manipulation, but for those who become deeply involved emotionally in a genre like soap opera, audiences want to maintain their independence and distance as much as possible while they enjoy it (Brown, 1994).

Ultimately, the major criterion for the justice of what the culture industry offers is the sense of identity and familiarity with the matter presented. Many follow certain genres such as sport or action adventure because these are areas that are important to them and areas they know something about. The whole complex of parallel media helps them know much more about, for example, the world of sport. These audiences feel involved with this cultural area and, because of the enjoyment, want to monitor its development.

Reevaluating the Cultural Capital of One's Favorite Media

Virtually every kind of popular culture is denigrated by some elite sectors: sports (its brutality), soap opera (cheap production quality, sentimentality), action adventure (violence), religion (gullibility), situation comedy (superficiality), and so forth. In the final analysis, this is a judgment on the people who enjoy this kind of media or genre, and the most direct expression of the denigration is conflict within the domestic circles. Husbands are denigrating wives for their "poor taste"; wives, their husbands; parents, their children; and children, their parents. There may be attempts to justify the interests in terms of the national culture, hegemonic as it is (soap opera, after all, is part of our melodramatic cultural tradition that expresses our common identity), or the group may simply seize upon the negated aspect as a symbol of independence and the right to particular tastes (Brown, 1994).

The right to independence in one's tastes and the affirmation of the equal value of all subcultures is at the heart of our postmodern cultural ethos. This is a rejection of the premise that our societal (national) unity depends on one overarching hegemonic cultural mythos. There is no culture with a capital "C." Everybody has a right to his or her own set of values. In this there is a great deal of exploration of the dimensions of cultural identities in terms of pleasure and how I feel about something. It is obvious that it is necessary in some degree to respect the cultural rights of others, but this affirmation of the value of what is denigrated becomes a form of testing the boundaries.

Affirming Independence from Dominant Cultural Patterns

Most members of the audience recognize that individually and collectively they are helpless to really change the content of the media offered to them and helpless to challenge the dominant culture. Fans of a particular genre are familiar enough with how the media industry makes decisions and fans recognize that they can have very limited influence, even though large fan organizations have made heroic attempts to override financial decisions of the media (Jenkins, 1992). Fans realize, more than other parts of the audience, that media are arbitrary, self-interested constructions and that they are not written on sacred tablets.

On the other hand, the media tend to present themselves solemnly as the fourth estate, the public forum, the foundation of democracy, and so forth. Most people have doubts about all this. But what to do? Deconstruction inevitably brings audiences to the point of action.

Traditionally, the "popular" classes have long discovered that it is important to always keep aware that power is pompous and a sham. The best way to keep this in mind and help remind the powerful that they are a sham is through the carnivalesque, the subtle ridicule, the calculated symbolic action of violation of sacred custom, the tongue-in-cheek love of the licentious and irrational pleasure, but especially the cynical parody with mock solemnity. This deconstruction strategy is to ridicule precisely those aspects that are clearly a manifestation of the political economic interests behind the media: the cheap production quality, the shifts in programming for financial reasons, the improvised scripting, the abuse of advertising, and all of the other hypocrisies of the media. Again, this is a cultural practice and what is being parodied is the culture itself. This is a declaration of independence from this version of the culture.

Oppositional and Resistive Readings

These are interpretations that clearly disagree with the media representation because it is perceived to be false, to be a deliberate attempt to denigrate the cultural identity of the people involved, and because it is self-serving. Anything that violates one's sense of self-worth will cause some negative reaction, but to the degree that the opposition is part of the subculture and the culture of this media network it may be very open and strong.

A variant of this is an identification and an affirmation of a representation that is, in itself, opposed to the hegemonic culture. Such clear oppositional readings are rare unless the audience is already part of a collective effort to construct an alternative text presenting an alternative reading of reality.

RECONSTRUCTION: THE CREATION OF ALTERNATIVE MEDIA TO EXPRESS IDENTITIES

By *reconstruction* I mean the development of an alternative subculture in which the rewriting of the text in terms of appropriated identities is implicit. Reconstruction also implies practices of celebration of the subculture that develops around alternative texts. I hesitate to apply the term "rewriting the text" in this case, because I think that articulation of popular culture into a broadcastable media text is an authorial skill that most fan groups do not have and do not pretend to. Audience reconstruction is much more playful and without the professional pressures. In some cases, there are among fans authorial skills with the ability to develop subcultural discourses into media texts that may substantially influence genres (Wallis and Malm, 1984). In some cases this alternative, oppositional rewriting of the text may extend into confrontation with media industry, trying to get the industry to keep a program on the air or change the text in accordance with audience pleasures (Jenkins, 1992). It is an empirical question as to whether reconstruction directly challenges the political economic structure, but I would argue that it is extremely rare.

The reconstruction of a text by the audience has already begun in the deconstructing process of evaluating the text in terms of identity. The audience is already saying that the text has not got it right. In part this is due to time lag. By the time the media has discovered where the audience last was, culturally and in terms of media articulation, the context has changed, the definition of identities has changed somewhat and the discourses of popular culture have changed. The media are compelled to continually try to catch up with audience identity changes if they are to meet audience expectations of "getting it right."

The reconstruction of text covers a wide gamut of activities. At one end of the continuum is simply the vague dissatisfaction of some audiences with what is presented, whereas at the other end we have producers, who are also members of the audience, coming up with new texts. Media studies have probably differentiated sender and receiver, producer and consumer, much too sharply. Just about everybody at some point in life is an entertainer or produces something that is recorded by audio or video, published, exhibited, or staged. All cultures involve people in ritual performances in some way, and our contemporary socialization and educational systems insist that a performative experience, even the experience of creating a media text, is part of growing up. With the multiplication of media channels, the decentralization of mass media, and the growing of number of people who are involved in some way with media studies, an increasing number of people are gaining an experience of reconstruction of the text. The great majority of people remain in the "gray area" of performance somewhere between the neighborhood barbershop quartet and prime-time television. Nevertheless, many of the people in this gray area are in some way involved with and do battle within the culture industry.

I would argue, however, that the formulation of media texts is a more intentional cultural practice which takes the raw material of cultural discourses and puts them into a specific media language with its established grammar. Even though there is a gray area between discourse and text, the construction of mass media texts requires the ability to encode discursive systems into the symbolic codes, genres, and formats that are consonant with practices of the mass media industry and which are decodable for at least large segments of the mass audience. As Hall (1977) and others have shown, cultural hegemony imposes itself precisely in the area of media language, and the degree of independence from hegemony depends on how alternative the media is (Wallis and Malm, 1984). I would like to focus here, however, on the gray area where the construction of mass media texts links with and emerges out of the discursive reworking stemming from deconstruction of texts.

Although there is considerable research on the production of mass media programming, we have relatively little systematic research on the gray area between discursive reworking and articulation of this audience reconstruction into mass media texts. Much of the most insightful research is on media fans who are toward the more active, creative end of the continuum. Some would question whether fan culture is typical of "audience culture" as a whole (Ellis, 1982; Grossberg, 1987: 28-45). The greater part of the audience, it is suggested, is much less involved emotionally, less self-conscious, less critical in terms of identities and, most important, much less active. This is an empirical question. There is evidence to suggest that some people become intensely involved with some series and then may be relatively passive with much other TV viewing. It is a thesis here that virtually everybody is a fan of some media at some time in their lives, and this relation between identity and media deconstruction-reconstruction remains part of their personalities.

The strategies of reconstruction of the text are much less clearly defined, but some indications are emerging.

From Collective Deconstruction to Collective Reconstruction

The entry into an active reworking of the subcultural discourse toward a recontextualized mass media text may be defined as the point where the media ceases to be just one topic of groups that come together for social solidarity and the group comes together primarily to discuss the media.

Reworking the media has become an end in itself, even if it means that people gather to enjoy the media together. Once the media are the focus of the group, the media begin to be worked into the subculture of the group, at least for these meetings and moments. It is at this point that the group begins to adopt special symbols of the subculture that are adapted to the subculture of *this* particular group with its identity.

What is happening here, I would suggest, is that the media text as it is deconstructed has become so expressive of the identities of the people, in a mass media environment that infrequently connects with the group identity, that the meetings are celebrating "being ourselves!" To some, putting on special clothing for these meetings, having special rituals, and so forth, may seem unexplainable unless we understand how satisfying it is to express identities. Virtually all subcultures adopt some form of symbol to dramatize their commitment to their identity, and to say to surrounding cultures that we think our identities are good. This echoes the Freirian pedagogy for cultural liberation.

Supporting and Promoting the Media

People who become deeply identified with a particular form of media begin to promote its use among others. This is more typical where the media represent a movement to transform society, as in the case of the televangelists or programming that espouses political causes. Those who have discovered what they consider to be their real identities in particular movements do, indeed, have a "born again" experience and will make great sacrifices so that others can have a similar experience. Followers of the televangelists will make great sacrifices to support and promote a program because they feel that it is the source of liberation for people today. They know that the whole movement is the cause of the transformation, but the media representation is the public symbol of this.

Attempts to Influence the Content of the Media

The classic example of the crossover from being a loyal, interested, members of the public to being a fan is that the fan begins to initiate communication with the producers. The producers often invite audiences to send letters, make visits, participate in the live audience, or to become part of a broader movement. Many educational, religious, and political broadcasts take a multimedia approach that includes receiving mailings of print materials, being part of associated local groups, or being part of an action movement. Entertainment media may consciously promote and orchestrate this sort of participation, but audience identities are always tussling with and escaping media attempts to situate them. Virtually all fan networks find themselves in various degrees of conflict with mass media organizations, and virtually all fan networks attempt to get the media to respond to their interests. Almost always financial or social control criteria have the final word (Jenkins, 1992).

The Alternative "Culture Industry" of the Audience Groups

As was noted above, there is an enormous gray area of involvement with performance, and usually amateurs borrow from the existing styles of media because this is what they know and it is what audiences will probably like. At the same time, these alternative productions bear the imprint of the subculture of the group. Jenkins (1992) notes that when people enter a fan group they gradually learn the styles and codes of the subgroup. He presents an extensive description of the scripts and video spinoffs from the series the groups are organized around, but in almost every case the alternative is a reflection of the identity of the subgroup— for example, the gay identity of the group.

Jenkins also notes that many of the people involved with the productions of fan groups are "overeducated" and bored with their jobs, looking for some kind of imaginative outlet in life at least on weekends and holidays. Some might use this alternative culture industry as a step further into the industry, but others prefer to remain in the alternative area.

Again, there is a continuum of members of the audience from those who gather simply to celebrate their alternative identities and interests around a text to those who are much more militantly interested in changing the tastes of the public or at least preserving what they consider to be better quality (Brower, 1992: 163-84).

LINKING MEDIA FAN NETWORKS WITH SOCIAL MOVEMENTS

The processes of deconstruction are of great political importance because they help in the definition and appropriation of cultural identities and in the critical disengagement with the hegemonic culture and society. The processes of reconstruction prepare the base for political project, especially in relationship to the media. As we noted above, the social organization of people around media becomes political action only if it is linked to an underlying social movement. There are various theories of the origins of social movements, but a general condition is a significant population that finds that its social, economic, cultural or other aspirations are blocked by the present organization of society and that the only solution is a mobilization to bring about changes in the society. Since communication to decision-making bodies is blocked, the aggrieved population forms an alternative network of communication among themselves to build a base of sufficient social, economic, and cultural power to force a change (White, 1996).

Freirian educational practice also recognizes that critical consciousness does not in itself bring about social change. It only clarifies the social vision and brings people to the point of social action and forming a movement on a local scale. It is presupposed that the hundreds of focal points of action must come together in a regional and national movement to bring about change (Festa, 1986).

The media networks can greatly strengthen movements because they bring the ability to develop new symbols and a new internal culture that welds together people of diverse cultural backgrounds. The media networks also bring the ability to create alternative mediated communication, which is necessary for a widespread movement.

REFERENCES

Brower, S. (1992) "Fans as Tastemakers: Viewers for Quality Television." In Lisa Lewis, ed. *Adoring Audience: Fan Culture and Popular Media*. London: Routledge.

Brown, M. E. (1994) *Soap Opera and Women's Talk: The Pleasure of Resistance*. Thousand Oaks, CA: Sage.

—— (1996) "Desperately Seeking Strategies: Reading in the Postmodern." In Debra Grodin and Thomas Lindlof, eds. *Constructing the Self in a Mediated World*. Thousand Oaks, CA: Sage: 55-67.

Cantor, M. C. and S. Pingree (1983) *The Soap Opera*. Beverly Hills, CA: Sage.

Ellis, J. (1982) *Visible Fictions*. London: Routledge and Kegan Paul.

Festa, R. et al. (1986) *Comunicación popular y alternativa*. Buenos Aires: Ediciones Paulinas.

Fiske, J. (1987) *Television Culture*. London: Routledge.

Freire, P. (1989) *Pedagogy of the Oppressed*. New York: Continuum Publishing Company.

—— (1990) *Education for Critical Consciousness-Extension or Communication*. New York: Continuum Publishing Company.

Frith, S. (1996) "Music and Identity." In Stuart Hall and Paul du Gay, eds. *Questions of Cultural Identity*. London: Sage: 108-27.

González, J. A. (1994) *Más (+) Cultura(s): Ensayos sobre realidades plurales*. México: Consejo nacional para la cultura y los artes.

Grossberg, L. (1987) "The Indifference of Television," *Screen, 28*(2), 28-45.

Hall, S. (1977) "Culture, the Media and the "Ideological Effect."' In J. Curran et al., eds. *Mass Communication and Society.* London: Edward Arnold: 315-48.

———— (1996) "Introduction: Who Needs Identity?" In Stewart Hall and Paul du Gay, eds. *Questions of Cultural Identity.* London: Sage: 1-17.

Harrington, C. L. and D. Bielby (1995) *Soap Fans.* Philadelphia: Temple University Press.

Hoover, S. (1988) *Mass Media Religion: The Social Origins of the Electronic Church.* Newbury Park, CA: Sage.

Horsfield, P. G. (1984) *Religious Television: The American Experience.* New York: Longman.

Jenkins, H. (1992) *Textual Poachers: Television Fans and Participation Culture.* London: Routledge.

Jensen, K. B. (1995) *The Social Semiotics of Mass Communication.* London: Sage.

Livingstone, S. (1990) *Making Sense of Television: The Psychology of Audience Interpretation.* Oxford: Pergamon Press.

Livingstone, S. (1998) "Relationship Between Media and Audiences: Prospects for Audience Reception Studies." In Tamar Liebes and James Curran, eds. *Media, Ritual and Identity.* London: Routledge: 237-55.

Louw, E. (1994) "Shifting Patterns of Political Discourse in the New South Africa," *Critical Studies in Mass Communication, 11*, 23-33.

Lull, J. (1988) *World Families Watching Television.* Newbury Park, CA: Sage.

———— (1990) *Inside Family Viewing: Ethnographic Research on Television's Audiences.* London: Routledge.

Martin, B. (1981) *The Sociology of Contemporary Cultural Change.* New York: St. Martin's Press.

Melucci, A. (1989) *Nomads of the Present: Social Movements and Individual Needs in Contemporary Society.* John Keane and Paul Mier, eds. London: Hutchison Radius.

Morley, D. (1992) *Television, Audiences and Cultural Studies.* London: Routledge.

Simpson, T. (1996) "Constructions of Self and Other in the Experience of Rap Music." In Debra Grodin and Thomas R. Lindlof, eds. *Constructing the Self in a Mediated World.* Thousand Oaks, CA: Sage: 107-23.

Wallis, R. and K. Malm (1984) *Big Sounds from Small Peoples.* London: Constable.

White, R. A. (1995) "Democratization of Communication as a Social Movement Process." In Philip Lee, ed. *The Democratization of Communication.* Cardiff: University of Wales Press: 92-113.

V

CASE STUDIES IN AUDIENCE RESEARCH

12

Modern Dilemmas: TV Audiences' Time Use and Moral Evaluation

Ingunn Hagen

> Meaning is constituted in human consciousness: in the conscious-
> ness of the individual, who is individuated in a body and who has
> been socialized as a person.
> —Berger and Luckmann (1995: 10)

The significance a person attributes to his or her TV viewing habits takes place in the intersection between individual and cultural consciousness. I want to explore firstly, how people position themselves as TV viewers and secondly, what discourses they draw upon in this creation of identity.

For this purpose I will provide examples from my recent study of audiences' TV viewing in the multi-channel situation in Norway.[1] In this

[1]This study was performed in Bergen, Norway, during the winter of 1994. I have also presented material from the project at the Nordic Conference for Mass Communication Research, Helsingør, 1995 (see Hagen 1995, and also 1996, 1998). I would like to thank Dan Y. Jacobsen and Anne-Marit Myrstad for con- structive comments during former drafts of this paper.

study, I have identified a moral tone in the interview accounts; especially related to TV viewing and how interviewees spend time in their everyday lives. Moreover, I will discuss what I interpret as interviewees' experience of dilemmas related to the positioning as TV users (*cf.* Billig et al., 1988).

As others also have noticed (e.g., Wilson, 1996), when people talk about television they frequently talk about how they view themselves and their lifestyles. Thus, TV viewing becomes a moral issue, in which viewers relate their viewing habits to standards of good and bad; and to what is a proper way of living.[2]

THE MEANING OF WATCHING TV

Watching television in many countries consumes more time than other leisure activities (see Argyle, 1992). Still, the amount of time spent on TV viewing in Norway is low compared to the average viewing time in many Western countries. Norwegians watch television a little more than two hours daily (in 1997 the average viewing time was 144 minutes).[3] Those with cable or satellite dish spend more time watching than those who do not have access to cable or satellite channels.[4]

The multichannel situation is relatively new in Norway. It was not until 1992 that many viewers got access to more than one channel (the

[2]To my knowledge this moral aspect of TV viewing has been most explicitly discussed by Alasuutari (e.g. 1991; 1992; 1996). Also, Tester (1994) is concerned with TV and morality in his book *Media, Culture and Morality*. However, Tester's focus is more on how media conveys moral issues, and how this impacts audiences' sense of moral duty and feeling of solidarity.

[3]This number is from the Norwegian TV-meterpanel report, *Fjernsynsseingen i 1997* (Rolland, 1998). The Norwegian TV meter research was (from 1992 to 1999) performed by the Markeds-og Media Instituttet (MMI). The average viewing time in 1997 of 144 minutes was a 6-minute reduction compared to 1996, when the national average viewing time was 150 minutes (Rolland, 1997). In 1995 the average viewing time was 143 minutes. This was an increase of 3 minutes from the year before, 1994, when the average viewing time was 140 minutes (Engen, 1996; Rolland 1996). The numbers of the National Bureau of Statistics (SSB) are lower than these numbers from MMI, because SSB uses a different age group in their sample (9 to 79 years compared to MMI's 12 to 79 years).

[4]In Norway, the public service channel NRK (the Norwegian Broadcasting Company) reaches almost the whole Norwegian population. For many years NRK only had one channel, but since August 1996 the license-funded institution started a second channel, NRK2.

state-owned Norwegian Broadcasting Corporation—NRK). The commercial TV2 started in September 1992, reaching about 60% of the population. Its distribution has risen quickly; at present TV2 reaches more than 90% of the population. In addition, the number of viewers getting access to satellite channels has steadily increased. In 1994, when I did my study, almost half of the Norwegian viewers had several channels to choose from.

The project I will draw my examples from was called "Television Reception, Everyday Life and Family Interaction: An Ethnographic Study of the Audiences' Television Viewing a Multi-Channel Situation." The primary goal of the project was to understand the meaning of watching television in this relatively new situation in Norway. I was concerned with what Corner describes as the third level of meaning: the attribution of significance, socio-cultural relevance and value (1991). For the purposes of this chapter, I focus more on the significance attributed to the act of watching than to particular programs.[5]

The significance attributed to TV viewing will vary some according to cultural context. In Norway, the audience has been accustomed to the monopoly situation with NRK for over 20 years.[6] However, since the early 1980s increasingly larger parts of the audience have gained access to multiple channels. In the 1990s the changes have happened so fast that the situation has been characterized as a media revolution.[7] The increasing number of channels available and particularly more entertainment programs actualize the examination of what TV viewing means for audiences.

In my study, I interviewed 15 households—altogether 30 people—of different educational and vocational backgrounds. I tried to interview people from a variety of social backgrounds and family situations. The households were recruited through a network procedure from three different neighborhoods.[8] I interviewed both children and adults in the household, if they agreed to be interviewed. Because generation or age

---

[5]This distinction is drawn by Radway, who argues that "it becomes possible to distinguish *analytically* between the meaning of the act and the meaning of the text as read" (1984: 210).

[6]The exception was the population in eastern Norway, who could also watch Swedish TV channels if they had a proper antenna.

[7]For a description of this change, see, for example, Stortingsmelding, 32 (1992-93, *Media i Tida*), Lundby and Futsæter (1993), and Høst (1993).

[8]These three neighborhoods consisted of first, a traditional working class area; second, a more mixed neighborhood with many students, artists, and immigrants; and third, a more wealthy middle-class neighborhood. The network procedure implies that I interviewed acquaintances and also let people I know recruit among their neighbors and friends.

was expected to be an important factor for TV use in a multichannel situation, I made attempts to have great diversity in age.[9]

TV was regularly watched during the evening by most of the households I interviewed. Many of the interviewees, especially those in the less-educated and elderly households, emphasized that they took great pleasure in watching television. The more educated and middle-class interviewees were more likely to devalue TV viewing.[10] Generally, however, the interviewees valued almost any activity they were involved in higher than watching television.

Thus, in the interview statements I could identify a value hierarchy, where watching television was located close to or at the bottom. For these interviewees, to watch television had mainly negative (rather than positive) connotations. TV viewing was perceived as something passive (as opposed to active). Watching television was regarded as a waste of time, in contrast to more utilitarian use of time. TV viewing became the opposite of life quality. Consequently, TV viewing was not an activity the interviewees gave priority to. This concurs with the findings in an English study, in which 60% agreed that they would "rather be out doing something [else] than watching TV" (Barnett, 1993: 113). The interesting question is what happens when watching television is not regarded very highly, but is still what is being done.

In the interview accounts of my study, TV viewing is often experienced positively, but still evaluated negatively. Let me illustrate this with the words of one interviewee, a 30-year-old woman:

> TV is not that stupid, actually there is much joy in TV. I guess it is the fact that you are sitting there passively. . . . You just sit there and watch a box where something is going on. Perhaps you do not realize how heavy you are in your body before you are getting up. And then you think "Oh, I was sitting there again."

To watch television is associated with laziness and hedonism; you sit there passively with a "heavy" body. "You just sit there and watch a box where something (vicarious experience?) is going on," instead of doing

---

[9]The importance of age for viewing habits and adaptation to a new TV situation was emphasized by Werner et al., 1984, and Høst, 1993, among others. In my project the range in interviewees' age was from eight to 80 years old. The households were also diverse in size and type, ranging from single-person households to couples with and without children, single parents, people who were married, living together, or divorced; young, middle-aged, and retired people, and so forth. The interviews were performed in people's homes, mostly in the evening.

[10]This tendency was also very clear in a former study of mine, where the focus was on TV news viewing (see Hagen, 1992).

something active in your own life. Watching out of fascination, it sounds like. Still, too much viewing is interpreted as having "wasted time." This frequently qualifies for having a bad conscience. Norwegians' moral consciousness often are rooted in the Protestant ethos with its emphasis on productivity (*cf.* Thorkildsen, 1995). Thus, such a nonutilitarian use of time is considered problematic. Actually, time is a major factor in determining the significance of TV viewing.

TV VIEWING AND TIME CONSUMPTION

The significance of watching television related to time can be seen when TV use is contrasted with, for example, radio use. Generally, people watch television in the evening, whereas the radio is used during the daytime. Radio listening often accompanies morning rituals and house chores. Television, on the other hand, is seen to require more focused attention. This can be illustrated by a 36-year-old woman who comments that compared to the radio,

> TV demands so much attention since you get information via both picture and sound. Radio is only sound and it actually follows you where you want to . . . since TV takes as much time as it does, if you want to watch it properly. If you want to really concentrate you cannot do much else than looking and listening. You are almost locked in the chair in front of it.

The problem with TV viewing is that it inhibits other actions, as it requires dual perceptual focus. To be "locked in the chair" does have involuntary connotations. This woman then formulates what seems to be the ideal of many interviewees; "When you turn it (TV) on, it should be in order to watch something. And then you should focus and concentrate on that." This expectation of attentive viewing is shared by most interviewees, except for two households in which the television seems to be on whether someone watches or not (their televisions were also on during the interviews). The ideal of a focused mode of viewing is a residual of the one-channel, NRK monopoly situation, quite different from, for example, American, more inattentive TV viewing (see Lull, 1988). Attentive TV viewing requires time, in contrast to the radio sounds that accompany other activities.

Moreover, too much TV viewing is regarded as a lack of ability to structure time. To structure time, to do something useful and goal-oriented—either involvement in culture or activities outside the home, or doing housework, homework, or cultivate a hobby—is attributed high value. The ideal seems to be to do things in an orderly fashion, to plan one's use of time rationally. Although the interviewees clearly vary in the extent to which they plan their TV viewing, planning is regarded as an ideal by most of them. One retired couple showed me—almost proudly— how they marked and also ranked in order of priority the TV programs they intended to watch from the newspaper TV menu. The husband even had a name for this—they were doing "quality control." Many of those who watched more accidentally and zapped between the channels to find something worthwhile to watch, often apologized or excused themselves for doing so.[11]

One of the main reasons that TV viewing becomes a moral issue is, in the expression of one interviewee, that it is a "time stealer." Modern people seem to feel that time is a limited resource. This was also the case in my interviews, even among the retired respondents. This is an interesting issue related to the expansion of cable channels. Several of the interviewees who expressed little interest in receiving more than two channels explained this by their lack of time. In a report on the future of television in England, Barnett (1993) saw audiences' "time famine" as the major problem of the TV industry. This notion of time famine implies that people experience that work and leisure make increasing demands on their time, so they have difficulties juggling different interests and responsibilities.

The hierarchical thinking related to TV viewing compared to other activities is also implicit in the way some of the older interviewees talk about the time before television. Some of the elderly interviewees contrasted their present viewing with past times—the days before the introduction of television. They claimed that then people talked more, read more books, performed handicrafts, and visited each other. The older interviewees, who have experienced "how TV changed one's life," view the time before television in a rather nostalgic light. Before TV, people supposedly took more interest in making proper food and in preparing for social occasions. Another claim is that there was more time available for playing games or other activities. Television is associated with modern times—with working women, dissolved families, and busy lives. Still, to many of the retired interviewees, television offers available pleasures in their leisure time, as they physically deteriorate and have less chances of being active in other ways.

---

[11]This moral attitude related to planning one's watching is also noticed in a Danish study by Jensen and his colleagues. Jensen et al. (1993: 58) explains this attitude as "one should plan in order to avoid wasting time." Such attitudes were found both among "planners and non-planners."

A SOURCE OF DILEMMAS AND CONFLICTS

In the interviewees' talk about their viewing habits, there are dilemmas between what they value and aspire to as ideals and what they actually do in their everyday lives. In a former study of mine (Hagen, 1992), I found that audience members to a large extent felt a civic obligation to watch TV news. To watch TV news—at the time of that study the only Norwegian national TV newscast—was a taken-for-granted duty.[12] In the present study I also find this positive evaluation of news and informative programs, which can be contrasted with the more negative view that interviewees hold of entertainment programs. My interviewees reiterate the common cultural dichotomies of information over entertainment, learning over experience, cognition over emotion, and verbal content over images, when they talk about their TV viewing habits (gendered dichotomies, indeed).

I will let a middle-class couple with three children illustrate this conception of a genre hierarchy, which is also integrated with a negative evaluation of TV viewing. The wife is 50 years old, the husband 45, and they are both teachers. The family lives in the more wealthy, middle-class neighborhood. I interviewed all three children, a 15-year-old girl and two boys, 14 and 8 years old. This family does only have access to NRK and TV2. The parents expressed that they were happy they live in a neighborhood where cable was not available. A satellite dish was out of the question for this family.

The wife in this family tells me that she watches the news, some debate programs, and also cultural programs. She ideally watches the latter—when she has time. The husband says that he watches news and also programs about sciences (he teaches biology). Generally, this couple has a negative attitude towards television; to watch TV is regarded mainly a waste of time, compared to other activities. They see this as a question of time priority. Time is something they both lack, as they often have work-related preparations to make at home. Exceptions are made for programs at the top of the genre hierarchy—news and factual programs. Along the same lines, this couple is quite morally disgusted with entertainment programs. Besides, they do not like to let their children watch commercials, as they find that advertisements promote values with which they disagree (consumer habits and superficial lifestyles).

In this family, there is an open conflict about TV watching. The parents describe the topic as the most controversial one in the family. The conflict is about regulation—what the children should be allowed to

---

[12]The TV news in question was *Dagsrevyen,* the main TV newscast of NRK, the Norwegian (public service) broadcasting institution.

watch. The parents prefer that the children should be involved in other activities rather than watching television. Entertainment programs, especially are not allowed. The children describe how on Saturdays—when Norwegian television usually broadcasts family entertainment programs—their parents forbid them to watch television at all. The parents prefer that the family should cook, talk, and play games together. With the exception of the youngest, who gets to watch children's TV, the children mainly get to watch news and debate programs, at the top of the genre hierarchy.

The children in this household are not too happy about the parents' regulations. The 15-year-old daughter however, seems to have internalized many of the standards of her parents; she only watches news and debate programs. She supposedly does not watch serials, that is "taboo in this home," as she says. She tells me that it used to be a problem for her related to her peers that she got to watch so few TV programs. However, she thinks that she could get to see programs if she really wanted to, because the parents have "become less strict than they used to be." But now she is less interested, so she "does not bother to stress . . . to nag, in order to watch," as she put it.

The 14-year-old son was quite upset when he talked to me. My impression was that he was on the verge of crying. I should mention that I talked to the children alone—the parents went out of the room and closed the door while I interviewed the children. The 14-year-old expresses that he feels that it is embarrassing or "stupid" that he does not get to watch the same programs as "everybody at school," because this makes him feel left out. He says he has chosen not to tell his friends about this. His parents allow him to watch news and sports without asking. He says he feels bad about having to ask, while "others just turn on TV in order to check if there is something fun to watch." Comic serials are his favorites. Thus, he and his brother are sneak watching *Mot i brøstet* (a Norwegian slapstick situation comedy) on TV2. This "sneak" viewing takes place in the evenings when their parents go out for a dance course. Actually, the parents seemed to be aware of this, telling me laughingly that the boys cannot wait to get them out of the house on those nights. The 14-year-old expresses a wish to watch more television, something that seemed to be a reaction to his parents' prohibitions.

It was the eight-year-old who was the most vocal critic of the parents' regulation policies. He expressed that he enjoyed entertainment programs and animated cartoons. He said that the family argues a lot about television and describes an argument like this:

> If we turn on TV to watch something we like for example, then they (the parents) will come and turn it off, and then we start arguing. Then

we, for example, say that they treat us badly or something like that. If they give in, we sometimes turn on TV2 and then my father becomes totally wild (the father has said he "cannot stand commercials").

The 8-year-old gets to watch nature programs together with his father. He comments: "He is a biology teacher so that is not so strange." The 8-year-old wishes that the family had more channels to choose from. But since they do not, he watches television at his friends' houses. Both his friends have cable television. He is aware that he is actually not allowed to watch, but says, "Since mom and dad are no longer nagging about it, I just do it." This 8-year-old is quite hedonistic; he expresses that he likes everything that is "fun to watch." If it were up to him, the family would have multiple channels, a video recorder, a stack of video tapes, and also a Super-Nintendo game.

As indicated, there are dilemmas and sometimes also full-blown conflicts related to television's place in the hierarchy of interests. The multichannel situation actualizes this, as more channels, and especially more entertainment programs, are becoming available. A number of these Norwegian households actively reject getting multiple channels. A formulation that I find in many interviews is that "two channels are more than enough." This was especially the case in the elderly households. Most of them find two channels sufficient, and are satisfied with one television. However, the wife in one of the retired couples on several occasions during the interview argues for buying another TV set. In her view, this represents the future. She argues that people have several phones and several radios, so they can have two television sets as well. Arguing for buying an additional television set could be interpreted as an indication of different program preferences, and as an attempt to avoid conflict.

"NOT A TV SLAVE, BUT . . ."

Why is it that television seems to be at the bottom in a hierarchy of leisure activities performed both at home and outside? The significance of watching television can be illustrated when comparing TV viewing to another type of media consumption—going to the cinema. When you go to the movies you do something active; you get out of your house and you pay for watching a particular film. Television on the other hand, is already available in your home; it is a "domesticated medium" (*cf.* Morley, 1992).

Since television is something (almost) everybody owns at least in Norway, it does not require much money or effort to watch. Besides, watching television does not require many qualifications, either. Most programs are easily understandable to a mass audience.[13] From film history we know that because film—as a visual medium—was available to the uneducated masses, it was regarded a low-brow medium. The film industry, especially in Hollywood, had to work hard to combat this low culture connotation by stressing art-film associations (With, 1992). Because television is easily available and comprehensible, it has maintained its low culture connotations. To rephrase Bourdieu (1984), watching TV does (apparently) not distinguish anybody.

Since TV viewing is regarded so low in the value hierarchy, "TV addiction" is something we associate with others. We ourselves have not fallen under the "spell of television." Thus, a major concern for many interviewees is who is the "master," TV or themselves? They think that television decides too much, especially for single people or "others." They themselves, however, go out of their way to emphasize that they are not "slaves of TV." In some interviews, this denial of being a "TV slave" is repeated several times. But the same person might at other points in the interview admit to the opposite.

An elderly, retired man, who several times rejects being a "TV slave," says "whether one wants to or not, one becomes very dependent on television. But luckily I have only two channels." He explains his "luck" in only having two channels by the fact that with more channels available he and his wife might just change channels. Thus, they might not even get to watch what they really want. His wife adds: "Besides, you should not forget to read a good book either."

The concept of "TV slave" was several times used related to disclaimers. According to Potter and Wetherell (1987), disclaimers are verbal devices used to avoid "obnoxious attributions." By saying "I am not a TV slave, but . . ." these interviewees are aware that what they are going to say may be interpreted as dependency on TV, so they disclaim such possible attributions. This device could be seen as an attempt to prevent the interviewer (me) from interpreting their accounts as a slave/(dependency)-relationship to TV by acknowledging the possible interpretation and then denying it.

In their recent study of Danish TV viewers, Jensen et al. (1993) suggest that there are three kinds of viewers, who vary in the degree to which they are under the "spell of TV": hedonists, moralists, and pragmatists. This typology is based on the viewers' evaluation of television

---

[13]Exceptions are, perhaps, parts of the news broadcasts that presuppose understanding of both politics, economics, social processes, and a certain vocabulary. Similarly, some cultural programs presuppose a certain cultural capital on the part of the viewers. However, in Norway the general level of literacy in the population is also rather high.

(mainly positive/negative) and on whether the viewing is planned or not. The hedonist has a positive attitude towards television and does not plan her/his viewing very carefully. The moralist, on the other hand, evaluates television rather negatively, and s/he has abstract ideals about TV and its role in life. The pragmatist has a more relaxed attitude towards television; it is a resource in the culture that one can enjoy when time allows. Jensen and his co-authors found 57% of their interviewees to be in the pragmatist category.

It can be fruitful to locate viewers in such typologies, because the ideal types can clarify some dominant patterns. I also found the same dimensions in my own material. However, the picture seems more complex. Of course, some interviewees are more negative in their evaluation of television, especially the highly educated and middle-class people. But I also found that the value attributed to television was very relative, for one and the same viewer, depending on the activity to which television was compared. Planning TV viewing was an ideal for most interviewees, even though the practice of this varied quite a bit. Planning would also vary for the same person. A person who might only watch the news or debate program on weekdays, might lie on the couch and watch almost anything on Friday night if s/he was tired after a long week.

DISCOURSES FOR EVALUATING TV USE

The underlying moral aspect of television that I have identified in the interview accounts actualizes an important question. What are these "subjective" statements that the interviewees have shared with me? Are these accounts their personal experiences and feelings? What about the nature of such TV experiences as cognitive and cultural processes?

Regarding experiences generally, Berger and Luckmann write: "each experience is related not to one another, but to a type of experience, a scheme of experience, a maxim, moral legitimation, etc., won from many experiences and either stored in subjective knowledge or taken from a social store of knowledge" (1995: 11). Similarly, I am interested in the subjective and social nature of TV experiences. I try to understand the relationship between people's individual thinking and the common script or schema for evaluating the experience of TV viewing.

Obviously, there are individual as well as social differences in the interviewees' relationship to television. But the similarities in the statements related to dilemmas, the value hierarchy of TV viewing versus other activities, and the genre hierarchy, suggest that this is more of a cultural script (see Silverman, 1991). One could call this orientation socially embedded "provinces of meaning" (Silverman, 1978[1970]),[14] which indicates to people that television might influence defenseless people, that it might alienate you.

People's orientations, Silverman suggests, depend on their aims and expectations. These ends and expectations depend on their various historical experiences and on their multiple role statuses at the time. In Norway, people's relationship to television has been formed by 30 years of the state-owned NRK's monopoly. The Norwegian politicians were from the beginning very ambivalent about television, accepting it only because they considered it an inevitable development (see Syvertsen, 1992). But the public service channel NRK and its ideals for enlightenment made TV viewing partly a civic duty.

During the last decades, European public service institutions have faced a legitimation crisis (cf. Ang, 1991). In Norway, NRK is loosing its stronghold to commercial, more entertainment oriented channels. The enlightenment goal of the monopoly had as its opposite a disregard for mass culture.[15] It seems that people are still paying tribute to these normative standards. Assumptions about potential damaging effects of TV viewing and especially of watching entertainment programs seem to underlie audiences' discourses. It seems that people pay "lip-service" to certain notions of TV viewing. Could it be that people experience television as fun, but because they fear that it is not doing them any good, they draw upon these cultural scripts or meaning structures?

These viewers' statements about television seem to be closely related to societal discourses regarding television. Linguists especially have realized the relationship between individual's everyday talk and practices and cultural images and meaning construction (cf. Andenæs, 1995). In conversations, as in interviews, people are negotiating identities. From a sociocognitive perspective on TV audiences, Höijer argues that "practically all human beings struggle with the dilemma to unite cultural and individual identities, and feelings of belonging go hand in hand with feelings of being an outsider" (1996: 17). Perhaps my interviewees try to portray themselves as sensible TV viewers. In this process, their draw upon cultural discourses about television.

---

[14]Silverman discusses orientations or finite provinces of meaning related to organizations. However, I find his discussion also enlightening with regard to audiences' orientations related to TV. The idea of finite provinces of meaning seems to be drawn from Berger and Luckmann's *The Social Construction of Reality* (1967), who develop the term based on Alfred Schutz's writings.

[15]Ien Ang characterizes the latter frame of reference as the "ideology of mass culture." According to this ideology, "some cultural forms—mostly very popular cultural products and practices cast in an American mould—are *tout court* labeled 'bad mass culture'" (1985: 94). It goes without saying that such products create negative associations.

John Corner (1995) has tried to characterize some of these discourses, related to the quality of television both broadly (what is TV good for?) and more narrowly (what is good TV?).[16] The first and primary concern is with television as a time waster. According to Corner:

> The appeal of television as a way of easily filling time is seen variously to work against the taking up of a more active, creative pastimes (including reading), the pursuit of social and community life outside the home and full engagement in family conversation and family recreation. (1995: 161)

The feared result is impairment of personal and social development. Second, television is regarded as a cultural invader in Norway like in many small Western countries (and also in Eastern Europe and the Third World). The heavily American origin of much imported TV material is seen to promote rather materialistic values.

Third, there is a concern with television as a source of taste debasement; a regular diet of standard TV and especially entertainment programs will have the effect of lowering the taste of many viewers. Thus, the fear is that the lowest common denominator strategy of television will develop into a cultural norm. Fourth, television is regarded as an extremely influential medium, whether its content is news, violence, or commercials. Fifth, one can often hear a cognitive impairment thesis related to television (especially promoted by psychologists and educators). In the words of Corner: "This takes the 'influence' argument in a particular direction, arguing not so much for any specific effect of form/content but for a general effect upon perceptual and cognitive processing skills" (1995: 162). This fear of reduced mental capacities argument is often related to the cultural deterioration discourse. Similarly, television is often seen to symbolize image-based culture, something which causes a fear of antiliteracy. All of these concerns, independently or in combinations, are regularly advanced in public debates about television. Thus, they easily become "common sense"; part of our common reservoir for meaning production. Several of these cultural discourses can be recognized in the statements of my interviewees.

CONCLUSION

I have argued that the interviewees discourses are based on an underlying moral hierarchy, in which TV viewing is estimated lower than most

---

[16]John Corner also talked about this theme at a lecture at the Nordic TV-days, Bergen, June 6-8, 1996.

other activities. Such moral values are intersubjectively constituted (see Luckmann, 1994). Moreover, such a hierarchy is closely associated with conceptions of good and bad taste, and of high and low culture. When the hierarchy is contradicted by actual behavior, some interviewees seem to experience dilemmas. In this chapter I have been concerned with analyzing the norms and ideals against which viewers evaluate their own TV viewing and how this enters into their descriptions of their daily viewing habits.

The dilemmas experienced concern the relationship between ideals and actual use of television. The interview accounts seem, as indicated, influenced by a Protestant ethic and modern enlightenment ideals. The value of productive use of time, including leisure time; the ideal of planning and structuring time; and the value attributed to information, were examples of the above. When interviewees differ from such ideals, they often provide reasons or apologies for this. I have tried to describe the reasons people give for their practices and to examine the base for the experienced dilemmas.

People juggle different roles and identities in front of the screen. They are citizens trying to become informed. They are "coach potatoes" trying to relax and to be entertained after a workday. They are consumers for advertised products. They are parents trying to educate children, including about TV viewing habits. In our everyday lives, as well as in our (interview) discourses about everyday life, we experience dilemmas—between ideals and everyday practices, between freedom and necessity, between individuality and collectivity. TV viewing is a question of time use, of life style, and of identity and identification.

I will let the citation from a 30-year-old female interviewee sum up my discussion. In the second interview, she restates what she had told me in the first interview session: "The essence was that I actually think TV is something nasty, and that only news and debate programs are worth watching for us conscious people." She admits that this was not what she actually did, but what she felt was right to say and also "in order to play on the team with those I want to play on the team with." In other words, her portrayal of TV habits relate to her group identification. But she admits that she uses television for many other purposes; she tells me that she often turns it on to see if there is "something exciting."

I think this illustrates quite well the dilemmas the interviewees struggle with; TV viewing is not considered a worthwhile activity, so it is not something you associate with yourself. This is especially the case if you identify with what is considered "good taste" and high culture in society (cf. Bourdieu, 1984). Such dilemmas can be identified in the interviewees' discourses, but also in their practices, and especially in the split between discourse and practices. Your TV viewing signals something about you to yourself and to others. Still, it seems that there is a kind of

psychological distinction going on, in which the interview situation acti-
vates social norms. The interviewer perhaps represents "good taste," by
virtue of being from the University. Thus, your TV habits become an indication of who you are, how you spend your time, what taste you have,
and how you educate your children. No wonder it is a moral issue.

REFERENCES

Alasuutari, P. (1992) "I'm Ashamed to Admit It, But I Have Watched
Dallas: The Moral Hierarchy of Television Programmes," *Media,
Culture and Society,* 561-82.
———— (1991) "The Value Hierarchy of TV Programs. An Analysis of
Discourses on Viewing Habits." In Pertti Alasuutari, Karen
Armstrong and Juha Kytömaki, eds. *Reality and Fiction in Finnish
TV Viewing.* Helsinki: Research Report 3/1991.
———— (1996) "Television as a Moral Issue." In Ian Crawford and
Sigurdjon Baldu Hafsteinsson, eds. *The Construction of the
Viewer: Media Ethnography and the Anthropology of Audiences.*
Højberg, Denmark: Intervention Press.
Andenæs, E. (1995) "Språklig konstituering av sosial identitet" [Linguistic
Constitution of Social Identity], *Konstituering av kjønn fra antikken
til moderne tid.* Oslo: Norges forskningråd.
Ang, I. (1985) *Watching Dallas: Soap Opera and the Melodramatic
Imagination.* London: Methuen.
———— (1991) *Desperately Seeking the Audience.* London and New
York: Routledge.
Argyle, M. (1992) *The Social Psychology of Everyday Life.* London:
Routledge.
Barnett, S. (1993) "The Future of Television." In *Media Futures.* London:
The Henley Centre.
Berger, P. L. & T. Luckmann (1967) *The Social Construction of Reality.
A Treatise in the Sociology of Knowledge.* New York: Doubleday
Anchor.
Berger, P. L. & T. Luckmann (1995) *Modernity, Pluralism and the Crisis
of Meaning. The Orientation of Modern Man.* Gütersloh:
Bertelsmann Foundation.
Billig, M., S. Condor, D. Edwards, M. Gane, D. Middelton and A. Radley
(1988) *Ideological Dilemmas: A Social Psychology of Everyday
Thinking.* London: Sage.
Bourdieu, P. (1984) *Distinction. A Social Critique of the Judgement of
Taste.* Cambridge, MA: Harvard University Press.

Corner, J. (1991) "Meaning, Genre and Context: The Problematics of 'Public Knowledge' in the New Audience Studies." In James Curran and Michael Gurevitch, eds. *Mass Media and Society.* London: Edward Arnold.

—— (1995) *Television Form and Public Address.* London: Edward Arnold.

Engen, G. E., ed. (1996) *MedieNorge 1995.* Nordicom/Norge, Institutt for Medievitenskap, Universitetet i Bergen [Department of Media Studies, University of Bergen].

Hagen, I. (1992) *News Viewing Ideals and Everyday Practices: The Ambivalences of Watching Dagsrevyen.* Dissertation, Department of Mass Communication, University of Bergen, August 1992.

—— (1995) *The Morality of TV Viewing—Dilemmas in People's Everyday Lives.* Paper presented at the 12th Nordic Conference for Mass Communication Research, Helsingør, Denmark, August 12-15, 1995.

—— (1996) "TV-Titting som morals dilemma" [TV Viewing as a Moral Dilemma]. In Gunnar Iversen, Stig Kulset, and Kathrine Shretting, eds. *As TIme Goes By.* Trondheim: Tapir.

—— (1998) "Creation of Sociocultural Meaning: Media Reception Research and Cognitive Psychology." In Birgitta Höijer and Anita Werner, eds. *Cultural Cognition. New Perspectives in Media Audience Research.* Göteborg: Nordicom: 59-73.

Höijer, B. (1996) *Audiences' Expectations on and Interpretations of Different Television Genres: A Socio-Cognitive Approach.* Paper given at IAMCR/AIERI/AIECS XX Scientific Conference in Sydney, Australia, 1996. (Published in this book)

Høst, S. (1993) *Daglig mediebruk—en oppdatert oppdatering* [Daily Media Use. An Updated Updating]. Volda: Møre og Romsdal distriktshøgskule.

Jensen, K. B., K. Schrøder, T. Stampe, H. Søndergaard and J. Topsøe-Jensen (1993) *Når danskere ser TV. En undersøgelse af danske seeres brug og oplevelse af TV som flow* [When Danes Watch Television. A Study of Danish Viewers' Use and Experience of TV as Flow]. Copenhagen: Samfundslitteratur.

Luckmann, T. (1994) "On the Intersubjective Constitution of Morals." In Steven Galt Crowel, ed. *The Prism of the Self. Philosophical Essays in Honor of Maurice Natanson.*

Lull, J. (1988, Ed.) *World Families Watch Television.* London: Sage.

Lundby, K. and K. A. Futsæter (1993) *Flerkanalsamfunnet. Fra monopol til mangfold* [The Multichannel Society. From Monopoly to Plurality]. Oslo: Universitetsforlaget.

Morley, D. (1992) *Television, Audiences and Cultural Studies.* London: Routledge.

Potter, J. and M. Wetherell (1987) *Discourse and Social Psychology. Beyond Attitudes and Behaviour.* London: Sage.

Radway, J. (1984) *Reading the Romance.* Chapel Hill: University of North Carolina Press.

Rolland, A. (1996) *Fjernsynsseingen i 1995. MMIs TV-meterpanel* [TV Viewing in 1995]. Oslo: Markeds- og mediainstituttet.

—— (1997) *Fjernsynsseingen i 1996. MMIs TV-meterpanel* [TV Viewing in 1996]. Oslo: Markeds- og mediainstituttet.

—— (1998): *Fjernsynsseingen i 1997* [TV Viewing in 1997]. *MMIs TV-meterpanel.* Oslo: Markeds- og mediainstituttet.

Silverman, D. (1978[1970]) *The Theory of Organisations.* London: Heinemann.

—— (1991) *On Throwing Away Ladders: Re-writing the Theory of Organizations.* Unpublished conference paper, "Towards a New Theory of Organizations," England.

Stortingsmeld. nr. 32 (1992-93) *Media i Tida.* Oslo: Kulturdepartementet.

Syvertsen, T. (1992) *Public Television in Transition: A Comparative and Historical Analysis of the BBC and the NRK.* Ph.D. Dissertation, Centre of Mass Communication Research, University of Leicester.

Tester, K. (1994) *Media, Culture and Morality.* London and New York: Routledge.

Thorkildsen, D. (1995) *Nasjonalitet, identitet og moral* [Natinality, Identity and Morality]. Oslo: Norges forskningsråd, KULTs skriftserie nr. 33.

Werner, A., S. Høst and B. P. Ulvar (1984) *Publihums realisiones pa satellitt-og lohaltiernsyn* [The Audiences' Reactions toward Satellite and Local Television]. University of Oslo: Institutt for presse-forshning [Institute for Press Research].

Wilson, T. (1996) *The Games People Play: Television and Cross-Cultural Identification.* Unpublished paper, University of Deakin, Australia.

With, A.-L. (1992) "Kvalitetsfilm og norsk kinopolitikk. Teoretiske og empiriske innfallsvinkler" [Quality Film and Norwegian Cinema Policy. Theoretical and Empirical Perspectives]. In *Om populær film og kvalitetsfilm.* Levende bilder nr. 3/92, Norges Allmennvitenskaplige Forskningsråd.

13

*Diasporic Identities: Chinese Communities and Their Media Use in Australia**

John Sinclair, Kee Pookong, Josephine Fox, and Audrey Yue

The current era of globalization is characterized by the massive movement not just of media content but also people across national borders,
and even from one continent to another. Diasporic emigrations from
China, India, Indo-China, and to a lesser extent, Thailand, all have created widely dispersed global markets for cultural products of all kinds from
these peoples' nations of origin. The social needs for communication
media in the circumstances of migration and the experience of cultural
difference become opportunities for media producers and distributors to
exploit. However commercialized, the various mechanisms through

*The research reported here forms part of a larger project supported by an
Australian Research Council Large Grant, "Audiovisual Media Use for Cultural
Maintenance and Negotiation by Diasporic Communities of Asian Origin in
Australia," in conjunction with Professor Stuart Cunningham of Queensland
University of Technology and the National Key Centre for Media and Cultural

which television programs and videos are distributed throughout the far-flung geolinguistic regions of the great diasporas still can be thought of as creating or at least maintaining imagined communities for them. The research reported here is concerned to find out about how immigrants, exiles, and also the longer settled communities of the Asian diasporas, might exhibit distinct patterns in their use of television and video, and do so in relation to different kinds of needs and identities.

It is part of work in progress that aims to map and analyze the systems of distribution of media within diasporas: how they work in Australia, and hence also their links to the international systems of which they form a part, thus tracing the whole chain from global production to domestic consumption. At the same time, the research also seeks to integrate direct household research on how audiences use this material and other media to deal with the psychological and sociocultural trans-formations of the diasporic experience, which are conceived as process-es of cultural negotiation. Thus, the project aims to fuse both the political economy of the production and distribution of diasporic media products and services with the ethnographic observation of the consumers at whom it is aimed. The specific case to be presented is of Chinese-speaking communities in Melbourne.

GLOBALIZATION AND DIASPORA

The patterns of Chinese migration represent one of the world's most impressive and complex cases of the phenomenon of diaspora. Originally referring to the dispersal of the Jews from Palestine in the first century after Christ, the concept of diaspora can now be usefully applied to the description and analysis of some of the major population move-ments of this century, and the complex processes of maintenance and negotiation of cultural identity in the age of globalization, especially the globalization of the media of communication that follow them.

Most definitions of diaspora emphasize the marginal status of those groups which, although they have settled outside their ethnic lands of origin, still maintain strong sentimental or material links (Esman, 1986;

Policy; Dr Manas Ray, also of the Key Centre; Dr Gay Hawkins of the University of New South Wales; Dr Glen Lewis of the University of Canberra, and other col-laborators.

Much earlier versions of this paper were presented to The Chinese in Australasia and Oceania conference, Chinese Museum, Melbourne, September 21-22, and the Culture + Citizenship conference, National Key Centre for Media and Cultural Policy, Brisbane, Sept 30-October 2, 1996.

Sheffer, 1986). However, the most essential element in the concept of diaspora is that of dispersal, which is expressed in its literal, etymological metaphor of the scattering of seed. Significantly, the concept of broadcasting is based on precisely this same metaphor.

Diasporic communities have sown themselves into several host nations, many in some cases, and can cover whole world regions, or even the globe. This sense of having taken root in a number of countries is one of the characteristics that distinguishes the diasporic from other kinds of emigration, in particular, from exile, which is forced expatriation, and perhaps to only one other country. Although certainly not excluding groups displaced by disasters, war, and political and ethnic expulsion, the concept of diaspora more significantly includes those whom current migration policy blandly labels as "economic migrants," that is, people wanting to improve their life chances, and willing to go and settle in any one of a whole range of countries in order to do so.

As far as communication media are concerned, there is a corresponding dispersal of audiovisual information and entertainment across borders. Indeed, such flows of media content and services are an integral part of what we are trying to define about the contemporary world when we use the now rather hackneyed term of globalization, along with flows of people, technologies, capital, and ideas (Appadurai, 1990). Like the flows of people, media flows travel not just from the metropolises to their peripheries, but can originate within and even help to define major world regions, including geolinguistic regions, that is, regions across which there are linguistic and cultural similarities. At least in the sense of forming a potential television audience, we can thus think of the worldwide diasporic communities of Chinese as an extension of Greater China (Sinclair, Jacka and Cunningham, 1996), an imagined community united if not through the time-space compression of satellite broadcasting, then at least by the portability and reproducibility of video.

Although both public and commercial television networks within national boundaries continue to assert their traditional role of generating a sense of national belonging and identity, the advent in Australia of "narrowcast" channels for specific markets, such as the New World Chinese service, as well as the more institutionalized government-run network SBS (Special Broadcasting Service) and other media forms such as video rental, can provide the means for people of Chinese origin to maintain their cultural links and orientation to their world outside their nation of residence.

It is within this tension between the national and the diasporic, the local and the global, that the research reported here has been developed. Its aims are to find out how audiovisual media, but especially television and video, are used in the everyday lives of diasporic communities such as the Chinese in Australia, with particular attention to the

simultaneous processes of maintaining cultural connections with the
Chinese world, while negotiating a place within the host culture. As well,
the project aims to incorporate a mapping of the sources of production
and the systems of distribution of audiovisual products and services that
emanate from the nations comprising Greater China, so as ultimately to
assess the actual patterns of consumption against the political economy
of production and distribution.

THE CHINESE DIASPORA IN AUSTRALIA

From the point of view of how immigrant communities can use the communication media, whether to maintain their cultural identity or to adapt
to a new environment, the Chinese in Australia are of particular significance. Because of the diversity of their origins and the different stages
at which they have arrived, Chinese groups in Australia present a micro-
cosm of the differences within the Chinese diaspora: differences in countries or regions of birth, languages, dialects, religions, and degree of
"desinicization" of values and behavior. The 1991 Census found 261,466
Chinese-speaking persons, out of an estimated 400,000 people of
Chinese ancestry in Australia. In Melbourne and its State of Victoria,
where a quarter of the Australian population lives, the largest Asian-born
grouping is from Vietnam, but in recent years, Mainland China has
become the top source country, and Hong Kong eighth (Department of
Immigration and Multicultural Affairs, 1997).

MEDIA USE AND IDENTITY OF DIASPORIC GROUPS

Benedict Anderson's seminal work on national cultures as "imagined
communities" (1983), bonded by a discursive sense of deep, horizontal
belonging to an imagined origin and a mythical past, is also relevant to
the various diasporas of the postcolonial era, and the imagi(nations) of
deterritorialized peoples. Repudiating any sense of culture as a closed,
impermeable, and unified object, and also rejecting the view that cultural
identity is an ideal, fixed condition that individuals seek to preserve,
Stuart Hall argues that the diasporic experience is lived and mobilized
more through "routes" rather than "roots" (1995). Cultures never remain
static, "pure," and true to their origin, particularly in the process of diaspora. The (original) "home" cultures of the displaced/marginalized
groups are obliged to negotiate with the (original)/"host" cultures of
other, dominant groups.

Postcolonial critic Homi Bhabha views such hybridity as the product of "cultural translation," in which diasporic identities are constantly being renewed and transformed through difference. Bhabha's concept of the hybrid, articulating both dominant and marginal discourses long associated with diasporas and other forms of postcolonial contact, opens the space for cultural strategies as active forms of resistance (1985).

Hamid Naficy's study of what he calls the "exilic" television produced by Iranians in Los Angeles in the 1980s is a model for how communication media can be used to negotiate the cultural politics of both both "home" and "host" (1993). By incorporating the industrial as well as the narrative features of the television services and program genres developed by the Iranian exile community, Naficy shows the relationship between the transnational experiences of displacement and migration (enforced in this case), and strategies of cultural maintenance and negotiation within the liminal slipzone between home and host, as seen on television.

Like the liminality of Iranian exilic television, the liminality of "Chineseness" within the diaspora can be seen as a slipzone of narration and identity, a process of cultural translation carried out under diverse local conditions to construct new and hybrid identities and communities. Clara Law's critically acclaimed film, *Floating Life* (1996), provides an excellent example of the diasporic Chinese experience as a narrative of displacement. The first-ever Australian Chinese-language film, *Floating Life* plots a Hong Kong family's journey of migration to Australia. Oscillating between the (imaginary) geoscapes of Hong Kong, Australia, Germany and China, the highly stylized narrative traces the multiple layers of deterritorialization and displacement.

In such contexts of dispersal, China, as the imaginary homeland, has become the absolute norm for "Chineseness," against which all other Chinese cultures of the diaspora must be measured. Postcolonial feminist Rey Chow has argued that Chinese from the Mainland might be seen as more "authentic" than those who are from Taiwan or Hong Kong, because the latter have been "Westernized" (1991). Depending on where one is situated with regard to the boundaries which mark out homes and hosts, it is conceivable that either privilege or disempowerment could be constituted by such notions as "too Chinese," or "not Chinese enough."

Cultural theorist Ien Ang offers an autobiographical staging of her own diasporic Chineseness as a strategy to illuminate the precariousness of identity, highlighting the very difficulty of constructing a position from which she can speak as an (overseas) Chinese (1992). Tracing the discursive otherness and the incommensurabilities of her life as an Indonesian-Chinese, Peranakan, Dutch-speaking and educated woman living in Australia, Ang argues against the hegemonic condition that "not speaking Chinese" signifies the loss of authenticity. She argues for the recognition of a heterogeneous Chineseness, the meaning of which is not pregiven and fixed, but constantly renegotiated and re-enunciated, both inside and outside China.

If on the one hand, Mainland China is too often mythologized as the "real" China, Hong Kong, a diasporic hybrid of East and West, as well as the world's third-largest producer of films after Hollywood and Bombay, can be seen as a kind of Chinese diasporic center for cultural maintenance and negotiation. Chinese communities in Asia, Australia, Europe, and North America form a geolinguistic region, or worldwide audience for the Hong Kong film industry. Its hybrid cinematic aesthetics fuse different genres and create a syncretism analogous to the constitution of hybrid identities. Its pre- and post-1997 preoccupations, which centered on such postcolonial themes as exile, displacement, and migration, offered almost an ethnography of the Chinese diaspora, and resonated with the diasporic sensibilities of loss, deterritorialization, and incorporation.

Cultural products such as films, and also television programs and services, attest to the the formation of transnational networks of media circulation and (re)production between home and host sites as the technological means for cultural maintenance and negotiation. In this context, Gay Hawkins has argued that New World Television, an Australian Chinese-language subscription television service, can be regarded as a form of diasporic television, because the "global Chinese" of Melbourne and Sydney are targeted as the sole audience for such a narrowcast service. Unlike the local material shown on the Iranian exilic television in Los Angeles, almost all the content of the New World service comes from Hong Kong, from which the channel takes its "look and feel." This "New York of the East" is thus presented as an important imaginary site for diasporic Chinese situatedness, although it is interesting also that Hawkins notes evidence of some audience demand for a stronger sense of local identification (1996a).

METHODOLOGY

The research reported here is a module in a larger study funded by the Australian Research Council, and undertaken in conjunction with Queensland University of Technology and other universities in Australia. As well as communities of Chinese origin in Melbourne, the full study will include communities of Indian, Vietnamese, and other Asian origin in Brisbane and Sydney.

The scope of the project extends from the international industrial structure of audiovisual production and distribution on the one hand, to the ways in which diasporic communities use the various media available to them in the context of immigration and settlement. We are also interested in both the theoretical and cultural policy implications of the study, but the emphasis in this chapter is on preliminary data gathered from a household questionnaire study that was conducted in Melbourne during 1996, and on the flows that we have been able to trace of Chinese-language media products and services from their origin to their audiences in Australia, and Melbourne in particular—from the global to the local.

A household study was chosen as the best means by which researchers could speak to respondents in the "natural" setting in which they made use of the audiovisual products and services to which they had access, and because the household as a site for this kind of predominantly qualitative research has become so thoroughly theorized in the literature (Morley, 1992; Silverstone and Hirsch, 1992). As well, a range of available research techniques has been developed around this ethnographic paradigm, and its privileging of domestic settings (Silverstone, Hirsch and Morley, 1992; Sinclair 1992). Additional ethnographic techniques also have been employed so as to complement the household interviews, and this work will be reported on as the study proceeds.

The interview schedule was designed for both adult and adolescent members of the household, asking them about their television viewing habits and preferences, though with particular attention to Chinese-related material. It also asked about their filmgoing and use of video, radio, karaoke, and computers. Further questions were to elicit birthplace, citizenship, and cultural identity, as well as socioeconomic status indicators such as occupation and education.

A target sample of 50 households was decided upon, composed of 10 households in each of five major Chinese-origin groupings. Given the inherent difficulties in winning the confidence of respondents and asking to be given both access to people's homes and a claim on their time (Sinclair, 1992), households were recruited into the sample principally through the personal contacts of the researchers, with some obtained through community organizations. Thus, the sample has no claims to be representative, but nevertheless is able to present data from a wide and systematic selection of households.

RESULTS OF HOUSEHOLD STUDY

As noted, households were recruited for the sample according to predetermined quotas for respondents from the People's Republic of China,
referred to here for brevity as Mainland China (MC); Southeast Asia,
namely Indonesia, Malaysia, and Singapore (SA); the Republic of China,
better known as Taiwan (TW); Indochina, comprising Vietnam,
Cambodia, and Laos (VC); and Hong Kong (HK).

Bearing in mind that the analysis is still incomplete, what we present here are apparent tendencies in the data so far, concerning how the
different groups use and relate to mainstream broadcast television, specialized television services, and nonbroadcast audiovisual media, especially
film and video, but including also radio and other domestic information and
communication consumer goods, such as karaoke units and computers.

Mainstream Broadcast Television

Mainstream broadcast television in Australia is a mixed system, with
Channels 7, 9, and 10 being the national commercial networks; the
Australian Broadcasting Corporation (ABC) provides its national network
out of public funds, and the Special Broadcasting Service (SBS) delivers
a multicultural service to the major capitals, funded by a combination of
sponsorship and government allocation.

When asked about the programs they regularly watched on television, there was quite a large number and wide range of programs mentioned, and without significant differences between groups, as shown in
Table 13.1. Programs in all genres were mentioned, from sport (the
Atlanta Olympic Games were on during the period of some of the interviews, of particular interest to Mainland Chinese) as one might expect, to
game shows, movies, series and serials, including the Australian soaps
like *Neighbours* and thoroughly global mainstream programs like *X-Files*.
News and current affairs programs of all types received frequent mention.

The number of times television programs in English were mentioned by all survey respondents suggests that language is not so much
of a barrier as might have been thought in watching mainstream television, even for the most recently arrived group: Chinese from the
Mainland are every bit as likely to watch the news, or a little less so, a
movie in English, as Chinese migrants from elsewhere.

Entertainment

On the other hand, the Mainland respondents' remarks about
their comprehension of television entertainment in English are illuminat-

Table 13.1. Number of English-Language Television Programs Named (All Types).

Mainland China	Southeast Asia	Taiwan	Indochina	Hong Kong
44	57	49	49	57

ing. One (MC 9) said about *The Oprah Winfrey Show*: "The English is fairly familiar and informal, that's why I've started to watch chat shows." Some of the Taiwanese respondents' remarks about television (and about video and film) display a similar concern with comprehension, but also with informing themselves about culture, and in surprising ways. One 19-year-old Taiwanese respondent (TW 8) said about the local variety show, *Hey! Hey! It's Saturday*, that "It gives Australian news and humor. Trying to assimilate into Australian culture—that's an indicator of how much you understand the language and the humor." About *Seinfeld*, he said: "You watch and you learn quite a bit about Western culture, the way friends speak with each other sometimes." Another respondent (TW 2) said, with a better sort of alibi, "Last month's women's group at La Trobe [University discussed] why *Melrose Place* attracts a female audience. Wanted to know why it's so popular."

News and Information

The parochialism of news and current affairs on Melbourne television was a regular cause of complaint from respondents of all national origins. For example, regarding the Channel 9 news in particular, one Mainland respondent (MC 1) said, "News content not bad but pays more attention to British, Anglo-Celtic people." A Cambodian-born respondent (VC 5) had a slightly more generous view of news: "They have very good news except that they are very limited, to Australian current affairs only. It would be better worldwide." A Hong Kong respondent (HK 5), asked if there was enough coverage of events of concern to Chinese people on the Channel 7 news, said: "I wouldn't say so. If I know something particularly is happening in China or Hong Kong I will turn to the SBS news."

The ABC news fared a little better, though it did not escape criticism. A Malaysian-born respondent (SA 9) said it "gives you more substance to the facts, more of a world view." A Mainland respondent (MC 2) thought the ABC news was "All right. [It has] a bit more [on China] than the commercial channels. They have their own correspondent in Beijing." Asked if there was enough news on Chinese topics on the ABC, a Southeast Asian respondent (SA 5) said, "No. Slightly better than commercial news format. News is presented too short and snappy to get the full picture."

The SBS news was best regarded for its international scope, but attracted different and sometimes contradictory charges of political selectivity. There were criticisms of the way in which news from China was framed. A Southeast Asian (SA 5) said, with some theoretical knowledge, "Chineseness is portrayed as, constructed as, other, exotic and different." Yet another (SA 3) said it was "Politically correct in Western terms—e.g., the Dalai Lama; anti-Chinese, pro-Western standpoint." One Taiwanese (TW 9) was more concerned with the host audience: "It lets me know how Western people look at my country."

Specialized Television Services

In addition to its evening news program in English, SBS broadcasts a number of news services in other languages, including Mandarin and Cantonese, in morning time slots. There were only five households that regularly watched the SBS news in English, one in each of the groups in our sample, although many more across all groups watched news in English on the other channels, as noted. Table 13.2 shows the numbers of households who watched the Chinese-language services.

The respondents' comments reflect a continued close engagement with the unfolding of events in East Asia, and irritation at the difficulty of staying adequately informed, reminiscent of, in another context, Naficy's observations of the "epistephilic desire" found in his study of the Iranian exiles in Los Angeles (1993). Several respondents, and not only those from the Mainland, complained of the pro-Communist Party character of the SBS Mandarin news, which is the national daily news broadcast of the Chinese state television network syndicated to SBS. One (MC 2) described it as "Not great. We just want to see what's going on. It's not the same as Australian news. A lot of propaganda." On the other hand, the Cantonese news was thought to be rather tame and insubstantial.

SBS entertainment programming also drew some comments. Asked about her favorite type of program on television, a Mainland respondent (MC 1) said "Sometimes SBS shows movies that are banned in China. SBS should do this more often instead of Hong Kong fighting movies. People in Australia think Chinese are stupid because of what's on TV and films in Chinese." This anxiety that media representations of Chineseness are going to create undesirable impressions within the mainstream culture is common.

Unfortunately, there was only one subscriber to the Chinese-language New World pay-TV service in the whole sample, and disappoint-

Table 13.2. Households Regularly Watching SBS Chinese-Language Services.

Mainland China	Southeast Asia	Taiwan	Indochina	Hong Kong
6	2	4	3	4

ingly few viewers of the Chinese programs on community television (Channel 31), attributed by several to poor reception in the suburbs further out. Nevertheless, what those few viewers did say points suggestively, if rather insubstantially, towards an analysis of Channel 31 use based on country of origin, or more specifically, on whether or not there is or has been an established, institutionally based discourse of ethnic identity and of interethnic relations in the countries from which the respondents have come.

Nonbroadcast Audiovisual Media

Video and Film

An apparent trend with regard to video and film use is that people from the Mainland watch appreciably less video material in English than people from any other origin, although there is no significant difference with film, as Table 13.3 shows.

At first sight, this is probably best understood as a reflection of the significant fact that the Mainland Chinese tend to have been in Australia for the shortest time, and to be the least fluent in English. However, one important qualification to be made about the data in Table 13.3 is that the Mainland sample is composed entirely of adults over 30, whereas all the other samples include teenagers and people in their early 20s, who are heavily represented as viewers of English video and film, as they went (or go) to school here, and participate in the usual social life of young people in Melbourne, which includes watching videos and going to films.

What about going out to films and renting videos in Chinese? Among residents of Melbourne of Chinese origin, those from the Mainland appear slightly more likely to go to the effort and expense of going out to see a film or renting a video in Chinese. This does fit the common wisdom that Chinese from the Mainland are rendered more marginal socially than others in Melbourne because of their relatively

Table 13.3. English-Language Films and Videos Named as Being Watched.

Videos				
Mainland China	Southeast Asia	Taiwan	Indochina	Hong Kong
3	8	13	8	17

Films				
Mainland China	Southeast Asia	Taiwan	Indochina	Hong Kong
7	9	10	9	8

poor level of English, combined with their relatively shorter length of stay in Australia and usually impoverished circumstances, and because of this they tend to continue to involve themselves in Chinese rather than Australian cultural consumption, as much by force of language as by personal choice.

Other Audiovisual Media Use

Radio

There are Chinese-language radio programs on the SBS AM station in Melbourne and the FM community service 3ZZZ, but these were listened to regularly in only a fraction of households overall, and several listened to no radio at all. However, those that did listen were concentrated in the Mainland and Indochinese groups. Most respondents overall tended to listen to mainstream music format radio, either classical, contemporary rock, or "light," depending on personal taste and age.

The Mainland respondents' comments are in line with certain characteristics that they displayed when talking about television and film: their close engagement with events in East Asia and an epistephilic desire to seek out information, an acute awareness of the implications of their Chineseness, and an uncertain grasp of English. Related to the last of these is their rather lateral use of Radio for the Print Handicapped, which appears as often for them as SBS radio as a source of linguistically accessible useful information. In the words of MC 7, "I listen to 3RPH sometimes. They read very slowly. I can pick up a word here and there."

Karaoke

In general, karaoke looks like something that Chinese-speaking people resident in Melbourne tend to acquire with length of stay and economic security, yet karaoke singing appears as much a social duty as an individual indulgence. There was one respondent (SA 9), who did not own karaoke equipment, but said "I've hosted a couple of CAV (Chinese Association of Victoria) karaoke evenings. I viewed it as community work," and proceeded to explain how she avoided having to sing. The low frequency of ownership and use among Southeast Asian respondents, even though they tend to be well off, is interesting, and suggests the karaoke fashion is less established in Indonesia and Malaysia than in Taiwan or Hong Kong, the respondents from which seemed to show more genuine enthusiasm.

Computer

Computer ownership was high across all the sampled groups: all ten of the Southeast Asian households had a computer of some sort; nine of the Taiwanese, and eight of each of the others. This is around three times the national average at that time, when less than a third of all Australian households had a computer, and just 262,000 of them were connected to the Internet (Bogle, 1996). When asked about use, most said that they used their computers for study, work, or letter writing without being more specific. Some respondents (all male) reported that they experimented with programming or generated graphics.

Concerning the Internet, there were six Taiwanese households with connection to the Internet, three Southeast Asian, two Hong Kong, and one of each of the others. Of these, three of the Taiwanese households mentioned keeping contact with friends and relatives overseas as one of their uses, as did a similar number (actually all) of the Southeast Asian households. Interestingly, SA 3 mentioned that he used the Internet to access a number of Southeast Asian newspapers.

On this evidence, computers are much more of a priority than karaoke for people of Chinese origin in Melbourne, particularly for those of Taiwanese background, although it is likely that there is a strong socioeconomic factor at play also, just as there is in the population at large, with regard to connection to the Internet.

DISCUSSION

Although further analysis of the data remains to be completed, we can expect that a good deal of the media-related behavior and attitudes we are observing among our different groups of respondents eventually will be able to be explained in terms of the patterns of difference and similarity regarding the sociopolitical orientation and linguistic skills that they bring from their homelands, and the socioeconomic status and generational experience that they accrue over time in Australia.

Thus for example, both Taiwanese and Mainland respondents relate to the media in a state of awareness of their own Chineseness. This awareness is due both to the collective historical experience characteristic of each group, and to the features of the new social environment with which they must deal. In the case of the Taiwanese, this might be seen as continuing to take the position of "Chinese subject," much as they would have done in Taiwan. The public political culture of Taiwan, in which Taiwan is set off ideologically against the PRC and the Communist Party as the sanctuary and the guardians of Chinese culture, arguably leads to Taiwanese migrants arriving in Australia with an already acute, if overdetermined, sense of the dutiful burden of Chineseness. In the case of the Mainland Chinese, few of them arriving in Australia in recent years would have identified themselves with the position of "Chinese subject" as used by the government of the PRC in the context of international power relations, but perhaps they tend to find the role of Chinese subject, often in its darker aspects, ascribed to them both by the operation of the official discourse of multiculturalism, and by its opponents, especially since mid-1996 when the interviews were conducted.

For apart from how their culture of origin has prepared them to respond to the quite new experience of their own racial and cultural difference, Australian society as a host can also make them aware of their difference, their "Chineseness," because of the still benign regime of multiculturalism, expressed in an immigration and settlement policy rhetoric that expects all immigrants not just to "have" a culture, but furthermore, to maintain it. This rhetoric valorizes an essentialist concept of "culture," manifest as language, food, and dance, but excludes politics.

However, for our respondents, watching a Chinese film is an act that carries political implications. We have noted how some former citizens of the PRC now living in Melbourne are interested in seeing films that were banned for political reasons in their home country. Their interest in Chinese politics is conscious, and they tend to speak readily and with some force about the positions they continue to take. On the other hand, even while continuing to speak as informed critics of the Chinese government, some respondents expressed resentment against those films that gave an impression of China as totalitarian, medieval, and poor. Perhaps distance also affects political convictions, but these respondents' unease may be attributable to a feeling that, in terms of the renewed debate about multiculturalism, they are somehow responsible for China as its subjects.

DISTRIBUTION OF CHINESE-LANGUAGE FILM AND VIDEO IN AUSTRALIA

In addition to the interview and ethnographic data from the 50 Chinese-origin households, the audiovisual media consumption of diasporic viewers in Melbourne was investigated through a series of interviews with videostore traders and a film distributor. These interviews were also intended to bring to light the circulation flows and distribution circuits of nonbroadcast media products (film as well as video) that connect the countries of origin of such material with their diasporic markets in Australia. More particularly, the purpose of interviewing videostore traders was to obtain inside information and opinion on the organization of the Chinese video business, including the relationship of videostore owners to the distributors; and to collect the traders' observations of the characteristics of the market for Chinese videos: its dynamics, its demographics, and any segmentation it might exhibit.

It should be noted at this point that diasporic viewers do not rely exclusively on videostores as a source of videos. Some of the household interview respondents did not rent videos from local stores at all, but did watch them occasionally when tapes were circulated amongst their informal kinship or other social networks. Videos are constantly brought into Australia by diasporic viewers themselves, or by visitors from their home countries, and then passed throughout such networks.

Furthermore, videos and other audiovisual products such as karaoke tapes are not just imported in a single, direct flow from the home country to Australia. Sometimes, they are involved in a lateral distribution circuit: for example, Hong Kong videos might first circulate in other parts of the Chinese-speaking world, such as Singapore, Malaysia, or China, before being brought to Australia. In other words, some of our household respondents in Australia, particularly Southeast Asians, would have acquired Hong Kong tapes from such other countries more than from Hong Kong. In some instances, especially when the tapes are acquired in Singapore, the original Cantonese vernacular is dubbed into Mandarin: in Singapore, Hong Kong material in Cantonese is not allowed to be distributed, so it is all dubbed into Mandarin.

In fact, this language difference, Cantonese being the language of Hong Kong and Mandarin of Mainland China and Taiwan, turned out to be a decisive determinant in the structure of the video business. The Mainland Chinese and Hong Kong video industries effectively run in parallel, each with its separate producers, distributors, rental outlets, and customers, with very little crossing over to the other side. This is for linguistic rather than business or political reasons. Thus, because Taiwanese videos, like those from the Mainland, are in Mandarin, they are also available in stores that rent Mainland videos.

Note, however, that the subtitling of exported Hong Kong as against Mainland Chinese and Taiwanese videos does allow for some crossing over, because the written language is much the same. Videos of cinema releases carry subtitles in Chinese characters, so that Chinese who do not speak Mandarin can follow a Mainland or Taiwanese film, and Chinese who do not speak Cantonese can follow a Hong Kong film. Some film studios, certainly those in Hong Kong, also give English subtitles to their cinema releases. However, it is interesting to note that television series and variety programs produced for domestic viewers in Hong Kong, China, or Taiwan and then marketed as videos are not subtitled, the expectation being that television product is less tradeable across national borders within the Chinese-speaking world than is film.

Distribution Circuits

Apart from its geopolitical position on the threshold to the motherland of China and its mythical status as the metropolis and global disseminator of Chinese popular culture, Hong Kong is in fact prominent in television production and distribution in Asia, based on its older preeminence in cinema production and export. Television production is based on the two networks that dominate the domestic market, TVB and ATV.

TVB (Television Broadcasts) is controlled by Sir Run Run Shaw and the Malaysian-Chinese entrepreneur Robert Kuok. Through its international arm, TVBI, it exports most of its domestic production, around 5,000 hours annually, in various forms and in several languages, but principally to diasporic markets. As well as having its own video outlets in Southeast Asian countries such as Malaysia, it also has cable subsidiaries in the United States and a satellite superstation aimed mainly at Taiwan. These are its major overseas markets (Chan, 1996; Lovelock and Schoenfeld, 1995).

As well as this vertical integration of television production and distribution on an international scale, TVB is horizontally integrated with Shaw Brothers (Hong Kong) Limited, a major distributor of cinema (Lent, 1990). After these, the next largest companies in Hong Kong active in media exports to diasporic and other overseas markets are built on similar vertically integrated models to TVB and Shaw Brothers, but are not related. These are the television network ATV and Golden Harvest, which is a major exhibitor as well as producer and distributor of films, well known in the West through one of its principals, Jackie Chan ("Hong Kong Films Conquer the World," 1997).

As for Mainland China, television production and distribution, both for the domestic and international markets, is centralized under CCTV (China Central Television), but there are also significant provincial and municipal stations in Shanghai, Guandong, and Sichuan. According to Chan (1996), all of these are active in program exports, both in their own right and coordinated through the export agency, CTU (China Television United). Films are marketed overseas through the Beijing Film Export Corporation. Thus, Mainland China as well as Hong Kong is active in pursuit of audiences of diasporic Chinese.

In Australia, our research has found that there are direct links between local videostores and the major distribution corporations of both Hong Kong and Mainland China. As well, the same major distributors also supply films to cinemas and programs to the specialist broadcast television services, evidencing how the patterns of horizontal and vertical integration in which they structure themselves in their domestic markets also extend out into their diasporic markets (see Fig. 13.1).

Video

To take video stores first, our research discovered that, in line with the market segmentation by language noted above, a video store would stock either Mainland Chinese videos in Mandarin (most are CCTV serials in fact), or would be tied to one or the other of the two Hong Kong major distributors by license agreement, and so stock either ATV or TVB Cantonese product.

Although both kinds of trader were suspicious of the project and gave answers with reluctance or evasion, we were able to establish that the Hong Kong video stores in Melbourne sign contracts with TVB or ATV, but not both: each distributor requires that a store deals with it exclusively. The contract with the distributor typically runs for a year, and can cost at least A$100,000 (about US$75,000). In exchange for this fee, the trader has access to TVB or ATV's entire past and present stock, which includes movies and all television genres, for the term of the contract, which may then be renewed with another fee. Video store owners cannot choose from catalogues, but must take what the distributor offers, a classic practice obviously advantageous to the distributor, particularly where distribution is vertically integrated with production. The trader is always given only one master copy, but authorized by the contract to make as many copies as necessary from his or her own blank tapes.

The Mainland Chinese side is organized on principles that generally follow the Hong Kong pattern. To quote one video store manager in Richmond, "There's a distributor in Melbourne. We sign a contract with a distributor each year who deals with all the Chinese state-owned TV serial producers. We give the distributors their fee each year and they give us a package. We can't choose." This store dealt only with the one distributor. Another trader named a distributor in Sydney, Tangfeng, and said he dealt only with them.

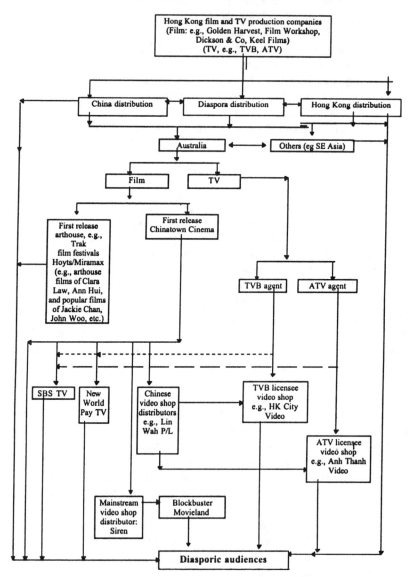

Flowchart of Distribution of HK Film, TV, & Video in Melbourne

Figure 13.1. Flowchart of Distribution of HK Film, TV, and Video in Melbourne

Although the Hong Kong stores are tied to either TVB or ATV, some do stock videos from other sources. For example, Anh Thanh Video is one of the biggest Chinese video chains in Melbourne. It has shops in the City (Chinatown Midcity Arcade), and those suburbs that have an above-average proportion of people of Chinese descent, namely Richmond, Footscray, Springvale, and Box Hill. Anh Thanh Video stocks not only ATV programs and shows (including gameshows, infotainment, music and variety shows, television serials, and news), but also a similar range of Mainland Chinese Mandarin-language programs and shows; popular Japanese material (such as television serials, mangas, music and variety shows); and popular Taiwanese television programs, serials, and shows in the hybrid dialect Minnanhua. Anh Thanh Video is exceptional in that it has a "parent" company called Lin Wah P/L with which it shares premises and a phone number. Lin Wah P/L is the licensee and main distributor of Chinatown Cinema videos to Chinese videostores in Melbourne, distributing Chinatown Cinema movie videos to both Anh Thanh and Hong Kong City TVB Video.

Chinese video shops are organized differently from mainstream video shops. Usually, there's a counter in the front of the shop, on which are several clear folders and photo albums of movie posters, surrounded by walls that are covered with hand-written lists, and more movie posters. Customers make their selection from the lists, posters, clear folders, and photo albums, rather than browsing around and picking up copies of empty tape covers like in Blockbuster and Movieland. More often than not, customers will have already heard of what they would like to have before going to the video shop. The trader usually charges customers about A$30 (US$22.50) for a refundable membership, which entitles them to rent tapes which cost A$2 (US$1.50) for old releases to A$4-5 (US$3-4) for new releases. There are no specific overnight loans, because the number of days that one is allowed to keep the tapes is dependent upon the number of tapes borrowed. For example, if a customer rents three tapes, all the tapes have to be returned in three days' time. If the customer rents seven tapes, they are returnable in seven days' time.

From this system, it follows that traders will usually want to make numerous copies of latest releases, as customers are allowed to keep them for over a week: hence, more copies to accommodate slower turnover. Also, there is an incentive to rerecord new titles over tapes of old ones when their popularity ebbs; so our questions about which types of videos did the traders find were in higher demand and of which did they have the least stock were irrelevant, because if traders found that they had higher demand for a particular tape, they would simply make more copies, and when their popularity faded, they would recycle the tapes for the next blitz of popular new releases. This practice is one reason for the extremely poor quality of the tapes, a matter on which most respondents in the household interview study made comment.

In these circumstances, piracy might become an issue: whether or not the store owner has continued to copy and rent out videos once the term of the contract that covered them is over, and the broader issue of whether or not the film or television producer's copyright has been infringed by the contract between the distributor and the video shop. However, because under the terms of the Berne Convention action against infringement of copyright must be initiated by the possessor of the copyright, the copying of Hong Kong videos in Australia passes without attention from the film and television producers in Hong Kong, who neither need to nor wish to spend money and time on small claims in Australia, and who, for the bulk of the content available, are also vertically integrated with the distributors in any case.

China is not a signatory to the Berne Convention, but piracy in the Mainland sector is alleged to come about through unauthorized taping of Chinese television programs in China directly from broadcast television, then exporting them. It was not possible to tell from looking at the tapes on the shelves in the three Mainland Chinese video shops visited whether they had been released under license by CCTV or not. Most were in sleeves with handwritten titles. This meant that they could have been pirate tapes, but also they could have been copies that the trader was authorized to make from the distributor's master tape under contract.

Cinema

Chinese-speakers in Melbourne can see first-release Cantonese-language Hong Kong films at the Chinatown Cineplex on Bourke Street, part of a national chain owned by Winston Leung. Tickets cost approximately A$8 (US$6) for a double feature, one being a first-release main feature; the other usually a rerun. These are the popular films such as many diasporic viewers would watch in their home countries, and those able to travel back there for business or to visit also watch such films when they have the opportunity.

There are also alternative arthouse cinema and film festival or other special event circuits that screen films from "auteur" Chinese directors like Clara Law and Wong Kar-wai, films that the Chinatown distribution circuit will not show, at least unless they prove popular on one of the other circuits. Chinatown's resistance can be attributed in part to the international (that is, non-Hong Kong-tied) nature of their funding, production, and distribution, as well as to the off-beat character of the films themselves (that is, commercially risky compared to proven genres).

For example, Clara Law's *Autumn Moon* (1992) was a Hong Kong film, but partly funded by a Japanese consortium. It was released in Cannes and picked up by the film festival circuit, and then distributed via the arthouse cinema circuit. Wong Kar-wai's masterpiece, *Fallen Angels* (1996), was not circulated via Chinatown Cinemas and its video outlets, but released in Melbourne and other capitals via the national arthouse group Palace Cinemas' Cine7 event.

It is interesting to note the cultural and commercial exchange that occurs between the arthouse and the Chinatown circuits over these Chinese auteurs. Because they are acclaimed and approved by international arthouse audiences, their most recent films bypass the Chinatown circuit altogether and go straight into the arthouse/film festival circuits. The response to this is for Chinatown then to screen their earlier films as popular cult reruns, which has happened with both the directors mentioned. A similar process occurs with films that fail with Chinese audiences but go on to enjoy international critical acclaim in the West. *Sex and Zen, Naked Killer,* and *The East is Red* are good examples that have enjoyed very successful queer film festival screenings, were then picked up by the international arthouse circuit, and only then screened by Chinatown.

Finally, there is the mainstream distribution circuit, at least over the last few years during which the West has become infatuated with the kinaesthetic martial arts comedy style of Jackie Chan. Of late, most of his films have been repackaged and rereleased in the West via mainstream cinemas and cult-fanboy specialist venues. In Melbourne, for example, *Rumble in the Bronx* (when bought, repackaged and rereleased by the multinational consortium, Miramax) was released (dubbed in English) through the mainstream national chain Hoyts in 1996. John Woo is another example. Having migrated to the United States from Hong Kong and become involved in joint productions with American companies, Woo's first American-produced film, *Broken Arrow* (starring John Travolta), was also released via the national chains in 1996.

From Chinese Cinema to Mainstream Video

Since about 1995, local videostores in Melbourne belonging to the major, mainstream English-language chains, notably Movieland and Blockbuster, which have been starting to stock a regular supply of popular Hong Kong films. These include the action cinema of Jackie Chan and John Woo, and also the internationally acclaimed arthouse and fantasy swordplay cult-types like Rouge, Centerstage, Saviour of the Soul, and Wicked City.

The manager of a local Movieland outlet in East Brunswick in inner-city Melbourne gave one of our researchers the contact number of Siren Entertainment as the main distributor of Hong Kong movies to these shops. He said that Siren marketed "a package of about 20 Hong

Kong films" as part of a distribution-marketing strategy for this kind of material. Hong Kong tapes in shops like Movieland and Blockbuster, when they are in the overnight category, cost only A$4 (US$3) per tape, compared to the rest of the mainstream overnight loans, which are in the vicinity of A$6 (US$4.50) per tape.

It transpires that Siren Entertainment has purchased a license from Winston Leung, the owner of Australia's Chinatown Cinema chains, to become the official distributor of Chinatown cinema movies to mainstream videostores. Siren gets rights to distribute a film on video only after, firstly, its initial release through Chinatown Cinema (which holds the sole rights for the first 12 months), and then, secondly, its video distribution to the Chinese-language stores, namely through Chinatown's licensee, Lin Wah P/L, which holds joint rights with Chinatown Cinema for the next 12 months). Thus, there is a waiting period of at least two years from a film's first local Melbourne Chinatown release before Siren can distribute it as a video.

Chinatown Cinema decides and advises on which kinds of film and by whom goes into the Siren package. So far, films in these packages fall into the acclaimed arthouse/cult/action genres with popular film-stars like Maggie Cheung. Directors include John Woo, Ringo Lam, and Stanley Kwan. Siren also has plans in the near future to introduce "Hong Kong Cinema" as a genre with its own shelf space, rather than letting Hong Kong films disappear obliviously into the nondescript weekly shelves.

The recent success of particular Chinese films with mainstream audiences, both cult/arthouse as well as popular, and the advent of Chinese videos in mainstream stores would seem to demonstrate that appreciation of Chinese culture is not restricted to the Chinese and their descendants. Rather, it becomes diffused into the host society, and appears particularly attractive to those whom we could call, without prejudice, "cosmopolitan." That is, Chinese media products, if made accessible to English speakers via dubbing or subtitling, can appeal not just to "communities of difference," but also "communities of taste" (Hawkins, 1996b). Second-generation Chinese, for their part, respond to these products in the context of whatever assimilation they would have received into the mainstream culture, so their media experience is hybrid, or crosscultural in the best sense.

CONCLUSION

There is a common-sense level at which patterns of media use are matter-of-fact and pragmatic, not at all difficult to explain. Chinese people in

Melbourne watch English media if their English is fluent, and watch Chinese media if their Chinese is much better than their English. As we have noted, they also make creative, selective, and adaptive use of both mainstream and specialized media. At this pragmatic level, their choices of television programs, films, and videos are not affected either by their own ideas of identity, nor by official or unofficial Australian perceptions of their identity. For example, the manifest preference for nonfiction television, and for "serious" and not "escapist" film and video apparent especially amongst Mainland and to some extent Taiwanese respondents, gives an impression of people who use audiovisual media deliberately to improve their English, and to provide themselves with factual information and cultural insight that they might use in negotiating a place for themselves in a new society.

The impression of the ethnopolitical dimension of audiovisual media use, as provided by the household interview respondents, is that they tend to remain closely interested in events in East Asia, find themselves out of the way of things in Australia, and wish to stay informed, even though they would not conceive of this continued engagement as cultural according to any theoretically essentialist or multiculturalist definition. Cultural negotiation in this light includes negotiation of the particular difficulties of migrating to a country in which culture is thus fetishized and foregrounded, and which can stand as a cipher for race. This means consciousness of difference is heightened in the search to satisfy culturally and circumstantially given needs for information and entertainment, including the phenomenon of epistephilia, seen in wanting more news than the mass media are prepared to give about the outside world, especially their former part of it.

In addition to further analysis of the household interviews, a number of more extended, ethnographic visits have been made to selected households, so there is more refined data to be distilled from these sources. When we are able to analyze in depth the whole of the data we have to hand, we expect to be in a position to explain how patterns of audiovisual media use reflect patterns of adaptation and adjustment which, when taken together, amount to the negotiation of new cultural identities in a lived, continuous process, not the maintenance of a museum exhibit.

REFERENCES

Anderson, B. (1983) *Imagined Communities*. Verso, London.

Ang, I. (1992) "On Not Speaking Chinese: Diasporic Identification and Postmodern Identity," Paper presented at Trajectories: A

Symposium for Internationalist Cultural Studies, National Tsing Hua University, Taipei, 5-19 July.

Appadurai, A. (1990) "Disjunction and Difference in the Global Cultural Economy," *Public Culture, 2*(2), 1-24.

Bhabha, H. (1985) "Signs Taken For Wonders: Questions of Ambivalence and Authority under a Tree Outside Delhi, May 1817," *Critical Inquiry, 12*, Autumn.

Bogle, D. (1996) "Consumers Slow their Rush to Worldwide Web," *The Weekend Australian,* September 14-15, 9.

Chan, J. M. (1996) "Television in Greater China: Structure, Exports and Market Formation." In John Sinclair, Elizabeth Jacka and Stuart Cunningham, eds. *New Patterns in Global Television: Peripheral Vision.* Oxford and New York: Oxford University Press: 126-60.

Chow, R. (1991) *Woman and Chinese Modernity.* Bloomington: Indiana University Press.

Department of Immigration and Multicultural Affairs (1997) *Population Flows: Immigration Aspects.* Canberra: Author.

Esman, M. J. (1986) "Diasporas and International Relations." In Gabriel Sheffer, ed. *Modern Diasporas and International Politics.* London and Sydney: Croom Helm: 333-49.

Hall, S. (1995) "New Cultures For Old." In D. Massey and P. Jess, eds. *A Place in The World: Places, Culture and Globalization.* Oxford: Oxford University Press: 47-8.

Hawkins, G. (1996a) "Chinese Television in Australia: Narrowcasting, Difference and Diaspora," Paper presented at the 20th biennial conference of the International Association for Mass Communication Research, Sydney, 18-22 August.

———— (1996b) "SBS: Minority Television," *Culture and Policy, 7*(1), 45-63.

"Hong Kong Films Conquer the World" (1997) *Asian Business Review,* March, 20-2.

Lent, J. (1990) *The Asian Film Industry.* London: Christopher Helm.

Lovelock, P. and S. Schoenfeld (1995) "The Broadcast Media Markets in Asia." In John Ure, ed. *Telecommunications in Asia: Policy, Planning and Development.* Hong Kong: Hong Kong University Press: 147-91.

Morley, D. (1992) *Television, Audiences and Cultural Studies.* London and New York: Routledge.

Naficy, H. (1993) *The Making of Exile Cultures: Iranian Television in Los Angeles.* Minneapolis: University of Minnesota Press.

Sheffer, G. (1986) "A New Field of Study: Modern Diasporas in International Politics." In Gabriel Sheffer, ed. *Modern Diasporas and International Politics.* London and Sydney: Croom Helm: 1-15.

Silverstone, R. and E. Hirsch (1992) *Consuming Technologies: Media and Information in Domestic Spaces*. London and New York: Routledge.

Silverstone, R., E. Hirsch and D. Morley (1991) "Listening to a Long Conversation: An Ethnographic Approach to the Study of Information and Communication Technologies in the Home," *Cultural Studies*, 5(2), 204-27.

Sinclair, J. (1992) "'Just Like Normal People': Towards the Investigation of the Use and Significance of Communication and Information Technologies in the Household," *CIRCIT Working Paper 1992/1*, Centre for International Research on Communication and Information Technologies, Melbourne.

Sinclair, J., E. Jacka and S. Cunningham, eds. (1996) *New Patterns in Global Television: Peripheral Vision*. Oxford: Oxford University Press.

14

The Popular Forms of Hope: About the Force of Fiction Among TV Audiences in Brazil

Thomas Tufte

In the form of a tango, a soap opera, a Mexican film or a cheap crime story, the melodrama taps into and stirs up a deep vein of collective cultural imagination. And there is no access to historical memory or projection of dreams into the future which does not pass through this cultural imagination
—Jesús Martin-Barbero (1993)

We know that struggles through cultural mediation do not yield immediate or spectacular results. But, it is the only way to ensure we do not go from the sham of hegemony to the sham of democracy: to block the reappearance of a defeated domination installed by hegemony in the complicity of our thoughts and relationships
—Nestor Garcia Canclini (1989)

The Spanish-Colombian media researcher Jesús Martin-Barbero synthesizes the main message of his book, *Communication, Culture and Hegemony—From the Media to Mediations* (1987, in English in 1993) on the last page: ". . . melodrama and television, by allowing the people as a mass to recognize themselves as the authors of their own history, provide a language for the "popular forms of hope" (Martin-Barbero, 1993: 240). He ends his book with an example from the presidential elections in Brazil in 1985, analyzing how people—after 21 years of military dictatorship and in their mourning over the newly elected President Neves' illness, death, and burial—rediscovered their citizenship, "reinventing their identity in a spectacle, fusing politics and carnival with the corporal presence and the movements of a crowd" (Martin-Barbero, 1993: 239-40). Contrary to the press, the radio and television took to the streets and participated in the complex, ambiguous, and popular movement of the Brazilian people mourning the loss of their beloved president who never actually took office.

Something stronger than mere manipulation obviously moved the four million mourners on the streets of Sao Paulo. What was the nature of the force moving these masses of people? How did it occur and why did it manifest itself in this way? Martin-Barbero uses this story as the final example and synthesis in his classical analysis of the history and development of popular culture in Latin America. In his book he develops, from a Latin-American point of view, a theory of sociocultural mediation, arguing for a profound contextualization of media analysis in cultural analysis. The book launches an approach to media analysis based on the concept of mediations, with mediations defined as "the articulations between communication practices and social movements and the articulation of different tempos of development with the plurality of cultural matrices" (Martin-Barbero, 1993). His approach opens up a more dynamic—albeit complex—understanding of audience reception, avoiding the classical dualisms such as the active/passive audience. Martin-Barbero's concept of mediations, to which I return later, is an enriching alternative not only to reception studies, but to critical media theory as a whole.

Based on my own empirical work in Brazil, I shall first analyze—within the framework of Martin-Barbero's sociocultural theory of mediation—how the consumption of TV fiction on a regular daily basis contributes to the articulation of cultures, identities and social (and political) practices in everyday life.

I next present two examples of spectacular events that on a mass scale manifested the force of fiction among the Brazilian television audiences. Both examples are events of mass social movement sparked by audience consumption of tv-fiction. One illustrates how a fiction series in 1992 influenced the fall of President Collor, and the other shows how the death of a telenovela actress evoked a massive emotional response among the viewers, a response that soon developed into a huge civic movement demanding a revision of the penal code in Brazil.

Finally, I discuss the concept of media ethnography vis-à-vis Martin-Barbero's concept of mediation, arguing for the relevance of giving more attention to serious ethnographical approaches when studying the relation between the media and their audiences.

TELEVISION FICTION AND EVERYDAY LIFE

> Would it be inappropriate to ask to what extent the success of the melodrama in Latin America is a commentary on the failure of those political institutions that have developed with an unawareness of this "other society" and are incapable of acknowledging its cultural density?
> —Jesús Martin-Barbero (1993)

Neighborhood Cultures and Hybrid Spheres

Can the success of melodrama in Latin America be ascribed to the struggle of the people to be recognized, be it socially, culturally, or politically? Jesús Martin-Barbero poses the question whether there might be "a secret thread" linking the melodrama and the history of Latin America, indicating "the weight that the other primordial society of relatives, neighbourhoods and friendships holds for those who recognize themselves in the melodrama" (Martin-Barbero, 1993: 225-26). In a study about the role of telenovelas in the everyday life of low-income urban women in Brazil (Tufte, 1999), it was revealed how the women's identity construction was based on socioemotional experiences evolving from the social relationships found in the women's neighborhood cultures.[1] Five main socioemotional elements influencing their identity formation were identified, elements reflecting the hybridity of the cultures they live in and are a part of:

1. A concern and responsibility for the family, towards all members of the household. The women possess a high degree of loyalty to people they have "blood" ties with, including the whole extended family to which they open their homes. The outspoken sense of responsibility among the women often results in them having two jobs: one at home, keeping the household, and the other outside of the house, earning money.

---

[1]For further presentation of the concept of neighborhood cultures, see Martin-Barbero, 1993: 198. See also Tufte, 1999, chapters 7 and 8 for the empirical introduction to a concrete neighborhood culture, that of 13 women from three low-income urban areas of Brazil.

2. A daily struggle, and often an ambitious goal, is to obtain a decent and beautiful home of their own. Their dignity as human beings is very much linked to the organization of their household, keeping it clean and orderly. This was also expressed in the decorations on the walls and in the cultivation of small plants and flowers in front of their houses.
3. The women all have a strong solidarity with each other, expressed in a strong social network. It is a clear survival strategy that has to do with fulfilling the minimum need of each others families, but is also a means to make their lives easier and more enjoyable.
4. Among the black women a racial discourse is present in their self-reflection, manifesting their regular experiences of racial discrimination when shopping, when waiting at the bus stop, and when applying for jobs.
5. In relation to the world around them, a class consciousness and a feeling of marginality is present among all of them. They are keenly aware of the fact that they are poor and belong to the less privileged group of society. Although they are aware of their social position, most of them have dreams and aspirations of social change—more specifically, social ascent.

These socioemotional elements that influence the audience's identity formation—rooted in the neighborhood cultures of the mass urban suburbs of large Brazilian cities such as Sao Paulo and Salvador—spring especially, though not exclusively, from the *hybrid sphere of signification* encountered elsewhere and in which watching television is also a central activity (Tufte, 1994: 301-78). It is a sphere that constitutes a special organization of time and space, linked with a special code of conduct and together these create a sphere, both symbolically and materially, that is central to the formation of Latin American cultural identity—heavily infused with emotion, and with the telenovelas as central agents.

The Brazilian anthropologist Roberto DaMatta has been a source of inspiration in my conceptualization of this special sphere. DaMatta has in his book *The House and the Street* (1991), carried out a thorough analysis of the concepts of time and space in Brazilian everyday life. He argues that in Brazilian society, parallel forms of time and space exist, and he distinguishes among three discourses of time and space: the house, the street and what he calls the other world. They are linked to three different spheres of signification, marked by different codes of conduct, each possessing a specific language.

The three spheres are complementary, and difficult to separate. However, one class-specific code of conduct may prevail. Each of the dominated social groups—be it migrants from the rural areas or maids or work-ers in the informal sector—tends to use what DaMatta calls the language of the house (DaMatta, 1991: 54), which is based mainly on moral values referring to a moral that seems to be given by a higher power, a God.

In contrast to this discourse, there is that of the dominating seg-ments of society who use "the language of the street" and would never use moral references, but focus instead on personal contacts and val-ues. To them, laws are the guiding principle, along with the impersonal mechanisms of the logic of the capitalist system—modes of production, class struggle, and market orientation. According to DaMatta, the "street" is a sphere with little security, a dangerous place, where the law impos-es equality. This might sound strange—depending on one's cultural background—but the law signifies something negative. You lose your personal identity, become anonymous.

Finally, DaMatta operates with the "language of the other world."

> . . . it concerns a system which in an intriguing way relates to the superficial equality and which is given in legal codes of foreign inspi-ration, generally separated from our social practice; it possesses a hierarchical structure, refusing to take one of the codes as its exclu-sive and dominating one and always preferring a relation between the two. (DaMatta, 1991: 56)

DaMatta's "other world" demonstrates religious connotations that refer both to the Catholic history of colonial Brazil and also to other forms of religious affiliation.

This categorization of social practices constitutes a special approach, under which all aspects of everyday life are lived—including watching and producing meaning of television programs. DaMatta's con-cept of three different spheres proves extremely useful when analyzing empirical data. However, this present analysis of the role of telenovelas in everyday life indicates the existence of an autonomous, hybrid sphere of signification defined along some specific *temporal* and *spacial* para-meters. This is explained in more detail in the following.

The Hybrid Sphere of Signification

When television and telenovelas in the 1960s and 1970s appeared in the homes of many Brazilians, watching television gradually replaced other social activities, especially other media habits, such as listening to the radio. Watching telenovelas quickly became a significant factor of everyday life, dominating prime time in Brazil almost complete-ly. The women in this study watched an average of more than three telenovelas a day, mainly between 6 and 10 pm.

As far as organizing time is concerned, the flow of telenovelas stimulated both a linear and a cyclical concept of time. On the one hand, people adapt their everyday routines to the program schedule, thereby becoming rationally aware of time as something concrete that can be either abundant or limited, as is the case with watching the scheduled telenovelas.

However, the overall rhythm of the telenovela is even stronger. The daily presence of a telenovela for 6-8 months, the identifiable personal dramas, the repetitive narrative, and the colloquial language all contribute to transcending the linear time perception and stimulate instead a cyclical understanding of time.

Raymond Williams labeled the continuous interlinked broadcasting of TV programs in the course of an evening as "flow," thereby indicating the lack of clear limits between successive programs (Williams, 1975: 90ff). However, whereas Williams dealt mainly with the character of flow in the *horizontal* broadcasting policy, the abovementioned findings emphasize the *vertical* nature of the flow. The narratives are linked from day to day, so the lack of limits tends to be between yesterday's, today's, and tomorrow's chapter of a specific narrative rather than between the three telenovelas shown one after another every evening.

If we consider the organization of space in this hybrid sphere, TV viewing is organized according to a certain social and cultural codex. All collective household activities take place in the hybrid sphere, interlinked with continuous visits from relatives, neighbors and friends. It is neither a private nor a public sphere, but more a collective sphere. Its mere existence challenges the classical concepts of the meaning of "public" and "private," as well as the concept of domesticity used by Silverstone in his comprehensive analysis, *Television and Everyday Life* (Silverstone, 1994), the understanding and application of which will be considered later.

A typical phenomenon in the low-income Brazilian homes included in this present study is that one steps from the street right into the living room. There is never an entrance hall or corridor first. In other words, there is a direct connection between the main room in the house—the living room—and the street, or at least the space outside the house. Furthermore, as long as somebody is at home, the front door is usually wide open, so the street can be seen from the living room and vice versa. The windows are often open, too, and it is not unusual if there is no glass in the windows, which are shuttered at night. So in the morning, when the shutters are opened, it is not only to let light into the house, but also an often unconscious establishment of contact between the life inside and outside the house.

In *favelas* (slum dwellings), it is only a short distance from the house to the street because of the very dense and compact building of the houses, but in spite of the limited space, many people in the *favelas,* and especially the women, use the front space for both practical and decorational purposes. They have some flowers there or an outdoor sink to wash clothes in or just an open space where visitors can stand and talk with the woman of the house, or where the children can play. Thus, the contact between the house and the street becomes very close and as a result the limit between the public sphere (the street) and the private sphere (the house) becomes indistinct.

On the other hand, there is often a curtain or a small corridor between the kitchen/bedrooms and the living room, clearly indicating that the private sphere is behind this curtain or on the other side of the corridor, in the bedrooms and the kitchen. In the smallest homes, with only one room, the distinction between spheres is impossible; the private sphere simply disappears as a consequence. In such situations, the limit between the street and the house is clearly marked—for example, the front door will be closed more often and so a private sphere is established in the house, thereby eliminating the hybrid sphere in a physical sense.

The TV set is almost always in the living room. This was the case in 12 of the 13 homes visited, where the television was situated so it could be seen from the street. None of the 13 homes had the television set on the same wall as the main entrance, where it could not be seen from outside. Let me illustrate this with an example:

Eighteen-year-old Crioula's home in Calabar lay on a small hill a couple of meters from the narrow path sneaking tortuously through Calabar's cramped area. There was no fence and no real front yard. Both the door and the window shutters were open every time I visited Crioula and her family in their house. From the street, one stepped right into the living room, which was rather long and narrow. There was a sofa on the left side and the TV set was placed in a shelf system to the right. It could be seen both from the window and the door, as well as from the dining table at the other end of the living room. From the dining room at the end of the house, you entered the more private quarters.

Thus, the entrance area, together with the combined living and dining room, constituted the physical boundaries of the hybrid sphere in Crioula's home, and this was the case in many of the other homes visited.

Furthermore, unlike many other spaces in everyday life, this "in-between sphere" is not gender specific. Whereas men get together in their bars or on street corners and in squares, and women dominate the kitchen, the back yards, and the market places, the hybrid sphere is a collective space for both men and women.

Finally, the hybrid sphere is characterized by being a collective space of sounds and smells. The sounds of the television set, talk, playing children, traffic noise, the coming and going of people, the noise and smell from the cooking in the kitchen—all merge creating a collective space, where it becomes impossible to note whether you are in a public or private sphere.

Relating the above concept of hybrid sphere—spatially, temporally, audibly, gender-wise, and physically delimited as above—to Roger Silverstone's analysis and discussion of the concept of domesticity, it is worth noting that Silverstone points out what I consider to be one of the most characteristic tendencies in the general development of modern societies, a tendency that may increasingly challenge the hybrid sphere as described above: the tendency towards an increased isolation and removal of domesticity from the mainstream of modern society. Here, Silverstone understands domesticity as a reality envisaged from three perspectives: home (the phenomenological reality), family (the social reality), and household (the economic reality). He also analyzes domesticity in a historical context, analyzing how domestic life developed and gained commercial and cultural prominence (in Europe) in the early 19th century.

In the process of isolation and removal of domesticity from the mainstream of modern society, the mass media, and especially television, play a fundamental mediating role between the public and private spheres, between tradition and modernity, between urban and rural environments, and between the individual and the collective. What is in fact happening, generally speaking, is that hybrid spheres such as the ones found in low-income urban areas of Brazil tend to become less collective, less open vis-à-vis the outside world, and with an increased role attributed to communication via the mass media. Mediated forms of communication have become crucial agents in the constitution of the organization of time, space, and social relations, resulting in domestic life becoming reachable only through technical and heavily mediated forms of communication (Thompson, 1995).

Reconsidering Public and Private Spheres

In the abovementioned development process, and in the theoretical reflection on the reconstitution of public and private spheres, Jürgen Habermas' book, *The Structural Transformation of the Public Sphere: An Inquiry into a Category of Bourgeois Culture* (1962), which was first published in English in 1989, has experienced a strong revival. Despite his seminal analyses of the history and development of the public sphere, it remains today, for several reasons, more a classical reference than an up-to-date recipe for an analysis of the public sphere. For example, the fact that his analysis is based mainly on print-based culture illustrates the lack of taking the enormous, however more recent, role of audiovisual media into consideration. Habermas' later works, especially *The Theory of Communicative Action* (1981, in English in 1984-88) represents a significant advance in his formulation of a social theory, where his concept of "lifeworld" (vis-à-vis the "system-world") attributes substantial significance to the active subject in the constitution of social order and social action. Interesting parallels between the lifeworld of Habermas and the "other primordial society" of Martin-Barbero can be drawn.

The hybrid sphere of signification should be seen, in this theoretical context, namely as an attempt to reconsider the classical distinction between public versus private spheres, seeking conceptualizations regarding the organization of time, space, and social relations that contemplate the protagonism of emotion (and melodrama) and that can grasp sociocultural differences within the complex contemporary societies of the modern world. In this context, Silverstone's analysis of domesticity remains central in analyses of boundaries and gray zones between public and private spheres, thereby helping us to understand the processes of mediation in modern societies.

However, in view of Roger Silverstone's (and David Morley's, with whom Silverstone originally developed the theoretical-methodological framework for a case study) apparent desire to generalize, there may be an implicit risk of falling into one of the ethnocentric pitfalls mining the territory of qualitative empirical media research. Consider, for example, the following quotation taken from Morley's and Silverstone's work with new technologies in domestic settings: "Behind *the closed front doors* (my italics—ed.) of western and other societies, television and other information and communication technologies are consumed and used, one imagines, in ways that are both common and unique" (Morley and Silverstone, 1990: 4). My empirical work from Latin America reveals the problem of ethnocentrism in Morley's and Silverstone's understanding of domestic settings: in many low-income domestic settings in Latin America the use and consumption of television takes place not only behind but also *in front of* the front door! This is particularly true for lower social strata, whose front doors are rarely closed.

The organization of place and space in my case study is obviously very different from that signalled in Morley's and Silverstone's quotation above. This physical distinction may seem to be no more that a detail, but it is in fact a first indication of how complex our domestic environments can be. Therefore, the complexity of our social reality should be explicitly reflected in our development of analytical frameworks, in the concepts we use, and in the design of our empirical research.[2]

---

[2]For a more thorough analysis of Roger Silverstone's concepts and their applicability in cultural settings other than the ones in which they are developed, see Tufte, 1997.

In my case in Brazil, the fact is that television is placed in the most social of the household spheres, a sphere which in many cases transcends the barrier that a front door may constitute in other socioeconomic and cultural settings. In the Brazilian settings described, people relaxed and enjoyed each other's company, and they would typically be involved in other social activities, while at the same time gathering around the TV set, sometimes sitting on the doorstep or leaning in through the window, chatting and watching a telenovela.

This mode of living with television, and telenovelas in particular, contributes to a specific way of being together, influencing the constitution of the hybrid cultures of the urban masses in Latin America. It is by analysis of everyday practices and the ones seen in the hybrid sphere of signification that we can transcend old conceptual dichotomies of active or passive audiences, of public or private spheres, and instead focus on the polysemies of reception and on the multiple forms of cultural articulation and social action that spring from media consumption.

Constructing the Symbolic Order of Everyday Life

If we look closer at the reception of telenovelas, my analysis is structured along the two dominating discourses present both in the texts and in the comments and reflections of the women I interviewed (see also Tufte, 1999, chapter 9). The first discourse is the "personal discourse," which covers the emotional association and identification with fellowships such as family and community, as well as an identification with certain women's roles. The love drama, being central in all telenovelas, opens up for this identification and engagement.

For example, concern with and responsibility for the family is central. It is present in female viewers' identification with the often conflict-oriented relations between parents and children, men and women, brothers and sisters. Values such as unity, love, and mutual understanding are the ones emphasized when the women were asked to give resumes of their favorite telenovelas and when asked to highlight positive elements. In many ways the personal complication, touching upon disrespect, betrayal, and personal traumas of all sorts, reflects their own social reality. It was characteristic for the women that they had experienced several relationships with men and had often a series of tough personal experiences.

In recent years, more and more themes previously regarded as taboo have become key issues in telenovelas: for example, a love affair between a married woman and a priest, or a love affair between two people who turn out to be brother and sister. These issues question the norms and values upon which personal relations in Brazilian society are based. They challenge relational structures and moral codes. However, embedded in identifiable settings and with realistic characters, the issues are not normally rejected, but get debated.

In summary, analyzing the personal discourse within the reception of telenovelas reveals an emphasis on values of family relationship, unity, and community, and at the same time strong moral values. Similar codes of conduct—as will be seen in the case stories discussed later—can be recognized in the Brazilian audience's moral rejection of their President's corruptive affairs inspired by a fictional television program. Reception processes are clearly polysemic and at the same time reveal ambiguities between identification and distance, albeit with a shared tendency of strong emotional engagement.

If we consider the other principal discourse, that of class, the social mobility of the principal female character is often a central element in the narrative, which stimulates identification among low-income women. Most of the women in my study possessed this ambivalence between on the one hand dreaming about an easier life, envying the telenovela characters, their houses, cars, and clothes, and on the other hand focusing on the positive elements among themselves and their equals. Eva, 32 years old, from the neighborhood Santa Operaria in Canoas in Southern Brazil, formulates this very clearly when she talks about the values, the love, and the unity found within the Brazilian people:

> We are all aware that we haven't chosen life ourselves. We have been put in it, and it is obvious that we fight the best we can to obtain a better life than this. We always try to improve our life, but the powers we are up against are too strong. We have accustomed ourselves to living a plain life, and then we are also happier with a simpler life. We have a greater mutual understanding, more harmony. We know that those who have all that wealth, they do not have what we have. (Eva, 32, Santa Operaria)

In spite of a tough daily struggle for survival along with a struggle for social change, Eva finds comfort in the strong norms of unity and love found in her social stratum. In her analysis of the rich, Eva characterizes them as unhappy people, struggling for power, prestige and a social status that can only be obtained through a constant, dishonest fight for money. Their basic values differ fundamentally from the ones Eva argues that she and her fellow low-income citizens possess. In my view, this tends to be an idealization of their own norms and values, together with a simplification of the norms of others, in order to explain the everyday struggle for survival.

Despite a clear class discourse both in program and readings, the physical portraits of the social classes in telenovelas are not as physically explicit as in real life. Slums are never seen, and workers' boroughs are almost unrecognizable as they are cleaner, more beautiful and always more bountiful and richer than in real life. Nevertheless, the viewer comprehends clearly who the "rich" are and who the "poor" are. The language is one of the indicators of class difference.

A social interpretation of the narrative is clearly perceived in the language the women use about the characters and the narrative in general. All of them use expressions such as "to rise in life", "up there-down here," "fight to get there," "rise-fall," and "ascend-descend." The aspect of suffering is often central in the women's interpretation of this social inequality, where the struggle to maintain their personal pride becomes essential. Human dignity and pride is the last thing a person possesses when everything else is lost or beyond reach. As Eva clearly expresses it:

> . . . the poor are very humiliated, very trodden upon. We are regarded as nothing, as animals. Society does not accept us and that is why we suffer as much as we do, you see. Her story was the same (Maria do Carmo, the protagonist of the novela The Rubbish Queen-ed.). She rose thanks to a lot of suffering, renunciation and everything. But before, when she still was poor, she was mobbed in school, like my children. . . . Generally, those who fight, those who raise their voice here in the world are us, us that suffer most. Meanwhile, we don't have anything to lose, we have lost everything already. The only thing we haven't lost is our struggle, our dignity. (Eva, 32, Santa Operaria)

A person may be poor, but she should still be treated with respect and dignity. This is the core of one of Latin America's most basic problems: many inhabitants in urban peripheries are socially, economically, and culturally so marginalized that in practical terms they lack a lot of the fundamental citizen's rights, which brings us back to the issue—inspired by Martin-Barbero—that I raised at the beginning of this article, namely that ". . . melodrama and television, by allowing the people as a mass to recognize themselves as the authors of their own history, provide a language for the popular forms of hope" (Martin-Barbero, 1993: 240).

In summary, understanding how telenovelas articulate hybrid cultures and provide a language for the popular forms of hope in contemporary Brazil and Latin America in general requires profound analysis of the specific Brazilian or Latin American constitution of society and culture. Telenovelas and their mediations into the practices of everyday life have deeps roots in the history of narration, in the history of the Latin American process of modernization, and not least in the personal life history and life conditions of the telenovela viewers. Furthermore, as we have seen above, the viewers' normative, moral, and religious attitudes and beliefs influence the construction of symbolic order and the general production of meaning articulated from consuming telenovelas.

Thus, telenovelas relate to the everyday experiences of the viewers despite the fact that they portray a material world far removed from the viewers' own everyday life. The identification lies in the common human universe—the feelings—that transcends class conflicts and material differences. The telenovelas mostly enrich everyday life, articulating social and cultural practices. In some cases, the identification with characters and themes from fictive narratives stimulates such a strong mobilization of energy and opinion that it can stir up transcending social movement, best illustrated in the two cases to be presented next: the first case will show how the audience's surprising interpretation of the mini-series *Rebellious Years* in 1992 played a pivotal role in a historical political event in the history of Brazil and of Latin America in general, articulating and generating popular and at times carnivalesque forms of hope among the participating people.

The second case will show how the emotional engagement in a telenovela, manifested in profound grief over the loss of a "fictive friend," can be transformed into a civic movement demanding political change.

TELEVISION, EMOTION AND SOCIAL CHANGE

The Impeachment of President Collor

President Fernando Collor de Melo, a good-looking, wealthy, and politically unknown 40-year-old, liberal—and populist—man from a traditional family, became the first directly and thus democratically elected president in Brazil after 29 years of military dictatorship without presidential elections. Collor defeated the socialist candidate, Lula, in December 1989, after a fierce campaign in which he counted on massive, explicit and very favorable support from the all-dominant national TV-network, *Rede Globo de Comunicacoes,* owned by the legendary now 90-year-old Roberto Marinho and his family. Two-and-a-half years later, the same Globo-network contributed in several ways—and in close and fundamental interaction with their audience—to what led to the fall of President Collor.

Rebellious Years (Anos Rebeldes, Globo, 1992) was a mini-series (12 chapters) written by Gilberto Braga about the Brazilian student movement and its political resistance to the military dictatorship in the late 1960s and early 1970s. It showed how young people dared to resist the repressive regime, even using at times rather radical methods such as kidnapping an ambassador. The story was very similar to events that had actually occurred in Brazil in the darkest years of dictatorship: 1968-73. As part of the story, some authentic black-and-white film strips documenting student demonstrations in Brazil in this period were used. They had never been shown on television before.

What then happened in 1992 was overwhelming and must be seen in connection with the actual political situation at the time of the transmission. *Rebellious Years* was aired by Rede Globo in July 1992, a few weeks after President Collor's brother, on Rede Globo's news broadcast, had denounced the corruptive affairs his own brother, the President, was involved in. It was a moment of both severe political as well as economic crisis in Brazil, with the government taking drastic and controversial economic decisions, and with a personal conflict between President Collor and his brother Pedro leading to the brother denouncing the President. Furious about the President's supposedly corrupt affairs, and clearly inspired by the student movement shown in the fiction of *Rebellious Years*, thousands of students took to the streets and became, as the respected Brazilian news magazine Veja stated on their cover page, "Rebellious Angels" (Portuguese, *Anjos Rebeldes* very similar to the title of the miniseries, *Anos Rebeldes*).

The social movement against President Collor started with high school students and quickly spread to universities. *Rebellious Years* practically sparked a massive mobilization against President Collor, who reacted on Rede Globo's news broadcast by encouraging a counter-demonstration under his green and yellow campaign colors (also the colors of the Brazilian flag) to emphasize support for him. Instead, this became a direct invitation to do the opposite. People of all social strata took to the streets that Sunday in the middle of August 1992 dressed in black, mourning the Collor scandal (furthermore, black became the fashion color of the clothes of the principal character, Yasmin, in the main prime-time telenovela that year, called *From Body and Soul*).

In August and September 1992, Brazil experienced the biggest demonstrations seen since the movement for democracy in 1984-85, with millions taking to the streets. By late September, the Congress decided to set up a council to investigate the President's alleged corruption. President Collor was impeached. Three months later, on 27 December, the council came to a conclusion: former President Collor would be charged with corruption. His political rights were suspended for a period of eight years. Now, more than six years later, Collor lives a relaxed and comfortable life in Miami, but the rebellious students obtained what they wanted—Collor's downfall.

Meanwhile, the day the final decision to charge the impeached President Collor with corruption was announced in the Brazilian media—on 27 December 1992—the news was overshadowed by another, and apparently more important event—the murder of Daniela Perez.

The Murder of Daniela Perez

On the morning of 27 December 1992, Daniela Perez, one of the main actresses in the 8 pm telenovela of the time, *From Body and Soul* (De Corpo e Alma) was found murdered on a deserted road in the outskirts of Rio de Janeiro. Initially, when news of the murder spread, people were confused. *From Body and Soul* was reaching its peak and final episode, after about seven months of daily prime-time transmission, six days a week, and viewers were asking each other whether the principal character, Yasmin, died in the telenovela or whether the actress playing Yasmin, Daniela Perez, really died? Was this fact or fiction?

This was fact, and to add to the confusion, the main suspect of the murder was her husband/partner in the telenovela, Guilherme de Pádua, and his wife in real life, Paula Thomaz. The murder sparked a social movement, led by the victim's mother, the author of telenovelas Glória Perez: she demanded a total revision of the penal code in Brazil in order to arrest the suspect quicker and more efficiently than the current penal code permitted. The peak of this social movement came eight months later, on 19 September 1993, when 70,000 people gathered at a football stadium in Sao Paulo to see the victim's mother hand to the government authorities 1.3 million signatures supporting the revision of the penal code. A moment later, the organizer asked for a minute's silence in memory of the murdered Daniela. This silence was then broken by the musical theme of the novela character Yasmin, Daniela's last role . . . everyone was crying and the whole event was transmitted "live" on radio and television.

Four years later, in 1997, Guilherme de Pádua and Paula Thomaz were sentenced to 19 and 18 years imprisonment for the murder of Daniela Perez. To my knowledge, the Brazilian penal code has not—at least not yet (spring 1999)—undergone the revision called for.

Emotional Engagement and Social Action

Both of the case stories given above are spectacular accounts that show how fiction programs—and their respective characters and actors—mediate into and influence the cultural, social, and political action of our everyday lives, in the above cases with significant political and "civic" consequences. The miniseries *Rebellious Years* was interpreted as an invitation to participate in political opposition to President Collor, an interpretation not at all foreseen by Rede Globo, which screened the series. The example indicates the complexity of the reception process in general and of the relationship between the viewers' interpretation of a TV-series and the socioeconomic and political realities in which they live in particular. Thus, it demonstrates the relevance and importance of contextualizing a reception analysis, linking microsocial analyses of the reception process with macroanalyses of the given socioeconomic and political structures. Today it is unlikely that *Rebellious Years* would have sparked a similar massive mobilization: the political, economic, and partly also the social situation in Brazil is more stable now than in 1992.

With reference to the second case, the murder of actress Daniela Perez, the emotional engagement in relation to her death reveals the degree of strong social relationship and emotional complicity that exists between Brazilian actors (actresses), especially those in telenovelas, and their audience. It documents the at times very strong parasocial relationship that can develop between TV characters and their audience. This was first identified by American psychologists Donald Horton and Richard Wohl in 1956 in their classic article "Mass Communication and Para-Social Interaction: Observation on Intimacy at a Distance." These parasocial relationships continue to exist, the case of Daniela Perez being an example of how "the loss of a friend" may lead to surprising social action.

Both case stories provide significant insights into the sociopsychic or political force that is inherently a reception process—in these cases a Brazilian television-fiction shown to a Brazilian audience. It is a force that fundamentally is *emotionally* driven, a force that at certain moments in time and space can lead to transcending massive actions.

In his substantial research on reception processes, the Chilean media researcher Valerio Fuenzalida has worked specifically with the emotional relationship the viewer has to television. His findings have shown that television, and especially TV fiction, can create substantial emotional engagement among the viewers when television tells stories of everyday life. *Recognition* is fundamental to this identification and subsequent emotional engagement (Fuenzalida, 1992b). Fuenzalida speaks of the testimonial form of television: "The testimonial form presents ordinary people's acting and protagonism, and thereby values audiences' daily life. In this televisual form many people may recognize themselves as actors in their daily story with their works and contingencies; which is the very story of most people" (Fuenzalida, 1992b). This was to some degree the case of the young TV viewers watching *Rebellious Years*. Collor's corruption demonstrated a profound disrespect towards the people of Brazil, which many young people found similar to the situation under the military dictatorship portrayed in *Rebellious Years*.

Fuenzalida's plea for taking emotion seriously makes him argue that telenovelas, due to their widespread popularity in Latin American countries, constitute a much more important and relevant educational instrument than, for example, news programs. As Fuenzalida states:

"The redundance of the serials makes its attraction rationally inexplicable; but the interest is exactly emotional" (Fuenzalida 1987: 25).

According to Tufte (1999), the protagonism of emotional engagement in TV fiction is confirmed, whereby the "talking to the heart" mastered by telenovelas became the key not only to identification with characters, situations, and themes, but became fundamental to understanding the formation of identity of the viewers. When the women in that study were asked for example about why they liked telenovelas, their statements confirmed the key role of emotional engagement in the consumption of telenovelas: "Oh, it was full of emotion" (Ana, 20); "the novela touched people a lot" (Clara, 27), or "it was very touching" (Ilda, 41). Ana's example below demonstrates this, when referring to the telenovela *Pantanal* (screened on the Manchete TV network in 1990):

I liked it, I loved it. It was a great novela. It was a very strong novela, a novela full of emotion. I liked it a lot.

Could you perhaps explain what you mean, when you talk about emotion?

It is something we like, something that makes us feel happy.

What is it in the novela that makes you feel happy?

When a couple quarrel and then return and settle down peacefully with each other, kissing, hugging and then they marry. Well, then we feel happy. Or when you are hoping two people get each other. Like in *Ana Raio and Ze Trovao* (Rede Manchete, 1991—ed), where I am hoping that Ana Raio and Ze Trovao get each other. Well, then I get happy.

(...)

Wouldn't you like a life with emotion like the people in the telenovelas?

I would like that, of course (laughing a little), right, but sometimes it is very difficult to obtain. I do want it. All girls think like this: they want a house, want a husband and want some children. But these days, I think it is impossible because the men don't want to. They don't want to have a family and sometimes they don't want to have the trouble with the wife and don't want children. I see many examples around here, where the girls aren't too happy in a relationship. They get pregnant and then their boyfriends leave them. And she has to have the child. All this leaves me sad. I want to avoid these things, so I prefer to remain single. (Ana, 20: all quotations from Tufte, 1999)

The Brazilian media researcher, Carlos Eduardo Lins da Silva, confirms that telenovelas—contrary to the largest news journal in Brazil, Jornal Nacional on Rede Globo—offered very personal and recognizable stories that made active and critical reception possible:

> The fact that the novelas are about universal problems of mankind means that they of all the programmes in the Globo prime time schedule best allow the viewer to compare what they see with real life. And this is precisely why telenovela is the genre that influences the critical consciousness of the viewer most. . . . Almost all the persons who watch telenovelas have experienced similar situations or at least situations structurally comparable with the characters of the narrative: falling in love, betrayal, love, hatred, death, birth, marriage, abortion, illness, migration, persecution, unemployment, etc. (da Silva, 1985: 120)

Telenovelas—and the similar genre of mini-series—take place in the emotional universe and deal with common human feelings and situations, which makes it possible to recognize feelings and events. In the case of *Rebellious Years*, this liberated sociopsychic energies based on both anger and disappointment towards President Collor. Most people can talk about and have an opinion about love, hatred, or family life, like for example Ana, whom I quoted above. Despite the fact that Da Silva had set out to study the reception of news among two communities, what he found was that telenovelas tell people more about reality than the news programs do, for the simple reason that they deal with issues most people know about and are concerned with, namely everyday life, feelings, and the family.

Da Silva's reception analysis contributes to Fuenzalida's argument about the centrality of emotion. According to Da Silva, the telenovelas appear to be more "real" than news! Fuenzalida goes further with this argument to say that not only TV fiction, but televised language as a whole is fundamentally emotional. According to him, "televised language is more fit for the narrative fiction and the emotional identification than for the abstraction and analysis; tv's associative language, polysemic and glamorous affect better the fantasy and the desire" (Fuenzalida, 1992a: 39)

Thus, in order to increase one's understanding of the reception and interpretation process, one must accept the emotional relation viewers have to television. This does not necessarily imply comprehensive psychological analyses, but can be viewed in the perspective of the other contextual elements in which the viewing takes place. Fuenzalida thus argues that a more profound understanding of the reception process should be sought in an analysis of the relevance that the program has for the viewer, combined with the concrete need the viewer defines (Fuenzalida, 1992b: 15).

Both examples given at the beginning of this article contain in their reception processes elements of recognition, relevance, and need. In the first case, the young students recognized in *Rebellious Years* the emotional conflict they were experiencing; they became morally enraged by President Collor's affairs and thereby felt the need to do something about it. Ultimately, they wished to save the young democracy of Brazil. In those terms, the screening of the program at that moment became highly relevant for Brazilian viewers.

In the second case, the murder of Daniela Perez, her death severed an emotional bond developed between the actress and her viewers in the course of 170-200 chapters of the telenovela *From Body and Soul.* At the same time, it was a great disappointment not to be able to see the end of story; that is, the last chapters of the telenovela in which she was the protagonist. The loss both of a "friend" and of the dramatic climax of a seven-month continuous narrative stirred up the emotional engagement that developed into a civic movement demanding the reform of Brazil's penal code!

Fuenzalida and my own examples, given above, thus support the argument for increased attention to the practices of everyday life, linking consumption of TV fiction with the cultural characteristics and socioeconomic conditions of the viewers and acknowledging emotions as an important phenomenon linking media flow, cultural practices, and social development.

FROM MEDIA TO MEDIATIONS—THE VIRTUES OF MEDIA ETHNOGRAPHY

It is necessary to abandon mediacentrism, for the system of the media is losing its specificity and becoming an integral part of the economic, cultural and political system.
—Richeri (1985: 60)

If the epistemological objective of one's research is to obtain knowledge of the relationship between mass communication, cultural practices. and social development, then a "mediation" approach has proven relevant and useful. The first part of this article has sought to exemplify this mediation approach, hopefully providing some insight into the strongholds and applicability of a mediation approach. With my own examples, I have implicitly argued for a decentering of the academic object from the narrow relationship between the media text and the audience to a broader analysis of cultural practices and everyday life.

Furthermore, as explicitly argued by many Latin American scholars (Canclini, 1989; Leal, 1985, 1986; and Martin-Barbero, 1993), studying popular culture should be closely linked to consideration of social development and change. The socioeconomic situation on most of the Latin American continent—marked by social inequality, poverty, marginalization, and so forth—makes such a social concern apparent. Consequently, (media) ethnographical studies that study popular culture, such as television fiction, should relate to the sociocultural, historical, and political conditions in which the specific audience and media exist. In this article I have illustrated different dimensions of social change articulated by the consumption of TV fiction among Brazilian audiences. Studying popular culture in a Latin American context, as Martin-Barbero, Canclini, and others do, places the recognition of popular culture and celebration of pleasure and polysemic reception in a broader concern for the processes of social and economic development

Media ethnography along these epistemological lines—which many reception researchers concerned with ethnography and context-based reception studies for many reasons do not follow, however—can benefit enormously from constructing a theoretical framework around Martin-Barbero's concept of mediations. As mentioned earlier, Martin-Barbero understands mediations as "the articulations between communication practices and social movements and the articulation of different tempos of development with the plurality of cultural matrices" (Martin-Barbero, 1993).

What is in play is a *culture analysis*, in which cultural practices and social action are analyzed in relation to how mass media interact with the audience in these contexts. The mediations should be understood as the set of influences that structure, organize, and reorganize the understanding of the reality the audience lives in, thereby also having the power to give value and meaning to this reality. The mediations produce and reproduce the social significations, thereby creating a "sphere" which makes the understanding of the interaction between production and reception possible. The hybrid sphere of signification that I found in my case study of telenovelas is an example of such a melting pot of mediations.

Mediations in this respect are explicitly linked to a notion of culture in terms of a concrete manifestation of social structures. The social facts become mediations between, on one hand the historical conditions that contextualize specific social facts, and on the other hand the complex structure of society. Cultural expressions are *bricolages* of various cultural elements, "created and recreated at different levels of signification—at the collective memory, at mind structure of knowledge, at the affective level of everyday life structures" (Leal, 1985: 31).

Martin-Barbero suggests three types of mediations: the daily life of the family, social temporality, and cultural competence. By studying these three mediations, one should be able to capture the "sphere" in which the production of meaning takes place (Martin-Barbero, 1993: 211-24). In Tufte (1999) these mediations are developed into analyses of the everyday life of the audience (the daily life of the family), the social uses of the media (the social temporality), and a substantial genre analysis—both the history and development of the genre and the cultural context in which they developed, thus treating different aspects of the third mediation suggested by Martin-Barbero, namely that of cultural competence. According to Martin-Barbero, "the genres, articulating the narration of the serials, constitute a fundamental mediation between the logic of the system of production and that of consumption, between the logic of the format and how that format is read and used" (Martin-Barbero, 1993: 221). The first part of this article synthesizes aspects and characteristics regarding the first two mediations (daily life and social temporality).

The point I wish to make here is that Latin American scholars of communication and culture have, in fact, developed innovative ethnographical approaches to media and culture studies vis-à-vis the Anglo-American trend of media ethnography. I see the Latin American approaches following a line of thought that can deliver inspiring theoretical and methodological perspective to our "domestic" reflections within the Anglo-American "tradition."

The first point is the critical political perspective, which was once very prominent in British Cultural Studies, but has since been subject to a process of dissolution in the increasingly emphasized microsociological focus within media ethnographical work (see a critical retrospective in Lull, 1996). Within the broad Latin American field of cultural studies, media ethnography has grown out of the explicit critical and political wish to understand the processes of development and modernization—in particular the sociocultural dynamics occurring in association with the increased spread and consumption of mass media and popular culture. The critical "search for identity" as Latin Americans is manifest in this process, as mentioned at the beginning of this article.

The second innovative aspect is that of understanding the media from the perspective of mediations, transcending old oppositions of text-context, active or passive audience, and so forth. The decentering of the academic object does not imply an either-or, quite the contrary. For example, Martin-Barbero's genre concept, based on genre as a strategy of communicability, implies a holistic approach that conditions attention to both textual and contextual aspects regarding a genre and its relation to the audience (Martin-Barbero, 1993: 220-28). Therefore, by maintaining a focus on mediations, media ethnography becomes critical ethnographical studies of the mediations that, let's say, "form the setting" in which sense-making processes take place. It could, as in my case study, be related to the consumption of TV fiction. The classical mediacentrism of reception studies is thus replaced by a focus on mediations. And with the perspective of social change present, it often becomes a study of the popular forms of hope.

Finally, given the predominantly urban societies today, with substantial cultural exchanges in time and place as well as in race, class and gender, the hybridity of culture must be taken into account, not forgetting that the cultural exchange occurring in the urban melting pots is hierarchically organized. Hybridization of cultures between the dominant culture and the dominated cultures is, however, a symbolic relationship that does not lead to the elimination of one of the cultures. Brazil is a unique example of this, where cultures from all over the world have merged into hybrid cultures, the Afro-Brazilian cultures being the classic example.[3]

Given the above characteristics, media ethnography is characterized predominantly as an anthropological and cultural sociological discipline, but with a heuristic approach and thus with interdisciplinary characteristics.

Politics of Ethnographic Research

In the aftermath of the "rediscovery of everyday life" within Anglo-American empirical media studies of the mid- and late 1980s, there has since developed a clear warning against narrowing the focus of analysis to the microsocial settings, eliminating the macrosocial settings and structures. Meeting these criticisms, David Morley makes clear what he considers to be the politics of ethnographic research, arguing for the necessity of combining analyses of the microcontexts of consumption with analyses of the macrostructural processes: "If one of the central functions of communications systems is to articulate different spaces (the public and the private, the national and the international) and, necessarily, in so doing to transgress boundaries (whether the boundary around the domestic household, or that around the nation) then our analytical framework must be capable of being applied at both the micro- and the macro-level" (Morley, 1992).

Ien Ang, who herself is a strong spokeswoman for media ethnography, warns us against romanticism and an overestimation of the

---

[3]Brazil has been an attractive field of investigation among many anthropologists, thus also inspiring the Brazilians' own tradition of anthropology. Roger Bastide lived in Brazil from 1938-1951 teaching at the University of Sao Paulo and attributing special empirical attention to Afro-Brazilian religions. Claude Levi-Strauss also spent many years in Brazil (mainly in the 1930s), in addition to Radcliffe-Brown, Robert Redfield, Donald Pierson, Charles Wagley, and Marvin Harris.

symbolic resistance which the audience is often attributed in reception studies: "There is a romanticising and romanticist tendency in much work that emphasizes (symbolic) resistance in audience reception. . . . It is a perfectly reasonable starting point to consider people's active negotiations with media texts and technologies as empowering in the context of their everyday lives (which, of course, is the context of media reception) but we must not lose sight of the marginality of that power" (Ang, 1990: 246-47).

Despite the warning, I consider Ang as having overestimated this potential in her own concluding chapter of her book published the year after the above statement (Ang, 1991), an overestimation that led the Danish media researcher Kirsten Drotner to characterize Ang's argument and agenda as *ethnographic fundamentalism* (Drotner, 1996). Obviously, symbolic resistance does not create revolutions—however, it should not be underestimated. It is precisely in the ability to actually express symbolic resistance that we find two important elements that should be emphasized both in critical ethnography of mediations and generally in studies of everyday life:

- The symbolic resistance which possesses the seed to further struggle for social change and improvement at all levels.
- The ability to resist, which explains in part how marginalized people—as for example, many of the inhabitants in the urban peripheries of large towns all over the world—can survive, with all the sociocultural, political, and economic odds against them.

As de Certeau argues in introducing his own investigation, the study of everyday life has the deeper meaning of seeking to understand the "other" logic, for example, the polysemy of the interpretations of TV programs experienced among the viewers (de Certeau, 1984). The presence of a silent majority formulating multiple and often creative and incomprehensive modes of action is not a reason for excluding studies of their lives from academic research—rather quite the contrary.

REFERENCES

Ang, I. (1990) "Culture and Communication: Towards an Ethnographic Critique of Media Consumption in the Transnational Media System," *European Journal of Communication, 5*(23), 239-60.
——— (1991) *Desperately Seeking the Audience.* London: Routledge.
——— (1996) *Living Room Wars—Rethinking Media Audiences for a Postmodern World.* London: Routledge.

Canclini, N. G. (1989) *Culturas Hibridas*. Mexico: Editorial Grijalbo.

———, ed. (1993) *El Consumo Cultural en Mexico*. Mexico: Consejo Nacional para la Cultura y las Artes.

DaMatta, R. (1991) *A Casa e A Rua*. Rio de Janeiro: Editora Guanabara Koogan S.A.

Da Silva, C. E. (1985) *Muito alem do Jardim Botanico: Um estudo sobre a audiencia do Jornal Nacional da Globo entre trabalhadores*. Sao Paulo: Summus Editorial.

de Certeau, M. (1984) *The Practice of Everyday Life*. Berkeley and London: University of California Press.

Drotner, K. (1996) "Less Is More: Media Ethnography and Its Limits." In P. Crawford, ed. *The Construction of the Viewer: Media Ethnography and the Anthropology of Audiences*. Hoejbjerg: Intervention Press.

Fuenzalida, V. (1987) "La Gente es lo mas importante," *Communicacion America Latina, 17*, 31-35.

——— (1992a) "Investigacion." Paper presented for UNICEF Conference, Rio de Janeiro: November 1991. Published in *Dialogos, 33* (1992): 36-40. Lima: Felafacs.

——— (1992b) "TV Broadcasting for Grassroot Development." Paper presented at the conference, "TV and Video in Latin America," Denmark, November 1992. Denmark: Danchurchaid.

Giddens, A. (1984) *The Constitution of Society*. Berkeley: University of California Press.

Habermas, J. (1962/1989) *The Structural Transformation of the Public Sphere: An Inquiry into a Category of Bourgois Society*. Cambridge, MA: MIT Press.

——— (1981/1984-88) *The Theory of Communicative Action*. 2 vols. Cambridge: Polity Press.

Horton, D. and R. R. Wohl (1956/1986) "Mass Communication and Para-Social Interaction: Observation on Intimacy at a Distance." In Gary Gumpert and Robert Cathcart, eds. *INTER/MEDIA—Interpersonal Communication in a Media World*. New York and Oxford: Oxford University Press.

Jensen, K. B. (1991) "Humanistic Scholarship as Qualitative Science: Contributions to Mass Communication Research." In K.B.Jensen and N.W.Jankowski, eds. *A Handbook of Qualitative Methodologies for Mass Communication Research*. London: Routledge.

Leal, O. F. (1985) *Mass Communication: Culture and Ideology. A Field Statement*. Berkeley: University of California.

——— (1986) *A Leitura Social da Novela das Oito*. Petrópolis: Editora Vozes.

Lull, J. (1996) "The Political Correctness of Cultural Studies." Paper presented to the Bi-Annual Scientific Conference of the International Association for Media and Communication Research, Sydney, Australia, August 18-22.

Martin-Barbero, J. (1987/1993) *Communication, Culture and Hegemony.* London: Sage.

Morley, D. (1992) *Television, Audiences and Cultural Studies.* London: Routledge.

Morley, D. and R. Silverstone (1990) "Domestic Communication: Technologies and Meanings," *Media, Culture and Society, 12*(1).

Richeri, G. (1985) "Nuevas tecnologías e investigación sobre la comunicación de masas." In M. De Moragas, ed. *Sociología de la Comunicación de Masas.* Barcelona: Gustavo Gili.

Silverstone, R. (1994) *Television and Everyday Life.* London: Routledge.

Thompson, J. B. (1995) *The Media and Modernity—A Social Theory of the Media.* Cambridge: Polity Press.

Tufte, T. (1997) "Televisión, Modernidad y vida cotidiana. Un análisis sobre la obra de Roges Silverstone desde contextos culturales diferentes," In *Comunicación y Sociedad, 31.* Universidad de Guadalajara, Mexico: 65-96.

——— (1999) *Living with the Rubbish Queen—Telenovelas, Culture and Modernity in Brazil.* Luton: University of Luton Press.

Williams, R. (1975/1990) *Television: Technology and Cultural Form.* London: Routledge.

15

Between the Normal and the Imaginary: The Spectator-Self, the Other and Satellite Television in India*

Anjali Monteiro
K. P. Jayasankar

. . . But one thing is certain after the introduction of the cable [television] . . . the fights between the neighbors have definitely reduced. That is for sure. Everybody is at home—everybody in their respective homes. They watch programs, they don't sit outside. Otherwise they [the women] would sit outside . . . remove lice from each other's heads and along with the lice, out would come all the stories, the gossip . . . [laugh] and that would start off fights . . . with the cable, all that is gone . . . much less fighting. . . . (F, Interview 9)

*Both the authors have contributed equally to the writing of this paper. They wish to thank Ms. Anita Mehta, who conducted several of the discussions and transcribed and translated all the recordings, Mr. S. Muralidharan for typing the interview transcripts, as well as the families and groups who participated in the discussions.

This is an attempt at beginning to answer, in a small, fragmented and partial way, the broad question of how global capital, as a cultural phenomenon mediated by satellite television, is negotiated by the diverse audiences that constitute the growing urban middle class in India in the post-liberalization period. The liberalization process, involving a dismantling of-state controls over the industry, foreign trade, and investment, was initiated in the mid-1980s by the Rajiv Gandhi government. It gathered momentum with the introduction of the Structural Adjustment Program, in July 1991.[1]

Satellite television is perhaps one of the most pervasive fall-outs of this phenomenon of globalization. The authors consider India a test case of what happens when the skies are "opened" to a large number of satellite networks, for, until the decade of the 1990s, in a country of 960 million people, there was only one state-sponsored channel. The notion of agency of the viewer assumes significance in such a scenario, which in India is invariably regarded as a "cultural invasion from the skies." In the process of exploring the complex relationships between audiences and television, this paper attempts to short circuit the debate concerning active versus passive audiences (and omnipotent media institutions) by pointing to the possibility that it is precisely this feeling of "agency" that constitutes a spectator-self and facilitates its assimilation into larger matrices of power. The spectator-self is the sum total of the strategic, sometimes conflicting subject positions that the viewer occupies in order to negotiate his/her identity as a continuum vis-à-vis the televisual discourse.

Drawing on unstructured interviews and discussions with families in Bombay,[2] the paper also aspires to map out some dimensions of the fluid terrain on which identities are constructed and reproduced within urban popular culture in India. The process of constituting the spectator-self in contradistinction to television is effected by constructing "others," both above and below the spectator-self, and by demarcating the boundaries across the "imaginary" and the "normal." The spectator-self appears to yo-yo between these coordinates.

---

[1]For a critical discussion of the implications of this process, see Singh, 1993, and Ghosh, 1994.

[2]A series of nine interviews and focus group discussions were conducted with families and groups of youth, between March and September 1996, in two neigbborhoods in Bombay, one a lower-middle-class slum locality in North Bombay, and the other, a relatively affluent housing colony in Central Bombay. The families were chosen with two criteria in mind, the first being cable connectivity and the second, the need to represent various linguistic/ethnic/religious communities. For a profile of discussion groups, refer to Appendix 1. The discussions dealing with themes such as perceptions of satellite television and uses of TV were recorded, transcribed, and translated. They were coded and analyzed by the authors.

THE LOCAL AND THE GLOBAL

Television in India was introduced in the 1960s as a state-run experiment, intended as a purveyor of educational and developmental messages. The rhetoric of development continued to characterize the functioning of Doordarshan (DD), the state-owned television network, through the 1970s and early 1980s; its reach remained limited. The first major expansion of DD took place in the 1980s, with satellite-based transmission. The logic of development-as-state program was substituted with the logic of marketing development and development as market expansion (Monteiro, 1993; Monteiro and Jayasankar, 1994). This process of going commercial allowed for the entry of private production companies and sponsorship by business houses, under state control. There was a circumscribed space, defined by the moral and political imperatives of the state, within which private, commercial producers could operate. This state control was most apparent and perhaps most resisted by viewers in the case of the news (Monteiro and Jayasankar, 1994; Jayasankar and Monteiro, 1998).

The expansion of DD facilitated the circulation, by the state, of a pan-Indian culture and an "Indian" identity organized around the primacy of consumption, the privileging of the modern, urban middle-class nuclear family, the conflation of the "Indian" with upper caste, Hindi-Hindu culture, and the acceptance of the "pastoral power" of the state (Foucault, 1986; Nandy, 1989). The strategies invoked by viewers to negotiate their own identities in relation to the subject positions normalized by DD have been explored elsewhere (Monteiro, 1993).

Until the inception of cable and satellite television in the 1990s, DD had only one channel and a second channel for the four metros in the country. In the 1990s, as liberalization gathered momentum, cable and satellite television proliferated. At the end of March 1995, of the approximately 46 million households, 30 million were in urban areas and 16 million, in rural areas. Of the former, a third, 10 million, were connected to cable and satellite channels (Audience Research Unit, Doordarshan, 1995). The Indian identity produced by DD encountered an intensified circulation of the cultural artifacts of Bollywood[3] and the marketing of a range of newly emerging subject positions, spawned by advertising, and new genres such as the music videos, the chat show, the American soap, and so on. DD countered the threat of its diminishing popularity among urban audiences with a two-pronged strategy. On the one hand, it encouraged more Bollywood film-based programming; on the other, it revised its strategy of unitary pan-Indian programming by

---

[3]The Bombay Hindi film industry is popularly known as Bollywood (as opposed to Hollywood) and the fare dished out projects a "pan-Indian" character.

establishing regional channels in most of the major Indian languages.[4] The discussions with audiences show that these regional channels are popular, particularly among the older viewers in the cities, many of whom are first-generation migrants. With the success of DD's regional channels, several regional language channels have emerged, particularly in the South Indian languages.[5] The availability of these channels has created diasporic viewer collectivities across the country. The regional and the national are not mutually exclusive and viewers slide between these identities effortlessly:

> V: One thing is for sure . . . people do watch Hindi films, songs . . . everybody irrespective of their regional background . . . they do watch these programs . . . Philips Top Ten and Countdown programs. Another thing is when they watch programs in their language . . . cable helps them establish their regional identity . . . that is certain. . . . (family discussion 6)

In an attempt to draw the boundaries of local identities even tighter, the local cable providers have started producing relatively amateurish programs on community events and news in Bombay. They have also introduced "interactive" game shows such as "Tele-housie,"[6] which are becoming increasingly popular.

India has one of the largest indigenous film industries in the world and cinema is an integral part of urban popular culture, with a wide reach in rural India as well. Hindi films have a market not only in the subcontinent, but also in the Middle East and the African countries. This popular culture mediates and refracts the entry of global culture via satellite television. For instance, direct imports of Hollywood films dubbed in Hindi have, with some exceptions, fared poorly at the box office. Locally generated clones of Hollywood films and American serials have to translate the narratives into local idioms that are culturally relevant. This imperative to be responsive to the sensibilities of audiences operates more strongly in the case of cinema, which, given the economics of the film industry, needs to draw mass audiences across the country. For example, almost every film

---

[4]India has 16 languages that are recognized by the Constitution, in addition to Hindi, which is the national language.

[5]The South Indian languages such as Tamil, Telugu, Kannada, and Malayalam have film industries probably as large as Bollywood.

[6]Tele-Housie is a game in which each household is given a card with a series of numbers on it. The organizer of the show draws out numbers by lot, which are announced on the program. The viewers have to cancel the individual numbers from their card. The top winner is the first one to complete the card. There are other consolation prizes, too. There are several local variants of this game.

has to pay homage to the primacy of the patriarchal family and other traditional kinship ties, however "modern" its situations and characters might be. In contradistinction, given the segmentation of television audiences, televisual representations tend to be more diffused and contradictory, at times allowing for a questioning of familial norms. However, even here, popular American soap operas, such as "Santa Barbara" and "Beverly Hills 90210," have a relatively limited viewership, not merely because of the unfamiliar language, but also because of the alien cultural context.[7]

There are close interlinkages between television and cinema in the Indian context. Television becomes a major source for the dissemination of films and film-based programming and constituted a major reason for families to opt for cable and satellite television. Cable providers have channels that primarily disseminate films, whereas satellite television offers both films and other genres of programming:

Daughter: We are not so interested in films . . . now we are tired of
            films . . . it's just a time pass. . . .
Mother: Earlier, it was because of the films that we got the cable
            connection. Why go and stand in long queues and end
            up buying tickets in the black. . . . With the cable we can
            all sit at home and watch the film. Later, with the
            increasing number of channels . . . we are more inter-
            ested in this, than in cable. . . . (family discussion 8)

A cross-fertilization of styles and genres across television and cinema appears to be taking place; film song picturization, an essential feature of popular Indian cinema, has been influenced by television commercials and music videos, count-down programs for Hindi film songs, and game shows based on film music are among the most popular television genres.

In the postliberalization period, the extension of cable and satellite television has become a major strategy for the expansion of global markets and consumer culture,[8] not only among the newly emergent prosperous and burgeoning middle classes, but also among relatively disenfranchised and increasingly marginalized sections of the urban populace. This reproduction of consumer culture takes place through several genres and strategies: advertising and telemarketing, game shows based on finance and commodities, soaps and film extravaganzas that celebrate conspicuous consumption, commercial sponsorship of

---

[7]Star Television Network (owned by Rupert Murdoch) experimented with dubbing its soaps like "The Bold and the Beautiful" into Hindi, however, with little success. It has recently reserved its prime time for programs in Hindi.

[8]Morley foregrounds the need to conceive of television viewing as both ritual and ideological practice (Morley, 1991).

popular television shows and films, marketing of sports and other events. All these strategies foreground the creation of identities defined primarily in terms of consumption and utilize dominant cultural motifs to surcharge commonplace products with incongruent value.[9] In so doing, on the one hand, they create a climate for the consumption of upmarket branded products and on the other, a burgeoning underworld of unbranded surrogates (popularly known as "duplicates"), which illegally carry a reputed brand name, or a clever cognate of the name.[10] More than products per se, what is being sold are lifestyles that transcribe modern consumption strategies in terms of popular traditions of celebration and consumption. Festivals like *Diwali* or *Dassera* afford opportunities for sustained marketing hype and frenzied consumption. As though unsatisfied with this, culturally alien, "modern" festivals such as Valentine's Day and Mother's Day are becoming a part of the urban upper-class imagination, generating ever new terrains of consumption.

> K: Earlier there was a limit . . . to lead a good life . . . one needs so
>   much . . . not any more . . . now one needs everything . . . many,
>   many things.
> J: It is increasing day by day . . . (youth group 1)

The 1990s have witnessed the phenomenal growth of the Hindu right-wing political parties, which have succeeded in making significant electoral gains. The Hindu right rode to victory on the plank of restoring the mythical glory of Hindu tradition and cleansing Indian society of the pollution of Western culture.[11] Nevertheless, it was the extension of commodity culture and the proliferation of communication technologies that played a crucial role in the packaging and marketing of the new brand of *Hindutva* (Hinduness), invented by the Hindu right.[12] Today, several

---

[9]Appadurai (1990), explores the notion of consumption as "eminently social, relational, and active rather than, private, atomic or passive." In other words, consumption becomes a mode of communication, a means of "sending" and "receiving social messages" (Appadurai, 1990: 31).

[10]We are indebted to Arvind Rajagopal for drawing this point to our attention.

[11]Some constituents of this coalition, such as Shiv Sena, have, nevertheless, ruthlessly utilized their new-found power to forge a nexus between their political agenda and that of the multinational conglomerates. The latest among other controversies is Shiv Sena's patronage of Michael Jackson's concert in Bombay, the proceeds of which are supposed to go to an arm of the party. It is interesting that the supremo of the party, Bal Thackeray, though no office bearer in the Shiv Sena-led government in Maharashtra, calls himself the "remote control"!

[12]See Rajagopal, 1994, for an insightful study of the place of communal discourse within commodity culture, in particular, the role of national television in creating a Hindu identity.

Bollywood products celebrate this marriage between consumer culture, upper-caste Hindu "tradition" and nationalist identity;[13] mythological serials on the lives of Hindu gods and goddesses dominate prime time on many cable and satellite channels; politicians on the far right, who were considered to be on the lunatic fringe a decade ago have become respectable figures, featuring in talk shows and on the news. This Hinduization of popular culture is not as all-pervasive as the foregoing account might seem to indicate. The ethnocentric conflation of tradition with parochialism and modernity with tolerance also needs to be questioned. As our discussions bear out, some viewers who regard themselves as Westernized and modern are staunch supporters of the Hindu right. The intertwining of the local and the global, as mediated by satellite television and interpreted by viewers situated in domestic time and space, is a complex, ever-changing matrix.

THE REMOTE CONTROL

As opposed to popular Indian cinema, satellite television, both through its very entry into the domestic space as well as through the nature of its programming, has resulted in a renegotiation of familial relations and has caused a moral panic among many parents:

> Mother: . . . we are always living in fear . . . on Star Plus and Star Movies, there are hardly any good films. There is always a fear that if children are at home alone and they switch on Star Plus, etc. . . . these channels show all rubbish. . . . We are worried when we go out of the house . . . we feel tense. . . . (Family discussion 8)

More than the effects of screen violence, parents are perturbed about the corrupting influence of sexually explicit programming on their offspring. In an environment where discussion of sex between the generations offends the codes of decency, watching television together as a family becomes an act potentially fraught with peril:

---

[13]Rustom Bharucha, 1995, in his analysis of the popular Hindi film "Hum Aapke Hain Koun?" points out that the film represents, with fetishized intensity, the pleasures of familial rituals—a quintessential celebration of consumption on an obscenely lavish scale. In so doing, it reinscribes the discourses of religion and patriarchy, reaffirming the time-tested values of familial sacrifice and duty above all.

R: I can't sit with my parents and watch Star Movies—I feel embar-
      rassed!
G: (Laugh) We really only watch under 15 films, when our parents
      are there.
S: I watch films on Star with my family at home. . . . I don't mind
      and my parents know I am not going to go out . . . sometimes, I
      feel a little uncomfortable . . . a little uneasy. I just scratch my
      head or some such thing. . . . (Male youth group 2)

With the entry of satellite television and the availability of a large number
of channels, differences in the tastes of family members, which were
hitherto never a source of conflict, now generate struggles over the control of the remote control. This struggle for the control over viewing
becomes, as it were, a struggle for recognition of one's personhood,
one's identity as a spectator-self. This emerges particularly in discussions in which both fathers and children talk about how the mother is
permitted her occasional hour of soap! Although daytime watching is a
field of negotiation between the mother and/or the children, it is taken for
granted, in most households, that when the father returns home, the
remote becomes his possession! Though his stated preference might be
for sports and news, he may relinquish his privilege in favor of any other
member of the family.

Q: *[Laugh] In every house there is an argument!*
Daughter A: Yes, if he wants to see sports, I may want to see a film,
              or if I want to see my serial, he may want to see anoth-
              er serial. . . .
Daughter B: And we cannot fight with Daddy . . . we have to see
              what he sees. . . .
Q: *He does not like serials . . . ?*
Son: No, not at all. He does not like serials or films . . . just
              once in a way . . . he sees it with us. How can he dis-
              please his wife, so he watches Tara once a way
              [laugh]! (Family discussion 8)

Some families, who have the resources, have resolved the problem by
opting for a second television set. Interestingly, television commercials
for 14-inch television sets market their product either as a panacea for
family conflict or as permitting the creation of private individual spaces,
connoting individual liberation, within the confines of the domestic space.

Father G: Before I bought the second TV, there was a lot of dis-
              cussion or in-fighting—I want to see this and that . . .
              and I have always wanted to see news, and sports and

> my children wanted to see star and film-based and all
> such programs. . . . Before I got the second TV, we had
> time-sharing, this is your time—when I am at home, I
> am the master, and they have to give me one hour, of
> my TV time—my time for BBC news and some sports
> program—But after the second TV in my bedroom—
> there are no problems. . . . (Family Discussion 3)

In a certain sense, the kinds of resolutions arrived at by the household over time sharing embody the regime of discipline and relationships of power within the familial space. Satellite television offers a new site of resistance to parental authority.[14]

Television becomes a marker of the very matrix of power relations that defines familial space and epitomizes, in particular, the tensions between generations. It also presents, for some viewers, a possibility of reiterating and accounting for the change in familial relationships, of constituting themselves as a "modern" family.

Q: *You think people are changing attitudes?*
Daughter A : Yes, like my parents have changed their attitudes, like
             now you talk about, a particular scene on TV, I don't
             think it is so bad. . . . I can watch it with my parents—
             like it is not like earlier . . . switch off the TV . . . or
             change the channel or walk out of the room. Now I
             don't feel embarrassed or anything. . . .
Mother A: They can talk anything to us. . . .
Father A: I talk to my children a lot . . . which my parents have
             never spoken to me. . . .
Daughter A: Like the attitude of my parents about me going for a
             date—I really had never been told—don't do this or
             that. . . . (Family discussion 3)

THE "IMAGINARY" AND THE "NORMAL"

One of the basic coordinates for the spectator-self is the relationship between the "imaginary" and the "normal." DD, at least in some viewers'

---

[14]Some of the other concerns that mediate television-viewing behavior are academic pressures. For the middle-class family, the secondary school leaving examination represents a warlike situation, that has to be combated by making their children slog at their studies. The common perception is that the child's entire career depends on the grades in this examination. The entire family gears up to meet the impending crisis and television is the first casualty of this process; many families even discontinue their cable and satellite television connection for that particular year.

accounts (*apna* or ours), comes reassuringly close to normalcy. Cable and satellite television, in contradistinction, are unknown, treacherous territory. A Muslim family (family 8), for instance, would not watch cable and satellite television during *Ramadan,* a month of abstinence, but would watch DD news![15] In its earlier avatar, DD was the counterpoint to popular cinema, which unlike the domesticated, "educative," staid DD, afforded "suspension of disbelief," an escape into a fantastic, larger-than-life world, which had to be sought, braving long queues in movie houses (Monteiro, 1993). Though DD has shifted its program strategy, with the onslaught of cable and satellite television, to cash in on the popularity of Bollywood, its reputation as the upholder of familial values has survived to some extent.

A new set of differences has replaced the earlier distinction between television and cinema. Indian popular cinema has come metonymically closer to the position of DD, and satellite television has probably come to occupy the position vacated by it, offering "imaginary" spectator positions that violate the "normal." Indian cinema, with its rabid avowal of patriarchal kinship positions, is in stark contrast to the promiscuous, nebulous cliffhangers of the soaps on satellite television. It is a well-worn formula, in Indian cinema, to ruthlessly disallow sexual subject positions extraneous to the monogamous (needless to say, heterosexual). If there is, for example, a love triangle, one of the characters conveniently gets killed towards the end of the film, leaving behind a monogamous, reassuring residue! The soaps, with their endless rounds of extramarital and premarital relationships, replete with children born out of wedlock, offer a sharp contrast. The talk show is another new genre that is redefining the boundaries of the private and the public.

> Daughter A: You know in these talk shows—so far everything was
> hidden, but now things have started coming out. It is like
> if it is there on TV . . . it is all so open, why can't we
> also—like Oprah Winfrey . . . like . . . if there it is so open,
> why can't it be like this in India? (family discussion 3)

With all this, the moral landscape of urban popular culture has become far more complex and problematic, engendering resistance of various kinds. It is not only the moral panic of the parents, which always existed vis-à-vis sexuality, that is significant here, but a schism that the spectator-self experiences in terms of not being able to adopt the positions offered by televisual images.

---

[15]The genre most affected by satellite television is television news. News on DD had a very wide viewership, as it was watched as part of a single channel flow. Refer to Monteiro and Jayasankar, 1994, and Jayasankar and Monteiro, 1998, for a further discussion on the reception of news.

J: It [the styles in soaps] cannot be imitated . . . nobody tries to imi-
tate . . . not in this area at least. Anybody who watches Tara . . .
she has short hair and she wears a sleeveless blouse. . . . I don't
think anybody in this area will even dream of imitating her—That's
something that they think is all right for TV . . . it has nothing to do
with us. . . . (youth group 1)

Sometimes the trappings become a part of the spectator-self, failing to
touch an immutable inner core, that is seen to be governed by the normal. Most viewers feel that if at all the media exercise any influence on
their lives, it is merely at the level of style, restricted generally to clothing
and appearance. They are insistent on the fact that their behavior is
determined by many other considerations, as there are social, community, and peer group norms that they have to comply with. Any change has
to be accommodated within these norms.

R: We cannot think like them [characters in Western soaps]. We
act like them. . . . We try to act like them. We cannot be that free
as guys are or as teenagers are there—no never!
Q: *So the V and MTV culture. . . .*
R: We have been brought up like that, we should not try to act like
somebody else. . . .
G : Even if I cut my hair short and wear earrings. . . . I cannot
become someone in 90210 Beverly Hills. . . .
Q: *We cannot become like them. . . . Are we under some pres-
sure . . . or we don't want to . . . ?*
S: No, I don't want to be like them. . . . (Male youth group 2)

For many housewives, caught in a humdrum, unromantic existence, with
little familial recognition of their contribution or desires, watching soaps
becomes not merely an escape but also an affirmation of their hidden
anger, their revolt against the image of a good mother/wife, as this discussion with two women on the soap *Hazratein*[16] demonstrates:

---

[16]The basic narrative of the soap *Hazratein,* according to M, is as follows:

M: The protagonist of the serial—her mother was married to a man old
enough to be her father, so she [the mother] eloped with a younger man.
She [the protagonist] was brought up by her aunt and uncle. And she
looks forward to a stable, married life. She finds a person of her choice
and once she has a child, she feels like going out. She isn't educated,
she has done her SSC. Her husband is a professor—he ridicules her, but
somehow she finds a job, and is promoted. Then she starts liking her
boss, who molds her way of thinking. He tells her to be more open about
herself and everything about herself changes, once she meets her
boss. . . . (female group 4)

D: In fact, I know of men who are against their wives watching it, because they think. . . .

M: They might get influenced!

D: They may turn rebellious because it is very true what they are showing . . .

M: . . . As women, everybody can identify with it, all the women I knew have been watching it—we always discuss—with other women—if we miss out one episode, we catch up with others.

D: I think if you watch the serial you don't feel guilty of your feelings, like you might be having some feelings which you don't want to show, but you see this program, you are not so ashamed . . . that guilt in you is little less. Okay like I am not the only one who has these feelings. . . . Like if the woman is giving in, she is accepted, but if she tries to rebel in any way, he tries to put her down some way or the other . . . that insecurity in men. . . . (female group 4)

The imaginary is also a space for women to explore forbidden subject positions as spectator-selves. This has bearing on Ang's discussion of the relationship between the world of reality and the world of fantasy:

[Fantasy] is a dimension of subjectivity which is a source of pleasure *because* it puts "reality" in parenthesis, because it constructs imaginary solutions for real contradictions which in their fictional simplicity and their simple fictionality step outside the tedious complexity of the existing social relations of dominance and subordination. (Ang, 1985: 135, emphasis in original)

Popular Indian cinema with its mandate for preserving the patriarchal family has always had its "negative" women, clearly polarized against its "heroines," untainted by any signs of "evil." Actors/actresses tend to get typecast into set roles of hero/heroine or villain/vamp. DD's earlier soaps have tended to comply with this code. With the likes of "Santa Barbara" and "Dynasty" and their Indian counterparts, the line between the good and evil has become blurred. Women admit to secretly admiring "bad" women, who are seen as "strong," as opposed to "good" women, who are regarded as "wishy-washy."

Q: *What do you think about the negative characters being portrayed by women?*

M: Maybe, I think, it is a deep down . . . all women, at some point of time, want to be like vamps . . . negative . . . and they want to behave that way, but because of the upbringing we have had, we have to be good, even if we want to go out and slap somebody . . . we are forced to be good, so, whatever of us that is

> repressed . . . when we see these negative characters on
> screen, we feel . . . what we could not do, she is doing. . . .
> (female group 4)

Indian marriages are generally arranged by the parents and relatives, within the boundaries of caste, religion, and many other complex systems of kinship and belief. Generally, in Hindi films, interreligious/intercaste marriages are not common. The popular film "Bombay" (1995), set against the backdrop of the Hindu-Muslim communal riots of 1992-93, in Bombay, is a love story of a Hindu boy and a Muslim girl. The screen representation of this transgressive relationship has been invoked by some youth, who resist the norm:

> L: The incidence of love marriages is increasing . . . There is a
>   "dar-ingness" [sic] . . . I mean after seeing "Bombay" . . . a
>   Muslim girl and a Hindu boy—earlier one could not think of . . . .
> J: To be frank, he [pointing to L] has a Muslim girl friend and even
>   he [pointing to K] has a Muslim girlfriend, and they have started
>   thinking that there is nothing wrong in that. . . .
> K: But that is not because of that film.
> J: No, no. But you got this "daring" [sic] from the film. Now you
>   have realized that this is also possible. . . . (youth group 1)

To another group of youth, such a relationship is unthinkable. They do not identify with the characters, but regard the film as merely an abstract moral lesson in brotherhood. This is perhaps related to the deeply ingrained stories of Muslim "atrocities," narrated to them by their elders, who came to India as Hindu refugees during the India-Pakistan Partition in 1947:

> S: What! A Muslim girl? Never—I will definitely not marry a
>   Muslim. . . .
> Q: *Somewhere you still think Muslims are different?*
> G: No, we only think that riots are unnecessary. . . .
> S: We should not fight. . . .
> G: Yes, we should not fight—it does not mean that we should be
>   too friendly to Muslims or marry Muslims, no, never!
> R: Any other religion, but not Muslims! (male youth group 2)

Given the current crisis gripping the Indian nation-state, and the growth of the Hindu right, the Muslim has become all the more demonized by the mainstream Hindu culture. The talk of Hindu-Muslim harmony remains a pious platitude that does not impinge on everyday choices. The discussions, with youth, on the film "Bombay" bear witness to the varied readings and strategic uses that viewers construct in relation to the discourses of the mass media, which can not be deduced from a study of the discourses per se. The representations of the transgressive, the imaginary, would be invoked only in situations where they relate to immediate struggles, as also in the case of women for whom soaps like *Hazratein* become an assertion of their resistance, of their spectator-selves. In other words, the imaginary tends to be judged by the yardstick of the normal, in the process affirming the latter; the distinction between the imaginary and the normal blurs when viewers perceive a coincidence between the "agenda of the text" (Morley, 1996) and their own agendas. A mere textual analysis would not negotiate this coincidence. Having said that, this paper does not seek to romanticize the ability of readers to put the agenda of the text to consistently subversive uses, nor does it advocate the notion of a "semiotic democracy" (Fiske, cited in Morley, 1996).

THE OTHER ABOVE, THE OTHER BELOW

A crucial element of the constitution of the spectator-self is the invocation of dividing practices (Foucault, 1986), which involve the identification of a normal "us," in contradistinction to a deviant "them." These dividing practices invariably surface in viewers' accounts when the "effects" of cable and satellite television are explored. Middle-class viewers regard themselves as free agents, capable of consciously regulating and mediating their relation to the mass media; they regard the "impact" of the media on their own lives and selves as limited. In contrast, they posit a "them" below, who are vulnerable, unable to ward off the ill effects of media representations, often by virtue of their lack of "education" and "class".[17]

> Q: *What do you think—the influence of romantic or violent films. . . .*
> S: It only affects the others.
> Q: *Who are the others?*
> S: The uneducated people. . . .
> G: . . . It is only the *wadiwalas* [the less affluent, who live in one room tenements], their way of talking changes . . . they will talk like *taporis* [loafers]. . . . (male youth group 2)

---

[17]This dividing practice is at the heart of the discourses of development communication and the very notion of development (Monteiro, 1993).

As opposed to the "modern" other above, the other below is constructed as a "traditional" being. The other below is also defined by a lack of finesse, taste, and above all, lacking knowledge of English language:

> P: It is not the good crowd, that goes and watch these films, it is for. . . .
> N : The locals
> P: Yes, the vernacs [derogatory term for vernacular language speakers]—who watch these films . . .
> N: Even we watch, but we don't like it, when in the films, the crowd is whistling and clapping. . . . (female youth group 5)

Interestingly, this invocation of an educated elite "us" who can see through the crudity of the Hindi movie versus an uneducated, lower-class "them," who are swayed by the violence and glamour of Bollywood is but a replica of the dividing practice employed by the adult world in talking about youth. It appears that impact is something that happens to someone who is looked down upon, the less powerful! Age becomes another dimension along which flows of power are organized.

> J: I think action films are a bad influence. Children start thinking that violence is a solution.
> K: It is all about taking revenge, actually . . .
> J: Yes . . . they think that if you are violent, you will be the winner . . . the hero does it, so even we can do it. (youth group 1)

The availability of programming from the West on a hitherto unprecedented scale has influenced definitions of what is considered "cool" among upper-middle-class youth.[18] There are peer group pressures to keep up with the latest (read Western). Even those who come from families with limited acquaintance with Western music and other cultural artifacts, are compelled to conform to the norm.

> N: I feel it is very necessary to know about English music, if you are a part of a group, otherwise if others are discussing music, you really feel left out . . . if you don't know about some songs. . . . (female youth group 5)

Many would be ashamed to admit that they enjoy the products of Bollywood and the Hindi soaps, particularly male youth. Schwarzenegger is mentioned as one of the "cool guys"; male youth would aspire towards a physique like his.

---

[18]The phenomenon of watching MTV, Channel V, and other English language channels appears to be restricted to educated, upper class youth.

S: Yes, we have become more Western . . .

R: I think it is because of the basic Western culture, this culture has come through the TV, through the media . . .

R: I think somewhere we are trying to look a little like them. . . .

Q: Like whom? Shahrukh Khan [a Bollywood actor]?

S: No, not the Hindi stars. . . .

G: [laugh] His haircut is like Arnold's [Schwarzenegger]. . . . (male youth group 2)

These youth are conjuring up an image of the "other above," located above Bollywood stars; the styles of the latter are only for the *taporis.* The stereotypical images of Western youth culture that appear on satellite television are difficult to emulate: "We cannot be that free as guys are or as teenagers are there [in the West]—no never. . . ." At one level, even when these youth claim that they do not choose to be like these Western stars, these claims appear to be tinged with a sense of envy.

THE SPECTATOR-SELF

The spectator-self is a position that emerges through a range of viewer strategies, including a process of "othering" and a negotiation with imaginary and normal subject positions. The axis of the normal and the imaginary intersects the relationships between the other above and the other below (Fig. 15.1). As the following discussion reveals, the spectator-self regards the other below as unable to situate itself as a knowledgeable entity vis-à-vis the televisual image; it can only posit those images as the unattainable imaginary that belongs to the world of the other above. On the other hand, the spectator-self, located somewhere between the other above and the other below, is able to see through the agenda of the text, the promise held forth by the imaginary.

D : I think these serials are pushing us to take our own decision—I think it is like cajoling. . . .

M : No, I don't think it is pushing anybody. There are many people who watch these serials who are not educated, not much forward [progressive] in their views . . . have not gone out in the world, so for them, it is something out of their reach. They can just watch the serial, watch the women. . . . Say, "Oh, how I wish I could be like these women," but they cannot be like those women. And other women who watch these women characters, it is okay for them, they are educated, financially secure and are not much carried away by these—they see the grey shades— the others may see the white or black. The women whom they

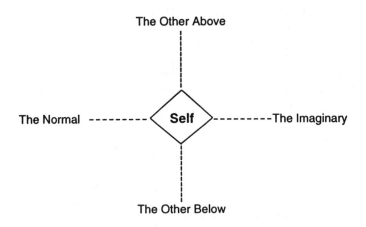

Figure 15.1. The site of the spectator-self

> want to influence, may not be influenced because they are not in
> a position to be influenced . . . and the others, they are not going
> to be influenced . . . because they are aware . . . their awareness
> level is quite high. . . . (female group 4)

Those women subjects, who should benefit from the influence of the
transgressive, are unable to make use of it, since they do not perceive
themselves as worthy of being influenced by it. It does not benefit the rest
either, because they are aware. In short, there is no point along these
axes that the spectator-self might occupy, where it would be affected by
the televisual discourse. The relative immutability of the spectator-self is a
recurrent theme in viewers' account about themselves. There are others,
and only others, who would suffer damage. In other words, the spectator-
self posits itself as a free agent, thus making this positioning an inclusive
proposition; every one seems to belong to this category. Their exclusivity,
in turn is guaranteed by "them," those who are corrupted by the televisual
discourse. The spectator-self is capable of setting its own agenda transcending that of the text, whereas the malleable and impressionable
'other' succumbs to it, transforming itself irreversibly.

What comes out as primary in viewers' accounts is this notion of
agency: although the spectator-self is not devoid of constraints, there is
a sense that within this space there are choices to be made. Moreover,
the effects of television on the spectator-self are seen as under its conscious control. It is precisely this sense of agency that facilitates the
incorporation of the spectator-self into the consumer culture of the

postliberalization period in India. Many television commercials play on this theme of the active discerning consumer, making the consumption of products a hallmark of privileged selfhood.

With the growing commodification of everyday life, there is a tremendous obsession with the packaging and presentation of the self. Aishwarya Rai, Sushmita Sen (Miss World and Miss Universe, respectively, in 1995) and their ilk have become icons of modern Indian womanhood and national honor.

> Daughter A: . . . I think overall attitudes have changed—like more youngsters are working now—even young girls—even the look is changing. I mean now people are more concerned about their look and how they present themselves while going to work—they are changing. . . . (family discussion 3)

These technologies of the self (Foucault, 1986) operate in an age where beauty queens in skimpy swim suits wax eloquent on how they want to save the children of the world or become like Mother Teresa. Appearance becomes paramount; giving the right answers, the key to success. This preoccupation with self-presentation pushes young people into streamlined modes of being.

> K: There is a sort of competition . . .
> L: It's like how many girls are looking at me . . . or even girls tend to think that way . . . how many boys are looking at us . . . [laugh]
> J: I can say about cosmetics . . . girls do tend to . . . even if there is no money or they cannot afford it . . . they want to look good . . . have good nails . . . use something good on the face. (youth group 1)

Given this apparently all pervasive global consumer culture and the media institutions that reproduce it (refracted and rewritten, no doubt, in indigenized terms, but consumer culture, nevertheless), where are the spaces for resistance and what forms does this resistance take? On the one hand, the televisual discourse appears, by and large, to be reiterating and facilitating consensus formation in terms of the larger relations of power that make for ruthless, uneven growth of a capitalist market economy.[19] On the other hand, viewers appear to be invoking aspects of the

---

[19]There are strands of resistance to consumerism and the redefinition of community and familial spaces, engendered by the media, which emerge in the accounts of older, first-generation working-class migrants.

against the power flows of their familial space, thus invoking a sense of agency in this process of resistance. Mass media representations are being employed by the spectator-self to legitimize its enactment of the imaginary: young people relating across religious and caste boundaries, women creating spaces for themselves within the confines of their homes, children resisting parental authority, and so on. The televisual discourse offers a site to mark and redefine the limits of the normal, the dominant, and the real, in opposition to what is imaginary, the other, the not-self.

> *Q:*   *Do you think that films have influenced you?*
> Son: I don't know whether films have influenced us, but we have influenced films. . . . After seeing "Rangeela" [a Bollywood blockbuster] I felt that films have started adopting our styles of speaking. . . .
> Mother: The film has imitated them. They have shown reality. . . . What is real in society. . . . (family discussion 8)

APPENDIX 1: PROFILE OF DISCUSSION GROUPS

1. Youth group, four males and one female, age group 20-25, all unmarried and currently unemployed, living in a slum in North Bombay. Education: High school to bachelor's degree. Discussion in Hindi.
2. Youth group, five males, age group 16-17, all students, living in a relatively affluent housing colony in Central Bombay. Discussion in English.
3. Two families: family A, consisting of mother 36, two daughters, 13 and 15; family B, consisting of father 44, mother 41, daughter 20 and son 15. Both families are related and run a joint family business, living in a relatively affluent housing colony in Central Bombay. Discussion in English.
4. Two women, M, housewife, with two young children, bachelor's degree in law, husband owns a travel agency. D, undergraduate, runs a business in fashion designing from home, two young children, husband is also a business man. Both living in a relatively affluent housing colony in Central Bombay. Discussion in English.
5. Youth group, seven girls, in their teens, all students, living in a relatively affluent housing colony in Central Bombay. Discussion in English.
6. Husband and wife, left-wing trade unionists and political activists, 46 and 43, three children in their twenties, living in a slum in North Bombay, Husband has a Ph.D., wife middle school. Discussion in Hindi and English.
7. Family of husband, wife, and two sons and a daughter, husband runs a petty business, one-room tenement, in a slum in North Bombay. Discussion in Hindi.
8. Family of mother in her mid-40s, two daughters and one son, all in their 20s, father owns small business, three-room tenement in a slum in North Bombay. Discussion in Hindi.
9. Individual interview with retired blue collar worker, 65, first-generation migrant from South India, living in a slum in North Bombay. Discussion in Hindi.

REFERENCES

Ang, I. (1985) *Watching Dallas.* New York: Methuen.

Appadurai, A. (1990) "Introduction: Commodities and the Politics of Value." In A. Appadurai, ed. *The Social Life of Things.* Melbourne: Cambridge University Press.

Audience Research Unit (1995) *Doordarshan—1995.* New Delhi: Doordarshan.

Bharucha, R. (1995) "Utopia in Bollywood—'Hum Aapke Hain Koun' . . . !," *Economic and Political Weekly,* April 15, 801-04.

Foucault, M. (1986) "Afterword: The Subject and Power." In H. J. Dreyfus and P. Rabinow, eds. *Michel Foucault: Beyond Structuralism and Hermeneutics.* Sussex: Harvester Press.

Ghosh, A. (1994) "Structural Adjustment and Industrial and Environmental Concerns," *Economic and Political Weekly,* Feb. 19, 421-26.

Jayasankar, K. P. and A. Monteiro (1998) "The News of the State and the State of the News." In K. B. Jensen, ed. *The News of the World.* London: Routledge.

Monteiro, A. (1993) "State, Subject and the 'Text'—The Construction of Meaning in Television." Unpublished Ph.D. Dissertation, Goa University.

Monteiro, A. and K. P. Jayasankar (1994) "The Spectator-Indian: An Exploratory Study on the Reception of News," *Cultural Studies,* 8(1), 162-82.

Morley, D. (1991) "Where the Global Meets the Local: Notes From the Sitting Room," *Screen, 32*(1), Spring.

———— (1996) "Populism, Revisionism and the 'New' Audience Research." In J. Curran et al., eds. *Cultural Studies and Communications.* London: Arnold.

Nandy, A. (1989) "The Political Culture of the Indian State," *Daedalus, 118*(4), 1-26.

Rajagopal, A. (1994) "Ramjanmabhoomi, Consumer Identity and Image-Based Politics," *Economic and Political Weekly,* July 2, 1659-68.

Singh, A. K. (1993) "Social Consequences of New Economic Policies," *Economic and Political Weekly,* Feb. 13, 279-85.

Author Index

323

Subject Index

active audience(s), 15, 16, 21, 41, 43, 119
advertising, 48, 57, 61, 80, 214
alternative cultures, 21
alternative media, 212, 214, 217, 223
anthropologist, 296n
anthropology, 73, 179, 182, 296n
anti-communism, 113, 114, 115
audience(s), 11, 13, 14, 15, 31, 32, 33, 34, 35, 36, 37, 38, 41, 43, 44, 45, 58, 97, 98, 106, 155, 169, 170, 180, 190, 191, 196, 203, 211, 214
audience commodity, 58, 59, 77

Birmingham Centre, 6
brand names, 77, 80, 107
British Broadcasting Corporation (BBC), 36, 48
broadcasting, 35, 36

CBS, 39
citizenship, 64, 276
class, 23, 37, 42, 43, 44, 45, 99 111, 119, 120, 126, 149, 193n, 278, 285, 286
commodification, 63
commodity(ies), 48, 49, 50, 51, 52, 54, 56, 57, 61, 109
    culture, 52, 54, 55, 56, 63, 64, 65, 306
    fetishism, 51, 56, 62
computers, 181, 261
conglomerates, 82, 83, 84, 87, 88, 118
consumer culture, 82, 83, 84, 87, 88, 118
consumer sovereignty, 104
consumption, 11, 13, 17, 48, 51, 55, 60, 63, 75, 76, 78, 79, 80, 82, 148, 306

cultivation analysis, 191
cultural
    anthropology, 73
    hegemony, 212
    identity, 18, 252, 255, 271, 278
    imperialism, 15, 23n, 96, 117, 120
    studies, 5, 6, 22, 42, 47, 48, 57, 59, 65, 95, 96, 169, 182, 295
culturation studies, 173, 189

Dallas, 195, 197n
decoding, 89, 168, 172, 219, 220
deconstruction, 218, 219, 222, 224, 226
department stores, 52, 53, 54, 56, 60, 61, 77
development communication, 115, 314n
diaspora, 250, 251, 252, 253, 254
diasporic communities, 18
domesticity, 282, 283
Doodarshan (DD), 303, 304, 309, 310, 312
Dynasty, 195, 317

emic, 17, 71, 73, 74, 75, 76, 88, 89, 132, 133
encoding/decoding model, 6, 7, 15, 19, 59, 123, 124
ethnography, 4, 8, 9, 14, 21, 42, 65, 71, 73, 74, 89, 126, 128, 131, 134, 135, 167, 168, 170, 182, 183, 255, 297
etic, 17, 73, 74, 89, 132, 133, 134
everyday life, 21, 106, 127, 139, 147, 149, 151, 153, 165, 172, 194, 232, 244, 276, 277, 278, 279, 284, 287, 290, 292, 293, 295, 296, 297

From Body & Soul, 289, 293
Falcon Crest, 195, 197*n*
fans, 14, 71, 72, 74, 75, 79, 80, 82, 83,
    84, 85, 86, 87, 157, 211, 213, 217,
    222, 223, 224, 225, 226
fan ethnographers, 71, 72, 73, 74, 75,
    89
fiction, 194, 195, 197, 199, 200, 201,
    202, 203, 276
films, 80, 81, 82, 83, 259, 263, 264,
    268, 269, 270, 271, 275, 305
film industry, 80, 303*n*, 304
Fordism, 65
Frankfurt School, 38
Freirian
    method/approach, 215, 216, 217,
    219, 227
    pedagogy, 225

gender, 37, 42, 44, 45, 74, 166, 175
genre, 150, 151, 157, 158, 166, 167,
    174, 189, 190, 191, 192, 193, 194,
    196, 197, 200, 202, 203, 204, 211,
    237, 295
globalization, 249, 250, 251, 302
Globo, Rede, 21

hybridization, 18

ideology, 6, 42, 75, 151, 196
Internet, 180, 261
intertextuality, 21, 174, 181, 195, 198,
    201

karaoke, 261
KDKA, 35

labor, 13, 14, 50, 58, 60, 88
leisure, 73, 75, 76, 77, 78, 79, 88, 127,
    150, 167, 244
market reserach, 105, 107, 112
mass communication(s), 32, 33, 34,
    35, 36, 37, 38, 39, 45
mass society, 38
media ethnography, 20, 166, 168, 169,
    170, 171, 173, 174, 175, 176, 177,
    179, 180, 181, 182, 276, 294, 295,
    296

melodrama, 151, 152, 153, 182, 188,
    275, 277
modernization, 115, 145, 295

narrative(s), 191, 192, 198, 201
"Nationwide" Audiences, The, 8, 126
news, 21, 141, 142, 192, 196, 197,
    199, 200, 201, 202, 237, 257, 290,
    292
newspapers, 57, 58
nationwide study, 7, 59
name brand, 73, 88

parades, 44
Paramount, 72, 83, 84, 85, 86, 87
Payne Fund studies, 37
Perez, Daniella, 21, 288, 289, 290,
    293
Princeton Radio Research Project, 37,
    39, 40, 45
pluralism, 6, 20
political economy, 10, 12, 13, 22, 23,
    57, 59, 63, 65, 72, 89, 95, 96, 97,
    210, 211
    of communication, 3, 4, 10, 11
polysemic, 19, 20, 59, 125
    texts, 16
post-Fordism, 65, 76
President Collor, 21, 287, 288, 289,
    292, 293
propaganda, 36
public sphere, 138, 141, 282

qualitative
    methodology, 175
    research, 5, 8, 168, 172, 255
    studies, 173
quantitative reserach, 166

race, 37, 42, 43, 44, 45, 74, 278
radio, 35, 61, 80, 81, 235, 260, 279
ratings, 41
Rebellious Years, 20, 287, 288, 289,
    290, 292, 293
reception
    analysis/theory, 3, 4, 5, 7, 8, 15, 19,
    20, 22, 119, 165, 168, 169, 170,
    179, 220, 290, 292
    research, 124